Shakespeare Without Class

Shakespeare Without Class
Misappropriations of Cultural Capital

Edited by Donald Hedrick and Bryan Reynolds

palgrave

First published 2000 by
PALGRAVE™
175 Fifth Avenue, New York, N.Y. 10010 and
Houndmills, Basingstoke, Hampshire, England RG21 6XS.
Companies and representatives throughout the world.

PALGRAVE™ is the new global publishing imprint of St. Martin's Press LLC
Scholarly and Reference Division and Palgrave Publishers Ltd (formerly Macmillan Press Ltd).

ISBN 0-312-22271-8 hardback

Library of Congress Cataloging-in-Publication Data to be found at the Library of
Congress.

A catalogue record for this book is available from the British Library.

Design by Westchester Book Composition.

First edition: November, 2000
10 9 8 7 6 5 4 3 2 1

Printed in the United States of America.

Contents

I Critical Introduction

Chapter 1   *Donald Hedrick and Bryan Reynolds:* Shakespace
and Transversal Power   3

II Acting Out From Under Authority

Chapter 2   *Robert Weimann:* Performance and Authority in
Hamlet (1603)   51

Chapter 3   *William Over:* New York's African Theatre:
Shakespeare Reinterpreted   65

III Adapting Ideologies

Chapter 4   *Curtis Perry:* Vaulting Ambitions and Killing
Machines: Shakespeare, Jarry, Ionesco, and the
Senecan Absurd   85

Chapter 5   *Bryan Reynolds:* "What is the city but the people?":
Transversal Performance and Radical Politics in
Shakespeare's Coriolanus and Brecht's *Coriolan*   107

IV Loving Otherwise

Chapter 6   *Laurie Osborne:* Sweet, Savage Shakespeare   135

Chapter 7   *Richard Burt:* No Holes Bard: Homonormativity
               and the Gay and Lesbian Romance with
               Romeo and Juliet   153

V   Disfilming Power

Chapter 8   *James Andreas:* "Where's the Master?":
               The Technologies of the Stage, Book, and
               Screen in *The Tempest* and *Prospero's Books*   189

Chapter 9   *Matt Bergbusch:* Additional Dialogue:
               William Shakespeare, Queer Allegory, and
               My Own Private Idaho   209

VI   Teaching Transversally

Chapter 10   *Leslie Katz:* Rehearsing the Weird Sisters: The Word as
               Fetish in *Macbeth*   229

Chapter 11   *Donald Hedrick:* Shakespeare's Enduring Immorality
               and the Performative Turn: Toward a Transversal
               Pedagogy   241

VII Afterword

Chapter 12   *Julia Reinhard Lupton:* Afterword: Shakespace on
               Marloan   277

Contributors   287
Index   289

Part I

Critical Introduction

Chapter 1

Shakespace and Transversal Power

Donald Hedrick and Bryan Reynolds

Prefatory Space: The Collection and Its Title

"Shakespace" is our name for the territory within discourses, adaptations, and uses of Shakespeare that is marked by a dynamic of what we call "transversality," a dynamic insufficiently captured by a term now familiar in cultural criticism, "appropriation," as in the appropriation of property. With apologies to our contributors as well as to what we think of as ourselves, for borrowing their essays for our own creative and commercial use, what is assembled here can hardly be thought of as our property, however, particularly since its use will transform over time. The aura of Shakespace is such that, in the immor(t)al words of its progenitor's own transversal slogan, one that might well stand as epigraph to this collection, "Property was thus appalled, / That the Self was not the same" (*The Phoenix and the Turtle,* 37–38).

These essays, chosen to address current issues of class, race, gender, sexual preference, postcoloniality, and pedagogy, were originally solicited so as to distinguish the volume from other treatments of Shakespearean adaptation by an emphasis on "dissident" responses to Shakespeare. Now, however, they seem to us rather more complicated in what they do. As it happens, dissidence, though important to the essays and by no means omitted from the overall ideological picture, constitutes only one type of response in an ensemble of actions, understandings, and affects—a broader field including, to name an area otherwise excluded from more strict usage of the term "dissidence," criminality. To the perennial question of how to do things with and to Shakespeare, the essays now speak less rigidly but more provocatively. The very fact of the difficulty of a sustained categorization of them seemed evidence that we needed a far more nuanced and expansive model of the kind we will theorize here.

Rather than providing reductive, homogenizing, and therefore dispensable summaries of the essays collected, essays that speak delightfully for themselves without benefit of abstract, and rather than giving a polite tip of our editorial hats to their infinite variety, we want to address the question of what is common to the following scenarios we find in them (presented in no particular order here) and in certain questions they provoke:

1. Women romance writers excluded from elite culture "marry" the supposed champion of that culture, William Shakespeare. Will the marriage work out for them? Will it change them both?

2. An Elizabethan actor must somehow assert his own expertise when handed golden words from the moneyed pen of William Shakespeare, a sometime dabbler in acting himself. What happens to either's authority in the process?

3. Risking contempt and even violence from a cultural elite, nineteenth-century African American actors adopt its very trappings and status by way of an alliance with Shakespeare. Does their double-voiced theater compel a new alternative vision of America?

4. A teacher and her students join together to play witches in improvisations of *Macbeth*. What are the new energies, both positive and negative, that get released from this shared transgressive performance, and from where do they come and go?

5. A modern dramatist of the absurd finds in the Senecan underpinnings of Shakespeare an experimental equivalent to his own practices. How does the earlier interrogation of heroism transform the contemporary one, projecting a sense of Shakespeare as contemporary or emergent?

6. A film director adapts *The Tempest* to display through images of the book the earlier era's use of writing and literacy as a powerful cultural weapon. How does it effect his investigation to conduct it with the new technology comparable to the book, namely the screen, the new technology of our age?

7. How is it that gay and lesbian renditions of *Romeo and Juliet,* by imagining a normalized homosexuality, go further than queer theorists do with their valorization of the camp and parodic critiques of "heteronormativity"? What exactly is the "post-queer"

space they thereby create, in which gender may no longer be legible or even matter?

8. A gay film director credits his gay-themed Shakespeare adaptation with an impudent acknowledgment that Shakespeare had a minor hand in the writing. How does this antinostalgia about his "collaborator" combine with a nostalgia for home and family, to form a new, countertradition of home and family for a new sexual era?

9. A teacher of Shakespeare responding to the renewed interest in the moral questions of literature is caught within the dilemma of either presenting moral certainties under canonical authoritarianism of a master, or treating teaching Shakespeare as show business without moral import. What Shakespeare would resolve this problem?

10. A dramatist adapts the text of Shakespeare to promote a Marxist ideology. How do parallel historical circumstances transform the text, without any adaptation, into a critique of class, through the medium of theatrical performance?

In each case, the encounter, or collision, or union with Shakespeare takes one, or one's interpretive community, outside oneself or that community, and outside the officially assigned space of one's subjectivity. Like dialogism, there may be collision or clash, but unlike dialogism, there is shared space for repositionings and transformations of more than voice alone. The family resemblance between these scenarios, therefore, is that the teachers, students, adapters, directors, and actors experience the encounter with Shakespeare in a collective, creative space not fully limited by their own interests, conceptions, or affects, and one in which new social arrangements are, if not actually produced or produced in miniature, at least become capable of being imagined. The particular scenarios we have included here thus constitute transversal cases that we have for the presentation of our book's contents provisionally catalogued as follows: acting out from under some authority; adapting historical ideologies by way of tactical contingencies; loving "otherwise" outside assigned subjective territory; "disfilming" or visually exhibiting and challenging hegemonic power; and teaching transversally or transgressively, as it were without a net—all with a view toward achieving salutary social and civic effects from certain theaterlike experiments in "being what you aren't."

Why "without class"? Here, we mean to be suggestive and exploratory rather than analytic and definitive. Like the infamous *Shakespeare Without*

Tears (Webster 1942), our title would at first seem to mark a naive ideal for customary ideological criticism, namely, the ignoring or bracketing of the pervasive factor of class in Shakespeare's England made somehow invisible in the plays. Or, equally, it might mark the removal of Shakespeare's high cultural status, the legacy of the highbrow/lowbrow split of the modern era, with a democratizing potential for the split's erasure (Levine 1988). Whether or not any such ideals may be approached, to imagine classlessness in such cases through the very movement itself across or through classes is what an encounter in Shakespace may in fact do. If so, the title operates in other, related senses as well, since "without class" might also refer to tastelessness and possibilities of transgression or disruption, as in some of the cases our contributors discuss. Even more broadly, however, our title points to the theoretical possibility of what is "without classification," the deterritorialization of conceptual spaces that may also occur in strong encounters with Shakespeare.

Why the keywords, "misappropriations of cultural capital"? The metaphor for literary and artistic value, and by extension for Shakespeare, as cultural capital is rapidly becoming commonplace. Thus, Shakespeare is regarded as a "banknote" (Holderness 1988, xi), or Shakespearean adaptation is seen in terms of the "costs as well as benefits in women's appropriations" (Novy 1993, 3). Yet, the theoretical mechanisms of adaptation are less often explored, and the term "appropriation" tends to enforce a neutralizing sense of the transformation, or one that implies some "normal" function of the Shakespearean text in typical acts of cultural domination. The transcendence of what we call "subjectivity territory" (to be explained below), however, will often involve transgression, insofar as that subjectivity is state-imposed or regulated. Thus, the now ubiquitous and somewhat neutral term "appropriation" does not sufficiently capture the transversal spirit whereby criminality, for instance, becomes a conduit for other actions against the state-imposed subjectivity, and thus how what is in effect a criminal subjectivity may be adopted, even without criminal behavior itself, for the transgressive, antistate effects ordinarily produced by criminality. For an image embodying this, we might take that of a picture of the Folger Shakespeare Library in Washington, D.C., with a SWAT team on its roof. Suggesting at first a range of criminal possibilities—from dissident Shakespearean scholars in a palace revolt inside, to alien terrorists holding Shakespeareans hostage—the actual event, the visit of Queen Elizabeth II to the library in May 1991, nevertheless suggests a space in which state power collides with whatever opposes it, and where transgressions thus become imaginable.

To take one instance of what we regard as a more limiting theoretical stance regarding appropriation, we find that the editor of the collection *The Appropriation of Shakespeare,* while acknowledging the key term's link to "usurpation," describes the encounter as "making sense of a literary arte-fact by fitting it into our own parameters" (Marsden 1991, 1). Through a rhetoric of "making it ours," "controlling," "possessing," and "fitting," Marsden's approach leaves us with the picture of a collision of autonomous and fixed entities or spaces, a binary separateness exacerbated all the more in the case of the traditional deification of Shakespeare, but in any case a picture systematically distorting certain aspects of subjective and artistic possibility.[1] We find instead that in what we are terming Shakespace, what may happen is a far more creative change, not a "making sense" of this lit-erary artefact but indeed going outside *someone's* sense. Misappropriation, moreover, does not necessarily entail misuse, but rather that a real value was accrued over time and in the investments of others (Shakespeare as only one of the investors in his art); and that one who takes this value, even if a kind of thief of value, can be transformed by the taking itself. Not a nega-tion of "appropriation," therefore, it does not entail a becoming-sequence of what should have been "yours" is now "mine," but suggests something far more complex and even indeterminate: what only seemed to be yours is now equally not mine, its new value apart from what may no longer be "me." Like another of Shakespeare's transversal slogans this time placed in the mouth of Viola: "what is yours to bestow is not yours to reserve" (*Twelfth Night* 168). Appropriation, on the other hand, is what Jean-Luc Nancy describes is the mode of self-love as the "love of possession . . . the love of the self as property" (Nancy 1991, 95); misappropriation is techni-cally therefore more, as we will see in what follows, like love.

One might be surprised to find as a strong exemplar of American mis-appropriation of Shakespearean capital the writer William Burroughs, who manages, furthermore, to represent a form of what we will explain as "transversality"; his misappropriation is a deliberate program against state-imposed subjective control. The early Beat experiences of Burroughs, who continued to cite Shakespeare with great frequency late into life, included Greenwich Village apartment performances of Shakespeare with Kerouac and others, and much banter with Allen Ginsberg over Shakespearean allu-sions. The experimental technique Burroughs developed with Bryon Gysin in the early sixties, the text-collage technique of the "cut-up," com-bines lines or words from the text of one author with that of another, as Burroughs himself does in cut-ups with Shakespeare's text. In effect, what his technique manages is the experimental alterity we call "transversality," using Shakespeare and one's own writing to create a subjectivity both out-side the self and, as Burroughs also believed, beyond the power of the state in forming such subjectivity, which is another of our understandings about the power of the transversal. In a letter to Gysin in February 1964, Bur-roughs suggests that one form of the technique would be to set authors' writings in newspaper-columns: "Set up Shakespeare, Conrad, Rimbaud in newspaper format," or to write novels in this way, to appropriate the power that newspaper columns have "to mold thought feeling and subsequent events" (Burroughs MSS). One could even do this with one's own writing (unpublished manuscripts of Burroughs sometimes involve his cutting up, say, of a letter to the *London Sunday Times* editor, rearranging its pieces, or even, as Burroughs also did, rearranging pieces of different dreams he recorded into a nonlinear narrative of sorts), in effect transcending one's own subjectivity by means of self-fragmentation and rearrangement. A fantasy scene from a draft of *The Wild Boys,* moreover, imagines a montage of juxtaposed images along the theme of "BEING MYSELF" and "BEING OTH-ERS": "You can do any number of takes along that line, first of course a pleasurable image of 'being myself' and then a very unpleasurable image of being others. And of course you can reverse this too. That is, 'To be Myself' can show starving or unfortunate people, and 'To be others' can show happy and prosperous people."[2] Arguably unreadable, Burrough's experi-ments nevertheless constitute a writing unpossessed, an image of the social creativity of the transversal.

Introducing Shakespace

As the instance of Burroughs' use of Shakespeare, more typical than one might first imagine, would indicate, the historical spaces through which Shakespeare has passed as an icon have been extraordinarily diverse and numerous. Shakespeare has stimulated, occupied, and affected countless commercial, political, social, and cultural spaces. These Shakespearean or Shakespeare-influenced spaces, however conventional, alternative, or some-times both, we refer to as "Shakespace," a term that accounts for these par-ticular spaces and the time or speed, the "pace," at which they move from generation to generation and from era to era. This volume of critical essays on adaptations of Shakespeare's work from the early modern period to the twentieth century is most concerned with the roles Shakespace has played at different moments in Anglo-American history. It is specifically interested in the uses and (mis)appropriations of Shakespeare, indeed the cultural constructions of Shakespace, that have produced the social creativity we call "transversal movements" out of "subjective territory" and into "transversal territory," as we have suggested in the family resemblances among the essays noted earlier. This set of concepts, to be elaborated in the discussion to follow, is not specific to Shakespace. But for historical reasons Shakespace is an especially strong exemplar of them, since within it are multiplied the epochal forces and transformations wrought by a multiplicity of forces: by early capitalism, by the great experiment of the new public entertainment industry in early modern England, by the interrogation of socially-prescribed gender roles, by aristocratic and legitimation crises, by the desacralization of absolutist sovereignty, by cross-cultural collisions and relativizations deriving from exploration and colonization, by the scientific revolution and its confounding of official knowledge, and—to take this space into our own time—by the recursive force of the canonical tradition itself on Shakespeare's work. It is no accident that all these constitute the sea changes explored in the early modern period and beyond.

The accumulation of such interacting forces gives additional transformative power to Shakespace, whether radical or conservative,[3] and hence produces what is often read as the ideological "complexity" of any object of critical and political scrutiny (Hedrick 1997). It is the argument of this introduction that both despite and because of the contradictory nature of Shakespace throughout history—from reactionary to complacent to radical—Shakespace has continued to expand into the twentieth century as simultaneously the manifestation of and the inspiration for transversal movements across convention's borders and outside of dominant sociopolitical parameters. It is through these transversal movements that Shakespace emerges as a culturally-imaginable space where Shakespeare may function without class in both the socioeconomic and aesthetic senses of the word. This is because Shakespace's cultural power, or Shakespeare-effect, resists and sometimes transcends all classification that is either reductive or totalizing. Shakespace becomes, as it were, a socially and historically determined playground on which class differentiation and class conflict sometimes slip transversally into an ambiguous space that makes possible and in fact encourages alternative opportunities for thought, expression, and development. Whereas Shakespace has certainly been, and frequently still manifests itself as, what we call an "official territory," and thus has worked to promote various organizational social structures that are discriminatory, hierarchical, or repressive (including structures in academia itself), it is perhaps most powerfully a transversal territory. That is, it has radiated territorially as a transportive, transformative space in which dreams have been made, pursued, virtualized, and realized.

Following a theoretical explication of transversality in terms of its resistance to state-power, our discussion of Shakespace and transversal theory will engage with Stephen Greenblatt's noted February 6, 1999 *New York Times* op-ed article on this year's Academy Award winning film, *Shakespeare in Love* (dir., John Madden 1998). Using his essay as a vehicle for exploring ideas of transformation in a particular context, we want to explicate three dimensions of transversality: the transcending of boundaries into different territory (such as from academia to the popular, from commerce to love, from one subjectivity to another); the possibility of transformation through space and/or time (Greenblatt's essay's juggling of era and location in order to produce something new); and love itself as a model and image of the transversal.

For the best parallel to the transformative power we speak of, we must turn to love. Love, as it happens, is not only the chief marker or signature of Shakespeare in the popular imaginary, but also the marker of resistance to a state-imposed subjectivity. Recognizing the critical importance of Shakespeare's *Romeo and Juliet* to contemporary Shakespace, for which the recent cinematic adaptations *Shakespeare in Love, William Shakespeare's Romeo and Juliet* (dir. Baz Luhrmann 1996), and *Tromeo and Juliet* (dir. Lloyd Kaufman 1996) are indicative, we want to outline a network of Shakespearean influences spatiotemporally distributed between academia, Hollywood, New Jersey, and early modern England. Throughout this distribution, Shakespace progresses substantially in transversal territory, with love at its heart, even when, or especially when, the ethos of capitalism pumps through its arteries—as in the present historical moment.

Transversal Theory[4]

The state machinery of all societies is an assembly of sociopolitical conductors: mental and physical movers, orchestrators, and transmitters. These include the educational, juridical, and religious structures, as well as the institutions of marriage and family. In agreement with its investment in cultural, social, political, and economic fluctuations and determinations, this organizing machinery functions over time and space, sometimes consciously and sometimes unintentionally, to consolidate social and state powers in order to construct society and "the state": the totalized state machinery. By referring to this conductorial assembly as "state machinery," a term that simultaneously connotes singularity and plurality, we are adapting Louis Althusser's conception of what he calls the "(Repressive) State apparatus" and fusing it with his subsidiary "Ideological State Apparatuses" to emphasize that the overall drive for totalization is fueled by diverse conductors of organizational power that are at different times and to varying degrees always both repressive and ideological.[5] This is a dynamic in which various conductors work, sometimes individually and sometimes in conjunction with other conductors, to substantiate their own positions of power within the sociopolitical field and, in the process, inadvertently or otherwise, advance the development and image of the totalized state. Hence, our use of the term "state machinery" should make explicit the multifarious and discursive nature of state power, and thus prevent the misperception of this dynamic as resultant from a conspiracy led by a monolithic state.[6] In fact, the monolithic, Leviathan, or absolute state can only ever be a fantasy-goal whose realization would preclude this dynamic.

Despite all inconsistencies or fissures in the "conduction," the dissemination, or the management of any social order, the state's organizing machinery needs to maintain its colonization of the range of thought or "conceptual territory" of the populace. The machinery needs continually to reestablish the range of personal experience and perception, or "subjective territory," of the populace so that notions of identity cease to be arbitrary and transitory, and acquire temporal constancy and spatial range for the subsistence of what is perceived to be a healthy individual and, by extension, a cohesive social body. It needs to imbue the subject population, however heterogeneous in actuality, with a common state-serving subjectivity, indeed an ideology, that would at the same time give this social body the assurance of homogeneity and universality.

Our term "subjective territory" schematizes personal conceptualization in spatial terms. It is related to Immanuel Kant's notion that it is our intuited acknowledgment of ourselves (as mental beings) as objects to ourselves within space and time that allows for both internal and external experience; our experiences are predicated on the understanding of ourselves as objects existing in space and time (Kant 1990, esp. 35–43). In regard to conceptualization, like Kant, but to a greater extent, we are privileging here the spatial over the temporal aspect of experience; hence our use of the word "territory" and our coinage "Shakespace." We are merging Kant's notion of space with that of Henri Lefebvre, who sees space as a mental, physical, and social determinant that is primary to personal experience. (See Lefebvre 1993, esp. introductory chapter). In this view, conceptualization encompasses space, and thus allows for expansion of, overlap with, trespass against, and flight from the conceptual territory of others. It is territory that permits occupation by subjects and objects. We posit subjective territory as a corrective to the idea of subjectivity as wholly individual, hermetic, or static, an idea that, as suggested earlier in different terms, may prop up the more limited "property" and "appropriation" models of the use of Shakespeare in adaptation.

Nevertheless, notwithstanding what within this viewpoint may in fact be liberatory in potential, subjective territory usually refers to the scope of the conceptual and emotional experience within any hegemonic society or subsociety (the university or criminal organizations, for example),[7] as well as to the subjectification by state machinery. It refers to those whose subjectivity has developed under the influence and auspices of what Pierre Bourdieu calls the "symbolic power" of a particular organizational social structure, whether mainstream, subcultural, or countercultural (Bourdieu 1991, 170). Subjective territory is delineated by conceptual and emotional boundaries that are normally defined by the prevailing science, morality, and ideology. These boundaries bestow a spatiotemporal dimension, or common ground, to an aggregate of individuals or subjects, and work to ensure and monitor the cohesiveness of this social body or, more precisely, as Benedict Anderson puts it, this "imagined community"—"imagined" because there are usually no actual social relationships or communal experiences connecting most of its members (Anderson 1983, 15–16). The boundaries demarcate the specific coordinates for the interaction of sociocultural and ideological centers and conductors. These conductors are usually the same evaluative assemblages that define the state machinery, such as the educational, juridical, and religious structures, that were implemented or appropriated by the state machinery to institute the conceptual and emotional boundaries in the first place. In short, subjective territory is the existential and experiential realm in and from which a given subject of a given hierarchical society perceives and relates to the universe and his or her place in it, working against the ability to imagine himself or herself as anything other than what he or she may already be.

To maintain their privileged status, the state's machinic constituents need to exercise their sociopolitical power carefully and strategically. Their power movements must play a state-serving role in the—much discussed of late—overall circulation of power and social energy within what Michel Foucault describes as the often clustering but ultimately acentered network of discursive "power-knowledge relations" within the sociopolitical field (Foucault 1979, 27–28). Every sociopolitical field is necessarily dominated by a particular ideology, such that its discursive ideological system controls significant conceptual territory. To this end, the state machinery supports and is supported by the dominant culture, so that this particular culture becomes "official" culture. However, since official culture is not always dominant in all circumstances, such as in a subcultural ghetto, official culture is primarily defined by its agreement with state power, and not by the pervasiveness and constancy of its superiority. For us, culture is the aesthetics, ideology, and sociopolitical conductors common to and cultivated by a certain group of people at a specific historical moment; and official culture is the distinguishable group of people, or imagined group, that is characteristically aligned with the culture that mutually supports state power. Official culture's sociopolitical conductors work to formulate and inculcate subjective territory with the appropriate culture-specific and identity-specific zones and localities, so that the subjectivity that substantiates the state machinery is shared, habitually experienced, and believed by each member of the populace to be natural and its very own; hence André Glucksmann's axiomatic goal for state philosophy, "I think, therefore the State is" (Glucksmann 1980, 112).

It is not surprising that the idea of a subjective territory dominated by state machinery finds an analogue in Marx, in an ideological analysis that would, as we might expect, not admit of an anarchist tendency to reduce repressiveness to the mechanisms of the state. What is surprising, however, is to find in Marx's resolution of this a strong outline of our concept of transversality in one key moment—the famous passage on the "hunter, fisher, shepherd, or critic." In this passage, Marx shifts from discussing the social production of individual consciousness to the division of labor, for which he describes an increasingly oppressive, perceived contradiction between individual and social interest, in the "exclusive sphere of activity" determined by state-imposed subjective territory. For our present purposes, this remarkable passage bears repeating:

> For as soon as the distribution of labor comes into being, each man has a particular, exclusive sphere of activity, which is forced upon him and from which he cannot escape. He is a hunter, a fisherman, a shepherd, or a critical critic, and must remain so if he does not want to lose his means of livelihood; while in communist society, where nobody has one exclusive sphere of activity but each can become accomplished in any branch he wishes, society regulates the general production and thus makes it possible for me to do one thing today and another tomorrow, to hunt in the morning, fish in the afternoon, rear cattle in the evening, criticize after dinner, just as I have a mind, without ever becoming hunter, fisherman, shepherd, or critic. (1978, 160)

As one of the rare moments in Marx where the philosopher gives some hint as to what the redeemed communist society would actually look like, the passage usually receives attention from Marxists as a question of the social organization he has in mind, of its distinctiveness as utopian or of its indebtedness to and limitations for an agricultural rather than an industrial epoch.

But it is also in a sense about love, our present figure for the transversal. Revealing its poignancy in Marx's rhetorical shift to personal desire—"just as I have in mind"—it exposes an "occupational unconscious" in Marx, as if imagining the possibility of career change, like the momentary pause in Derrida when he interjects that he would like to become a Shakespeare expert—if there were time (Derrida 1992, 67). In his own take on "subjectivity," Marx's treatment of love is thus about love of work, of work and of more work, a performative through activity instead of simply through consciousness. Supporting our transversal slogan to "Be what you aren't," by means of the impulse to "Be all that you can't be," and yet in a far more positive manner than in Lacan's version of desire as lack, Marx is nevertheless aware that this relation is structural. That is, given historical conditions at present, being what one isn't may be precluded by others being what they are. Marx thus implicitly opposes, in his own terms of love, a transversal subjective power to an enslaving, "objective power above us," which we associate with state-power and which Marx sees as a "fixation of our own social activity" by which the state becomes "divorced from the real interests of individual and community" (1978, 160). For the purpose of placing transversality's oppositional potential in relief, however, we bracket here our understanding of the way actual state power operates by internal contradictions and self-contestations.

Marx's alternative conception to this subjective territory is not, however, a postmodern utopia of fluidity and indefiniteness, abstractions that might just as well be exemplified by the increasing casualization (Bourdieu 1998) of work in our contemporary moment, with its downsizings, part-timing, outsourcing, and rationalized "flexibility." This "late capitalist" scene is rather a degraded version of transversality in the positive sense, though perhaps helping to ward off a premature valorization of the concept by acknowledging even within it a certain capacity for repressiveness. Proliferation and undecidability at any rate are not values in themselves, whether in transversality or in love.

This Marxspace, comparable to our Shakespace, is again a space without class in both the sense of disordering both social class as well as classification itself. (No longer would one be able to "List occupation here.") Marxspace describes a field in the spatiotemporal dimensions of transversality, as he envisions the activities of work broken down into the times of the day—morning, afternoon, evening, and after dinner—and time therefore implicitly spatialized into locations of forest, stream, field, and house. These territories and their connection to subjectivity are neither boundless nor indefinite, but processual from one to the other. None are inherently in structural domination over the others as privileged times or spaces.

As Marx comes up with his own vision of an alternative to subjective territory, so may anyone. In political philosophy, certainly, the antistatist philosophy of anarchism comes to mind, whose philosophical underpinning, as is sometimes forgotten, is the concept of "mutual assistance," and therefore, once again, of something like love. Of course, current evidence of the multiplicity of imagined alternatives is cultural theory itself, with its debates about competing models of resistance, subversion, counterhegemony, dissidence, and so forth. Sometimes overly invested in an assumed, automatically liberatory potential of these models, cultural theory tends to treat them as candidates for some ever-receding, unified theory of ideological opposition, instead of viewing them, as we do here, as instances of a catalogue of historically contingent and sometimes local ways in which acts of transversality occur. This may account for the way in which the Shakespeare text can promote a complexity that is transformative rather than maintaining of the status-quo.

Call them what you will, resistances are induced when there are efforts to configure and fix any subjective territory, and in effect to consolidate a narrowly defined social body and nation-state. There is almost always resistance of some kind when people are forced to think, value, and desire the "proper" things. (There has yet to be implemented a mode of hegemony that can fully control or sufficiently accommodate the relative unpredictability and diversity that seems fundamental to the experience of all things.) Resistance occurs in such diverse forms of unconventionality as occultism (witchcraft and paganism), random and organized crime (mugging, prostitution, racketeering), and sexual immorality (fornication, adultery, sodomy—roughly the triumvirate of socially transgressive forces in Shakespeare's works). Simply put, resistance occurs because the boundaries of subjective territory are challenged, altered, or expanded by either the individual, a social collective, or an external source of transversal power. Like the disparate and often diffuse sociopolitical conductors that support official culture and state power, those that resist the state machinery need not work together as part of an instituted or monolithic movement against the state, even though collaborative resistances and even traditions are common. Like the state machinery, conductors of resistance are typically discursive and not necessarily deliberate; but unlike the state machinery, whose conductors point toward an idealized totality, these conductors, collectively, point toward a plurality or a decentralized power. They are structurally related in that they defy convention, but hardly related in regard to overall purpose. To be a conductor of resistance or of state power, one, or more appropriately, one's practice or expression neither has to be wholly against or supportive of the official ideology, nor against or supportive of this ideology at all times. To be identifiably influential, however, sociopolitical conductors must be predominantly and recognizably on one side at a given moment. Furthermore, regardless of whether an individual who practices a dissident act, such as adultery or witchcraft in early modern England, does so intentionally as an act of resistance to state power, such behavior, because of its symbolic power within the sociopolitical field, nonetheless constitutes resistance, the effect of coalition, as it were, even without coalition. The fears of the Renaissance antitheatricalists were thus grounded, not so much in the imitation of the transgressive acts or characters portrayed on stage, but in imaginative coalition whose effects would be achieved by different means. These effects, moreover, might be intentional or not, as it is frequently the case that people inadvertently oppose or support a power structure, and thus unwittingly contribute to their own emancipation, on the one hand, or oppression, on the other.

Many new historicist and cultural materialist critics—who have dominated Shakespeare studies for the last two decades—argue that early modern England's hegemonic forces, inadvertently or otherwise, fostered dissidence only eventually to suppress it and thereby further reinforce the dominant power structure.[8] Despite the fact that such entrapment is characteristic of all state machinery, this subversion/containment paradigm does not account for or acknowledge the full complexity of the sociopolitical situation at hand, no more than it is fully transferrable, as some argue, to any historical period. It is especially significant that this paradigm, as it is often applied, tends to preclude or ignore microsubversions, or small revolutionary changes of the sort that a transversal model allows. In some cases, the state machinery may have manufactured or inspired these changes, but either chose not to contain or else was unable to contain them. Further, while uncontained microsubversions did occur on various sociopolitical levels, they occurred most importantly at the level of conceptuality. If a particular microsubversion, such as female-to-male transvestism, was thought-provoking and generated polemics and legal action, it was more consequential than a different microsubversion, such as a seditious but esoteric play that generated little or no response (we are thinking of the "positive value," as Terry Eagleton puts it, of the witches' subversiveness in Macbeth).[9] Both the contained and uncontained dissidence of early modern England's public theater (Reynolds 1997a), received tremendous attention and generated vehement conceptual and physical responses from both popular and official sources. The public theater was so influential that, as Reynolds argues, it developed into and was developed by transversal territory. And, as discussed above, it is from the participation of Shakespeare and Shakespeare's plays in such important historical developments that what we call the Shakespace phenomenon evolved.[10]

Initially introduced by Félix Guattari, the terms "transversal" and "transversality" were used rather narrowly without the theoretical enlargement presented here. In his collection of essays (1971–1977) entitled *Molecular Revolution: Psychiatry and Politics* (1984), Guattari uses these terms to discuss the phenomenon of group desire, in particular the way in which the degree of awareness of others in space and time serves to govern movement and change. Guattari's metaphor for this is a field of horses that wear blinkers, whose awareness of what is outside themselves depends upon the degree to which the blinkers are open or shut, which in turn determines their collisions, avoidances, maneuvering, and movements in general. Related to collective fantasy, Guattari thus writes of transversality as "the whole aspect of *social creativity*" less evident in Marx's ideas of subjectivity (Guattari 1984, 26, italics added), except in such a case as his adumbration of transversality discussed earlier. Helpful, too, is a brief borrowing of the term by Gilles Deleuze, in his rejoinder to being criticized once for capitalizing in his theoretical positions by means of the figures of drug users, alcoholics, lunatics, and others without having had their experiences himself. He thus responds that transversality insures that "any effects produced in some particular way (through homosexuality, drugs, and so on) *can always be produced by other means*" (Deleuze 1995, 11). While Guattari's initial use of the term is incorporated in our own, we extend his definition of transversality to conceptuality and its territories, and apply it to the existential processes of individuals as well as of groups getting outside themselves through various means.

As with our use of the word "territory," we are expanding the *OED (Oxford English Dictionary)*'s spatial definitions of "transversal" as "something lying athwart" and a "deviation" to include conceptual spaces. Transversal territory is thus the nonsubjectified region of one's conceptual territory. It is entered through the transgression of the conceptual boundaries, not necessarily real-world ones, and by extension, the emotional boundaries of subjective territory. Most conceptual and emotional boundaries, like those of subjective territory, function like Bourdieu's "habitus":

they are historically- and socially-determined modi operandi that decide, normalize, and monitor individual and collective conceptualization and experience of the world; as a result, these same modi operandi are often successfully perpetuated throughout space-time.

But transversal territory is entirely different. Although also firmly linked to its sociohistorical moment, transversal territory neither requires determination or regulation, nor does it serve any specific structures, conductors, dispositions, methods, or objective outcomes.[11] In a sense transversal territory is an anti-habitus—an antisubjective territory: the power of transversal thought produces or informs the transgressive *modi vivendi* of sociopaths, schizoids, criminals, philosophers, artists, and all sorts of social, cultural, and political nonconformists. Foucault illuminates the transversal threshold when he proclaims, "Transgression opens onto a scintillating and constantly affirmed world, a world without shadow or twilight, without that serpentine 'no' that bites into fruits and lodges their contradictions at their core" (Foucault 1977, 37). Transversal territory ensues from and signifies a deterritorialization of or a subversive intersection with subjective territory. Its "transversal power," as a mechanism for experiential alterity, energizes and is energized by the enunciation and amplification of transition states, from criminal acts to natural disasters. Consequently, transversal territory transcends, fractures, or displaces the "scintillating and constantly affirmed world" of subjective territory. By extension, since subjective territory is a mechanism of subjectification for the state machinery, transversal territory threatens an ideological "official territory": the ruling proprieties and legalities within a social body. The "rational State," as Glucksmann opines, is a Machiavellian "machine consciously organized on the basis of permanent awareness that the fatherland, that is, the State itself, is in danger" (Glucksmann 1980, 106). Clearly, transversal territory is not a mechanism of this machine; it is not a hobgoblin that the state needs and constructs paranoiacally or strategically; it is not simply a factor in a subversion/containment operation. Instead, transversal territory is diametrical to the state machinery and a *real* enemy of state power, whatever the progressive or nonprogressive status of that power might be. It is reflected in the great metamorphic themes and *topoi* of Shakespearean narratives: ruler into commoner, woman into man, actor into citizen, and clown into philosopher—the innumerable instances of spectacular, experimental alterity.

Shakespearean characters, and characters from life, occupy transversal territory when they defy or surpass the conceptual boundaries of their prescribed subjective addresses, opening themselves, as it were, to subjective awareness outside the self. Transversal territory invites people to deviate from the hierarchicalizing assemblages—whether vertical or horizontal—of any organizational social structure. Its transversal power inspires multiplicities of conjunctions and disjunctions within official territory, and may even motivate the production of a counterculture, which is to say a subculture that actively and intentionally challenges official culture. Of course, transversal power need not stop at a single social formation: a counterculture itself would, by the logic of the transversal, be subject to a further movement leading members outside the subjective territories of a hegemonic subculture. In short, transversality is the indispensable traveler's aid, inducing travel conceptually and emotionally across the organized space of subjectivity, to expand subjective territory and thereby enter a disorganized and perhaps unlimited space through an ambiguous or explosive processual movement, by means of performances of iconoclasm, impropriety, immorality, criminality, insanity, or other acts we summarize as being distinctly "without class."[12]

Desire, under the regime of subjective territory, may also be constructed and manipulated by and for state power, in order to perpetuate official culture. By contrast, transversality, as might be expected, produces and expresses desire in the dynamic form of what Gilles Deleuze and Félix Guattari term "becoming."[13] Becoming is a desiring process by which all things (energies, ideas, people, societies) change into something different from what they are. If those things had been identified and normalized by some dominant force (such as state law, religious credo, or official language), then any change in them is, in fact, a becoming-other. The metamorphosis of becoming-other-social-identities confounds such concepts as the essential, the normal, the unified, and the universal, which are often fundamental to subjective territory, together with the binary constructs, so often under deconstructive pressure in Shakespeare, that we find culturally and historically widespread—male and female, good and evil, normal and abnormal, natural and unnatural, real and unreal.[14] The occurrence of identity becomings corresponds to a negotiation and transformation in the modes of power and knowledge from which official models for subjectivity are drawn. Considering the social and political potential of becomings, it is important to remember that neither revolutionary change nor containment or return, whether individual or collective, need happen instantaneously or totally. Rather, they may happen as a result of various microsubversions and microcontainments, the space of Shakespearean adaptation providing one, with its future state no more autonomous than a past one. In contradistinction to subjective territory, transversality necessitates the conceptual space-time for identity becomings, and evokes and advances the antistate concepts of heterogeneity, mutability, performance, nomadism, expansion, and indeterminacy.[15]

Finally, one can even imagine a kind of transversal universality: the ideal state in which transversal power is pure and pervasive and in which everyone acknowledges and respects difference, transformation, and indeterminacy; hence what we might imagine to be the transversal chorus: "We think, therefore we can be anything." The ideal is more like Gonzalo's ideal commonwealth in *The Tempest* than one might expect, for Shakespeare represents his narrative there as itself subject to transversality. In other words, while Gonzalo imagines what he would do with the isle if he were "king on't," his imagination soars as he eliminates in turn riches, poverty, legal contract, work, and, finally, sovereignty itself (2.1.157). While Sebastian and Antonio, misreading the speech as a logical treatise and thus sneering at the apparent contradiction of a king who declares there will be "no sovereignty" in his realm, it is old Gonzalo's own forgetfulness of the first part of his speech as he arrives at the latter part that is instructive. His act produces an effect that narratively embodies transversal performance: a non-king becoming a king, crossed by the figure of a king becoming no king by successive, imaginative, and even revolutionary microsteps, in a rhetorical wandering through a topic that replicates the discursive mode of the same speech's source, the Montaignian essay, which is the Renaissance embodiment of transversality as a literary genre. The political ideal, like the subjectivity of its kind speaker, is founded, it appears, on love or, rather, on transversality in love: the consciousness of having been nothing but becoming everything.

Star-Crossed Shakespace

Where, then, does the becoming-other of transversality cross the experience of Shakespace? Here we will consider the transversal nature of a certain discourse regarding the film, *Shakespeare in Love,* together with the film itself, as illustrations of aspects of transversality. In the process of this presentation, it will become clear that rather than serving as an instance of transversality, as we have interpreted it here as constituting a figure of love, the film reveals itself to possess a different transversality altogether.

In contrast to the film's Academy Award-winning combination of sophisticated entertainment and taste, however, we want briefly to consider what might be thought of as its virtual opposite, the teenexploi film *Tromeo and Juliet* (1997, dir. Lloyd Kaufman), a tasteless, campy adaptation with signature excesses of graphic sex and gore, a film that few have seen or perhaps would want to see, popular only in a niche market where it is nevertheless wildly popular. Richard Burt in his consideration of this film and others like it, regards them as symptomatic of a certain combination of both elevating and erasing or dumbing down Shakespeare in contemporary culture, in films that, like this one, are so far from the Shakespearean text as barely to be able to be termed adaptations at all. Although many might indeed find the film unwatchable, its link to Shakespeare decidedly tenuous, it may be that its nature is, for our present discussion, quite instructive.

In his introduction to the video of *Tromeo and Juliet,* director and co-screenwriter Lloyd Kaufman informs us that the film will include "the car crashes, the kinky sex, the dismemberment, all the wonderful ingredients Shakespeare always wanted but never had" (1998). While this sort of statement is a traditional apologetic for wildly imagined adaptations disclaiming full directorial responsibility, it certainly may be that in some transversal sense, "kinky sex"[16] is more Shakespearean than highbrow taste would admit, as the history of Shakespearean Bowdlerization and censorship would attest (Hedrick 1994). Certainly the excesses of gore in *Titus Andronicus,* often dismissed or forgotten in reverential elevations of Shakespeare, would confirm Kaufman's self-justifying take on the Bard. Indeed, the tasteless gore in Kaufman's Troma Company films seems to have trickled upward in tastefulness as well, into several derivative moments of camp violence in Julie Taymor's recent film *Titus,* a serious blockbuster production boasting top actors such as Anthony Hopkins and Jessica Lange, a film whose ultraviolent ending draws from the shlock style of the Troma films, just as the BBC's earlier version of the play drew explicitly from the graphic representation of gore in *The Texas Chainsaw Massacre* (the killing of Chiron and Demetrius staged in a slaughterhouse setting). The permeability of high and low culture is hardly unidirectional where entertainment value is concerned, where the high cultural mode may experiment with the alterity of trash—transversally experiencing the benefits of trash without its stigmatized social location.

A brief sense of the shock intentions of the adaptation would convey its New York City subcultural realm of heavy metal, pornography, and leather, depicted with an astonishing array of graphic language, sex, and violence: nipple piercing, chopping off of fingers in a paper cutter, cacophonous flatulence of Romeo's father, murder by skull-bashing on a fire hydrant, eye stabbing with a tattoo needle, lesbian sex between Juliet and her punk-metal-rocker female cook, masturbation by Romeo to Shakespeare porn on CD-Rom, wife-beating by Juliet's father, Juliet's bondage and sexual abuse by her father, a dream-assault against Juliet by a monster penis, self-flagellation by Juliet's fiancée with cow carcasses, and Juliet's transformation into a barfing-head-spinning pig-girl with a long dangling greenish penis. The film ends with a virtually Jacobean revelation that Romeo and Juliet are actually brother and sister, a discovery that does not however thwart their love, and it concludes happily with a future domestic scene of the two at a family backyard barbecue with the deformed, mutant children from the inbreeding of their union.

While Kaufman maintains that his cinematic adaptation of *Romeo and Juliet* is truer to Shakespeare's wishes than Shakespeare could realize, implying limitations imposed by technology as well as by government and social control, his joking relation to the Bard continues with the claim of a personal connection, namely, that "Shakespeare's spirit entered my body at Stratford" (Kaufman 1998). In effect, what Kaufman describes in this quasi-joke about poetic inspiration is one aspect of transversality, namely, the ability to achieve the effects of a certain subjectivity without having to inhabit that subjectivity.

What Kaufman describes, therefore, is particularly transversal. Beyond the topos of the muses, it is possession, by demons or otherwise, that conveys the transversal spirit of poetic furor. If seriously intended, the claim would, of course, be skeptically received today. Nevertheless, despite the skepticism of early moderns such as Reginald Scot and others, there was, according to Stephen Greenblatt in a provocative essay entitled "Shakespeare Bewitched," ready belief available in Elizabethan London, to which "Shakespeare was willing to present witchcraft as a visible, credible practice," such as in *Henry VI* and *Macbeth,* but also that Shakespeare himself was a witch (Greenblatt 1993, 108–35, esp. 122, 127). Regardless of whether or not Shakespeare was really a witch, as Kaufman's remarkable possession might also suggest, the very possibility of a witch-effect—perhaps better demonstrated through Kaufman's *Tromeo and Juliet* than by either Greenblatt's historiography or his proposed movie about Shakespeare that makes no mention of Shakespeare being a witch—is what most fuels Shakespeare's transversal influence. To be more precise, it is the believed possibility, as Marjorie Garber observes, that Shakespeare, transformed and transforming, is supernatural or at least superhuman (hence his ability to work such extraordinary "magic" on the minds and hearts of so many people), that imbues Shakespace with peculiar ideological power:

> He is—whoever he is, or was—the fantasy of originary cultural wholeness, the last vestige of universalism: *unser Shakespeare.* From the vantage point of

a hard-won cultural relativism, a self-centered de-centering that directs attention, as it should and must, to subject positions, object relations, abjects, race-class-and-gender, there is still this tug of nostalgia, the determinedly secularized but not yet fully agnosticized desire to believe. To believe in something, in someone, all-knowing and immutable. If not God, then Shakespeare, who amounts to a version of the same thing. (Garber 1998, 168).

And if Shakespeare in fact spoke from the position of the witch, as Kaufman and Greenblatt suggest, the transversality of the practice would be apparent, requiring no further elaboration.

Yet another aspect of *Tromeo and Juliet* is crucial to its inheritance of transversality, thus making it, as we ourselves want to believe, truer to Shakespeare's wishes; it is truer to the nostalgia most responsible for Shakespeare's persistent popularity and attested universalism. *Tromeo and Juliet* virtualizes with a newly-recovered teen idealism and flair the romantic concept of love that is Shakespeare's trademark, which brilliantly overrides the play's sordid world and its jaded view. Indeed, love may be a buried subtext throughout the film, as in the otherwise odd moment (odd given the raunch conventions expected from its designated audience) of Tromeo's masturbation scene that the porn announcer on the screen, at Tromeo's height of passion, begins chanting how she *loves* him. At the film's end, unlike in Shakespeare's play, Tromeo and Juliet's love transcends all opposition and is gloriously victorious, so much so that despite its sordid and chaotic grotesquery one may become at the end (as the response of at least some of our students suggests) even exhilarated, despite the absurdity, by another level in the madness of true romantic love, that is, through Tromeo and Juliet's love's overcoming not only mutant deformity but also the deep but fascinating deformity of suburban New Jersey existence. *Tromeo and Juliet* thus takes us on its own transversal journey, but with a historical depth-of-field linking it to Shakespeare's own London.

Returning to our consideration of the phenomenon of the film *Shakespeare in Love,* we observe that it was produced in an era of an explosion of Shakespace in a more literal sense. These include venues for performance, such as the rebuilt Globe Theatre in London, and numerous films and adaptations, both mass-marketed and alternative. There have been more cinematic versions than in any other decade to date.[17] The adapted plays that have received widespread media attention include: *Hamlet* (dir. Franco Zeffirelli 1990, and dir. Kenneth Branagh 1996); *The Tempest* (as *Prospero's Books,* dir. Peter Greenaway 1991); *Henry IV* (as *My Own Private*

Idaho, dir. Gus Van Sant 1991); *Much Ado About Nothing* (dir. Kenneth Branagh 1993); *Othello* (dir. Oliver Parker 1995); *Richard III* (dir. Richard Loncraine 1995 and as *Looking for Richard,* dir. Al Pacino 1996); *A Midsummer Night's Dream* (dir. Michael Hoffman 1999); *Titus* (dir. Julie Taymor 1999); and anticipations at the present moment of *Hamlet, Othello, Love's Labor's Lost,* and *Twelfth Night.*

As Richard Burt illustrates in his contribution to this volume, however, the play of Shakespeare's that has been of highest interest and profile is *Romeo and Juliet.* Not only has the play been adapted into one mass-marketed Hollywood film, Luhrmann's *William Shakespeare's Romeo and Juliet,* with Leonardo DiCaprio as Romeo (1996), one mass-distributed cult film, Kaufman's *Tromeo and Juliet* (1996), and three films for the adult heterosexual and gay male video markets, *Juliet and Romeo* (dir. Joe D'Amato 1996), *Romeo and Julian* (dir. Sam Abdul 1993), and *Romeo Syndrome* (dir. Jim Enright 1995), but Shakespeare's *Romeo and Juliet* also provides the storyline underlying the 1998 Academy Award-winning account of Shakespeare's life, *Shakespeare in Love* (dir. John Madden 1998). More recently the love tale becomes frame for a Hong Kong style action-film, *Romeo Must Die* (dir. Andrzej Bartkowiak 2000), with Hong Kong star Jet Li as the Romeo character caught between Chinese, African American, and white families and mob lords in a struggle over waterfront property sought for the development of a sports arena. Strikingly, for our present purposes, the latter film deemphasizes the romantic relationship (the Romeo and Juliet characters Han Sag and Trish never in fact kiss) developing between the interracial couple, making it more platonic, with the depth of feeling shifted transversally to *alliance* and *affiliation,* as they conspire with each other and against family in order to solve and revenge the murder of a brother. Although they never kiss, they have a fight scene together, with Shakespeare's story furnishing a transformative Shakespace by which the effects of love are achieved in another sphere altogether, as we will show them to be achieved in the following extended discussion of the recent film *Shakespeare in Love.*

Thus, Shakespeare's virtual identification with love itself is again thoroughly cemented in the current cultural sphere. In *Shakespeare in Love,* Shakespeare, the most famous playwright and poet who ever lived, who is most celebrated for his profound understanding of love, is characterized through the plot of his most beloved love story, *The Tragedy of Romeo and Juliet,* intercut with a fictionalized version of his own love life. As a candidate for a contemporary reading of transversality, the film, appearing to crystallize the concept of love as a driving force of transversal power, is thus remarkably well-situated. But as the present analysis will demonstrate, its transversality tells a different story in unexpected comparison with *Tromeo and Juliet,* for in *Shakespeare in Love* the love is, in effect, not worth fighting for, since, as Greenblatt summarizes in his *New York Times* op-ed piece, it is a film not about Shakespeare finding the love of his life, but one in which "the poet has found his muse" (Greenblatt 1999, A29).

Yet this considerably classy movie, as we suggest, itself creates a Shakespace, not the least for the discourse around it, as will be exemplified by a discussion of its relation to the figure of Stephen Greenblatt, the era's most famous Shakespeare scholar, whose scholarship has itself provoked considerable transversal and dissident movement through academia (literary scholars as historians practicing, as it were, without a license). In Greenblatt's consideration of the film we see various transversal movements in the Shakespace of which Greenblatt's op-ed piece is both participatory and illustrative.

Greenblatt: The Essay

Greenblatt's *New York Times* op-ed uses the identity of the Renaissance scholar and the image of history in distinctive ways, as the piece narrates an ironic but nostalgic history of his brush with the film's initial conception. Apparently, Greenblatt was solicited several years back for advice by the co-writer of *Shakespeare in Love,* Marc Norman, who visited him at UC Berkeley seeking ideas to write a screenplay about Shakespeare's life. A comic tale of his suggestions dismissed, the piece recruits the reader with a longing for a more radical Shakespace linked to a less radical, popular longing to reveal the mystery of Shakespeare's identity, life, and genius. The op-ed tells the story of how Greenblatt's idea for the main angle of the movie—why not make up a story of Shakespeare in love with Christopher Marlowe?—was quickly rejected by Norman, since "no studio would buy it." The essay's rhetorical point is, in effect, about failed alterity—the lack of influence on the entertainment industry by the idealistic scholar proposing an idea that would have made the film more progressive.

Shakespeare in Love ultimately, as Greenblatt implies, plays it pretty safe, sex-wise. It is, moreover, largely heteronormative even as it employs comic cross-dressing, though perhaps with some canny resistant touches, such as the failure of the company of actors during rehearsal to raise eyebrows about Shakespeare's close relation to this actor—actually Viola de Lesseps disguised as Thomas of Kent—playing Juliet in his new play, or indeed in Shakespeare's initial interest in the boy. While not pressing his suggestion,

Greenblatt uses his suggestion to address the film's chief occlusion, namely the question of Shakespeare's own sexual orientation. This he addresses by citing the moment when its aspiring Shakespeare, newly inspired by an affair not with Marlowe but with the fictitious noble woman Viola de Lesseps, runs off (as he is so often seen in this film as *running*) to write Sonnet 18 to her—"Shall I compare thee to a summer's day?" Perhaps a little in-joke (certainly the hand of Tom Stoppard in the screenplay would lend itself to such playfulness), the scene allows Greenblatt to refresh the memory of the *New York Times* reader, who may have forgotten for a moment the Shakespeare class he or she took at Amherst or Colgate, with the hardly arcane information that this sonnet, like most of the sonnets, was written not to a young noblewoman but to a young nobleman, and a pretty one at that.[18]

Yanking back the reader of the *New York Times* to this past knowledge, Greenblatt bursts the bubble of heteronormativity that perhaps pervaded that bygone Shakespeare class but which is recuperated anew, against the current of the time, in *Shakespeare in Love*. Exposing the Hollywood machine for its sell-out in misrepresenting Shakespeare, he "outs" or "re-outs" Shakespeare. For the moviegoers who were relieved to learn that Shakespeare's alleged same-sex love was only ever rumor, Greenblatt's authoritative reminder must have been disillusioning at best. And for his other audience, moviegoers who felt betrayed by the film's heteronormalizing of Shakespeare, Greenblatt's intervention may have been intended as a welcomed, transversal reempowering of the Shakespace legitimating same-sex love, countering the very state machinery that would under other circumstances underprop Shakespeare's cultural capital. Moving eloquently across space-time in this little misappropriation, Greenblatt's meddling begins with an explanation of the mixed attitude of Shakespeare's historical era toward same-sex love, which he introduces by way of a droll citation of Senator Trent Lott's malevolent comparison of homosexuality to alcoholism and kleptomania.

Shifting then to his meeting with Norman, Greenblatt stresses that Shakespeare's personal life, little known about and even less spectacular, would require much embellishment if it were to become "cinematic." To that end, Greenblatt first suggests writing a story about Shakespeare's imagined involvement in religious intrigue of the time, something like what turns into the other current historical movie about early modern England, *Elizabeth*. Greenblatt then offers his perhaps even less convincing suggestion, namely to imagine, given Shakespeare's "ambiguous" sexuality, Shakespeare's arrival at literary greatness. When this suggestion is rejected as well,

Greenblatt's conclusion shifts away from historical explication to contemporary cultural analysis, after the fact of the movie's success. Here, the figure of the naive academic momentarily tries on a market-savvy identity; he opines—quite accurately we believe—that the theme that actually made the movie a success was not even its romantic heterosexual love, but the only theme that "all Americans can celebrate"—that of *success,* our national preoccupation. Acknowledging that the "canny" character of the screenwriters in rewriting and fabricating Shakespeare's emotional history and life was very much like Shakespeare's own "fiddling with facts," Greenblatt's self-excuse ends, however, with a reassertion of his rejected idea for the plot. He ends up defending it *after all,* and doing so on the moviemakers' own marketing terms: that they may have underestimated the ability of Americans' obsession with success to override any unease with a same-sex love story.

Returning to his "own" identity, Greenblatt implies that his cultural analysis might, as it were, have produced not better historiography but a better *movie,* as he shifts transversally between a popularizing and a historicizing role. Of course, such a film would have been more provocative and complicated in its response: appealing to people who privilege commercial success above everything—including love; disturbing people who think love, whether heterosexual or same-sex, is most important; engaging to those approving the "fact" of Shakespeare's homosexual love of the young nobleman; and distressing those who privilege, say, traditional family values over any accomplishment by an individual, whether motivated by love, prestige, or money.

Greenblatt's ingenious rhetorical design shifts from critique to apology to critique again, excusing his own lack of influence in this case with an account of a time-machine alliance forged between those shrewd marketeers Shakespeare and Hollywood. The shrewdness is captured by the movie's representation of Shakespeare in quite contemporary commercial terms, not so much as aspiring but as hustling young writer, who steals ideas from the street, from other actors, and from rival playwrights; who is discovered practicing the writing of his signature when he has a play due; who jockeys with and fakes the offers of the theater owners to buy his yet-to-be-written or even to be conceived play, "Romeo and Ethel, the Pirate's Daughter." The essay's rhetorical voice, moreover, delicately shifts between the authoritative demeanor of the scholar, implicitly the very reason for the writer's visiting such a top-gun Shakespearean in the first place, and a deferential submission to Hollywood, with Mr. Norman, mogul-like, taking him out to something like a power lunch. Greenblatt even adopts the registers of the entertainment realm rather than the scholarly one, when his bright idea is torpedoed: "Never mind," is his hip response, invoking the historical memory of Gilda Radner on TV's *Saturday Night Live.*

Along with this staged deference to pop culture, Greenblatt somehow indirectly manages deference to the scholarly audience as well, as he presents what are more or less historical commonplaces within the field about the era. The resulting identity of the scholar here that Greenblatt transverses into is that of a "good enough" not a groundbreaking scholar, a scholar for hire, as it were, who is competent to furnish basic information, the scholarly equivalent of the hack authors inhabiting *Shakespeare in Love.* Perhaps this scholar is even one who is, as Hollywood might expect him to be, somewhat imagination-challenged, like the movie's Shakespeare, whose inspirational quill, as he bawdily complains to the comically transported Elizabethan shrink, has dried up of late. The competing authorities—Hollywood and academia—are both presented in their overconfident realms of expertise, only to be challenged at the end of the piece by the concluding suggestion of a realm of cultural "mystery": what the public *could* love. Nevertheless, it is the scholar who owns a secret key to the entertainment industry.

Of course, the story of Greenblatt's rejection, like that of *Shakespeare in Love,* has its positive though bittersweet side, for his narrative makes us privy to what Greenblatt apparently, in his rejected suggestion, provided as a real basis for the film, although the essay never explicitly acknowledges his role: the film does indeed use the fiction of a hack commercial writer's pivotal transformation into a great writer and a commercial success (though itself not a novel idea), a transformation achieved through the agency not of the mind but of the heart. Love, it would at first seem, is the force of transversal power in the film that moves people out of their stagnating subjective territories, where their range of conceptual and emotional experience had seemed unalterably blocked, and into realms of greater emotional and conceptual possibility. The movie thus parallels several love-motivated transformations: Shakespeare is transformed to greatness; Viola de Lesseps is transformed from social conventions; the theater is transformed from aesthetic conventions; the Queen's cynicism is transformed in the discovery that commercial poetry can represent true love; and the money-lenders and whores are transformed from their jaded worldliness. The multiple levels of transformations could only have been even more pronounced had Greenblatt's essay complicated the discussion more transversally with a greater parallel: why not tell a story of new historicism's enormous success, the accomplishment producing both Green-

blatt's dual rhetorical stature as historian and critic of contemporary culture, as one inspired by its own transformative personal relation? Why not,
indeed, imagine new historicism's transversal founding on love?

Greenblatt: The Movie

The desire to have a hand in making a story more "cinematic," whether by
way of the influence either of traditional boring scholarly knowledge or
else of hip cultural critique, suggests a transversal way of looking at Greenblatt's essay, that is, cinematically rather than rhetorically. Thinking of it this
way might help bring into relief the general relationship between Greenblatt's historicism and the cinema, as well as to provide some understanding of the difference between the creative historiographical moves of
Greenblatt and the commercial ones of *Shakespeare in Love*. Such a comparison will also allow us to elucidate other contradictory Shakespaces now
dominated by the competing interests of Hollywood and academia.

If a subtext of Greenblatt's film is, in effect, the self-reflexive one, a will
toward *directing,* what it points toward is the manipulation of what Gilles
Deleuze refers to as the "time-image" of contemporary cinema, a change
occurring after postwar film that, we think, may have provided a condition
of possibility for a new historicism. Significantly, film direction, according
to François Lyotard, is among the most *political* of acts (Lyotard 1989, 176),
and hence authorizes consideration of the political force of Greenblatt's
cinematic orchestration of sociocultural movement and his time, here
alluded to as Greenblatt formulates an antihomostigmatic project to
counter conservative U.S. Senator Trent Lott and his specific influence on
state power. To do so, Greenblatt must pass through the ideological spaces
of Hollywood, commercial capitalism, and historical London.

In what might be viewed as a cinematic supplement to our theory of
transversality, Deleuze analyzes "images" (camera shots and shot sequences),
and differentiates between the "movement-image," the "action-image," and
the "time-image."[19] Movement-image refers to the interaction among vari-
able elements (characters and objects) that are not the focus in a scene, of
the camera's gaze: we watch background characters snicker at a romantic
moment between two lovers. Action-image refers to the interaction
between elements that are the camera's focus and other elements, those that
are periphery or simply not the focus: we watch a character (an action-
hero) singlehandedly overcome an onslaught of "bad guys." Movement-
images and action-images, as the mobile sections of a cinematographic
duration, typically indicate sequential or causal connections between the

objects or events depicted: a character shoots a gun and another falls, objects or characters depart from point A and arrive at B. Both movement-images and action-images represent time as actual, contiguous, passing, and measurable. To do this, they must achieve a plausible linkage and seemingly chronological coherence of sensory-motor relations within the image (among objects and characters) and between the image and the viewer (so that the viewer not be confused or doubtful of the order of events represented).

In contrast, time-image refers to a virtual presentation of time, when the image's elements and events appear simultaneous, random, or simply without chronology. This is achieved only through a frustration or break up of the image's sensory-motor schemata (the expected and tractable interactions among characters and objects) in the form of a purely optical and sound situation. Comprised of apparently chance relations, the time-image does not extend logically or comfortably into action or reaction, any more than it is stimulated by these processes: we see incoherent montage cuts and sequences, dissolves, deframings, superimpositions, intricate camera movements—all techniques mirroring the radical displacement of the transversal, broken up like the revolutionary cut-up technique of Burroughs, itself cinematically driven. Whereas there can be, and usually is, interaction among focused and periphery elements within a time-image, the image is predominately nonchronological and amorphous or hallucinatory, such that the internal movement cannot be centered or contextualized with certainty in relation to other elements (cuts or objects) within the time-image. Because of its inherent ambiguity, the time-image must be "read" as much as it is seen (and heard); it produces what Deleuze calls "any-space-whatever": disconnected space that demands contemplation and allows for greater freedom of interpretation, and thus challenges the viewer's analytical capacity. With the concept of an "any-space-whatever" Deleuze describes a transversal space into which moviegoers wander, though only temporarily while viewing the film, when made to straddle or venture beyond the thresholds of their subjective territories by the transversal power of a time-image.

As a potent mode of expression, the time-image frequently emerges at pivotal moments in the filmic narrative. This is often done, as in Greenblatt's essay, in the form of a "recollection-image" or a "dream-image," such as in a flashback, premonitory, fantasy, or hallucinatory sequence. Recall Greenblatt's speedy oscillation among his commentary on *Shakespeare in Love*'s (mis)representation of Shakespeare, his account of early modern English attitudes on same-sex love, his critical invocations of Trent Lott's outspoken prejudice against homosexuality, his recollection of the power lunch with Mr. Norman, his own meditations "over dessert and coffee," and his imaginary love affair between Marlowe and Shakespeare. Together, in the span of just several paragraphs, these musings and images create any-space-whatever. In addition to a feeling of timelessness that Greenblatt's essay creates through not only nonchronological historiographical montage, but also as a result of the preexisting Shakespace in which it moves, that is, the accepted timelessness of Shakespeare that today's Shakespace adamantly promotes, Greenblatt's movie must be "read," literally: it is an essay, one that depends on both Greenblatt's and its audience's recollection-and dream-images. Recollection-and dream-images, according to Deleuze, are virtual images of events (often related to a character's past, future, or unconscious experiences) that are made accessible by the actual sensory-motor schemata of the corresponding movement-and action-images. For instance, Shakespeare's sonnet, "Shall I Compare Thee to a Summer's Day," that Shakespeare writes in an action-image for Viola de Lesseps in *Shakespeare in Love* reappears in a recollection-image in Greenblatt's movie-essay as the sonnet scholars know that Shakespeare wrote for a "fair-haired, wealthy young man." However, recollection-and dream-images are not by definition time-images. For them to be time-images, as in Greenblatt's imaginary scenario in which Shakespeare and Marlowe are lovers whose romance leads to both the historical facts of Marlowe's tragic death and Shakespeare's commercial success, the virtual must interact with the actual such that the image is double-sided and mutually engaged. Moreover, also as in the case of Greenblatt's imaginary scenario, if this engagement becomes convoluted or united to the point that the actual and the virtual are blurred, and thus the meaning of the relationship between the two is unclear, the time-image is in fact what Deleuze calls a "crystal-image."

In the crystal-image, the any-space-whatever crystallized by the coalescence of the actual and the virtual is a gateway for what Deleuze calls "the powers of the false" with which all images are potentially imbued. Put differently, the crystal-image influences the viewer with the idea that things are not as they appear, that the narration may be false: truth is questionable. According to Deleuze,

> By raising themselves to the indiscernibility of the real and the imaginary, the signs of the crystal go beyond all psychology of the recollection or dream, and all physics of action. . . . What is in play is no longer the real and the imaginary, but the true and the false. And just as the real and the imaginary become indiscernible in certain very specific conditions of the image,

the true and the false now become undecidable and inextricable: the impossible proceeds from the possible, and the past is not necessarily true. (Deleuze 1995, 274–75)

It is in this any-space-whatever of Greenblatt's movie-essay that Shakespace's past and present are possibly just as uncertain as its future; here the powers of the false inspire transversal movement through the primary "cinematic" effect of the op-ed essay on *Shakespeare in Love*—the crystal-image; but transversal movement is also inspired through the "depth of field" effect that Deleuze believes to be a crucial component of the time-image of contemporary cinema.

Deleuze gives this effect a historical sense comparable to a visual one. That is, depth of field in its full importance is "a function of remembering . . . a figure of temporalization" (1989, 110). Layers of history, in one aspect of this technique, are brought into simultaneous focus for the duration of the shot, and hence become, for the time being, commensurable, either as an actual image of someone's recollection or as an "invitation" to recollection (1989, 109–10). The technique is therefore linked to memory itself, either as the juxtaposition of disparate "sheets of the past," or, when employed with more complexity, as in the work of Robbe-Grillet and the filmmaker Alain Resnais, as a "simultaneity of peaks of the present," that is "a present of the past, a present of the present, and a present of the future":

It is the possibility of treating the world or life, or simply a life or an episode, as one single event which provides the basis for the implication of presents. An accident is about to happen, it happens, it has happened; but equally it is at the same time that it will take place, has already taken place and is in the process of taking place; so that, before taking place, it has not taken place, and taking place, will not take place. (Deleuze 1989, 100–1).

The shot sequence of Greenblatt's movie begins with an establishing shot within *Shakespeare in Love,* the particular moment of the writing scene followed by a flashback to the historical "fact" of the sonnet audience, then followed by another pairing of the broader historical contexts of each of those shots—the juxtaposition of particularly Elizabethan attitudes toward sexual orientation (legal intolerance, indifferent enforcement) to the contemporary sociopolitical scene of more tolerant laws but less tolerance, exemplified by Trent Lott's invidious comment comparing homosexuals to alcoholics and kleptomaniacs. This jammed double set of historical pairings, both historical sheets and "peaks" of the present, is then followed by juxtaposing the current moment of the film with the story of its origin, the screenwriter's pilgrimage to the—great, or good enough—Renaissance scholar, and finally by the paired suggestions rejected in turn by the proper movie man. As we compare stretches of time that are generally commensurable, we become aware of sequence in the piece, in such a way that a larger duration of time seems evident, rather than a particular time. This juxtaposition tends then to give an image of time itself, an open space, Deleuze's any-space-whatever, the hope of a transformative possibility for a homophobic political culture. In considering Greenblatt's op-ed essay, we begin to realize that the device of the anecdote—that much vexed and often derided signature of the new historicist essay—is best understood not as a literary or historicist methodology but as a cinematic device.

The historical juxtaposition within the film *Shakespeare in Love,* however, establishes a space chiefly for individual, not social, transformation. The rather limited progressive act of a woman's playing her own gender in the professional theater—undoubtedly a positive social change but one with little direct analogue or political leverage for the present—is brought up to the present, however, in Queen Elizabeth's pronouncement upon discovering that Thomas of Kent is a disguised woman, namely, that she herself knows what it means for a woman to play a man's role in a man's world. Despite the razor-edged pointedness of Judi Dench's delivery of the lines (a delivery that earned her an Academy Award for supporting actress for less than ten minutes of screen time) in terms of the broader picture of social relations, the historical collisions and playful anachronisms in the film produce a less real collision of positions. In effect, the perspective created has a much shallower depth of field; that is, it is not so much by a juxtaposition of contemporary gender relations with early modern ones, or even early modern ones before the "woman's debate" of the early seventeenth-century, as it is of a pre-1970s feminism, with its drive toward equality, against the less-defined yet more disturbing potentialities of later feminism and postfeminism. The shipwreck fantasy of Viola echoes screenwriter/director Jane Campion's *The Piano* as a trope of liberation; her wandering alone on the shores of the "vast and empty" land of cinematic America is like Deleuze's cinematic any-space-whatever. Imagined by the film for purposes of telling a love story, therefore, is some relatively brief historical moment in which only so much reform is needed so as to get women onto the stage (and into the gaze of the Oscars), and to end arranged marriages—a nonthreatening historical practice to which we are smugly superior. In a sense, this limited depth corresponds ideologically to the backlash phase or conservative restoration of the present, with its political reversion to the "pragmatic," the space in which contemporary feminism so often finds itself positioned.

The first sociocultural space of the beginnings of the early modern entertainment industry, London, is not so much juxtaposed to as actually identified with the final location of this industry and the hustling embodiment of the future of capitalism, Los Angeles. Thus, through historical displacement, the film allows Los Angeles to be conceived not in its conventional noir or even tragic form, as we must needs conceive it now (as superbly unpacked in the work of Mike Davis, 1990, 1998), but rather as a site of romantic screwball comedy. The movie thus treats through farcical fashion the potential ruthlessness of entertainment rivalry. This happens not only in the competition of companies with their mafia and thug overtones (the opening torture of the theater owner by the moneylender, echoing the dark sides of films such as *Bugsy* [Eggert 1997] and *Casino*), but also in the rivalry of authors and studios themselves (as in *The Player*). Consider that Shakespeare's deflection of his rival's vengeance onto his rival, by momentarily pretending to be Marlowe himself, signals the way that the game is to be played from now on, the deception leading—or so Will thinks before the matter is comically cleared up—to the death of his admired competitor, all in a screenwriter's nod to Greenblatt's plot proposal.

While the LA/London superimposition certainly reflects the film's and Greenblatt's competition, as established and intensified in Shakespeare's own time, between love and business—the latter presciently termed by John Donne as "the worst disease of love"—it is largely in the surface plot that the reconciliation occurs. Love, it would appear, triumphs over commercial triumph, while paradoxically ensuring its success. The performance we see of *Romeo and Juliet* thus transfixes the audience, who had earlier been bred on the supposedly cheap previous entertainments promoted by Henslowe as "love and a bit with a dog," a dog bit shown in the film as wildly entertaining the crowd, including our tough Queen. Of course, the victory of *true* love appears on all fronts: Shakespeare wins the play's wager with the old cynic Elizabeth, who had earlier denied that poets could represent love truly; the producer-money-lender Fennyman transcends his entrepreneurial blinkers as he is called upon to play the part of the apothecary (a producer learning the subject position of an actor), so caught up in the role that he steps on Romeo's lines in his breathless submission to the play's story; and, in the comic image summing up the reconciliation, the painted whores in the audience are shown sobbing at the play's tragic conclusion. The structure of the film is thus an *a fortiori* one, that is, if love (represented, real) can transform even *this* jaded audience, what will it do for one less jaded?

"It's a mystery": Henslowe's line explaining how the scruffy, incoherent bricolage of theater adds up to something greater than itself, becomes the tag motif of the entire movie. It would seem simply to assert the resolution of romantic conflict in idealized terms, but it seems to apply more to the question of commerce than to the question of love. Love, as it happens, is largely unproblematic and straightforward throughout the film, with no real questions about who's in love or not, or about what the love *means*—standard Shakespearean *topoi*. Clearly it is business, not love, that constitutes the *ultimate* mystery, befitting its current U.S. status as what Noam Chomsky terms is our only "national religion" in the U.S. Nowhere, as it happens, is there the sense that the new religion *requires* a revolution in theatrical representation signaled by Shakespeare's transformation of theater. But the market, as we are given to understand, could never on its own achieve this level of transcendence. In terms of the shallow depth of historical field represented here, London in effect stands in not only for Los Angeles but for Los Angeles in two relatively close "sheets" of time, that is, as the movie industry at the early inspirational moment when it begins to define itself (the commercial sets the groundwork for the arts) and at a later moment of decay, emptiness, and inspirational impoverishment (when the commercial impoverishes art). The implicit story of nostalgia is, therefore, not the development of an art from a primitive "love, and a bit with a dog," but rather its declension into that form. (Love, and a bit with an ocean liner, as we might translate.) The past becomes regarded as a trashbin of possibilities, virtually a benighted, unkempt "third world" from which to ransack materials for the present. The past may be mirror to the present, but transversally, reversing a present sense of the decay of the popular arts into a past sense of their continued progress. Rather than view the crypto-locale of Los Angeles as loss of both love and art, we forget this future, for a short moment perhaps even entertaining the fantasmatic possibility that in their joint *furor poeticus* Shakespeare's rejuvenated pen impregnated Viola prior to her untimely departure.[20] If so, their alien love child she conveyed aboard, its secret pedigree "compounded" equally in passion and commerce, arrives as our last, best hope: the joyous miracle of entertainment. Some of us may even be— so the collective fantasy goes that joins American Hollywood to American Academe—the true descendants and heirs of Shakespeare.

Greenblatt's cinematic memory theater, with its juxtapositions of history and its moments of revelation of excluded history (Shakespeare's actual life, Greenblatt's idea for a story), itself deploys a cinematic "out of field," to use Deleuze's notion, in proposing a movie to the screenwriter. The cinematic status of homosexual love, occluded in the movie proper, is itself troubled in Greenblatt's movie. Greenblatt summarizes in Shakespeare a life of work regularity ("he wrote two plays a year for his company"), of propriety (unlike Jonson and others, Shakespeare "stayed out of prison"), and of prudence (Shakespeare "made money, invested prudently, and retired to his hometown, where he had bought one of the best houses"). Such a narrative would be "from the point of view of the movies: a major yawn." Enter the new historicist to jazz things up, first noting the "murky, dangerous world of religious struggle" (the Armada, secret Catholics, exorcisms, assassination plots, executions of Jesuits), in an idea the writer doesn't happen to "warm to."

The list of descriptives for Marlowe that Greenblatt uses to introduce his second suggestion is especially revealing: Marlowe is, as Greenblatt writes, "the really spectacular life of the late 16th century . . . spy, blasphemer, atheist, violent brawler, double agent, homosexual, as well as brilliant playwright and poet, murdered at the age of 29." Drawing on the mob film paradigm, Greenblatt goes on to explain the two historical versions of his Marlowe's suspicious murder (like two possible movie versions available): first, as tavern dispute over the bill, resulting in the knife thrust over the eye; and then, as later evidence suggests that the murder may have been a "deliberate hit, possibly planned by the head of Elizabeth's secret police, Thomas Walsingham." The list momentarily leaves undecidable again the question of exactly which time-frame is it we are observing in this shot sequence—ours or Shakespeare's age? What creates the effect of intrigue in either case?

Greenblatt's summary of Marlowe's life, moreover, places, probably unintentionally, homosexuality in the realm of the lurid and scandalous. It does so perhaps for ostensibly practical reasons, linking it, syntactically, to atheist or brawler rather than to "brilliant playwright and poet." Or at least it seems *primarily* linked to those, placed in a liminal position between them and the phrase of artistic success. The point here is that the brilliance stands as a separate shot, not part of the whole or as part of a uniform montage of scenes from Marlowe's lurid life. That is, Marlowe's playwriting brilliance is detached from, rather than integral to, his life and his affective experience. Is he brilliant, then, *despite* these lurid elements of his life, such as homosexuality? Just as, on the opposite hand, Shakespeare might furnish us with lurid spectacle despite his yawn of a life. Like a visual sequence, the mere list does not necessarily give instructions on how the montage works.

We might recall from earlier in the essay, however, that it is Trent Lott the senator, not Stephen Greenblatt the director, whose comparison of homosexuality to "alcoholism and kleptomania" initially raised the possibility of its link to social disorder or mental disease, a lurid and unsavory spectacle. While Lott writes the rhetorical spectacle for political ends, obviously functioning in state machinery, Greenblatt does so for cinematic ends, aptly demonstrating once again Lyotard's notion that film directing is a *real* form of politics.

The reason for worrying this detail here is that both *Shakespeare in Love* and Greenblatt's fantastic idea for the film are indistinguishable in proposing (for Greenblatt at least at the outset), an affective life not apart from but integral with artistic success, indeed one that itself *produces* artistic success. And the reason that this is crucial, in turn, is that Greenblatt has proposed, in his rejected version of the film, that Shakespeare both has a homosexual affair and that that affair produces the upward turning point of his professional career. What in Greenblatt's case is "out of field" and tugging his audience toward transversal territory, is the actual link in Greenblatt's movie between the "spectacular" homosexual theme and the "success" story he argues that the American public would value—even to the extent of accepting the representation of this kind of affair in a Hollywood feature film. Or, are we to infer that the homosexual theme—the same one whose problematic status is demonstrated by its placement in his Marlowe list between the criminal and the conventional—is *not* to be thought of as crucial to the career transformation, as it is crucial to the transformations in *Shakespeare in Love?* All of this problematizes immensely and revealingly the comic finale of Greenblatt's movie-essay, which speculates about the public's taste being more tolerant, or at least more educable, than that of either the Hollywood studios or the Elizabethan judicial system, the two time-travel alternatives he offers the reader. What he chooses especially to praise in *Shakespeare in Love,* moreover, shows that he recognizes how central is the narrative of artistic development, when he writes how much easier it must be "to dramatize the stupendous increase in a basketball player's skill than in a poet's." While the theme of homosexuality as career motivation remains completely out of field, a failed transversality, closer to view is the possibility that the market itself (both movies' central player) produces the change. As Greenblatt observes somewhat ambiguously and ambivalently (another "mystery" realm), "this spectacular display of talent is . . . in the seething, capitalist marketplace," with "seething," rather neutrally describing what elsewhere Greenblatt might term cultural "energy," as the equivocation of choice for the parallels of Shakespeare's time to ours, a figure perhaps translating the cauldron of Shakespeare's witchcraft with that of the modern market. What is even further out of field, however, is the aspect of the film called to mind when were we to imagine what Greenblatt the director would stage as visual alternative to the love-making scenes between Shakespeare and Viola. Would a studio replace those scenes by love-making scenes between Shakespeare and Marlowe, as in *Shakespeare in Love,* crosscutting the bedroom dialogue with the stage dialogue from *Romeo and Juliet* or lines from the Sonnets?

Despite Greenblatt's concluding suggestion, it is hard to believe the studios, hardly post-queer yet, would buy such a shock, unless Greenblatt's movie were to exclude the very aspect of the story that he had argued was excluded by the intolerant climate of the present historical moment. Greenblatt's America might accept the film if it showed Shakespeare becoming a success in spite of his sexuality; yet, would we, Greenblatt's us, accept it if it showed Shakespeare's success was *because* of his homosexuality? What is deliberately or nondeliberately placed out of field in Greenblatt's movie, and prancing through transversal territory, thus makes the historical depth of field look a little like a shell game using historical periods, calling into question the entire point of the proposal in the first place. Too, it calls into question Greenblatt's defense of the pragmatic new historicism's cultural analysis that weighs public acceptance on the basis of interpreted cultural values of the moment. Entirely unresolved, then, would be the moviemakers' presumed problem of exactly how to link spectacular display of talent with spectacular display of homosexual affect. Just what's a movie to do?

Feelings, as it happens in this case, are difficult to represent with juxtapositions of depth of historical field. The relation between feelings and history, the transformation of intimacy through historical periods, is given by Deleuze a filmic equivalent, which points toward the cinematic nature of the sort of memory Greenblatt has employed:

> If feelings are sheets of past, the thought, the brain, is the set of non-localizable relations between all these sheets, the continuity which rolls them up and unrolls them like so many lobes, preventing them from halting and becoming fixed in a death-position. (Deleuze 1989, 125)

By focusing on the rejection of his idea, Greenblatt's directorial intervention conceals its role in imagining an entertainment about Shakespeare as one about his love life. In a sense, he has touched on the perennial icon of Shakespeare's in the popular imaginary, not as authority about wisdom in general, but rather as one about *love*. From the Sonnets to *Romeo and Juliet* and beyond (perhaps even to the images of marriage that, as Stephen Orgel finds (1996), so often are bad or work out badly), the figure of Shakespeare is, as suggested earlier, identified with that of love. But the vexed status of this fact for Greenblatt's new historicism is revealed in a startling way in Greenblatt's recent introduction to the new Norton Shakespeare, where in the section on Shakespeare's life the only reference to his impassioned outpouring of subjectivity in the Sonnets, arguably his most personal expression of love, is a sentence or so, buried mid-paragraph, that only glances at Shakespeare's "admiration" for the young nobleman of the Sonnets (Greenblatt 1997, 52).[21] Even more amazingly, given the recovery of Shakespeare's sexuality in the op-ed piece, is Greenblatt's further editorial burial of the sexuality question related to these love poems—a rhetorical omission that could largely occlude the question for the next generation of college students who might on the biography of this textbook or even on the not entirely dissimilar occlusion in *Shakespeare in Love*.

Cannily removing in a number of ways his high-cultural status, as well as the back-projected romantic image of the creative genius, *Shakespeare in Love* does so in part by selecting Joseph Fiennes to act Shakespeare, a decision to lower Shakespeare's receding hairline and high forehead (in the Folio and other images) as a signifier of high IQ and highbrow art, and to amplify his kissing over his intellectual potential—Fiennes selected as perhaps the current actor with the greatest ratio of lip to face. As the movie represents the love as inspirational, we see even the *loss* of it becoming inspirational at the end, as Viola, comforting Will as she prepares to embark for her new life with her husband in Virginia, turns from actress to amateur screenwriter, proposing the crucial suggestions for the story of the shipwrecked maiden Viola, landing on an unknown shore, dressing up like a boy, falling in love, and so on.

It is here that Will, unlike his despairing Romeo, swiftly and comically gets over his love loss, warming to Viola's narrative with approving remarks and quickly becoming wrapped up in developing the storyline—a little bit of a jerk, but no cad. Another teasing canonical joke, about the compositional inspiration of *Twelfth Night,* the moment also exposes the movie's effort to create what we can now more clearly see, from the perspective of its failed transversal representation of love, as virtually a commercial sublime, replacing what we saw as Marx's love of work with love of career. This transformation will be neither the realm of business from Shakespeare's own time as the "disease of love;" nor the next possibility of business as a realm apart from the love that transcends it; nor even business as a realm in which affect can thrive *despite* its oppressiveness. Instead, the transformation will be one that, itself as foundational mystery, is the actual *source* of affect and of love. In the historical transformations of intimacy, like the development of sales pitch over centuries that helped lead to the triumph of capitalism, the last stage may be to regard the commercial, by way of the entertainment industry, not in opposition to love (an opposition that both the poetry and the economic treatises of the early modern period might be evidence for); nor as the existing condition under which all alienated social relations of the time must take place (Marx); nor even, romantically, as what must be transcended for love to occur (as both *Shakespeare in Love* and Greenblatt's movie-essay would like it). But rather, as we see in the faultlines of both movies and what distinguishes them from early modern love, as the source and model of affective relations, this last stage may consider the commercial as a new feeling unrolling frame-by-frame, an imagined continuity linking an imagined past to an imagined future, our new cinematic labor of love.

We began by expecting that, as a film about love, Shakespeare in Love would exemplify theoretical dimensions of transversality, itself the strong theoretical analogue of love. Through the surprising juxtaposition of an exploitation film's take on true love, and through the maneuverings of a scholar venturing into moviemaking, maneuverings that themselves served to outline transversality more clearly, we now find that while *Shakespeare in Love* does indeed constitute another of the many historical and contemporary cut-up Shakespaces of this volume, a collection of experimental alterities, it is one where the transversal movement outside the self does not proceed through love but through the now sacred realm of the commercial. True Love, as we think, resides in a Shakespeare without class, perhaps in New Jersey, in a transversal territory where the self is not the same. As with its social and political analogues , it must be looked for in all the wrong spaces.

Notes

1. A recent work of scholarship, *Shakespeare and Appropriation,* ed. Christy Desmet and Robert Sawyer (London and New York: Routledge 1999) advances the concept of appropriation further in the direction of the present theorization. Helpfully categorizing kinds of appropriation, and privileging the small or "local" appropriations involved in "talking back to Shakespeare" (like the "microrevolutions" we speak of in the present essay), the emphasis of this work's introduction and of many of the essays points toward a Bakhtinian model, one of "dialogue with the alien" (Desmet 1999,

9). But Desmet becomes more explicitly transversal at times, as when she notes that "Something happens when Shakespeare is appropriated, and both the subject (author) and object (Shakespeare) are changed in the process" (Desmet 1999, 4). To this we naturally concur, but would supplement the suggestion with a radical dimension in which subject and object become indistinguishable or shift places.

2. From unpublished Burroughs correspondence in the archives of the Arizona State University library. We acknowledge and thank James Grauerbach of Burroughs Communications of Lawrence, Kansas for permission to cite.

3. For a striking, current instance of the latter, with ramifications for the fetishization of the commercial we will explore in our following discussion of the film *Shakespeare in Love,* see Norman Augustine and Kenneth Adelman's book of Shakespeare-based tips for CEO's: *Shakespeare in Charge: The Bard's Guide to Leading and Succeeding on the Business Stage* (New York: Hyperion, 1999).

4. Parts of this theoretical section are adapted from Bryan Reynolds, "The Devil's House," (1997a). For examples from the essays of this anthology which could serve as further illustrations of the theory, see Index entries for transversality, subjective territory, and Shakespace.

5. See Louis Althusser (1971).

6. Here, Donald Hedrick would, from a more vulgar Marxist position, qualify our joint claim in order to question a full Foucauldianism by which there are only strategies without strategists. State power in the current U.S. example, for instance, not only involves discursivities, but also internal contradictions, on the one hand, as well as the actual collaborative decisions by live corporate and political leaders, on the other hand. For this reason Noam Chomsky must not be forgotten even if we strategically forget Foucault. There may, moreover, be a totalitarianism deriving not from the top down from the bottom up, as Baudrillard suggests as a possibility for newer forms of repression, within the very micropolitics, linked in our essay with transversality, that are otherwise capable of forms of resistance. Agency need not be involved in some repression, but need not be ruled out of all repressiveness either.

7. In addition to the overall hegemonic society promoted by the state machinery, there are usually subsocieties, such as those of a university or a criminal organization, which are also hegemonic. For discussion on hegemony, see Raymond Williams (1983, 144–46), (1977, 108–114).

8. For discussion on the subversion/containment paradigm, see, among other sources, Dollimore (1991, 81–91); Bristol (1990, 189–211); Montrose (1989, 20–24).

9. See Eagleton, (1986, 2). In addition to the conceptual influence of the practices of transvestism of gender and class on and off the public stage, we are thinking of the huge conceptual influence of Puritan radicals and belief in the occult. About Puritan influence, see Christopher Hill (1980), and

Patrick Collinson, *The Elizabethan Puritan Movement* (Oxford: Clarendon Press, 1990). About occult influence, see Alan Macfarlane (1970) and Christina Larner, *Witchcraft and Religion: The Politics of Popular Belief* (Oxford: Blackwell, 1984). For political discussion on *Macbeth,* see Bryan Reynolds (1993, 109–27), and Alan Sinfield (1992, 95–108).

10. We are indebted to Félix Guattari for the terms "transversal" and "transversality," concepts we have much adapted for our own explanatory and theoretical purposes. In his collection of essays, *Molecular Revolution: Psychiatry and Politics* (1984), Guattari uses these terms to discuss the phenomenon of group desire. While his use of the term is incorporated in our own, we extend his definition of transversality to conceptuality and its territories, and allow it to apply to the existential processes of individuals as well as of groups, as we explain. See also Guattari's collection of essays (1965–1970), entitled *Psychanalyse transversalité* (1972).

11. See Pierre Bourdieu (1990, esp. 54–56).

12. In our continuing discussion about the concept and its political implications beyond "Shakespace," Donald Hedrick and Bryan Reynolds do not fully agree about the broader implications of transversality. For Reynolds, transversality often accounts for the historical fact of heterogeneous social configurations and asymmetrical or erratic social development. Reynolds agrees with the Lacanian post-Marxists Ernesto Laclau (1990, 79; 5–17) and Slavoj Žižek (252), who respectively identify this fact as a "radical indeterminacy" that is historically conditional and necessarily challenges all attempts to effectuate hegemonic order. But he disagrees with their claim that this fact originates in and is symptomatic of, as Žižek puts it, humankind's traumatic acknowledgment that "there is no return to the natural balance" and the consequent "radical antagonism through which man cuts his umbilical cord with nature, with animal homeostasis" (1989, 5). For them, it is this "pure antagonism" (Laclau's phrase), caused by humankind's estrangement from nature, that inspires all social change (Laclau 1990, 79). In contrast, Reynolds sees the sociohistorical process as a phenomenon fueled by humankind's desire to control its own experience *in relation to* the natural world. And Reynolds sees transversal power, however present and potent in different historical moments and situations, as a major player behind heterogeneous social evolution. Although transversal territory may surface as a result of antagonism between humans or between humans and natural events (atrophic, seismic, or meteorological transformations), it cannot be defined against or in response to nature. This is because transversality reflects nature's apparent capriciousness and multifariousness as transversality operates adjacent to nature.

While accepting transversality as a formal and contingent rather than an essential mode of change or becoming, and, like Reynolds, questioning human antagonism as the source of heterogeneous social developments, Hedrick would also question whether some essential human component renders transversality a transhistorical phenomenon marking a desire for harmony with the natural world. The history of attempts at domination of nature, the faultline within Marxism now investigated by the ecocriticism, would also at the very least cast doubt on some such broad claims for transversality, not to mention the history of dominations of some by others. Transversality's particular explanatory power, for Hedrick, consists in attending to the modes of subjectivity-shifting and ideology-shifting common to both an insurrectional misappropriation and revolution as well as to love, constituting a form of what Antonio Negri and Michael Hardt have called "affective" or "immaterial" labor (Hardt and Negri 1994, 12–14 et passim). Through its concept of social creativity, it provides a needed supplement, for instance, to Althusserian interpellation with its more fixed sense of a subjectivity imposed, or to political models of desire based on incompleteness and lack.

13. For more on becoming, see Gilles Deleuze and Félix Guattari (1987, especially the chapter "Becoming-Intense, Becoming-Animal, Becoming-imperceptible . . .") and the chapter "Becoming a Woman" in Guattari (1984). Identity becoming is rarely a singular, one-dimensional process, that is, when a person becomes directly something else that is specific and readily identifiable. For this reason, we follow Deleuze and Guattari by pluralizing the term becoming (as in "identity becomings" and "becomings-child") when speaking generally about a teleological category or direction for becoming rather than an ontological destination.

14. For discussions exploring such binaries, see Archer (1991); Bristol (1989); and Bushnell (1990).

15. One should acknowledge, however, that these characteristics are as likely to be themselves appropriated by the state, under the conditions of global capitalism with its self-serving interest in breaking down of boundaries, hierarchies, and stabilities (sometimes of the identity and power of the nation-state itself), as Fredric Jameson and others have argued to be the situation for the logic of postmodernism at the present historical juncture.

16. For an argument that Shakespearean perversity goes beyond notions of "bawdy" into a more indefinite and transformative realm of "deep bawdy," see Donald K. Hedrick, "Flower Power" (1994).

17. See the extensive treatment and review of pop and sub-pop Shakespeare, provocatively construed in relation to contemporary "loser culture" by Richard Burt (1998).

18. In *Symptoms of Culture,* Marjorie Garber comments eloquently on this peculiarly academic kind of Shakespearean nostalgia: "That Shakespeare *is* the dream-space of nostalgia for the aging undergraduate (that is to say, for just about everyone) seems self-evidently true, and, to tell the truth, not all bad" (1998, 168).

19. For more in depth discussion of Deleuze's time-image providing parts of the present discussion, see Bryan Reynolds, "Untimely Ripped" (1997), which analyzes the sociopolitical impact of both Roman Polanski's 1971 film version of *Macbeth* and Shakespeare's *Macbeth* in light of Deleuze's film theory and Artaud's performance theory.

20. We gratefully acknowledge this suggestion by D. J. Hopkins.

21. The remarkable and instructively coy passage is as follows: "This Patronage, or at least Shakespeare's quest for it, is most visible in the dedications in 1593 and 1594 of his narrative poems *Venus and Adonis* and *The Rape of Lucrece* to the young nobleman Henry Wriothesley, Earl of Southampton. It may be glimpsed as well, perhaps, in the sonnets, with their extraordinary adoration of the fair youth, though the identity of that youth has never been determined. What return Shakespeare got for his exquisite offerings is likewise unknown" (52). As in *Shakespeare in Love,* representing love as a tangle of the commercial and the romantic, Greenblatt reiterates our ignorance of this "return" (Greenblatt's own bawdy equation of sex with money) in another glancing reference when, explicating the Renaissance legal and social situation of homosexuality, he parenthetically notes that the sonnets, as record, are "opaque" as indicators of the extent of homosexuality, presumably referring to Shakespeare's (26–27).

Works Cited

Althusser, Louis. 1971. "Ideology and Ideological State Apparatuses (Notes Towards an Investigation)." In *Lenin and Philosophy, and Other Essays.* New York: Monthly Review Press.

Anderson, Benedict. 1983. *Imagined Communities: Reflections on the Origin and Spread of Nationalism.* London: Verso.

Archer, Ian. 1991. *The Pursuit of Stability: Social Relations in Elizabethan London.* Cambridge: Cambridge University Press.

Bourdieu, Pierre. 1998. *Acts of Resistance: Against the Tyranny of the Market.* New York: Norton.

———. 1990. *The Logic of Practice.* Stanford: Stanford University Press.

———. 1991. *Language and Symbolic Power.* Ed. John B. Thompson. Cambridge: Harvard University Press.

Bristol, Michael. 1989. *Carnival and Theater: Plebeian Culture and the Structure of Authority in Renaissance England.* New York: Routledge, Chapman and Hall, Inc.

Bristol, Michael. 1990. *Shakespeare's America, America's Shakespeare.* London: Routledge.

Burroughs, William. n.d. Unpublished correspondence. Arizona State University archives.

Burt, Richard. 1998. *Unspeakable Shaxxxpeares: Queer Theory and American Kiddie Culture.* New York: St. Martin's Press.

Bushnell, Rebecca. 1990. *Tragedies of Tyrants: Political Thought and Theater in the English Renaissance.* Ithaca and London: Cornell University Press.

Collinson, Patrick. 1990. *The Elizabethan Puritan Movement.* Oxford: Clarendon Press.

Davis, Mike. 1990. *City of Quartz: Excavating the Future in Los Angeles.* New York: Verso Press.

———. 1998. *Ecology of Fear: Los Angeles and the Imagination of Disaster.* New York: Random House.

Deleuze, Gilles. 1989. *Cinema 2: The Time-Image.* Trans. Hugh Tomlinson and Robert Galeta. Minneapolis: University Minnesota Press.

———. 1990. *Negotiations 1972–1990.* New York: Columbia University Press.

Deleuze, Gilles and Fèlix Guattari. 1987. *A Thousand Plateaus: Capitalism and Schizophrenia.* Trans. Brian Massumi. Minneapolis: University of Minnesota Press.

Derrida, Jacques. 1992. *Acts of Literature.* New York and London: Routledge.

Desmet, Christy, and Robert Sawyer. Eds. 1999. *Shakespeare and Appropriation.* London and New York: Routledge.

Dollimore, Jonathan. 1991. *Sexual Dissidence: Augustine to Wilde.* Oxford: Clarendon Press.

Eagleton, Terry. 1986. *William Shakespeare.* New York: Blackwell.

Foucault, Michel. 1977. *Language, Counter-memory, Practice: Selected Essays and Interviews.* Ed. Donald F. Bouchard. Ithaca: Cornell University Press.

———. 1979. *Discipline and Punish: The Birth of the Prison.* Trans. Alan Sheridan. New York: Random House.

Garber, Marjorie. 1998. *Symptoms of Culture.* New York: Routledge.

Glucksmann, André. 1980. *Master Thinkers.* Trans. Brian Pearce. New York: Harper & Row.

Greenblatt, Stephen. 1999. "About That Romantic Sonnet . . ." *The New York Times* (February 6): A15.

———. 1993. "Shakespeare Bewitched." In *New Historical Literary Study: Essays on Reproducing Texts, Representing History.* Princeton, New Jersey: Princeton University Press.

Guattari, Félix. 1984. *Molecular Revolution: Psychiatry and Politics.* Trans. Rosemary Sheed. New York: Penguin.

———. 1972. *Psychoanalyse transversalité.* Paris: Maspero.

Hardt, Michael and Antonio Negri. 1994. *Labour of Dionysius: A Critique of the State Form.* Minneapolis: University of Minnesota Press.

Hedrick, Donald K. 1997. "War is Mud: Branagh's *Dirty Harry V* and the Types of Political Ambiguity." In *Shakespeare the Movie: Popularizing the Plays on Film, TV, and Video.* Ed. Lynda E. Boose and Richard Burt. New York and London: Routledge.

———. 1994. "Flower Power: Shakespearean Deep Bawdy and the Botanical Perverse." In *The Administration of Aesthetics: Censorship, Political Criticism, and the Pub-*

lic Sphere. Ed. Richard Burt. Minneapolis and London: University Minnesota Press.

Hill, Christopher. 1980. *The Intellectual Origins of the English Revolution.* Oxford: Clarendon Press.

Holderness, Graham, ed. 1988. *The Shakespeare Myth.* Manchester, UK: Manchester University Press.

Kant, Immanuel. 1990. *Critique of Pure Reason.* Trans. J. M. D. Meiklejohn. Buffalo: Prometheus Books.

Kaufman, Lloyd. 1998. *Tromeo and Juliet.* DVD, Troma Entertainment.

Laclau, Ernesto. 1990. *New Reflections on the Revolution of Our Time.* London: Verso.

Larner, Christina. 1984. *Witchcraft and Religion: The Politics of Popular Belief.* Oxford: Blackwell.

Lefebvre, Henri. 1993. *The Production of Space.* Ed. and trans. Donald Nicholson-Smith. Oxford: Blackwell.

Levine, Lawrence W. 1988. *Highbrow/Lowbrow: The Emergence of Cultural Hierarchy in America.* Cambridge, MA: Harvard University Press.

Lyotard, Jean-Francois. 1989. "Acinema." In *The Lyotard Reader.* Ed. Andrew Benjamin. Oxford: Blackwell.

Macfarlane, Alan. 1970. *Witchcraft in Tudor and Stuard England: A Regional and Comparative Study.* London: Routledge.

Marsden, Jean, ed. 1991. *The Appropriation of Shakespeare: Post-Renaissance Reconstructions of the Works.* New York: St. Martin's Press.

Marx, Karl. 1978. *The German Ideology.* In *The Marx-Engels Reader.* 2nd edn. Ed. Robert C. Tucker. New York and London: Norton.

Montrose, Louis. 1989. "Professing the Renaissance: The Poetics and Politics of Culture." In *The New Historicism.* Ed. Aram H. Veeser. New York: Routledge.

Nancy, Jean-Luc. 1991. *The Inoperative Community.* Ed. and trans. Peter Conner. Minneapolis: University of Minnesota Press.

Novy, Marianne. 1993. *Cross-cultural Performances.* Champaign-Urbana: University of Illinois Press.

Orgel, Stephen. 1996. *Impersonations: The Performance of Gender in Shakespeare's England.* Cambridge: Cambridge University Press.

Reynolds, Bryan. 1993. "The Terrorism of Macbeth and Charles Manson: Reading Cultural Construction in Polanski and Shakespeare." *The Upstart Crow* 13: 109–27.

———. 1997. "The Devil's House, 'or worse': Transversal Power and Antitheatrical Discourse in Early Modern England." *Theatre Journal* 49.2 (May): 143–167.

———. 1997. "Untimely Ripped." *Social Semiotics: A Transdisciplinary Journal in Functional Linguistics, Semiotics and Critical Theory* 7.2 (August).

Rodowick, D. N. 1997. *Gilles Deleuze's Time Machine.* Durham and London: Duke University Press.

Shakespeare, William. 1974. *The Riverside Shakespeare.* Ed. G. Blakemore Evans. New York: Houghton Mifflin.

Sinfield, Alan. 1992. "*Macbeth:* History, Ideology, and Intellectuals." In *Faultlines: Cultural Materialism and the Politics of Dissident Reading.* Berkeley: University of California Press: 95–102.

Webster, Margaret. 1942. *Shakespeare Without Tears.* New York and London: McGraw-Hill.

Williams, Raymond. 1983. *Keywords: A Vocabulary of Culture and Society.* New York: Oxford University Press.

Williams, Raymond. 1977. *Marxism and Literature.* New York: Oxford University Press.

Žižek, Slavoj. 1990. "Beyond Discourse-Analysis." In *New Reflections on the Revolution of Our Time.* London: Verso.

———. 1989. *The Sublime Object of Ideology.* London: Verso.

Part II

Acting Out
From Under Authority

Chapter 2

Performance and Authority in *Hamlet* (1603)

Robert Weimann

lthough *Hamlet,* as Anthony Scoloker noted in 1604, was perceived as a play that "should please all"(1930, 2: 215), its textual
history tells a different story. If, as Philip Edwards observed, the
"study of the early texts of *Hamlet* is the study of a play in motion" (1985,
8), the element that is most in question (and in motion) is the circulation
of cultural authority itself. At issue is the fluid, composite source of this
authority, its unsettled and dispersed locations between the writing and the
production of the play. The unstable linkage between the texts and the performances of *Hamlet* can perhaps best be explored at the point of intersection between the early textual history of the play and its own
intervention in the forms and functions of playing. At this crucial point,
authority in the text of the play appears profoundly and irretrievably
entangled with what authority or legitimation is behind respective "purpose[s] of playing" (3.2.20).[1] In the so-called "bad" quarto, relations of
writing and playing find themselves in a particularly blatant state of both
entanglement and differentiation. Such entanglement and differentiation, at
least to a certain extent, continue to inform the more subdued difference
between the authorial amplitude of the Second Quarto (1604) and the
more theatrical qualities of the Folio text (1623).[2] Between these texts,
there resonates a cultural preference in response to either the literary needs
of "goose-quills" or the practical requirements of "common players"
(2.2.344;349). This preference, as Harold Jenkins has shown, almost certainly connects with "the fickleness of a public favour which readily transfers itself from the old established to the upstart" (1982, 472). This
fickleness attests to some of the submerged changes that went hand in hand
with an imminent process of cultural differentiation and reform. But while

Hamlet's own preference in the Folio text appears to be in defense of those berattled "common stages" (342), the lines of social divergence and cultural interest appear far more confusing and potentially divisive as soon as our view of the "play in motion" includes the traditionally underestimated "suspect" text of the First Quarto (1603).

In this version, the recasting of the most hallowed soliloquy in the play and its *mise-en-scène* is a case in point. Here, Polonius (in the First Quarto called Corambis) prepares for Hamlet's entrance and King Claudius provides the cue, but five lines after Hamlet has entered, the King's withdrawal is yet to come (the future tense is unmistakable).

Cor. [. . .] Your selfe and I will stand close in the study,
There shall you heare the effect of all his hart,
And if it proue any otherwise then loue,
Then let my censure faile an other time.
King. See where hee comes poring vppon a booke.
Enter Hamlet.
Cor. Madame, will it please your grace
To leaue vs here?
Que. With all my hart.   *exit.*
Cor. And here *Ofelia,* reade you on this booke,
And walke aloofe, the King shal be vnseene.
Ham. To be, or not to be, I there's the point,
To Die, to sleepe, is that all? I all:
No, to sleepe, to dreame, I mary there it goes,
For in that dreame of death, when wee awake,
And borne before an euerlasting Iudge,
From whence no passenger euer retur'nd,
The vndiscouered country, at whose sight
The happy smile, and the accursed damn'd.
But for this, the ioyfull hope of this,
Whol'd beare the scornes and flattery of the world,
Scorned by the right rich, the rich curssed of the poore?
The widow being oppressed, the orphan wrong'd,
The taste of hunger, or a tirants raigne,
And thousand more calamities besides,
To grunt and sweate vnder this weary life,
When that he may his full *Quietus* make
With a bare bodkin, who would this indure,
But for a hope of something after death?
Which pusles the braine, and doth confound the sence,
Which makes vs rather beare those euilles we haue,

Than flie to others that we know not of.
I that, O this conscience makes cowardes of vs all,
Lady in thy orizons, be all my sinnes remembred.

Ofel. My Lord, I haue sought opportunitie, which now I haue, to redeliuer
to your worthy handes, a small remembrance, such tokens which I
haue receiued of you.[3]

Although this version presents us with an unusual, indeed perfectly outrageous degree of departure from what, according to Q2 and F1, Shakespeare wrote in the longer versions, we should be wary of dismissing it, as
generations of editors did, as "corruption" *tout court.* What Hamlet's speech
epitomizes in miniature is, more than anything, a reduction in the authority of the author in the playtext. We are confronted with highly mobile and
thoroughly contingent relations of authority between the poetics of writing and the exigencies of playing. My reading of the passage, moving from
what it says to how it is staged, will emphasize three points.

Semantically, in its uses of language, this version of Hamlet's "To be, or
not to be" speech foregrounds a perspective on the hardness of ordinary
living that is markedly different from what we have in the received soliloquy. Eliding the question "Whether 'tis nobler in the *mind*" to "take arms"
against hostile circumstances (3.1.56;58), the utterance replaces the purely
intellectual, stoical, and culturally elevated forms of resistance by an
entirely plain, everyday horizon of harsh living, one that at least in part is
inspired by an awareness of social conflict. "Scorned by the right rich, the
rich curssed of the poore" moves in a world that verbally as well as socially
is far below "the proud man's contumely," the "law's delay," and the "inso-
lence of office" (3.1.70–72). If the oppression of the "widow" and the
wrong of the "orphan," not to speak of the "taste of hunger," is more predictable, it is for all that more physically concrete than the mixed metaphor
of using weaponry against a "sea of troubles" (58). In the longer versions,
the repeated imagery of battle ("shocks/ That flesh is heir to" [61–62])[4] is
subsumed under a naturalized and socially elevated notion of inheritance.
The First Quarto avoids this; rather than debating, in Edwards's phrase,
"which of two courses is nobler" vis-à-vis the continuous punishing hostility of life itself, the early quarto abridges the text, characteristically without letting go of the indiscrete language of the body, as in "To grunt and
sweate under this weary life."

Dramaturgically, the differences in Q1 are even more significant. The
mise-en-scène of the speech, inseparable from its uses of language, reveals an
extraordinary, swift, even perhaps blunt directness, an acceleration of stage

business that presupposes a sovereign command of and an extreme fluidity in the uses of theatrical space. There is none of the preparatory action motivating and anticipating the withdrawal of Gertrude, Claudius, and Polonius *before* Hamlet's entrance ("*King.* Sweet Gertrude, leave us two [. . .] *Pol.* Withdraw, my lord." [3.1.28;54]). Instead, his entrance *precedes* their withdrawal. There results a simultaneity in the staging of the scene that does not automatically integrate the stage representation of Hamlet's presence into the scene at large. Rather, Hamlet's entrance provides, as it were, a cue for the subsequent withdrawal of the others. It is as if there is no need for him, as yet, to honor an iconic frame of reference marked by represented characters such as Corambis or the Queen. It is only six lines later, through the act of speaking the speech, that a fully representational status accrues to his performance practice. Thus, Gertrude can take her leave, Corambis find his place in hiding, and Ofelia assume her pose, all *after* the player playing Hamlet, here the observed of all observers in the audience, has come onto the stage. Far from constituting the unified site of a dramatic scene that, in a fiction, would be dominated by the signs of symbolic action, Hamlet enters and lingers on the threshold between role-induced perception, seeing and hearing, and an actor's more neutral presence, for whom the unity of place and the logic of symbolization do not obtain. At the frontiers of his absorption by the symbolism of a fully integrated space of dramatic action, the player, as it were, can resist his being lost in a unified scene until the last moment. It is as if the physical presence of the leading actor on stage helps defer what closure we have in this scene. Literally, the visible player comes first, the fiction of "invisible" concealment second, not vice versa. The demands of performing on an open stage go hand in hand with a dramaturgy that, after almost 400 years, appears far from inefficient, let alone despicable. Thus, a modern actor (Peter Guiness) playing the role of Q1 Hamlet can express his "joy to have that muscularity and directness," while another performer of the same role (Christopher McCullough) observes that "There are all sorts of clues in the play about how actors were working; [. . .] we are seeing the possibilities of theatrical energy, of the way space was used, of how actors related to audiences" (Loughrey 1992, 125).

Finally, in the entire cast of the "To be, or not to be" speech, we can observe how *audience contact and response* are entertained by a specific mode of transaction, a mode of presentation that is part of and yet different from that representation that, in the strict sense of the word, constitutes the inward self through a soliloquy. As modern actors like Guiness and McCullough have suggested, for Hamlet to say, "I there's the point," is to address spectators rather than his own interior state of mind. His altogether abrupt turn to Ofelia (in his last line) indicates that little or no transition is required to return from a *platea*-like address to genuine dialogue. The presentation of this speech can be viewed as the enabling condition of a transaction whereby the action, representation itself, comes to fruition in a moment of display, which *is* the act of delivery.

In the First Quarto, as we shall see, the lines of division between drama, show, and ceremony can more easily be blurred. This blurring of boundaries between dramatic action and theatrical display, representation and presentation, may well have been in response to, but also in aid of, circumstances characteristic of the itinerant stage. As the *Records of Early English Drama* and other archives (to which I shall return) indicate, Elizabethan traveling players continued to rub shoulders with all sorts of jugglers, dancers, singers, tumblers, and related showmen. Performers such as these were relatively unconcerned with the symbolic, let alone iconographic, dimensions of their actions. Their concern was to get the show across, that is, to privilege vis-à-vis the audience an immediate—literally an iconographically and symbolically "unmediated"—space for delivery. Thereby, the responsiveness of spectators was implicated in the very transaction itself, in the sense that the skill and competence in the speaking of the speech were offered to them as worthy of public display.

If I may here anticipate my further reading of the play, the circuit of authority in Shakespeare's *Hamlet* must be viewed as dispersed and "distracted" (4.3.4), as participating in the nexus of unruly and still unsettled relations of production (especially when compared to the authoritative order of the Elizabethan guild system). In the theater, a diversity of cultural interests and labor must have been particularly pronounced wherever the imaginary world-in-the-play, that is, the dramatic representation, engaged and was engaged by the material and economic logistics of playing-in-the-world of early modern England. As I would suggest for further investigation, the threshold between the stage-as-imaginary-world and the stage-as-stage was crucial; at least in part this threshold overlapped with the line of "cultural difference" that Leah Marcus has persuasively traced between "orality and writing as competing forms of communication within the Renaissance playhouse"(1996, 132–176).[5] But if the gap between these two types of cultural production and communication was social and educational, as well as poetic and epistemological, how did it affect the "nexus" of authority inside the Elizabethan theater? Could it be that there was a link between the instability of the Shakespearean text and its openness to diverse production requirements?

As a provisional answer, I propose to look more closely at the first printed version of *Hamlet* for what evidence we can glean about this "open" circulation, in the production process, of diverse cultural energies, interests, and functions. From the point of view of such circulation of authority among the Lord Chamberlain's Men, Hamlet's advice to the players is perhaps the most tantalizing scene in Shakespeare's theater—a scene in which the administering of cultural authority itself is staged and dramatized. In the First Quarto, this site is marked, uniquely, by an astonishing difference in what, in Q2 and the Folio text, is called "the purpose of playing" (3.2.20).

> And doe you heare? let not your clown speake
> More then is set downe, there be of them I can tell you
> That will laugh themselues, to set on some
> Quantitie of barren spectators to laugh with them,
> Albeit there is some necessary point in the Play
> Then to be obserued: O t'is vile, and shewes
> A pittifull ambition in the foole that vseth it.
> And then you haue some agen, that keeps one sute
> Of iests, as a man is knowne by one sute of
> Apparell, and Gentlemen quotes his ieasts downe
> In their tables, before they come to play, as thus:
> Cannot you stay till I eate my porrige? and, you owe me
> A quarters wages: and, my coate wants cullison:
> And, your beere is sowre: and, blabbering with his lips,
> And thus keeping in his cinkapase of ieasts,
> When, God knows, the warme Clowne cannot make at iest
> Vnlesse by chance, as the blinde man catcheth a hare:
> Maisters tell him of it.   (F1–F2)

As Harold Jenkins pointedly observes in a note, the First Quarto "provides, ironically enough, an instance of the thing complained of"(1982, 289) in Hamlet's advice. The Prince, "thus" performing a clown's "cinkapase of ieasts" and, with another "thus," so "blabbering with his lips," is telling the player what not to do by doing it himself. Thereby, he can in one and the same speech collapse two different orders of authority in the purpose of playing. One follows classical mimetic precepts associated with Donatus and Cicero, the other—in the teeth of their rejection—the contemporary practices of Tarlton and company. By formally rejecting the latter while actually cashing in on them (even, as George Ian Duthie has shown, drawing on jests that Tarlton is on record as having used) (1941,

232–237),[6] the First Quarto exemplifies one important aspect in the cultural genealogy of what, taking a phrase from *Troilus and Cressida,* I propose to consider as "bifold authority."

Hamlet, in his rehearsal of the clown's stale jokes, proceeds to do what his humanist alter ego declares to be against "some necessary point in the Play." When Hamlet's advice culminates in the Prince dis-playing the clown, even the empathy-cherishing, Stanislavski-inspired critic will have difficulty accounting for this in terms of representational cogency. The least that can be said is that the quasi-performance of these jests indecorously exceeds the purpose of instructing the players; these "jestures" (Richard Jones' term) certainly do not serve the protagonist's disguise or any other strategy of concealment or revenge. If anything, this specimen of clowning is "far unmeet" for that "matter of worthiness" (Jones 1981, 111) that, in the longer texts, Hamlet's plea for a poetics of representation and discretion seeks to convey to the players. In fact, the Prince's demand, "mend it all together" is more than contradicted by Hamlet's "cinkapase of ieasts." Even if, as is likely, the Prince through overemphasis burlesques these jests, his travesty is in line with an ancient, almost ubiquitous practice of unscripted, unsanctioned performance. Prince Hamlet himself embodies a site on stage where—to anticipate Polonius' phrase—the "law of writ and the liberty" (2.2.401) of the performer clash. Rather than unambiguously disapproving (as the Q2 Hamlet does) of what in both the moral and the social sense of the word is "villainous" (3.2.44) in clownage, the "suspect" Hamlet is double-dealing somewhat in the vein of Ambidexter in *King Cambises,* who says, "Now with both hands will you see me play my parte" (Adams 1924, l.783; cf. lines 151, 701, 744). As, handy-dandy, the princely agent and the villainous object of reform exchange places, there emerges a "bifold authority" in Hamlet's own purpose of playing. The ambidextrous capacity for both recommending and undermining the self-contained Renaissance play aids both the representation of character and the presentation of such conceits as befit the fond sport and frivolous game of jesting mother-wits. Although Hamlet's duplicity is not nearly as blatant as that of the old Vice Ambidexter, the cultural difference is within the configuration of the protagonist himself. Since this difference here clearly affects his own "purpose of playing," it goes significantly deeper than the contrast, in the texts of the Second Quarto and the Folio, between Hamlet the humanist courtier and Hamlet the "rogue and peasant slave," the "John-a-dreams" (2.2.550,568).

Here, the First Quarto, in recasting a given text, does not invalidate its writerly authority from any ideological or social point of view. Ideology clearly does not offer what Kathleen Irace in her recent edition of the play calls, "unequivocal evidence pointing to the reasons behind the differences between Q1 and the longer texts" (1998, 18).[7] Nor can the text be viewed as an aggressive counterversion indicating "actor's voice." What theatrical practices, agencies, and interests are here projected already participate in a moment of cultural "reform" and differentiation. Even so, the culturally inclusive uses of language—unsettling, at least momentarily, the identities of prince and clown—collude with an instability in both the text and the purpose of playing; thereby they affect both the staging and, closely connected with it, the meanings of the text. Here we have very much a "mixed" composition that, in Hamlet's advice to the players, slides easily between the representation of character—the character of a princely Maecenas—and the presentation, à la Tarlton, of "such conceits as clownage keeps in pay"(Jones 1981, 2). Between them, there is no single, overriding, unified "purpose of playing." Again, I am deliberately using the phrase from Hamlet's advice to the players in Q2 and F1 in order to suggest that the singular form ("the purpose," as used by the Prince) is far from being an adequate description of late Elizabethan performance practice.

In order to study the coexistence, even interaction of diverse modes of playing, I propose to look at the Nunnery scene in the First Quarto, where—to use a distinction made earlier—the presentational purpose of playing throughout commingles with the representation of character. In this scene, where the protagonist is shown in his most eccentric moments, his eccentricity must have displayed something eminently worthy of show, an exceptional kind of exhibit. Accordingly, Ofelia is made to *present* the Prince of Denmark to the audience a few lines after his "To be, or not to be" speech, where, in Q2 and F1, his "unmatch'd form" is said to be "Blasted with ecstasy" (3.1.159–60).

> *Ham.* To a Nunnery goe, we are arrant knaues all,
> Beleeue none of vs, to a Nunnery goe.
> *Ofel.* O heauens secure him!
> *Ham.* Wher's thy father?
> *Ofel.* At home my lord.
> *Ham.* For Gods sake let the doores be shut on him,
> He may play the foole no where but in his
> Owne house: to a Nunnery goe.
> *Ofel.* Help him good God.
> *Ham.* If thou dost marry, Ile giue thee
> This plague to thy dowry:

<pre>
        Be thou as chaste as yce, as pure as snowe,
        Thou shalt not scape calumny, to a Nunnery goe.
Ofel.   Alas, what change is this?
Ham.   But if thou wilt needes marry, marry a foole,
        For wisemen know well enough,
        What monsters you make of them, to a Nunnery goe.
Ofel.   Pray God restore him.
Ham.   Nay, I haue heard of your paintings too,
        God hath giuen you one face,
        And you make your selues another,
        You fig, and you amble, and you nickname Gods creatures,
        Making your wantonnesse, your ignorance,
        A pox, t'is scuruy, Ile no more of it,
        It hath made me madde: Ile no more marriages,
        All that are married but one, shall liue.
        The rest shall keepe as they are, to a Nunnery goe,
        To a Nunnery goe.   exit
Ofel.   Great God of heauen, what a quicke change is this?
        The Courtier, Scholler, Souldier, all in him,
        All dasht and splinterd thence, O woe is me,
        To a seene what I haue seene, see what I see.   exit   (E-E2)
</pre>

With the exception of one truly dialogic phrase ("At home my Lord"), Ofelia's utterances, being neither addressed to nor received by Hamlet, are dominated by a presentational *gestus* throughout. Referring to Hamlet in the third person, she qualifies her distance from participation in the represented scene by an articulation of dismay about the eccentric actions of the Prince of Denmark. In her early interjection, "O heauens secure him," and, even, "Help him God," the figures of Christian invocation and compassion that characterize her response (and involvement), may yet predominate. This is very much the case Q2 and F1, where Ophelia's interjections are distinguished by even stronger signs of pity and piety ("O, help him, you sweet heavens!" [3.1.133]; "Heavenly powers, restore him!" [140]). However, it is only in the First Quarto that Ofelia, in her reference to Hamlet, proceeds to a purely demonstrative "this" as something pointed at rather than spoken to: "Alas, what change is this?"—"Great God of heauen, what a quicke change is this?" It is true, the rhetoric of interjection continues to draw on figures of piety and perplexity, but the iteration itself reduces the capacity for effectively subsuming the presentational *gestus* within a characterizing representation, on Ofelia's part, of pious concern and consternation.

All this while, Ofelia is made to point out, even perhaps point at, a virtuoso display of mad humor. With gender relations as his theme (always a favorite of audiences), Hamlet himself performs an outrageous piece of misogamy, richly dressed with misogyny. While the texts of the two quartos here are more or less identical, in only the First Quarto does Hamlet go to the length of a sevenfold iteration of "To a Nunnery goe"—using the phrase like a refrain or a signature tune, not unlike Iago's "put money in thy purse," or the harping of Vice figures upon the titular theme of the play in *Like Will to Like* or *The Tyde Tarrieth No Man*. And whereas Q2, not irretrievably crossing the frontiers of dialogic representation, has, "I say we will have no moe marriage" (3.1.147), Q1 is closer to F1 in that Hamlet's use of the plural form distinctly swerves from a dialogic stance. Almost certainly, the plural in his "Ile no more marriages" correlates to an open stage, *platea*-like position, as does the enhanced iteration of the refrain that juggles with two meanings ("nunnery" could, of course, also denote a brothel). From this spatial position, the protagonist in Q1 can more consistently ignore the conventions of represented dialogue and harangue a plurality of spectators, among them, men ("wisemen know [. . .] What monsters you make of them") but especially the women (the plural form in "your paintings" is unmistakable, as it is in "you make your selues another" [face], where F has "your selfe"). The resulting effect must have been an uncanny blending of alarm and laughter, extreme dismay and reckless merriment.

There is then, as the briefest comparison could establish, more of a fluidity in relations in the First Quarto between "author's pen" and "actor's voice." Such a comparison is especially revealing if we assume, as I think we must, that Q1 *Hamlet,* "a version specially abridged for performance on tour" (Irace 1998, 100),[8] was adapted and reconstructed by traveling members of Shakespeare's own company. In the circumstances, the instability of the text can be established as inseparable from an obvious area of divergence in the purpose of playing. The point is that the underlying difference in authority and legitimation affects both the arts of writing and the styles of performance, respectively. In the Second Quarto, the authority of the writer is more firmly established; hence, the emphasis is on "the necessary question" of dramatic composition. But in the case of *The Tragicall Historie of* HAMLET *Prince of Denmark* (Q1), where the author's authority is either partially absent or short-shrifted, the realities of performance practice in the provinces are strongly asserted and appear to inform at least some of the features of the play. Thanks to the work of scholars like Sally-Beth MacLean, Alan Somerset, and contributors to the *Records of Early Eng-*

lish *Drama* series, we have of course come to revise "the anti-provincial bias" of a previous generation of critics: provincial touring, we must assume, participated in "an astonishing amount of entertainment activity" in the country; even when it may seem too emphatic to think of it "as a working holiday" for the traveling company, it can no longer be viewed as "the enforced banishment to the bucolic backwaters that touring has often been taken to be"(Somerset 1994, 50; 60). In regard to the provincial venue that the First Quarto almost certainly was associated with, we need to take into account that a considerable amount of the established playing places in the country—'Somerset reckons more than two thirds (1994, 59)'—were indoors.

Even so, playing in the provinces was, at the turn of the century, almost certainly in the absence of the playwright. In its remove from a stringently sustained authorial authority, the so-called "bad" quarto would more easily foreground the presentational voice and delivery of the performer. The play was thus reshaped by the practical exigencies of multiple purposes of playing that, even when transgressing the poetics of self-contained representations, would remain hugely indebted to a unique "author's pen." Here we have, in Thomas Clayton's acute observation, "a far from homogeneous, 'mixed' text, excellent in part but also divided against itself and apparently in 'authority'"(1992, 23). In other words, the First Quarto in particular drew on a hybrid authority, one that was as "divided against itself" as the double-dealing poetics that simultaneously informed Hamlet's antic clowning and his own advice against it.

Notes

1. Unless otherwise noted, all quotations of Shakespeare are taken from *The Riverside Shakespeare,* 2nd ed., ed. G. Blakemore Evans (Boston: Houghton Mifflin Company, 1997). (The *Riverside* copy-text of *Hamlet* is based on Q2.)
2. See, e. g., Paul Werstine, "The Textual Mystery of *Hamlet,*" *Shakespeare Quarterly* 39.1 (1988): 1–26.
3. My text is *The Tragicall Historie of Hamlet Prince of Denmarke,* (At London printed for N.L. and Iohn Trundell, 1603), reproduced in facsimile from the copy in the Henry E. Huntington Library (Cambridge, Mass.: Harvard University Press, 1931). For modern editions that, for systematic comparison, conveniently assemble all variants and passages unique to Q1, see the New Folger Library *Hamlet,* ed. Barbara A. Mowat and Paul Werstine (New York: Washington Square Press, 1992); or, even more complete, *The Three-Text* Hamlet, ed. Paul Bertram and Bernice W. Kliman (New York: AMS Press, 1991).

4. See the editor's note to 3. 1. 62, defining "shocks" in the "primary sense of 'clashes of arms.'"

5. As against "editorial practice in mainstream editions of *Hamlet*," Marcus in her provocative chapter "Bad Taste and Bad *Hamlet*" provides an important new perspective on "the strong movement [. . .] to rehabilitate Q1" (135) in terms of the play's remarkable "position on the register between orality and literacy" (Marcus 1996, 176). This perspective should be read in conjunction with Eric Rasmussen, "Setting Down what the Clown Spoke: Improvisation, Hand B and *The Book of Sir Thomas More*," *The Library* 13.2 (1991), 126–136; Kathleen Irace, "Origins and Agents of Q1 *Hamlet*," *The* Hamlet *First Published* (Q1, 1603); *Origins, Form, Intertextuality,* ed. Thomas Clayton (Newark: University of Delaware Press, 1992), 90–122; the same author, *Reforming the 'Bad' Quartos. Performance and Provenance of Six Shakespearean First Editions* (Newark: University of Delaware Press, 1994); Laurie E. Maguire, *Shakespearean Suspect Texts: The 'Bad' Quartos and their Contexts* (Cambridge: Cambridge University Press, 1996); among others.

6. But note John Dover Wilson's repeated opinion that "this addition must be a personal attack upon a particular clown" (*Hamlet:* "The New Cambridge Shakespeare," [Cambridge: Cambridge University Press, 1934], p.197), which appears to modify somewhat his earlier assumption, upon discovering the Tarltonic source of two of the clown's "cinkapase of jests," that the passage in question was the dramatist's attack on Tarlton himself (*The Library*, 1918; 240–41). As against Dover Wilson, Chambers argued that the passage "can only be a theatrical interpolation" (*William Shakespeare,* 1:418–19). Duthie at some length considers Brinsley Nicholson's suggestion (*Transactions of the New Shakespeare Society, 1880–82,* Part I, 57–59), that the attack was leveled at William Kempe; but then he shows conclusively that we have "no clear evidence in Q1 for the existence behind it of anything that might be called a Shakespearian first draft" (237).

7. Although, unfortunately, the "New Cambridge Shakespeare" Quarto edition refuses critically to pursue the connection between the play's provenance and its dramaturgy, there are, indisputably I believe, trenchant traces of a difference in the authorization and *mise-en-scène* of the First Quarto in comparison with the two other versions.

8. According to her conjectural reconstruction, "a few of Shakespeare's colleagues, including 'Marcellus,' may have had an unexpected need for a *Hamlet* playtext while on tour; it might have been quicker—or safer—to reconstruct the play rather than return to plague-ridden London for the promptbook" (ibid.). Cf. Kathleen Irace, *Reforming the 'Bad' Quartos,* and her "New Cambridge" edition of *Hamlet* (1603) (cit. in note 14), where she suggests that "the players might also have responded to a special request [. . .], like Hamlet's for *The Murder of Gonzago,* so that Q1 "was reconstructed as well as adapted [. . .] for an audience outside of London" (19).

Works Cited

Adams, Joseph Quincy, ed. 1924. *Chief Pre-Shakespearean Dramas.* Boston: Houghton Mifflin. l.783; cf. lines 151, 701, 744.

Clayton, Thomas, ed. 1992. Introduction to *The 'Hamlet' First Published.* Newark: University of Delaware Press; London: Associated Presses.

Duthie, G. I. 1941. The 'Bad' Quarto of Hamlet; A Critical Study. Cambridge: Cambridge University Press.

Edwards, Philip, ed. 1985. *Hamlet: Prince of Denmark.* "The New Cambridge Shakespeare." Cambridge: Cambridge University Press.

Evans, G. Blakemore, ed. 1997. *The Riverside Shakespeare.* 2nd ed. Boston: Houghton Mifflin Company.

Irace, Kathleen, ed. 1998. *The First Quarto of Hamlet.* Cambridge: Cambridge University Press.

Jenkins, Harold, ed. 1982. *Hamlet. The Arden Shakespeare.* London: Methuen.

Jones, Richard. 1981. Preface to *Tamburlaine the Great.* Ed. J. S. Cunningham. Manchester: Manchester University Press.

Loughrey, Bryan. 1992. "Q1 in Recent Performance: An Interview." In *The Hamlet First Published (Q1, 1603). Origins, Form, Intertextualities.* Ed. Thomas Clayton. Newark: University of Delaware Press.

MacLean, Sally-Beth. 1993. "Tour Routes: 'Provincial Wanderings' or Traditional Circuits?" *Medieval and Renaissance Drama in England* 6 (1993): 1–14.

Marcus, Leah. 1996. Unediting the Renaissance: Shakespeare, Marlowe, Milton. London: Routledge.

Scoloker, Anthony. 1930. "Epistle to *Daiphantes.*" Cited by E. K. Chambers, *William Shakespeare: A Study of Facts and Problems.* Oxford: Clarendon Press.

Somerset, Alan. 1994. "'How chances it they travel?' Provincial Touring, Playing Places, and the King's Men," *Shakespeare Survey* 47.

Trundell, N. L. and Iohn. 1603. *The Tragicall Historie of Hamlet Prince of Denmarke.* (At London, reproduced in facsimile from the copy in the Henry E. Huntington Library.) Cambridge, MA: Harvard University Press, 1931.

Chapter 3

New York's African Theatre: Shakespeare Reinterpreted

William Over

Viewing nineteenth-century blackface parodies of Shakespeare in America, Kris Collins (1996) concludes that they "organized Shakespeare and African Americans as occupants of separate (and certainly *not* equal) social/cultural spaces, and in doing so staged an essential boundary between the two cultures" (95). White performers travestying black Shakespeareans codified a racial taxonomy that identified Shakespeare with whiteness, a process that developed throughout the nineteenth century. But what would be the effect of a uniquely African American staging of Shakespeare? The struggle to present Shakespeare to an African American audience in antebellum New York City involved more than merely introducing "literary classics" to a varied but largely uninitiated audience. I hope to demonstrate that New York's African Theatre, under the management of Henry Brown, challenged prevailing conceptions of racial definition and elitist notions of high culture by representing Shakespeare not only with all-black casts but with its own style and actor/audience alliance.

The identification of high culture with New York theatre in the 1820s remained precarious, as American dramas were few and British imported plays and players prevailed (Hill 1986, 11). American plays and performers were as yet unable to depose the tradition of British touring companies (Hodge 1971, 4–6; McDermott 1993, 9–10). New York's defensive position toward perceived rivals of cultural definition made the city a relatively intolerant venue, as African American performers of Shakespeare were to discover. For instance, Ira Aldridge, apprenticed at the African Theatre, was only successful after he left America for England and the Continent, where he became world famous (Marshall and Stock 1968, 48–69; Lindfors 1994).

By placing the African Theatre within the cultural spectrum of New York City during those years, I hope to demonstrate how African Americans reinterpreted American culture for its own purposes. I also hope to show that Brown's theatre company expressed a political agenda that went beyond its intention to redefine the limits of elitist theatre.

In 1820s New York, Black cultural agency was made commensurate to white enterprise by imposing upon it an imitative rather than a creative identity. However, the African Theatre under Brown and James Hewlett redefined its "imitative" status, putting into question the originative nature of mainstream (white) theatre. This was accomplished in a way similar to Bertolt Brecht's Epic Theatre: "by mentally switching off the motive forces of our society or by substituting others for them . . . thus allowing the real motive forces to be shorn of their naturalness and become capable of manipulation" (Brecht 1964, 191). In fact, New York's African Theatre and Brecht's theatre show significant parallels, as I hope to demonstrate.

"never to act Shakespeare again"

A former ship's steward, Brown probably built his acting company from the evening entertainment supplied for the African Grove, a tea and ice cream garden for free African Americans in New York. The New York *National Advocate* first mentions the Grove in its August 3, 1821 issue, where it is described as a garden for evening refreshment and relaxation. The same paper reports what may have been the first production of the African Theatre, a performance of *Richard III* (September 21, 1821, 1). Throughout September and October 1821, New York papers reported on the company's productions. Their descriptions of the individual acting performances conformed to traditional white conceptions of black physicality and behavior, and were almost entirely visually oriented: "the agony of the appalling Richard, the rolling eyes, white gnashing teeth, clenched fists and frenzied looks were all that the author could wish" (*National Advocate,* September 21, 1821, 1)

Brown's theatre company was under constant harassment from the local police after opening *Richard III.* Ending a review with what was probably intended as a humorous anticlimax, the *National Advocate* reporter commented succinctly, "Richard and Catesby were unfortunately taken up by the watch" (October 27, 2). The same article makes an oblique reference to the increased presence of whites at the African Theatre: "They have graciously made a partition at the back of their house, for the accommodation of the whites." Whether the company actively sought white patronage, or devised separate seating as a means of appeasing local authorities and minimizing racial friction is not clear. In either case, the restricted audience areas did not prevent disruptions. The company was unable to prohibit or control its white patrons, and the theatre was closed by the police within a few months, reputedly because of white harassment (New York *American,* January 10, 1822, np). A performance of *Richard III* was interrupted and the entire cast detained at a police station until they agreed "never to act Shakespeare again" (Snipe 1822, 1).

The African Theatre soon reopened after its forced closure. Simon Snipe, a white New York journalist, gave an account of a performance of *Othello* by Brown's company in the summer or early autumn of 1822 (Snipe 1822, 2). Snipe attempts to create a farcical story from his own experience of the production and relies upon prevailing white conceptions of African American identity. In line with the *National Advocate,* the *New York American,* and the *New York Evening Post* reportage, a serious effort to criticize the production was never part of Snipe's coverage. However, as Aldridge (1849) commented years later, "people who went to ridicule remained to admire" (11). Aldridge further claimed that Stephen Price, the competitive manager of New York's preeminent Park Theatre, had been personally responsible for the hiring of the rowdy elements in the audiences of Brown's theatre before its first closing (6).[1] Recently, Samuel Hay has identified the editor of the *National Advocate,* Mordecai Manuel Noah, as a chief instigator of antiblack voting issues in New York state. A powerful politico, playwright, and friend of Price, Noah wrote negative reviews of *Richard III* to arouse feelings against the liberalization of voting requirements at the 1821 New York Democratic Convention (Hay 1994, 7–8). In his reviews Noah associated African American performance of elite culture with political activism:"They now assemble in groups; and since they have crept in favour in the convention, they are determined to have balls and quadrille parties, establish a forum, solicit a seat in the assembly, or in the common council. . . . They can outvote the whites, as they say" (*National Advocate,* September 25, 1821, 2).

The company persisted after the forced closure, but abandoned its Shakespearean repertoire to perform dramas with contemporary political themes. On June 20 and 21, 1823, *The Drama of King Shotaway* was performed. Written by Brown himself for his benefit performance, *King Shotaway* was described in its playbill as "Founded on facts taken from the Insurrection of the Caravs in the Island of St. Vincent. Written from experience by Mr. Brown" (qtd. in Odell 1928, 3:70–71). Its subject was the 1795 uprising against the British government on St. Vincent, West Indies. Later that month, *Tom and Jerry* was given, based on a New York mainstream production of that play, but with an added scene of the Charleston slave market, featuring slaves and auctioneer (Odell 1928, 3:71). The representation in early nineteenth-century America of a slave auction and a slave rebellion against a white colonial authority clearly violated mainstream American values.

As the leading actor in Brown's African Theatre, Hewlett appeared as Othello and Richard in the Shakespeare plays and as King Shotaway in Brown's play. New York newspaper reviewers were more considerate of Hewlett than of other cast members. Noah in *National Advocate* conceded that "The person of Richard was on the whole not amiss" in its September 21 review of *Richard III*. He learned his acting "under those celebrated masters [George Frederick] Cooke and [Thomas A.] Cooper, which he followed as a servant boy, and stole their actions and attitudes" (New York *Star*, December 22, 1825, 2). When Hewlett gave "imitations" on his own, he drew from the acting styles of Cooke, Edmund Kean, Charles Mathews, the Kembles, and other British stars who visited the Park Theatre on their American tours after 1810. Most of the programs advertising Hewlett listed these actors as sources for his "imitations." However, Hewlett reappropriated Shakespeare by constructing an African American identity where "imitations" of white performers identified black performers with Shakespeare's cultural status, even as they moved beyond the cultural norms they "imitated." The particular elements of this originative performance style I will discuss later.

With the final closing of the African Theatre after the production of *King Shotaway*, Hewlett performed "imitations" at the assembly room of the Military Gardens. The New York *Star* announced that this would be his last performance "prior to his return to London, to fill his engagement at the Cobourg Theatre" (December 15, 1825, np). But his name appeared several years later, in March 1831, when he "imitated many" and was given a benefit performance on March 7 in New York (Odell 1928, 3:536). George Odell states that the actor "failed after this" and comments cryptically that after July 1831, Hewlett "gave imitations and took exhilarating gas . . . Herein lurks a real tragedy of a negro's thwarted ambition" (Odell 1928, 3:536). The only other reference to his misfortune came from Aldridge, who lamented, "They confuse me with poor Jim Hewlett" (qtd. in Marshall and Stock 1968, 39).

"my 'mind or my 'visage'"?

Hewlett was probably in England during most of 1824 and 1825. A December 1825 American playbill announced him with the comment, "A grand Entertainment prior to his return to London, to fill his engagement at the Cobourg Theatre." The English comic actor Charles Mathews claimed that Hannibal Hewlet [*sic*] gave a performance of *At Home* for "two or three nights" at the Theatre Royal, Liverpool on January 13, 1825 (Mathews 1839, 3:26). If this were so, then Hewlett planned his acting piece to follow Mathews' own star performance of *At Home*. Mathews also claimed that Hewlett "went to London . . . to challenge me for ridiculing him in a part" (Mathews 1839, 3:29). Mathews had in fact ridiculed an African Theatre *Richard III* performance in his stage act and in his popular memoir, *Trip to America*. His target was probably Hewlett, but later critics confused him with Aldridge (Mathews 1823, 9), such that later in his career Aldridge would parody in turn the Mathews parodies attributed to him.[2]

Hewlett's eloquent reply to Mathews's parody in an open letter for the *National Advocate* is his only known personal correspondence: "Now, when you were ridiculing the 'chief black tragedian' and burlesquing the 'real Negro' melody, was it my 'mind' or my 'visage' which should have made an impression on you?" (May 8, 1924, 2). Hewlett applies Desdemona's justification for her attraction to Othello, "I saw Othello's visage in his mind" (1.3.252), to implicate the predominant racial motives of Mathews. Desdemona, anticipating the objections of Venetian society, affirms the inner qualities of Othello over the culturally charged outward qualities of his skin color and form. In his Shakespearean roles, Hewlett was consistently objectified by mainstream reviewers and commentators, so that his "visage" was obsessively regarded while his "mind"—the inner qualities of character interpretation and verbal expression—was ignored. Hewlett uses Shakespeare as cultural authority to call Mathews to account for moral and aesthetic myopia. His open letter demonstrates the malleability of the cultural icon, reinterpreted by oppressed groups for their own defense and affirmation.

"his imitations were recognized as correct"

Endowed with a lengthy and relatively varied dramatic tradition, the English theatre of the early nineteenth century had the capacity to tolerate and even applaud, within limits, potentially disruptive representations. That the limits seem comparatively broad is evidenced by the stage career in England of Aldridge, who often played Othello opposite white Desdemonas.[3] By comparison, New York theatre was small, much less varied, and decidedly provincial. The newly built Park Street Theatre was the city's largest and leading playhouse, holding 2,500 spectators, but it was run by Stephen Price, who kept tight control over his dramatic fare and preferred British touring stars to resident companies (Brockett 1977, 58, 402; Nagler 1959, 524). As the national identity of the United States during the 1820s was formative, New York's cultural spectrum remained comparatively narrow. White audience rowdiness and scornful publicity by journalist and well-known white performers could hold tight rein on black performers of Shakespeare in New York. Direct police action—an arrest and a prohibition on performing Shakespeare—accompanied the cultural reaction, which associated blacks-playing-Shakespeare with criminal behavior. The *New York Evening Post's* description of the theatre closing reveals, with some smugness, the black actors' loss of status following their arrest: "the whole dramatic corps were actually taken to the watch-house, with all their tin-selled honours upon them" (January 10, 1822, 2). Black actors were deprived of their histrionic capability, a quality that implied equality with white performers. Such cultural enforcement reaffirmed the originative identity of whiteness in America.

Even in Europe, Aldridge's dazzling success was something new. Theatre history cites very few black people in roles of any color on the British stage until Aldridge, and the century-long debate among prominent drama critics over whether Shakespeare's Othello was intended to be "black," swarthy, Moslem, or North African, reveals the tensive relation of race to Eurocentric cultural institutions.[4] In America, representations of Shakespeare by a politically and racially suspect group—free Northern blacks—could not elicit rational debate from its elitist institutions. To attempt a rational analysis of the African Theatre's acting interpretation and subject matter would acknowledge its cultural status, a perspective unacceptable to the dominant ideology of a nation that still owned or profited from African American slavery. Thus the reputation of Brown's Shakespearean productions did not motivate mainstream argumentative discussion of Othello's racial identity and, hence, of the racial foundations of social power in America. However, Mathews' popular "imitations" of black Shakespearean performers served only to draw attention to alterity in 1820s New York; their parodic elements reproduced racial stereotyping that acknowledged, rather than denied, the Other. Mathews' travesties eventually became a source for the black-faced minstrel form in the United States and Great Britain (MacDonald 1994, 235; Browne 1960, 374–91).

Considering Foucault's view of state power, that it "renders manageable what might be otherwise too unwieldy or complex, and what, in its complexity, might defy the limiting and substantializing ontology presupposed by [power]," how did the dominant culture of New York respond to Brown's performances? White newspaper reportage typically assumed a visual orientation in the presence of black actors, whose racial difference appeared most obvious through the scopic sense. The visual bias denied more meaningful responses.

> How delighted would the Bard of Avon have been to see his Richard performed by a fellow as black as the ace of spades . . . . It was perceived that the actor [Hewlett] had made the King hump-backed instead of crooked back, having literally a hump behind his neck little less than a camel's. (*National Advocate,* September 21, 1821, 1)

The descriptions of audience members also took a scopic approach, often to the point of fetishism:

> The gentleman, with his wool nicely combed, and his face shining through a coat of sweet oil, borrowed from the castors; cravat tight to suffocation, having the double faculty of widening the mouth and giving a remarkable protuberance to the eyes; blue coat, fashionably cut; red ribbon and a bunch of pinch-beck seals; white pantaloons, shining boots, gloves, and a tippy rattan. (*The National Advocate* August 3, 1821, 2)

Such caricatures denied the creative power of black stage performers, who were powerful carriers of social coding, and rejected the status of their black theatre-going patrons.

Even relatively sympathetic reviewers reduced Hewlett's performances by categorizing them as "imitations," much as an apprentice actor might imitate his mentor. In such reviews, histrionic correctness prioritized white standards. The only extant portrait of Hewlett, as Richard III, is also derivative. It shows Hewlett in costume and pose similar to the lithograph portrait of the American actor Junius Brutus Booth as Richard III, dated May 9, 1817.[5] In fact both performers appeared in New York as Richard in October 1821 (Odell 1928, 3:2). The tendency to fix Hewlett as an imitator of white performers is retained even by the twentieth-century biographers of Aldridge, Marshall and Stock (1968), who continue without critical comment to describe Hewlett's acting performances in New York as "imitations" (38).

White New York journalism acknowledged the reappropriation and transformation of Shakespeare by African Americans, but not without heavy sarcasm: "It appears that the sable managers, not content with a small share of the profit and a great portion of fame, determined to rival the great Park Theatre" (New York *American,* January 10, 1822, 2). The ironic tone of the hyperbolic "great portion of fame" hardly conceals the article's anxiety over the trespass of cultural boundaries. Moreover, the disruption of *Richard III* by white outsiders witnessed the extent to which the redefinition of race by an objectified group threatened the prevailing racial ideology of antebellum America. Under the circumstances, the claim by an anonymous source that the disturbances were not spontaneous but the result of premeditation only underscores the unanimity of elitist reaction. Local police action paralleled the newspaper attacks of Snipes and Noah, an instance of the close alignment of cultural and political attitudes against threatening alterity. Finally, the agreement whereby the cast was required "never to act Shakespeare again" (Snipe 1822, 1) directly enforced the association of class and race, since African American performers of farcical comedy and popular musical forms were not subjected to such strictures in the nineteenth century.

Black actors playing powerful white characters (*Richard III*) and a black character in interracial intimacy (*Othello*) confused the objectification of blackness. Of Ira Aldridge's successful representations of Othello later in the century, Joyce Green MacDonald (1994) has observed that "[a]s a black man playing the role of a black man, Aldridge forged a new link between signs and meanings. His performance . . . challenged the relevance of previous centuries' efforts by white actors to 'act black'" (232). Even Aldridge's bold bits of acting business—such as dragging his (white-acted) Desdemonas by the hair around the stage in the death scene—were accepted with only minor critical comment by European audiences (Kendal 1890, 30). Although parodies of Aldridge's acting style by white performers did occur early in his acting career, he successfully countered such public attacks with his own parodies, as in the case of Charles Mathews. By contrast, the African Theatre could not prevent even the most overt physical disruptions. From its inception Brown's company suffered systematic denigration by white authority—negative journalism, police action, and travesties by star performers—machinations that Aldridge's interracial productions at elitist theatres managed to elude. The cultural challenge of the African Theatre—Shakespeare re-presented by a black management in its own theatre for its own audiences—was more fundamental, if less successful, than Aldridge's, since the latter's productions were usually incorporated into elitist establishments. Moreover, as a completely independent institution founded for the free African American community of New York, the African Theatre raised more directly issues of cultural enfranchisement and authorization.

Perhaps in response to the tendentious commentary of New York journalists and political figures, Hewlett's own advertisements pointedly promoted his status as a Shakespearean; by doing so he hoped to personalize his stage career in an effort to avoid his own objectification by mainstream journalism, which identified blacks at best in low-comic and song-and-dance roles: "a young man who, notwithstanding the thousand obstacles which the circumstances of complexion must have thrown in the way of improvement has, by mere dint of natural genius and self-strengthened assiduity, risen to a successful competition with some of the first actors of the day."[6] Its straightforward acknowledgment of racism suggests that a sympathetic audience existed in 1820s New York, just as its self-promotion indicates the obstacles facing Hewlett's "circumstances of complexion." Some playbills designated Hewlett "Shakespeare's proud Representative," a title intended to counter preponderant claims to white exclusivity.[7] By casting himself as the "Representative" of Shakespeare, Hewlett redefined the boundaries of cultural authority, which no longer could be seen as white only.

Hewlett's efforts to realign race and high culture eventually led to his own marginalization—quite literally into side rooms of major American theatres, such as New York's Spruce Street Theatre (Odell 1928, 3:224). Given the racially segregated audience areas of the New York mainstage theatres, these literal side shows continued to keep audiences racially separated. African American performers of high culture were contained under the economic authority of white theatre establishments, while performances in black-managed establishments were eliminated.

"imitative inmates of the kitchens and pantries"

White attitudes toward the growing African American population of antebellum New York remained ambivalent. Brown's audience was probably composed of African American ship stewards and city workers together with their spouses, although one source described his clientele as holding "respectable and responsible positions" (Smith 1860, 27). Hay's contention that they were "apolitical and irreligious" seems unfounded, especially given Brown's risky repertoire (Hay 1994, 11). As Brown challenged proprietary notions of culture by offering original alternatives to a nontraditional audience, mainstream New York papers were motivated to attack his patrons quite as much as his productions. One such strategy involved an ironic plea on behalf of the African Theatre that trivialized its assertions of cultural independence:

> and thus were many of our ebony friends excluded from a participation in those innocent recreations to which they were entitled, by virtue of the great charter that declares "all men are equal." These imitative inmates of the kitchens and pantries, not relishing the strong arm of the law thus rudely exercised, were determined to have some kind of amusement. (National Advocate, September 21, 1821)

White New York also attacked Brown's own management of the African Theatre. Noah's articles against Brown project a racial orientation that fears the violation of its own cultural sanctions.

> It appears that the sable managers, not satisfied with a small share of the profit and a great portion of fame, determined to rival the great Park The-atre, belonging to Messrs. Beekman and Astor, and accordingly hired the Hotel next door to the theatre, where they announced their perfor-mances. . . . The ebony-colored wags were notified by the police that they must announce their last performance, but they, defying public authority, went on and acted nightly." (New York *American,* January 10, 1822)

The characterization of subaltern cultural production as overblown and bumbling demands a contrastive rhetorical strategy wherein elitist institu-tions are endowed with ultimate standards of perfectibility. The sympathetic review did appear at times in the New York papers when Hewlett became better known as a marginalized, and therefore less threatening, side-room monologist. However, even these reviewers tended to stress his "imitative" nature: "Hewlett must have had a natural talent for theatrical performances, and an excellent voice, or he never could have surmounted his early diffi-culties. . . . His imitations of Kean, Matthews, Philips and others were rec-ognized as correct, and evincing a nice discrimination and tact." The reviewer's emphasis on outward qualities, "natural talent," and faithfulness to white Shakespeareans demonstrates the subordination of African Amer-ican performers to white standards, which are presumed originative and prior to other standards. The African Theatre's "great portion of fame" was not conceived within its own context and form, but as derivative of white performers at such dominant institutions as the Park Theatre, from which Hewlett "stole their acting and attitudes" (New York *Star,* December 22, 1825, qtd. in Odell 1928, 3:293). By imposing upon it an imitative rather than a creative identity, black cultural agency was made commensurate to white enterprise, thereby removing the threat of alterity. Noah spoke directly to this: "People of colour generally are very imitative, quick in their conceptions and rapid in their executions; but it is in the lighter pursuits requiring no intensity of thought or depth of reflection" (*National Advocate,* August 3, 1821, 2). Noah's hidden agenda was to characterize blacks as imitative and therefore subject to the control of the white Federalist Party leaders he opposed as a Democrat. This party line was also expressed in the keynote address of the 1821 Democratic Convention: "[African Americans] are a peculiar people, incapable, in my judgment, of exercising that privilege [of voting] with any sort of discretion, prudence, or independence" (Fox 1965, 259).

Brown's selection of plays further threatened white notions of exclusivity. Since *Richard III* concerns an ambitious and forceful nobleman who earns power through his own force of personality quite as much as through his considerable martial ability, a black man representing "the mighty duke" could not be given legitimate status. By representing Hewlett's Richard as an unintended travesty of white performances, mainstream journalism maintained dominant racial categories. In *Othello,* Hewlett played a powerful black man in an interracial marriage. Although stripped of his *gravitas* as a military leader and adventurer, Shakespeare's Othello still possesses tragic stature. The choice not to take the African Theatre *Othello* and *Richard III* seriously can be understood as a strategy of containment by the white power structure. To acknowledge black performers representing characters of such tragic stature implied an affinity with "the great charter" of racial equality, a position that mainstream New York journalism would not uphold in the 1820s.

"tarnation conceit and considerable effrontery"

Perhaps the most threatening element of the African Theatre experience for antebellum New York was the transformative capability of the black actor and actor-manager, who broke boundaries by reappropriating Shakespeare for an African American context. On this point the 1849 *Memoir of Ira Aldridge* reflects, "Certain Yankees, with a degree of illiberality peculiar to some 'liberals,' had no notion of such indulgences being allowed to Negroes, whose 'tarnation conceit and considerable effrontery licked nature slick outright'" (qtd. in Marshall and Stock 1968, 40). The black performer's right to play Shakespeare—restricted to white, and most successfully to British, performers—appeared so culturally disruptive as to go against nature, it "licked nature slick." Implicit is the essentialization of black and white sensibilities, with black natural to popular and folk culture, white natural to all categories, but dominating elite, originative culture.

Brown's Shakespearean productions involved more than a change of cast from white to black. Contemporaries described a performance style and actor/audience relationship that differed markedly from the New York mainstage productions.[8] Mathews, Snipes, and other critics document an overt interaction between performer and spectator, what has been termed "audience/performer pairing," akin to the "call/response" tradition of African American performance and religious celebration.[9] For instance, Hewlett breaks from the role of Othello to speak directly to the audience or to deliver songs, either related to the dramatic scene or evoked by spontaneous audience response. The malleable structure suggests a unique African American staging of Shakespeare.

The white coverage of the African Theatre overlooked alternative meanings, styles of performance, and audience responsiveness. Mathews' racial bias overlooked the individuality of the actor—witness Aldridge's lament that "they confuse me with old Jim Hewlett" and Mathews's own disregard of which black actor he was reviewing (see above, pp. 9–10). Similarly, Mathews' reading of the performance overlooked the validity of an alternative style derived from an African American tradition steeped in oppositional strategy and tactical innuendo.[10] His account has Hewlett move quickly from the 3.1 soliloquy of Hamlet to singing "Opposum Up a Gum Tree," which Mathews recognized as "the national air, or sort of 'God Save the King' of the Negroes." What escaped Mathews was its significance as a protest song of slavery. For instance, the second stanza, never recorded by Mathews, begins:

> Massa send we Negro Boy
> Board a ship, board a ship,
> There we work and cry, "Ye hoy"
> Cowskin whip, cowskin whip,
> Negro he work all de day,
> Night get groggy, night get groggy,
> But if Negro he go play
> Massa floggy, Massa floggy (qtd. in Marshall and Stock 1968, 42)

Roger D. Abrahams' definition of "signifying" describes this tradition: "a technique of indirect argument or persuasion . . . a language of implication" (1970, 66–67). Zora Neale Hurston's important analysis of African American culture, "Characteristics of Negro Expression," offers other elements of this tradition: a tendency for "mimicry," the "will to adorn," "asymmetry"—which would explain Hewlett's sudden break from the linearity of Shakespeare's script to the situational context of audience demand (Gates and McKay 1997, 4). Other characteristics include a reliance on group creation and improvisation. Moreover, Hewlett's performance shows a unique form of intertextuality common to African American expression, where other voices and traditions are critically parodied or assessed. To describe this style, Henry Louis Gates quotes Bakhtin: The word "becomes 'one's own' only when the speaker populates it with his own intentions, his own accent, when he appropriates the word, adapting it to his own semantic and expressive intention" (Gates 1988, 1, 4).[11]

The African American signifying tradition and Brecht's Alienation Effect (*Verfremdungseffekt*) reveal certain parallels: the direct relation between actor and audience—"[The actor] acts in such a way that nearly every sentence could be followed by a verdict of the audience and practically every gesture is submitted for the public's approval" (Brecht 1964, 95); the nonlinearity of dramatic structure—"The unexpectedness of logically progressive or zigzag development, the instability of every circumstance, the joke of contradiction" (Brecht 1964, 277); and the frequent use of parody and irony in song and narrative. While Brecht attempted a "scientific" theatre that would transform the commercial theatre on a wide scale, Brown and Hewlett adapted their theatre for the free black subculture of New York, which in 1820 numbered 8,400 out of a total city population of 124,000.[12] Both theatres, however, attempted to transform the ideology of power by changing the form of its cultural reproductions—"by mentally switching off the motive forces of our society or by substituting others for them" (Brecht 1964, 191). As this was accomplished in the African Theatre, its secondary status as an "imitative" theatre was transcended.

Taking back the "tinselled honours"

Jean Baudrillard (1981) observes that objects become carriers of a social and cultural hierarchy, "but precisely for that reason there is every occasion to think that far from following the injunctions of this code undeviatingly, individuals and groups use it to their advantage. . . . That is to say, they use it in their own way: they play with it, they break its rules, they speak it with their class dialect" (37). On the same point, Michael Bronski (1984) finds that a subculture "creates and recreates itself—politically and artistically— along with, as well as in reaction to, the prevailing cultural norms. No counterculture can define itself independently of the dominant culture"

(7). However, Alan Sinfield (1994) explores the levels of freedom through which subcultural groups operate within dominant culture: "[S]ubcultures may return from the margins to trouble the center. They may redeploy its most cherished values, abusing, downgrading, or inverting them; willy-nilly, they exploit its incoherences and contradictions. So they form points from which repression may become apparent, its silences audible" (79). The futility of censoring or outlawing an art form is that, by its very nature, artistic expression challenges dominant culture. All art has this potential of "internal distantiation" by revealing the dominant ideology from which it departs, as Althusser (1971) observed (204). Brecht's *Verfremdungseffekt* and Brown's African Theatre are conscious attempts to distance artistic performance from "the motive forces of our society."

The African Theatre dissented from mainstream New York's cultural practice by incorporating within its formal elements innovations and disguised or overt political allusions, in this way freeing itself from subordinating ideologies. Although severely delimited by the white establishment of New York, Brown and Hewlett discovered through Shakespearean performance the means to overcome such restrictions. The African Theatre embodied what Judith Butler (1997) terms the "performative contradiction," which takes place "when one with no authorization to speak within and as the universal nevertheless lays claim to the term. . . . One who is excluded from the universal, and yet belongs to it nevertheless, speaks from a split situation of being at once authorized and deauthorized." Hence, subcultural performance calls into question all totalizing foundations: "Speaking and exposing the alterity within the norm . . . exposes the failure of the norm to effect the universal reach for which it stands" (91). Moreover, attempts by white New York journalists to cast the African Theatre in a derivative role by referring to its "imitations" and by performing parodies of its Shakespearean performances only questioned the originative nature of white cultural identities. As Butler (1993) observes, "*imitation* does not copy that which is prior, but produces and *inverts* the very terms of priority and derivativeness" (313). I suggest that a similar dynamic was present in the African Theatre, where subversive possibilities were presented by Brown and Hewlett through their "imitations" of well-known white performers. These mainstream performers were, as we have seen, British models who, in the 1820s, were challenging (white) Americans to develop their own Shakespearean style. Hewlett's "signifying" performance style, together with Brown's selection of plays and efforts at black audience development, challenged the originative nature of mainstream New York theatre. If white New York sought, using Butler's term, to "naturalize" its idealization of American Shakespeare performance, making it unnatural for black performers to play Shakespeare, then the presence of a black theatre company surely threatened such strategizing. At times this presence was directly accusatory. Aldridge himself would later challenge the originative status of Mathews and other white stars by performing parodies of their parodies. Similarly, Hewlett's open letter to Mathews used Shakespeare's words to implicate the white objectification of black Shakespearean performance—"was it my 'mind' or my 'visage' which should have made an impression on you?"

The African Theatre presented critical alternatives to Shakespeare that used intertextuality in a covertly political way. It broke the boundaries between high and low culture—combining Shakespearean verse with folk lyrics—and circumvented Shakespeare-as-cultural-status-quo by using the innuendo of political protest and the subversive possibilities of "imitation." Although white Americans would soon attempt to restrict black identity through the development of the nineteenth-century minstrel show form and the burlesque of black performances, the brief phenomenon of New York's African Theatre demonstrated that Shakespeare's cultural capital could no longer be considered strictly a white holding.

Notes

1. For an account of the predatory nature of Price and the highly competitive nature of New York cultural life during the period, see Hewitt (1971, 108–09).
2. Aldridge denied it was he Mathews parodied. The evidence points to Hewlett as the object of ridicule, although Marshall and Stock do not make the connection. See Marshall and Stock (1968, 40–44, 82, 150).
3. Recent documents reveal that Aldridge had several affairs during his marriage to Margaret Gill and in 1855 was sued for adultery. Even so, the negative publicity affected his career only temporarily. See Bernth Lindfors (1994).
4. For an account of the ambivalent views toward Othello's race in British theatre performance, see Ruth Cowhig (1979).
5. The Hewlett portrait is from the Raymond Mander and Joe Mitchenson Theatre Collection, reproduced in Marshall and Stock (1968, 40). The Booth portrait is opposite the title page, Odell (1928, vol. 3).
6. New York *American,* April 27, 1825, signed "A Friend of Merit," for a performance at the Spruce Street Theatre, room number 11.

7. Playbill for a performance at Saratoga, New York, n.d. Cited in Marshall and Stock (1968, 32).

8. Yvonne Shafer's otherwise insightful article assumes that the African Theatre shared the same performance concept as white Shakespeareans. See Shafer (1977, 393).

9. For a discussion of the call/response tradition in African American culture, see Gates (1997, 4–5). Dewberry (1982) recognizes the presentational style and the independent musical insertions typical of early black minstrelsy (131).

10. For a study of the African American tradition of oppositional strategy and double-entendre, see Gates (1988), especially definitions of signifying (66–67). Of particular relevance is the subversively parodying speech from traditional tales.

11. A current example of the misinterpretation of the African American signifying tradition in performance has been observed by Gates in "An Album is Judged Obscene; Rap, Slick, Violent, Nasty and, Maybe Helpful." *New York Times,* June 17, 1990, p. 1.

12. Census report from the *New York Evening Post,* February 16, 1821, 2.

Works Cited

Abrahams, Roger D. 1970. *Deep Down in the Jungle: Negro Narrative Folklore from the Streets of Philadelphia.* Chicago: Aldine Publishing.

Aldridge, Ira. 1849. *Memoir and Theatrical Career of Ira Aldridge, The African Roscius.* London: J. Onwhyn.

Althusser, Louis. 1971. "A Letter on Art in Reply to Andre Daspre." In *Lenin and Philosophy and Other Essays.* Trans. Ben Brewster. London: New Left Books. 201–8.

Bate, Jonathan. 1989. *Shakespearean Constitutions: Politics, Theatre, Criticism 1730–1820.* Oxford: Clarendon Press.

Baudrillard, Jean. 1981. *For a Critique of the Political Economy of the Sign.* Trans. and Introduction by Charles Levin. London: Telos Press.

Brecht, Bertolt. 1964. *Brecht on Theatre.* Trans. John Willett. New York: Hill and Wang.

Brockett, Oscar G. 1977. *History of the Theatre.* 3rd. ed. Boston: Allyn & Bacon.

Bronski, Michael. 1984. *Culture Clash.* Boston: South End Press.

Browne, Ray B. 1960. "Shakespeare in American Vaudeville and Negro Minstrelsy." *American Quarterly* 12: 374–91.

Butler, Judith. 1997. *Excitable Speech: A Politics of the Performative.* New York: Routledge.

———. 1993. "Imitation and Gender Insubordination." In *The Lesbian and Gay Studies Reader.* Ed. Henry Abelove and David M. Halperin. New York: Routledge. 298–319.

Collins, Kris. 1996. "White-Washing the Black-a-Moor: *Othello*, Negro Minstrelsy and Parodies of Blackness." *Journal of American Culture* 19 (Fall): 87–102.

Cowhig, Ruth. 1979. "Actors Black and Tawny in the Role of Othello—and Their Critics." *Theatre Research International* 4: 133–46.

Dewberry, Jonathan. 1982. "The African Grove Theatre and Company." *Black American Literature Forum* 16 (Winter): 128–31.

Foucault, Michel. 1977. *The History of Sexuality*. Trans. Robert Hurley. New York: Pantheon.

Fox, Dixon Ryan. 1965. *The Decline of Aristocracy in the Politics of New York*. New York: Harper & Row.

Gates, Henry Louis, Jr. and Nellie Y. McKay, eds. 1997. *The Norton Anthology of African American Literature*. New York: Norton.

Gates, Henry Louis, Jr. 1988. *The Signifying Monkey: A Theory of Afro-American Literary Criticism*. New York and Oxford: Oxford University Press.

Hay, Samuel A. 1994. *African American Theatre: An Historical and Critical Analysis*. Cambridge: Cambridge University Press.

Henderson, Mary C. 1973. *The City and the Theatre: New York Playhouses from Bowling Green to Times Square*. Clifton, NJ: James T. White.

Hewitt, Bernard. 1971. "'King Stephen' of the Park and Drury Lane." In *The Theatrical in England and America*. Ed. Joseph W. Donohue. Princeton, New Jersey: Princeton University Press: 105–119.

Hill, Errol. 1986. *Shakespeare in Sable: A History of Black Shakespearean Actors*. Amherst: University of Massachusetts Press.

Hodge, Francis. 1971. "European Influences on American Theatre." In *The American Theatre: A Sum of Its Parts*. London: Samuel French. 3–5.

Kendal, Madge. 1890. *Dramatic Opinions*. Boston: Little, Brown.

Lindfors, Bernth. 1994. "Nothing extenuate, nor set down aught in malice': New Biographical Information on Ira Aldridge." *African American Review* 28 (Fall): 457–72.

Marshall, Herbert, and Mildred Stock. 1968. *Ira Aldridge: The Negro Tragedian*. Carbondale: Southern Illinois University Press.

Mathews, Charles. 1839. *Memoirs of Charles Mathews*, 4 Vols. Edited by Mrs. Mathews. London: Richard Bentley.

———. 1823. *Sketches of Mr. Mathews's Celebrated Trip to America*. London: J. Limbird.

MacDonald, Joyce Green. 1994. "Acting Black: *Othello, Othello* Burlesques, and the Performance of Blackness." *Theatre Journal* 46: 231–249.

McDermott, Douglas. 1993. "The Theatre and its Audience: Changing Modes of Social Organization in the American Theatre." In *The American Stage: Social and Economic Issues from the Colonial Period to the Present*. Ed. Ron Engle and Tice L. Miller. Cambridge: Cambridge University Press. 6–17.

Nagler, A. M. 1959. *A Source Book in Theatrical History*. New York: Dover.

Odell, George C. D. 1928. *Annals of the New York Stage*, 15 Vols. New York: Columbia University Press.

Shafer, Yvonne. 1977. "Black Actors in the Nineteenth-Century American Theatre." *CLA Journal* 20.3: 387–400.

Sinfield, Alan. 1994. *Cultural Politics—Queer Reading.* Philadelphia: University of
Pennsylvania Press.

Smith, James McCune. 1860. "Ira Aldridge." *Anglo-African Magazine* (January): 27.

Snipe, Simon. 1822. *Sports of New York: Containing an Evening at the African Theatre.*
New York: New York Historical Society.

Part III

Adapting Ideologies

Chapter 4

Vaulting Ambitions and Killing Machines: Shakespeare, Jarry, Ionesco, and the Senecan Absurd

Curtis Perry

In an interview from 1966, Ionesco acknowledged Shakespeare's relevance to the theater of the absurd in such a way as to deny any more specific personal influence:

> Didn't he say of the world that "it is a tale told by an idiot" and that everything is but "sound and fury"? He's the forefather of the theatre of the absurd. He said it all, and said it a long time ago. Beckett tries to repeat him. I don't even try: since he said do well what he had to say, what can we possibly add? (Bonnefoy 1970, 49)

Disclaimers notwithstanding, Ionesco could not resist repeating Shakespeare. His *Macbett,* first produced in 1972, restages Shakespeare's *Macbeth* along lines sketched by Jan Kott and anticipated by Alfred Jarry's notorious farce *Ubu Roi* (1896): "My *Macbeth* is somewhere between Shakespeare and Jarry; it is close to *Ubu Rex*. . . . It was my friend Jan Kott's book *Shakespeare Our Contemporary* which showed me the way" (Lamont 1993, 182). As its pedigree suggests, *Macbett* is intended to be a doubly radical revision of Shakespeare, eager both to demonstrate absurdist elements in Shakespeare's play, and to render ridiculous those heroic aspects of the play that might obscure the meaninglessness of its violence. Accordingly, as several critics have noted, *Macbett* elaborates Shakespeare's suggestion that rebellion and tyranny may be part of an endless cycle of political violence.[1] When Macol (the Malcolm figure) seizes the throne at the end of the play, his final speech is cobbled together out of the avowal of sin that Shakespeare's Malcolm uses to test the loyalty of Macduff ("My poor country shall have more vices than it had before" [Ionesco 1985, 103–4]).[2] *Macbett* thus ends with the promise of "confineless harms" to come (Ionesco 1985, 104).

Macbett, however, is at its most heavy-handed when bent on illustrating what Kott calls the "grand staircase of history," with its inevitable cycles of political violence (Kott 1964, 75). The earnestness of its political message coexists only uneasily with its flights of parodic whimsy: even Martin Esslin, generally one of Ionesco's champions, tactfully described the play's depiction of the political machine as "far from sensationally original" (1973, 54–55). Beyond its depiction of state violence, however, Ionesco's play is interested in anatomizing the kinds of desires that fuel this political machine, an emphasis borrowed perhaps from Jarry, whose *Ubu Roi* reduces the *Macbeth* story to a farce of unchecked infantile appetite. Ionesco's sense of Shakespeare as "the forefather of the theatre of the absurd" is based in part on the way that Macbeth's actions are motivated by desires that lose their objects, so that what begins specifically as ambition to rule morphs into a vague and ultimately insatiable wish to be "Whole as the marble, founded as the rock, / As broad and general as the casing air" (3.4.21–22).[3] This transformation in Shakespeare's title character provides a starting point for the absurdist farces of Jarry and Ionesco, with the result that analysis of absurd desire in *Ubu Roi* and *Macbett* can still (almost four decades after Kott's book) illuminate ways in which Shakespeare seems both radical and contemporary.

Why Shakespeare? Partly of course because of the familiarity and accessibility of Shakespeare's plays.[4] Partly because attacking Shakespeare's cultural status has its own inherent shock value. But more importantly, because of Shakespeare's participation in a strand of Renaissance dramatic experimentation that is in some regards analogous to the drama of Jarry and Ionesco. I call that strand the "Senecan absurd" because it seems to me to be part of the thematic inheritance of the Senecan tradition in Renaissance drama best described by Gordon Braden. Briefly, Braden argues that Seneca's tragic heroes strive toward total autonomy, attempting to establish "personal identity as a force that transcends its origins and contexts" by the sheer magnitude of their passionate will (Braden 1985, 34). But, at the same time, these heroes—spurred on by mimetic rivalry—require acknowledged dominion over those around them and thus rely for satisfaction upon the very contexts they aspire to transcend. Hence the restlessness that Braden finds at the core of Senecan ambition (Braden 1985, 60–62). Though Braden's analysis emphasizes the period's interest in greatness of spirit, it seems to me that this same inheritance leads as well to a series of experiments with more nearly absurdist concerns. That is to say that a fair amount of the period's Senecan experimentation explicitly probes the limits of personal autonomy and the instability of mimetic desire, thereby emphasizing both the final inseparability of desire and context, and the radical dehumanizing of autarkic aspiration. The tragic protagonists in such plays—brutal, insatiable, and finally stripped of human feeling—anticipate the concerns of Jarry and Ionesco. Shakespeare's Senecanism makes him Ionesco's "forefather."

Absurd Desire in *Ubu Roi* and *Macbett*

Jarry's humor is sometimes called Rabelaisian in acknowledgment of its emphasis on lower bodily appetites and functions (Esslin 1961, 255; LaBelle 1980, 66–70). From the play's notorious first word—"Merdre" (*merde* with an extra letter, translated by Barbara Wright as "Shittr")—the play is obsessively scatological.[5] Pere Ubu features an enormous gut ("he looks like an armed pumpkin" [90]), and an appetite to match. And indeed the play does contain elements of the Rabelaisian worldview described by Mikhail Bakhtin. Here, for example, is the exchange after Mere Ubu first suggests regicide to her husband:

> *Pere Ubu*: Oh! Mere Ubu, you insult me, and you'll find yourself in the stewpan in a minute.
> *Mere Ubu*: Huh! you poor fish, if I found myself in the stewpan, who'd mend the seats of your breeches?
> *Pere Ubu*: Well, what of it? Isn't my arse the same as anyone else's [*N'ai-je pas un cul comme les autres* (35)]? (11)

The emphasis on the lower/open body is used here, as in Rabelais, to suggest that everybody is fundamentally the same—wrapped in the same fleshy bodies and driven by the same basic urges. For Jarry, as for Rabelais, this is above all a rhetoric of de-idealization: what is the meaning of manners, rank, decorum if what's important about a person is of the register of appetite and "arse"? Everyone's are the same as anyone else's.

In Rabelais the de-idealizing motifs of the open/lower body are used to criticize pretensions of serious culture in favor of the values of the carnivalesque: communality, festivity, the primacy of the body. The universality of this register leads to a demystifying of desires based on power, position, wealth, and so on, desiderata that fade to relative insignificance next to the urgency of the body in grotesque realism. Not so, however, in *Ubu Roi*. In Jarry's play, Rabelaisian motifs of grotesque realism coexist with and are even seen as integral to murderous ambition lifted from the story of *Macbeth*. The exchange quoted above continues as follows:

> *Mere Ubu*: If I were you, what I'd want to do with my arse would be to install it on a throne. You could increase your fortune indefinitely [*augmenter . . . tes richesses* (35)], have sausages whenever you liked, and ride through the streets in a carriage.
>
> *Pere Ubu*: If I were king, I'd have a big headpiece made. . . .
>
> *Mere Ubu*: And you could get yourself an umbrella and a great big cloak that would come right down to your feet.
>
> *Pere Ubu*: Ah! I yield to temptation. Clod of a shittr, shittr of a clod, if ever I meet him on a dark night he'll go through a bad quarter of an hour.
>
> *Mere Ubu*: Oh good, Pere Ubu, now you're a real man. (12–13)

Instead of debunking political ambitions, Pere Ubu's lower-body appetites seem inextricable from them. He pursues office with the same boisterous infantile greed that makes him gobble up Mere Ubu's cooking before the king arrives in the play's second scene.

This exchange is typical of Jarry's play in that it cobbles together three different kinds of desire: Pere Ubu's appetite for sausages (the stuff of grotesque realism); his desire for more wealth (mundane bourgeois aspiration); and his interest in the trappings of public authority (carriage, headpiece, umbrella, cloak). Everybody is subject to appetites of the belly, and most people want more money, so Ubu's desire for the outlandish props that represent authority seems the most absurd and the least familiar of Pere Ubu's desires. But the exchange, in which the promise of such props makes Ubu yield, suggests that they capture Ubu's imagination. As a farce of Shakespearean ambition, this accomplishes two things. First, it associates political ambition with the least heroic and most familiar kinds of appetites (the bodily and the bourgeois). Second, it renders the objects of ambition so trivial as to be manifestly not worth striving for. In the world of this farce, ordinary men driven by enormous appetites kill each other for trifles.

By emphasizing the outlandish triviality of the objects Ubu craves, Jarry literalizes what Macbeth himself comes to feel only too late: "There's nothing serious in mortality: / All is but toys" (2.3.93–94). Accordingly, Jarry strips the political ceremonies between Ubu and King Venceslas of the stateliness characterizing the equivalent scenes in *Macbeth*. The following exchange from *Macbeth* is a ritual exchange of loyalty and reciprocal support that represents an ideal of civility:

Macb.:   The service and the loyalty I owe,
         In doing it, pays itself. Your highness' part
         Is to receive our duties; and our duties
         Are to your throne and state children and servants;
         Which do but what they should, by doing every thing
         Safe toward your love and honor
Dun.:   Welcome hither!
         I have begun to plant thee, and will labor
         To make thee full of growing. Noble Banquo,
         That hast no less deserv'd, nor must be known
         No less to have done so, let me infold thee
         And hold thee to my heart.
Ban.:   There if I grow
         The harvest is your own. (1.4.22–33)

Jarry stages a similar scene, but mocks the display of reciprocal loyalty as just another exchange of toys:

The King: Pere Ubu, I want to recognize your numerous services as Captain of the Dragoons, and I am making you count of Sandomir as from today.
Pere Ubu: Oh Monsieur Venceslas, I don't know how to thank you.
The King: Don't thank me, Pere Ubu, and be present tomorrow morning at the great Review.
Pere Ubu: I'll be there, but be good enough to accept this little toy whistle [ce petit mirliton (47)].
            (He presents the king with a toy whistle)
The King: What do you expect me to do with a toy whistle at my age? (29)

Ubu treats the whistle as if it stood for his loyalty and gratitude, and as if it were an adequate requital for Venceslas's generosity. And though Venceslas is taken aback, the title of Count of Sandomir seems equally trivial. Everywhere in *Ubu Roi*, public life is represented as the traffic in trifles and toys. Later in the play, the power of Ubu's monarchy is vested in yet another set of comic props: a hook for executing enemies and a cart called "the phynancial conveyance" (75) for carrying off their money. It is possible that Jarry had in mind Macbeth's own anguished discovery that the props of monarchy—"fruitless crown" and "barren scepter" (3.1.60–61)— add up to nothing in and of themselves. Only in Jarry's play their fruitlessness of such objects is obvious and everybody wants them anyway.

Ubu becomes king at the start of Act 3: "By my green candle, here I am, the king of this country and I've already got myself indigestion and they're going to bring me my big head piece" (59). Ubu's indigestion results from a grasping hunger that, in keeping with the play's conflation of different kinds of appetite, makes him gobble up sausages as readily as he grabs the throne. As king, his grasping appetite leads him to have all the nobles killed in order to take their property. Then, having killed his magistrates and officers, Ubu himself is forced to drag the phynancial conveyance "from village to village" to collect taxes. As he explains his taxation to reluctant subjects, he offers a glimpse of the fantasy that drives his enormous greediness:

> I've changed the government and I've had it put in the paper that all the existing taxes must be paid twice, and those that I impose later must be paid three times. With this system I shall soon have made my fortune, then I'll kill everybody and go away. [*Avec ce système, j'aurai vite fait fortune, alors je tuerai tout le monde et je m'en irai* (78)]. (76)

This is a key moment in the farce, since it is the only instance in which Ubu offers any explanation for his ambition beyond the kind of overtly trivial proximate objectives we have been looking at: the carriage, the head piece, the umbrella, the cloak, and so on. But of course this genocidal fantasy is no less absurd. Since the wealth that Ubu extorts is valuable only in relation to an economy involving other people, his greediness is literally inconsistent with his fantasy of universal destruction. Ubu wants to triumph in his world—to monopolize the goods and props that are understood to be valuable and prestigious—but only as a means to achieve a kind of impossible autonomy that would destroy that world itself. We might think of this as a kind of political analogue to Ubu's indigestion: both are included to demonstrate the degree to which his appetites are driven by sheer greediness, and divorced from any pragmatic end (satiation of the body, pleasure, political influence, etc.).

Though crudely (and amusingly) put, this moment in Jarry's play strikes me as a sophisticated response to the paradox of ambition in *Macbeth*. For Macbeth too strives for the crown only to find that it is a proximate goal standing unsatisfactorily for a fantasy of total autonomy. One wonders, for example, why Macbeth should be so suddenly upset about Banquo's heirs in 3.1, since he knew about the witches' prophesy before killing Duncan and since he has no children of his own. It seems that Macbeth's anxiety has to do with the idea of successors in general. Or, more generally, that he chafes at anything that proves him to be other than "perfect, / Whole as the marble, founded as the rock, / As broad and general as the casing air" (3.4.20–22). Macbeth—like Ubu—grasps hungrily at triumph over others while dreaming of total autonomy.[6]

We might describe this as the paradox of mimetic desire: so long as value is given mimetically by competition with others, total victory can only diminish the desirability of the end. In *Ubu Roi* and *Macbeth*, the fantasy of unlimited power and autonomy remains in conflict with the mimetic desire that shapes its approximations. Consequently, as each protagonist aspires toward his impossible fantasy of perfect autonomy, he can do so only by exercising the kind of power over others that comes with domination in the social sphere. The gap between aspiration and action renders political power absurd. What's more, the need endlessly to exert power over others in search of this fantasy transforms both men into dehumanized killing machines. After ascending to the throne, Macbeth vows to act violently and without reflection ("From this moment / The very firstlings of my heart shall be / The firstlings of my hand" [4.1.146–48]); Ubu—once he yields to temptation at the beginning of the play—kills gleefully, repeatedly, and without a second thought.

But where Shakespeare treats this struggle for autonomy as a tragic aspect of exceptional heroic ambition, Jarry caricatures the mimetic structuring of desire. Moreover, though the earthy, Rabelaisian elements in *Ubu Roi* may remind us of bodily appetites that can in themselves be satisfied, there is no sense that a character like Ubu can ever stop short of indigestion. Jarry himself described his play as an "exaggerating mirror" designed to reflect back the vices of his Parisian audience. As such, it uses Ubu's pure greed to lampoon the restless hunger of bourgeois aspirations perceived to have lost all moorings in bodily pleasure or true need (Jarry 1961, 174). This then is Jarry's revision of *Macbeth*: in order to lampoon the conventionalized aspirations of his audience, he transforms it into a play about the uneasy relationship between mimetic desire for various conventional objects and the essentially self-centered and absolutist impulse behind competitive desire as such. The unbridgeable gap between the former (desire for power over others, for a crown, for money, for esteem) and the latter (desire to be "perfect" in *Macbeth*, or to "kill everybody and go away" in *Ubu Roi*) renders the immediate objects of ambition absurd, and commits the desiring subject to a project of serial approximation that goes on without meaning or end.

Jarry studied with Henri Bergson at the *Lycèe Henri IV* in Paris. It is likely, therefore, that *Ubu Roi*'s penchant for broad caricature and repetitive drives owes something to Bergson's famous theory of comedy as "something mechanical encrusted on the living" (Bergson 1980, 84). In particular, one can imagine Bergson's ideas influencing Jarry's depiction of Pere Ubu as a killing machine, acting on impulse without introspection or conscience. Such elements of Bergsonian farce may also explain Ionesco's interest in *Ubu Roi*, since similar ideas lie at the heart of his dramaturgy. Thus, when asked about the mechanical aspects of his plays—the way lines are repeated, for example, or the way that characters' patterns of speech can seem to be driven by cliché—Ionesco too alludes to Bergson:

> I realize now that this isn't just a formula or a dramatic device. It's a mode of being. At the start, you have "a little of something mechanical encrusted on the living." It's comic. But if the mechanical gets bigger and bigger and the living shrinks and shrinks, things become stifling and then tragic, because we get the impression that the world is slipping from our mental grasp. (Bonnefoy 1970, 108)

Tragedy for Ionesco is the acceleration of the mechanisms of farce in order to imitate the experience of an alienated "mode of being." In *Macbett*, these mechanisms are structured and driven by mimetic desire: each of the play's characters is driven to repeat the atrocities of his predecessor while striving for the same inconsequential triumphs. While Jarry is interested in the aggressive and autarkic impulses that find mimetic expression, Ionesco is concerned to show how the conventionality of aspiration dehumanizes his characters. As the objects of their desire lose specificity, the characters in *Macbett* are rendered interchangeable and reduced to cogs in an automated system of emulation and violence.

Ionesco depicts the mechanized and undifferentiated nature of his characters by relying heavily upon repetition. Macbett and Banco, for example, each deliver the same long and gruesome soliloquy during their initial battle with the rebels ("The blade of my sword is all red with blood" [14–18]). Similarly, denunciations of Duncan first spoken by Candor and Glamiss are later repeated, with only the slightest variations, by Banco and Macbett (4–5, 68). The relationship between the play's repetitiveness and the vacuity of mimetic desire is evident in the exchange in which Glamiss and Candor talk each other into rebellion against Duncan:

> *Glamiss*:   He's no better than we are.
> *Candor*:   Worse, if anything.
> *Glamiss*:   Much worse.
> *Candor*:   Much, much worse. (5)

Such repetitions evacuate the conspirators of individual personality while, at the same time, the indignation of each conspirator feeds off of the other in a way that underscores the degree to which such attitudes are reinforced by the stated opinions of others. The rebellious impulse, in short, stems from an interchangeable and mimetically structured ambition. This introductory representation of ambition sets the stage for Macbett's rebellious ambition later in the play, about which the same might be said:

Macbett: Yes, he's a good king. Though he should be more appreciative of his impartial advisors—like you for example.
Banco: Or you.
Macbett: Like you or me.
Banco: Quite.
Macbett: He's a bit of an autocrat.
Banco: Very autocratic.
Macbett: A real autocrat! (66)

All who want the crown are conspirators; all conspirators want the crown because the crown is what is wanted. They are interchangeable and mutually reinforcing pieces in a system of recurring rivalry and violence.

Beyond this general anatomy of ambition, Macbett's own desires are given a more thorough treatment in the play. There is no Lady Macbeth, in Ionesco's version, to goad her husband to murder. Instead, there is a composite figure—both Lady Duncan and the lead witch—who seduces Macbett and simultaneously gives shape to his rebellious imagination. The crucial scene is staged as a strip tease: the first witch removes a mask and reveals herself to Macbett as the beautiful lady Duncan; then she strips down to a "sparkling bikini" in the manner of a dancer at "la Lido Club or Crazy Horse Saloon" (1985, 56; see also Lamont 1972, 245).[7] The smitten Macbett offers to be Lady Duncan's "slave," to which she replies:

(*holding out the dagger to him*) I'll be yours if you wish. Would you like that? Here is the instrument of your ambition and our rise to power. (*seductively*) Take it if that's what you want, if you want me. But act boldly. Hell helps those who help themselves. Look into yourself. You can feel your desire for me growing, your hidden ambition coming into the open, inflaming you. You'll take his place at my side. I'll be your mistress. You'll be my sovereign. (56–57)

Macbett's ambition is given as a kind of irresistible erotic desire, an equation that alludes to Lady Macbeth's association of regicide with manliness.

Here, to seize the dagger means to desire Lady Duncan and therefore to be a real man. Such manliness is enfeebling, though: the scene ends in a darkness through which we can see only Lady Duncan's "glistening body" and Macbett rolling at her feet (58).

Many of the play's critics have obscured the function of this scene, either by failing to examine the kind of erotic desire invoked or by decoupling ambition from eros. Nancy Lane does both, for example, when she argues that "the lure of feminine sexuality, rather than political ambition, is the driving force behind Macbett's actions (Lane 1994, 179). In fact, though, what lures Macbett is not "feminine sexuality" so much as the spectacle of the female body in its most objectified and commercially packaged state. A strip tease artist should be simultaneously—and more or less equivalently—desirable to all present. And since in their commercial setting such performances are repeated over and over, their venues operate on the premise that one dancer will do more or less as well as the next: the package is the product in this kind of erotic exchange. Ionesco's emphasis on the sparkles of Lady Duncan's bikini and the glistening of her skin underscores precisely this point. This in turn means that Macbett is seduced not by the specific allure of a specific body and the erotic promise that it holds, nor by "the lure of feminine sexuality" as such, but instead by an empty, ritualized, and universally consumable spectacle.

In the theater, Lady Duncan's costume is bound to seem comically inappropriate, rendering Macbett's erotic desire ridiculous. This effect underscores the scene's serious point: that Macbett's desire is in no way idiosyncratic or personal, since its object is only a conventional trope of desirability. This is in keeping with the play's characteristic use of repetition in that it tends to evacuate the protagonist of individuality, demonstrating that Macbett's erotic desire is just like everybody else's. In fact, Ionesco links erotic desire and political ambition here precisely because the two are similarly structured within the play: Macbett strives for the throne because it's what one strives for; similarly, he lusts after Lady Duncan simply because she transforms herself into an icon of what one lusts after. Taken together, these offer an anatomy of fully mimetic desire in that the allure of each object is finally based on its very conventionality.

Such conventionality, in *Macbett*, strangles feeling. One of the characteristic comic techniques in this play—and in Ionesco's work generally—involves the juxtaposition of horror and brutality with the most exaggeratedly conventional behavior. As the play's first battle rages in the wings, a woman crosses the stage unconcernedly on her way to do some shopping (19). Candor's army is guillotined on stage while Duncan, Lady

Duncan, Macbett, and Banco sit down to high tea (31–36). Banco and Macbett each conclude their descriptions of the carnage of war with the banal observation that "It's been quite a pleasant day" (16, 18). These horrific scenes are designed to convey a deadening of feeling that is in turn part of the play's analysis of the way its characters—forged in the crucible of convention—are driven by the same desires as everybody else.

Ionesco does not lavish attention on Macbett's tyranny in the manner of Shakespeare's play. The scenes that follow Macbett's ascension are comically truncated, as is his fall. But Ionesco does retain some of Macbeth's forceful bravado in the face of all challenges. When his coronation banquet is disturbed (in this case by the ghosts of Duncan *and* Banco) Macbett responds with self-reliant disdain: "I don't need anyone's help. (*To the guests*) Get out, you slaves" (98). When Macol appears, backed by a powerful Carthaginean army, Macbett's response is "I fear no one" (99). His confidence, like Macbeth's, is bolstered by a prophesy that seems to promise invincibility: "Silly little sod. Shoo! I killed your fool of a father. I wouldn't like to have to kill you, too. It's no good. You can't hurt me. No man of woman born can harm Macbett" (99). Ionesco ties up some of Shakespeare's loose ends by revealing that Macol is in fact the biological son of Banco and "a gazelle that a witch transformed into a woman," subsequently adopted by Duncan (99). When Macbett finally realizes that the prophesies are coming true, his response is a tribute to Jarry: "Shit" (101)!

In the context of the play's hasty and intentionally outlandish wrap-up (a gazelle!), Macbett's heroic bravado sounds silly. This is precisely the point, of course. Macbett is most sure that he has achieved something triumphant at the very moment when everything in the play seems most ridiculous. The hastiness of the way these events unspool nicely conveys the vacuity of conventional ambition, compressing Macbett's sense of victory together with the audience's feeling that the game itself has been empty and trivial. For this reason, the nod to Ubu is apt as well. For like Jarry—who makes a farce of the gap between the absolutism of ambitious desires and the trivialized objects that come to stand in for them— Ionesco's comic effect here hinges on the fact that the objects of mimetic desire (the throne, the "sparkling bikini") necessarily fall short of the kind of triumph Macbett imagines them to represent. Though Macbett is revealed to be striving toward the perfect autonomy of victory ("I don't need anyone's help"), he can do so only by striving for the conventional, the banal, the ephemeral, the absurd. This is the central paradox of mimetic desire in each of these plays. But where Jarry is concerned with the way social convention structures the expressions of a more primitive selfish aggression, Ionesco emphasizes simply the all-pervasiveness of conventionality. That is why there is no one character in *Macbett* as vivid as Pere Ubu: where Ubu represents a primal and competitive self-regard that motivates conventional aspiration, Ionesco's play sees nothing prior to the conventionality that so interchangeably structures the play's motivating desires.

Emulate Pride and The Senecan Absurd

Like Ubu or Macbett, Shakespeare's Macbeth strives toward perfect autonomy from within the mimetic structure of political competition. Indeed, from the moment he has it, Macbeth recognizes that the crown cannot be "the be-all and the end-all" (1.7.5). His seemingly pragmatic wish to be safely enthroned quickly gives way to the more explicit and impossible fantasy of being "perfect / Whole as the marble, founded as the rock, / As broad and general as the casing air" (3.4.20–22). Awareness of the impossibility of this desire finally reduces Macbeth's aspirations to "a tale / Told by an idiot, full of sound and fury, / Signifying nothing" (5.5.26–28). Macbeth's willingness to explore and to articulate for us the paradoxical nature of such tragic striving is what allows him to hold our interest, and perhaps our sympathy, even after he has become a killing machine.

The most vivid instance of this occurs just after the fiasco of the banquet in Act 3, as Macbeth sets out to revisit the witches:

> For mine own good
> All causes shall give way. I am in blood
> Stepp'd in so far that, should I wade no more,
> Returning were as tedious as go o'er.[8] (3.4.134–37)

According to the *OED*, "tedious" could mean something like "painful" or "slow," but its primary meaning, then as now, was more like "wearisome." I prefer to understand Shakespeare's use of the word in the last sense, for this makes it a remarkable expression of Macbeth's growing sense that his actions signify nothing. To describe mass murder as merely tedious bespeaks a colossal desensitization, dismissing horrible actions like the killing of Macduff's family as motions that simply need to be gone through. As with Macbeth's allusion to the "bank and shoal of time" earlier in the play (1.7.6), a spatial metaphor stands in awkwardly for moral and temporal registers here. What matters, though, is the directionlessness of the way Macbeth imagines himself by this point in the play. The meaningful directive of his earlier ambition (to "o'erleap" obstacles and achieve the throne [1.4.49]) is replaced with a weary recognition that no direction will lead to the (impossible) end. Except, perhaps, self-destruction: Braden describes how Macbeth's "pursuit of . . . radical integrity" must culminate in "an annihilation of himself and of all around him, a suicide of the soul (Braden 1984, 292).

This I think is the reason that Jarry and Ionesco found Shakespeare to be contemporary, and why they both returned to *Macbeth*: not just the play's cynical depiction of state violence, but the way it explores the paradoxes of ambition and mimetic desire, the tragic necessity of the gap between the fantasy of absolute autonomy and the conventional objectives that must stand in for it. Shakespeare himself offers a marvelously compact phrase that captures precisely this irony when, in *Hamlet*, Horatio describes the heroism of Hamlet's father as being driven by "a most emulate pride" (1.1.83). The heroism of Old Hamlet, as Horatio's phrase unwittingly makes clear, involves two simultaneous and contradictory desires: the desire to be better than other men and the need to imitate their objectives. The same phrase describes Macbeth's predicament, the way his pride's transcendent aspiration is confined by the sheer conventionality of its approximations. For "emulate pride," more generally, is Shakespeare's name for the mimetic desire that drives masculine ambition, and this in turn is what is developed in the absurdist revisions of Shakespeare offered by Jarry and Ionesco.

But in this regard, Shakespeare is merely the most familiar of the many Renaissance dramatists who seem contemporary. For while the richness of Macbeth's meditations is unique, interest in the heroic pursuit of "radical integrity" and its necessary limitations is in fact something of an obsession in renaissance English drama. The best examples—both of this pursuit and of its absurdity—are found in Marlowe's studies of outsized ambition, in which, as Stephen Greenblatt has nicely described it,

> the objects of [the hero's] desire, at first so clearly defined, so avidly pursued, gradually lose their sharp outlines and become more and more like mirages. Faustus speaks endlessly of his appetite, his desire to be glutted, ravished, consumed, but what is it exactly that he wants? By the end of the play it is clear that knowledge, voluptuousness, and power are each mere approximations of the goal for which he sells his soul and body; what that goal is remains maddeningly unclear. (1980, 217)

This is very like the trajectory of Macbeth's impossible desires, which cannot be satisfied by any of the serial murders he undertakes in search of the be-all and the end-all. The fantasy of Barabas (the protagonist of Marlowe's

Jew of Malta [~1590]) to enclose "infinite riches in a little room" (1.1.37) bespeaks a worldly greed that, like Ubu's or Macbeth's, is driven by a desire for transcendent autonomy. The absurdity of this desire is registered, in Marlowe, by means of repetition: Marlowe's heroes, driven toward impossible ends by emulate pride, pursue them by means of serialized contests with rivals. Indeed, Marlowe—with his flair for brutal farce and "the mechanical encrusted on the living"—is much closer to the manner of Jarry or Ionesco than is Shakespeare.[9]

Since this kind of emphasis on the ironies of mimetic desire is evidently part of what Ionesco finds compelling in *Macbeth*, then Shakespeare is "the forefather of the theatre of the absurd" partly because he participates in this larger Renaissance interest in the absurdity of emulate pride. To make this claim is to argue for some intellectual continuity between this radical strain in Renaissance drama and the equally radical theater of Jarry and Ionesco. In each case, the drama reduces conventionally ambitious political actions to the quixotic pursuit of an impossible dream of completion. And though the process can be treated as tragedy or farce, in each case the actions themselves become mechanical and trivial as they are revealed merely to be serial approximations of this fantasy. The intended effect, in each case, is a powerful exposé of conventional ambition, an attempt to lay bare its self-delusions, its destructiveness, and its basic inhumanity.

I call this strain in Renaissance drama the "Senecan absurd," for it has its roots in Seneca's hugely influential tragedies. On the one hand, Seneca's tragic protagonists strive always to achieve a unique style of transcendent self-realization, and often—as Braden describes—by means of terrible atrocities: "heroic evil is the ultimate autarceia, enforcing and exploiting a radical split between the self's needs and the claims of its context" (Braden 1985, 47). On the other, Senecan drama is full of intimations that the fantasy of transcendent autonomy is necessarily delusional, since such pursuit also requires the world as witness. *Thyestes* is Seneca's richest exploration of emulate pride, and in the interests of brevity I will confine my remarks about the Senecan absurd to a discussion of that play's murderous desires.

The action of the play pivots around the archetypal sibling rivalry of Atreus and Thyestes, a pair of brothers who have been locked for a lifetime in competition over the kingdom of Mycenae. Thyestes was the first transgressor—seizing his brother's land and wife in the play's prehistory—but he has paid for it since with a long and impoverished banishment. Nevertheless, Atreus castigates himself bitterly for his failure to harm his brother further since, as he puts it, "crimes thou dost not avenge, save as thou dost surpass them.[10] It quickly becomes clear that this is a story of competitive pride, not a story of justice. Indeed, Atreus seems determined not only to harm to his brother, but also to commit the ultimate crime. In particular, he strives to outdo the revenge of Procne, who killed her children and fed them to their father in retribution for the rape and mutilation of her sister. But, characteristically, competition and imitation are closely linked in Atreus's imagination. His attempt to top Procne is in fact a reenactment of her revenge. After luring Thyestes back to the palace with talk of forgiveness, Atreus kills Thyestes's children and feeds them to their father.[11] When the deed is done, Atreus is eerily (if briefly) exultant: "Peer of the stars I move, and, towering over all, touch with proud head the lofty heavens" (163). In keeping with Braden's generalizations, Atreus imagines the sheer horror of his actions as a kind of self-creating transcendence.

The connection between competition and emulation is similarly evident in the delusional way Atreus imagines his brother throughout the play. As Atreus plans his revenge, he suggests on several occasions that Thyestes would happily commit equivalent atrocities if given the chance: "I know what thou complainst of," Atreus declares in his moment of triumph, "thou grievest that I have forestalled thee in the crime, and art distressed, not because thou hast consumed the ghastly feast, but because thou didst not offer it to me" (181). There is no reason to think that this is accurate, since Thyestes is depicted as a timid man attempting to reconcile stoic precepts with a desire for comfort. But it becomes clear, over the course of the play, that this delusional understanding of his brother's intention is absolutely essential to Atreus's self-fashioning.

Atreus's willful distortions lie at the heart of Seneca's didactic purpose, for they cast light on the disfiguring nature of competitive psychology. Atreus needs to feel that his horrid actions represent a total victory over his brother. The absoluteness of this victory is what allows Atreus to feel himself "towering over all." But in order to feel that his atrocities represent a victory, Atreus needs to believe that his brother has in fact been competing. Atreus's assertions about his brother seem strange because they seek to serve each of these somewhat contradictory psychic needs: they assert simultaneously that Thyestes has been the mirror image of Atreus—cut from the same cloth, plotting the same revenge, invested as heavily in the contest—and that Atreus's victory has been total. Since the Thyestes we see is not competing, Atreus needs first to assert that there has been a contest, and then that he has won. Once again "emulate pride" seems an uncannily precise description of this pathology, capturing as it does the way that the pride of victory is contingent upon similarity and emulation. Atreus commits his crime in pursuit of a fantasy of self-realization that requires a symmetrical rival in Thyestes.

The last exchanges between Atreus and Thyestes are enormously difficult to unravel.[12] Atreus vacillates between triumph and the uneasy recognition that even this cannibal banquet has been too little:

> Crime should have limit, when crime is wrought, not when repaid. E'en this is not enough for me. Straight from the very wound I should have poured the hot blood down thy throat, that thou mightst drink gore of thy living sons—my wrath was cheated by my haste. (175–77)

In fact, Atreus finds satisfaction only by asserting that watching Thyestes's torment has proven the legitimacy of his own children: "Now do I believe my children are my own, now may I trust once more that my marriage bed is pure" (179). Atreus's concern with the question of legitimacy goes back to the play's prehistory, in which Thyestes has eloped with Atreus's wife. But his certainty here is puzzling because there it has no logical basis: nothing has been said or done to prove the legitimacy of the children. This too underscores the delusional quality of Atreus's mania for revenge. Perhaps Atreus, imagining that his brother too is obsessed with emulate competition, assumes that he would have taken this moment to declare his paternity? There is no indication that Thyestes wants to claim paternity of Atreus's children, so we might say that in this instance, as in the larger revenge plot, Atreus invents a contest in order to declare himself unquestioned victor. Because Thyestes remains unconcerned with the rivalries Atreus invents, however, the impulse behind them cannot be fully satisfied.

The story of Atreus's unsatisfiable appetite is framed, in Seneca's fiction, by the eternally unsatisfied appetites of his ancestor Tantalus—whose horrific afterlife (always hungry and thirsty, food and drink recede from his grasp eternally) makes him a figure for "ever-gaping hunger" (93). The play's first act shows a reluctant Tantalus forced by a Fury to rekindle the cycle of family violence that has plagued the family:

> *Ghost of Tantalus*: Here will I stand and prevent the evil deed. Why with thy scourge dost fright mine eyes, and fiercely threaten with thy writhing snakes? Why deep in my inmost marrow dost rouse hunger pains? My heart is parched with burning thirst, and in my scorched vitals the fire is darting—I follow thee.

The Fury: This, this very rage of thine distribute throughout thy
house! So, e'en as thou, may they be driven on, raging to
quench their thirst each in others blood. (99)

This amounts to an almost hydraulic account of Atreus's hunger for
vengeance: the Fury fills Tantalus with hunger and thirst; these force him
to follow; the pangs are discharged into Atreus where they become murderous bloodthirstiness. Tantalus thus serves a quasi-allegorical function in
relation to the play's main plot the play, as a representation of the kinds of
"ever-gaping" competitive appetites that drive the family toward atrocity.
This also fits the didactic purposes of Seneca's stoicism, depicting emulate
pride not only as delusional but as inherently restless and dissatisfied.
Hence, too, the play's interest in structures of endless repetition: since emulate pride cannot find release in total victory, its rage is never spent. By con-
textualizing Atreus's story with the allegorical nod to Tantalus, Seneca
associates this restlessness with endless repetition, eternal grasping at an
impossible goal. The implication is that, from one perspective, Atreus and
all the cursed killers of his family are killing machines, repeatedly generating horrors in serial approximation of a fantasy of infinite revenge, total
victory, and transcendence.

One Genealogy of the Absurd

Once *Thyestes* is described in these terms, it is easy to see how the exploration of ambition in Renaissance plays like *Macbeth* or Marlowe's tragedies
extends Seneca's bitter critique. For these plays share with Seneca their
depiction of ambition as an "ever-gaping hunger" for a kind of triumph
over the world that can never be realized within it. One important implication of this is that Renaissance dramatists were very sophisticated readers of Senecan tragedy, able to mine it for a radical critique of public
aspiration applicable beyond the specific excesses of Nero's Rome. It is
only because this kind of influence is difficult to pin down that debates
over the influence of Senecan tragedy have centered instead on borrowed
phrases and comparatively trivial formal elements (Kiefer 1977; Miola
1992, 3–9). More particularly, *Macbeth* transposes Senecan concerns in (at
least) two ways. First, by taking the story out of the family and moving it
more overtly into the political sphere. By doing so, the play makes Seneca's
critique of mimetically structured ambition more explicitly a critique of
public aspiration in general. Second, it builds Seneca's interest in repetition
more directly into the plot. Macbeth takes the place of the whole house of

Atreus, committing a series of atrocities in an increasingly dehumanizing attempt at perfection. Each of these formal innovations expands upon what is merely allegorical in Seneca's scheme.

Jarry, recognizing in *Macbeth* a fierce attack on the complacency of social convention, retells it as farce. Ubu takes his cues as to the value of items and positions from others, but his enormous selfishness is driven by a desire to destroy and transcend the world around him. In keeping with this perspective—which allows for no inherent value in the objects of mimetic competition—the objects fought over in Jarry are hilariously trivial. This generalizes Macbeth's ruminations on the meaninglessness of the crown, stripping the story of specific political context and supplying instead a perspective within which any and all public ambitions are mocked.

Ionesco's *Macbett* keeps Jarry's focus on the triviality of conventional desires but shifts the focus once again. Instead of looking at the selfish and trivial desires of one character, Ionesco emphasizes the degree to which all desires are trivial because conventional. As a result, Ionesco's is a play of interchangeable parts: the endless hunger of Tantalus, Macbeth, and Ubu is replaced by a murderous society in which everyone has the same murderous appetites as a matter of course. This approach emphasizes most fully the dehumanizing tedium of repetitive violence stoked by conventional ambition. Within this world of trivial and violent interchangeability, Macbett's boasts of autonomy and triumph are designed to ring with bitter, Senecan irony.

The formal innovation of Renaissance Senecanism—which makes endless repetition into part of the plot—is extended still further in Ionesco's absurdist revision: in addition to shaping the actions of the plot, mimetic repetition structures the way Ionesco's characters think, talk, and relate to one another. The fantasy of transcendence that generates this repetition in earlier Senecan drama is further attenuated here by the total failure of individuality, but Macbett's hollow ambition is still to stand alone as a fully triumphant and self-sufficient king. Indeed, if one thinks of such repetition as a major formal innovation of the theater of the absurd, used to express a modern alienation from what Ionesco calls "transcendental roots," then perhaps the affinity between theater of the absurd and Senecan drama will seem almost inevitable (Esslin 1961, xix). I am struck, therefore, by the fact that Camus's influential essay on the Absurd turns to Sisyphus—doomed forever to roll a stone up a hill, doomed to fail, endlessly trying—as an emblem of the Absurd hero. That Seneca and Camus both use the endless torments of the classical underworld to represent the emptiness of worldly action is a coincidence that underscores a real continuity between Absurdist and Senecan concerns.

Literary history is always overdetermined. Shakespeare and Seneca are not the primary influences upon Absurdism, nor would Ionesco or Jarry have necessarily conceived of their relation to Shakespeare in the terms I have proposed. But these affinities do offer some explanatory context for the uncanny sense that Shakespeare is in dialogue with some of the most radical innovations of modern drama. That is to say, they begin to explain what in *Macbeth* seems modern and why Shakespeare was doing it. More importantly, sketching this chain of influences is designed to demonstrate Shakespeare's participation in a much larger tradition of radical dramaturgy that owes its staying power to a remarkably powerful, adaptable, and therefore vital critique of the absurd desires beneath public ambition. It is my hope that recuperating this genealogy strengthens it, lending a greater cumulative weight to its insistent exposé of emulate pride.

But in order to make use of this perspective, we must attend to the alternative models of desire implicit in these plays. For despite their shared emphasis on eating (the cannibal banquet in Seneca, Macbeth's disrupted feast, Ubu's gourmandizing, tea and carnage in *Macbett*), these plays tend to lack depictions of healthy appetite. Hunger, we might say, leads directly to indigestion. This too may have Senecan origins: Thyestes's return to court, for example, is depicted as a kind of fatal weakness for comfort, a failure of stoic indifference that makes Atreus's crimes possible. More generally, Braden has argued for a close analogy between the stoic's dream of perfect indifference and the kind of transcendence aimed at by Atreus: both are driven by a desire "to keep the self's boundaries under its own control (Braden 1985, 23). Both, in short, have a fundamental hostility to the demands of neediness. The same hostility permeates the world of *Macbeth*, where the drunken porter alone stands as an attenuated but crucial gesture toward a Rabelaisian perspective that celebrates instead the self's openness.

The coarseness of Jarry's farce ensures that the registers of bodily need are always present. This means that though Ubu's greed is driven by a fantasy of transcendence, the play's audience can intuit a Rabelaisian alternative to his Senecan drive. But this possibility is forestalled in Ionesco's *Macbett*, a play that reduces bodily appetites to convention and thus to emulate pride. In doing so, Ionesco reproduces a hostility to pleasure that leaves its audience once again with only the stark choices of Senecan tragedy: destructive emulate pride or complete withdrawal from the world. This nonchoice may explain why audiences have found *Macbett* comparatively unsatisfying as a piece of dramatic art. For indeed, the grim emphasis on the destructiveness of mimetic desire throughout these incarnations of the absurd underscores for me the importance of an alternative model of desire not based on competitiveness and mimesis. While recovering this Senecan tradition may provide us with a radical and long-standing critique of ambition, it should also lead us to look beyond stoic hostility to need, and to celebrate instead the more immediate desires and satisfactions of the body.

Notes

1. On Shakespeare's interest in cyclical violence see Booth 1983, 91–92, and Sinfield 1986. On Ionesco's reinscription of Shakespeare's political violence see: Lamont 1972, 231–53; Kern 1974; Sessa 1978; Scott 1989, 72–88.
2. See *Macbeth*, 4.3.46–100.
3. All citations from Shakespeare's *Macbeth* will appear in this form.
4. Even in France, which did not have a strong Shakespearean tradition until the eighteenth century (Jusserand 1899; Heylen 1993).
5. For the French see Jarry 1962, 33. For the translation see Jarry 1961, 9. I use these editions throughout.
6. This basic argument has been made in several critical vocabularies. See for example Adelman 1992, 130–46, Braden 1984, and Brooks 1948, 22–49.
7. Lamont 1972, 245.
8. On the Senecan heritage of this passage see Miola 1992, 93.
9. On paradoxes of desire throughout the Marlowe canon, see Tromly 1998.
10. Seneca 1961, 105. I use this text throughout. On the excessiveness of revenge in Senecan drama see Kerrigan 1996, 114–17.
11. As has been remarked, this Senecan motif of child killing symbolizes the desire of the hero to kill the future—that which is beyond control, that which necessarily limits perfect autonomy—and is picked up by the images of children and child killing in *Macbeth*. See Braden 1984, 291–92, and Miola 1992, 108.
12. Perhaps in order to elaborate some of what seems elliptical, Jasper Heywood's translation of *Thyestes* (1560) adds one final speech in which Thyestes calls for self-punishment. See Kerrigan 1996, 111–12.

Works Cited

Adelman, Janet. 1992. *Suffocating Mothers: Fantasies of Maternal Origin in Shakespeare's Plays, Hamlet to The Tempest*. New York: Routledge.

Bakhtin, Mikhail. 1984. *Rabelais and His World*. Trans. Hélène Iswolsky. Cambridge: MIT Press, 1968. Reprint, Bloomington: Indiana University Press.

Bergson, Henri. 1980. "Laughter." In *Comedy*. Ed. Wylie Sypher. Garden City: Doubleday, 1956. Reprint, Baltimore: The Johns Hopkins University Press.

Bonnefoy, Claude. 1970. *Conversations With Eugène Ionesco.* Trans. Jan Dawson. New York: Holt, Rhinehart and Winston.

Booth, Stephen. 1983. *King Lear, Macbeth, Indefinition, and Tragedy.* New Haven: Yale University Press.

Braden, Gordon. 1984. "Senecan Tragedy and the Renaissance." *Illinois Classical Studies* 9.2: 277–92.

———. 1985. *Renaissance Tragedy and the Senecan Tradition: Anger's Privilege.* New Haven: Yale University Press.

Brooks, Cleanth. 1948. *The Well Wrought Urn: Studies in the Structure of Poetry.* New York: Harcourt, Brace & World.

Camus, Albert. 1969. *The Myth of Sisyphus and Other Essays.* Trans. Justin O'Brien. New York: Alfred A. Knopf.

Esslin, Martin. 1961. *The Theatre of the Absurd.* Garden City: Anchor Books.

———. 1973. "Review of *Macbett.*" *Plays and Players* 20.12: 54–55.

Greenblatt, Stephen. 1980. *Renaissance Self-Fashioning: From More to Shakespeare.* Chicago: University of Chicago Press.

Heylen, Romy. 1993. *Translation, Poetics, and the Stage: Six French Hamlets.* London: Routledge.

Ionesco, Eugène. 1985. *Macbett.* Trans. Charles Marowitz. In *Exit the King, The Killer, and Macbett: Three Plays by Eugène Ionesco.* New York: Grove Press.

Jarry, Alfred. 1961. *Ubu Roi.* Trans. Barbara Wright. New York: New Directions.

———. 1962. *Tout Ubu.* Ed. Maurice Saillet. Paris: Librairie Général Française.

Jusserand, J. J. 1899. *Shakespeare In France Under the Ancien Règime.* London: T. Fisher Unwin.

Kern, Edwin. 1974. "Ionesco and Shakespeare: *Macbeth* on the Modern Stage." *South Atlantic Quarterly* 39.1: 3–16.

Kerrigan, John. 1996. *Revenge Tragedy: Aeschylus to Armaggedon.* Oxford: Clarendon Press.

Kiefer, Frederick. 1977. "Seneca's Influence on Elizabethan Tragedy: An Annotated Bibliography." *Research Opportunities in Renaissance Drama* 20: 17–33.

Kott, Jan. 1964. *Shakespeare Our Contemporary.* Trans. Boleslaw Taborski. Garden City: Doubleday, 1964.

LaBelle, Maurice Marc. 1980. *Alfred Jarry: Nihilism and the Theater of the Absurd.* New York: New York University Press.

Lamont, Rosette C. 1972. "From *Macbeth* to *Macbett.*" *Modern Drama* 15: 231–53.

———. 1993. *Ionesco's Imperatives: The Politics of Culture.* Ann Arbor: University of Michigan Press.

Lane, Nancy. 1994. *Understanding Eugène Ionesco.* Columbia: University of South Carolina Press.

Marlowe, Christopher. 1994. *The Jew of Malta.* Ed. James R. Siemon. London: A & C Black.

Miola, Robert. 1992. *Shakespeare and Classical Tragedy: The Influence of Seneca.* Oxford: Clarendon Press.

Scott, Michael. 1989. *Shakespeare and the Modern Dramatist*. Houndmills, Basingstoke, Hampshire: Macmillan.

Seneca. 1961. *Seneca's Tragedies*. Trans. Frank Justus Miller. Vol. 2. Revised edition, London: William Heinemann.

Sessa, Jacqueline. 1978. "Deux Avatars Derisoires de *Macbeth: L'Ubu Roi* de Jarry et le *Macbett* de Ionesco." In *Travaux Comparatistes*. Ed. Lucette Desvignes. Saint-Etienne: Centre d'Etudes Comparatistes et de Recherche sur l'Expression Dramatique, 135–53.

Shakespeare, William. 1974. *The Riverside Shakespeare*. Ed. G. Blakemore Evans. Boston: Houghton Mifflin.

Sinfield, Alan. 1986. "*Macbeth:* History, Ideology and Intellectuals." *Critical Quarterly* 28: 63–77.

Tromly, Fred B. 1998. *Playing With Desire: Christopher Marlowe and the Art of Tantalization*. Toronto: University of Toronto Press.

Chapter 5

"What is the city but the people?": Transversal Performance and Radical Politics in Shakespeare's *Coriolanus* and Brecht's *Coriolan*

Bryan Reynolds

BIG TIME, LOST
I knew, that cities were being built
I didn't go there.
That belongs to statistics, I thought—
Not to history.

But what are cities, built
Without the wisdom of the people?

—Bertolt Brecht[1]

Shakespeare's *Coriolanus* and Brecht's adaptation of it were written during historical periods of high cultural anxiety and frustration.[2] Both works reflect and comment on social, economic, and political problems contemporaneous to their conception. Whereas Brecht makes his purpose for creating *Coriolan* explicit in his nonfictional writings, he does not reveal the direct correlations between his play and, as he calls them, the "dark times" in which he wrote. To do this would have been dangerous for Brecht while living in a newly formed East Germany that was indirectly governed and closely monitored by Soviet forces. Similarly, despite the obvious topicality of its subject matter, Shakespeare gives no clear indication of his political investment in *Coriolanus,* and censorship was an issue that Jacobean dramatists were compelled to consider.[3] In this essay, I compare *Coriolanus* and *Coriolan* in light of their historical contexts in hopes of bettering our understanding of both the actions of the plebeians and Coriolanus' negotiation of his own subject position in response to the changing sociopolitical environment in Shakespeare's play. I aim to propose a new reading of *Coriolanus* that emphasizes performance rather than literal possibilities for the play-text.

Historical Contexts, Critical Approaches

The Soviet Union made the years immediately following the establishment in 1949 of the German Democratic Republic (GDR) dire for East Germany's working class. It extracted resources and goods from the GDR and continued to do so until war reparations were formally settled in August 1953.[4] The extractions caused depression and the rationing of staple products like fat, sugar, and meat; consumer durables remained scarce and expensive. Although wages increased for people employed by the state, living standards for the majority were terribly low.

The predicament culminated on June 16, 1953. After several years of inefficient and disruptive negotiations between the workers and the government, the people's unrest escalated into an angry protest comprised of approximately 10,000 demonstrators.[5] By noon of June 17, the protest approached intractability. Violence between the police and the malcontents became more frequent and unmanageable. Finally, the Soviet military commander proclaimed a state of siege, and heavy artillery was mobilized into the cities' centers. Confronted with overwhelming military power, the insurrection was soon suppressed.

During these difficult years, Brecht wrote *Coriolan,* completing it sometime between 1952 and 1955.[6] Given Brecht's dedication to the needs of the proletariat and to the promotion of Marxist ideology and aesthetics, it is not surprising that with his adaptation he planned to represent and champion Germany's working class by celebrating the communal empowerment of the plebeians depicted in the play.[7] Brecht says of *Coriolan,* that "we must at least be able to 'experience' not only the tragedy of Coriolanus himself but also of Rome, and specifically of the plebs" (1973, 374). Brecht's partiality for the proletariat is confirmed by another work that he wrote shortly after June 17. As historian Henry Ashby Turner, Jr. states in his account of the June 17 workers' uprising, "the foremost Communist literary figure of East Germany, Bertolt Brecht, gave expression to sentiments of many in a poem he secretly circulated" (1987, 123). The sar-

castic, propagandistic poem, ironically entitled "The Solution," illustrates
Brecht's strong support of the proletariat at the time:

> After the uprising of the 17th of June
> The Secretary of the Writer's Union
> Had leaflets distributed in the Stalinallee
> On which one could read, that the people
> Had forfeited the trust of the government
> And could win it back only
> By redoubled efforts. And so, would
> It not be easier if the government
> Dissolved the people
> And selected another? (1984, 1009–1010)[8]

Brecht's devout Marxism can be seen in all of his work,[9] and, as I hope
to demonstrate, Shakespeare's *Coriolanus* was a ready vehicle for the promotion of his politics. By examining Brecht's *Coriolan* as an interpretation
of *Coriolanus,* I want to argue that *Coriolanus* was predisposed to Brecht's
purpose, both textually and historically, and that it could easily be performed, and possibly was originally performed in early modern England,
in line with Brecht's politics, that is, *without* textual adaptation.

When writing his version of the Coriolanus legend, Shakespeare too
considered the plight of the working class, or rather, the "common people," as they were referred to in early modern England and in his play. The
potential for Shakespeare's *Coriolanus* to serve Brecht's enterprise without
alteration is informed by the fact that it, like *Coriolan,* was written in an era
of fervent sociopolitical conflict resulting in a revolt led by plebeians. In
England, beginning in 1607 and culminating in 1608 (probably the year
Shakespeare's *Coriolanus* was originally performed),[10] the increasing cost of
corn and the accompanying dread of famine were serious, manifested concerns. A consequence of this distressing situation was the Midlands insurrection of May, 1607. "A great number of common persons"—up to
5,000, says John Stow in his *Annals,* gathered in various Midlands counties,
including the county of Warwickshire where Shakespeare usually resided,
to dig up and level enclosures and to protest the dearth of food (1631,
890).[11] Like the East German protesters, the early modern English protesters damaged properties and threatened wealthy landowners (whose position
resembled that of political conformists in the GDR, where there were no
landowners).[12] And, as in the workers' revolt in East Germany, the Midlands
crisis was eventually quelled by military forces and trailed by executions.

The Midlands insurrection differed from the riots that took place in the preceding century, under Queen Elizabeth's rule, in that it "was purely and nakedly a demand for economic redress," while the earlier riots were provoked by "economic and social grievances" mixed with "religious and political issues" (Pettet 1950, 34). As Karl Marx and Friedrich Engels describe what they call "the proletarian movement"—a concept that anticipated the June 17 uprising—the Midlands revolt was wholly a "self-conscious" action taken *by* "common people" for the benefit of the "common people" (1982, 92). Thus, the Midlands insurrection may have been a significant event foreshadowing the revolution of the 1640s, a war that was largely motivated by the people's desire for a more equitable distribution of wealth and a form of government allowing them greater representation.

Yet, unlike Brecht, who openly, though only to a select few, discloses his partiality for the workers in his post June 17 poem, there is no record of Shakespeare having so frankly expressed his opinions on any sociopolitical issue. This is why it is difficult to discern from Shakespeare's writings his relationships to various matters of his day. In the case of *Coriolanus,* however, the evidence showing a correlation between the play and the people's uprising of 1607 is substantial. This can be found in Shakespeare's departures from Livy's and, more importantly, Plutarch's version of the Coriolanus legend, the latter being the main source from which Shakespeare contrived his play.[13]

Whereas there is often ambiguity regarding the reasons for Shakespeare's divergences from his sources (such as in the abundance of departures in the three parts of *Henry VI*), the evidence here seems straightforward. As noted by Pettet, "This particular divergence is a very marked and peculiar one: Shakespeare has reduced the grievances of the plebeians to the one matter of scarcity of corn (which he entwines with the fear of Coriolanus' absolutist temper), and he has set this grievance prominently before us in the first scene of the play, declining to follow Plutarch's account of a rising against the oppression of usury" (1950, 37). Shakespeare's reduction of the people's complaints to a single, highly charged point of contention establishes an association with the recent socioeconomic problems and subsequent revolt. By giving *Coriolanus* this conspicuous topicality, Shakespeare constructed a relationship between the play and issues important to its early modern audience, making the play more compelling, and the audience ready for a relevant political statement on the Midlands crisis. Regardless of Shakespeare's actual intentions, doing this transposed the theater into a political arena, and the stage into a platform from which the ideology delineated in the play was expressed without pretext, subterfuge, or mystification. This means that any framing of the performance, as a play, say, mainly about the historical figure Coriolanus and ancient Rome, was breached. In effect, the audience was keyed into another (additional) framing of the play as germane political commentary.

Examining criticism published on *Coriolanus* since Charles Gildon (1710) and Samuel Taylor Coleridge (1815) and especially over the last 50 years, quickly leads to the discovery of what appears to be an interpretive consensus. Of the claims shared by this consensus, the following assertions are most pertinent to the issues I am discussing here: (1) Shakespeare's *Coriolanus* vents hatred for the plebeians, or it is at least unsympathetic to their needs (Gildon 1710; Coleridge 1817; Brockbank 1976; Farnham 1963; Grass 1964; Huffman 1971; Ide 1980; MacCallum 1967; Pettet 1950; Rabkin 1967; Rossiter 1961; Simmons 1973; Zeeveld 1962); and (2) the play condemns the notion of democracy, or it is at least in favor of an absolute monarchy (Gildon 1710; Coleridge 1817; Farnham 1963; Grass 1964; Honig 1951; Huffman 1971; Kishlansky 1986; Phillips 1940; Rossiter 1961; Simmons 1973; Zeeveld 1962).[14] Recently published alternative readings to the ones just listed are by Adelman (1980), Bristol (1987), Dollimore (1984), Jagendorf (1990), Patterson (1989), Scofield (1990), and Sorge (1987); except for those by Jagendorf and Scofield, which do not address in any relevant way the concerns of this essay, I will refer to these readings as my analysis progresses.[15] For now, however, it is sufficient to note that these readings, insofar as they deal with issues relevant to the assertions listed above, are alternative mainly in that they either sympathize with the plebeians, suggest that the play sympathizes with the plebeians (if only in passing), do both of these things, or maintain that the play is ambiguous, politically, in its handling of the plebeians' situation.

In my view, *Coriolanus* welcomes a performance-oriented interpretation that differs greatly from the apparent consensus and affirms some of the suggestions made by the alternative readings. As many critics have pointed out, Shakespeare's *Coriolanus*, like Brecht's *Coriolan*, is primarily about two powerful conflicts: (1) the tragedy of a great pathological individualist (Coriolanus) existing in contradiction to his social world, and (2) the struggle for solidarity between the "common people" and the ruling oligarchy. In analyzing what seems to be *Coriolanus'* endeavor to resolve these two conflicts, I will argue that Shakespeare's play parallels Brecht's *Coriolan* in its criticism of the notion of an irreplaceable leader or absolute monarch. This parallelism is especially clear when the play is analyzed as a performed text situated within the historical context of its initial performance for the early modern English audience. It is my hypothesis that the original production accomplished this critical feat by prompting the audience to identify and thereby empathize—rather than sympathize—with the plebeians. As a result, Shakespeare's *Coriolanus* encouraged the audience's support of the plebeians' wish for a more democratic form of government, both within and beyond the Roman world represented in the play. Moreover, I want to make the corollary argument that through its treatment of the concept of indispensability in its depiction of Coriolanus, the play most powerfully posits as viable sociopolitical enterprises not only replaceability but also the changing and expanding of identity through what I call "transversal movements."

Communist Commoners?

The field of sociopolitical forces operating in both *Coriolanus* and *Coriolan* is explicitly exemplified in the first scene, which sets the plot and tone for the plays. In a lively parley among the First Citizen, the Second Citizen, and a chorus of others, we are invited to share the plebeians' craving for justice. From their conversation we learn that the plebeians are willing to sacrifice their lives while fighting to free themselves from the deprivation imposed on them by the upper class; they are "all resolved rather to die than to / famish" (1.1.3–4; cf. *Coriolan* 59).[16] They all agree that "Caius Martius [Coriolanus] is chief enemy / to the people" (1.1.6–7; cf. *Coriolan* 59), but settle upon this conclusion only after they consider "what services he has done for / his country" (1.1.29–30). We are told that the plebeians are motivated by their "hunger for bread, not in / thirst for revenge" (1.1.24–25) and by their desire to be self-governing: "we'll have corn at our own / price" (1.1.9–10; cf. *Coriolan* 59). Despite the fact that their logic during this initial scene is a little fuzzy, "the people's belief that the death of Coriolanus would allow them to have corn at their own price is," as Janet Adelman observes, "eventually sustained by the plot, insofar as Coriolanus opposes the giving of corn gratis" (3.1.113–117; cf. *Coriolan* 100–101) (1980, 136).

The plebeians' declarations, that also reflect Brecht's point of view, are echoed by Marx and Engels in a decisive statement about the Communists: "They openly declare that their ends can be attained only by the forcible overthrow of all existing conditions" (1982, 120). Like the Communists, the plebeians of *Coriolanus* and *Coriolan* want "To unbuild the city and to lay all flat" and therefore equal (3.1.196; cf. *Coriolan* 104). Furthermore, when Menenius inquires of the angry citizens: "Will you undo yourselves?" (1.1.63)—asking them if they will risk everything in an attempt to take on the "Roman state" (1.1.68)—the First Citizen wittily yet honestly responds, "We cannot, sir, we are undone already" (1.1.64; cf. *Coriolan* 61). The First Citizen's contention is similarly argued by Marx and Engels in *The Communist Manifesto:* "The proletariat have nothing to lose but their chains. They have a world to win" (1982, 121). Like the proletariat that Marx and Engels are concerned with, the proletariat of Shakespeare and Brecht, heading for starvation, have nothing to lose by revolting except the chains of their oppression (1.1.83; *Coriolan* 61). Although these similarities between Shakespeare's *Coriolanus* (and Brecht's *Coriolan*) and *The Communist Manifesto* are not elaborate, I note them because they testify to an ideological compatibility between *Coriolanus* and *The Communist Manifesto* with regard to governmental matters and the concept of an indispensable leader, at least insofar as the plebeians represent the particular ideology promoted by Shakespeare's play.

Initially, Menenius tries to shift the responsibility for the "soaring prices" of food and the people's accompanying "misery" (61) away from the government and onto the gods: "Your suffering," he tells them, "in this dearth, you may as well / Strike at the heaven with your staves . . . For the dearth, / The gods, not the patricians, make it" (1.1.66–72; cf. *Coriolan* 61). However, Menenius is not taken seriously. The First Citizen ignores his mention of the gods and angrily responds by stating exactly how the patricians oppress the "common people." He says that they "Suffer us to famish" while "their store- / houses crammed with grain;" they "support usurers" and "repeal daily any wholesome act / established against the rich, and provide more / piercing statutes daily, to chain up and restrain the poor" (1.1.79–84; cf. *Coriolan* 61). These allegations demonstrate sharply the gravity of the situation, especially as they are contrasted against Menenius' feeble attempt to hold the gods responsible for the starving people, while the rich have plenty of food.

Without addressing the complaints of the First Citizen, complaints that are incidentally never addressed by the patricians throughout the plays, Menenius goes on to deploy a new strategy; he endeavors to assuage their animosity with a parable. But, as Marx explains in his own critical commentary on Shakespeare's *Coriolanus,* "when the Roman plebeians struck against the Roman patricians, the patrician Agrippa [Menenius] told them that the patrician belly fed the plebeian members of the body politic. Agrippa failed to show that you feed the members of one man by filling the belly of another" (1975, 106). Furthermore, as Thomas Sorge writes in his astute account of the failure of Menenius' "pretty tale" (1.1.89; 61), a second look at the way the First Citizen parades the conventional rhetoric of the fable's underlying analogy shows how he turns the tale in the plebeians' favor by stressing that the different members are after all oppressed "by the cormorant belly" [1.1.120]—a move which forces Menenius both to interrupt him and to beg for more time and "Patience awhile" [1.1.125] before he can tell them the belly's already well-known answer. And it is no surprise that the answer eventually comes as an unsatisfactory anticlimax. (1987, 234–235)

The First Citizen responds sarcastically to Menenius' answer, "It was an answer. How apply you this?" (1.1.146; cf. *Coriolan* 63). The tale does not influence the First Citizen, and thus this is the plebeians' first victory; they successfully resist this first effort to suppress their insurrection. But the power they gain in this rhetorical battle is quickly diminished by the entrance of Coriolanus. Apart from one satirical comment made by the First Citizen in response to Coriolanus' denigrating the plebeians (1.1.165), Shakespeare's plebeians, unlike Brecht's, are silent for the duration of the scene. But this silence, I think, does not signify defeat or concession.

In Brecht's *Coriolan,* Coriolanus enters "unnoticed except by Menenius" and "escorted by two armed men" (63), and he does this some 20 lines earlier than indicated by the stage direction in Shakespeare's text, which only calls for the entry of "Caius Martius [Coriolanus]." Brecht provides an explanation for this alteration in his brilliant analysis of the first scene:

I'd suggest having Marcius and his armed men enter rather earlier than is indicated by Agrippa's [Menenius'] 'Hail, noble Marcius!' [1.1.163]. . . . The plebeians would then see the armed men looming up behind the speaker, and it would be perfectly reasonable for them to show signs of indecision. (1964, 258)

Staging the action as Brecht proposes would also explain Menenius' "sudden aggressiveness" toward the First Citizen (1964, 258). Having Menenius willing to risk acting in this manner because he feels empowered as well as safeguarded by the presence of Coriolanus and his soldiers would stress that his ideology, like that of Coriolanus, welcomes the threat of violence, and must be reinforced by this threat in order for the plebeians to submit to it.

Although Brecht's work on the opening scene reveals how he developed successfully for his purposes, with much textual alteration, what is already in Shakespeare's text, I aim to show that it was unnecessary for him to change any text, including the stage direction, to achieve the effects he describes. In fact, this scene could be staged in a variety of ways without any alteration to the text. It could be staged just as Brecht proposes. Menenius could be made to see Coriolanus in the distance (with or without the armed men), yet only acknowledge Coriolanus when his presence is verging on the obvious, as Brecht would have it. Or, to give another possibility, Menenius' sudden hostility toward the First Citizen (and his fellow mutineers) could be staged as a defensive measure caused by the embarrassment and anxiety he experiences as a result of his failed parable. In this case, Coriolanus' entrance comes as a relief to him, and may prevent him from being injured by the angry rabble of citizens.

Moreover, Shakespeare's plebeians, notwithstanding their silence following the First Citizen's sarcastic remark, can be seen as continuing actively to protest Coriolanus even after his arrival. They mock him with their silence—by ignoring his authority. This act of dissidence could be made blatant with gesture, such as with smirks, nudges, backslapping, and cupped whispers. Furthermore, by remaining silent like the audience, the plebeians' dilemma is more identifiable; the audience becomes aligned with the plebeians, both being spectators to Coriolanus' ruthlessness. Such a staging is actually reinforced by Shakespeare's and Brecht's texts: when Coriolanus commands the plebeians to leave ("Go get you home, you fragments!" [1.1.221; cf. *Coriolan* 65]), they do not respond to him verbally and there is no stage direction calling for their departure. Finally, after Coriolanus ridicules the plebeians with his request that they be permitted to go to the "Capital" to prepare for war with the nobles, we are told by the stage direction that the "Citizens steal away" (Brockbank 1976, 114). This stage direction is frequently cited to illustrate the play's belittlement of the "common people." For example, John Dover Wilson says that Shakespeare has the plebeians steal away in order to demonstrate their pusillanimity (Wilson cited in Brockbank 1976, 114). Nevertheless, as in the instance of Coriolanus' entrance, the text invites more than one interpretation.

Perhaps the plebeians exit stealthily not out of fear but as protest; they actively oppose, with much irreverence, Coriolanus' enticement ("The Volsces have corn. . . .Worshipful mutiners . . . follow" [Shakespeare 1.1.248–250]) by departing quietly, indifferently. This is plausible considering, as noted above, that they ignore his command for them to leave. To broaden our perspective on the implications of this stage direction, we must consider the positioning of the plebeians on the stage throughout the whole first scene. Shakespeare's Coriolanus delivers the news of the newly appointed Tribunes for the people solely to Menenius; consequently, he and Menenius are the only ones to discuss the ramifications of these appointments. So, to insure that the plebeians are denied access to this private conversation they must be positioned (within the stage illusion) out of hearing distance from Coriolanus and Menenius. After all, why would they stand close enough to Coriolanus—an enemy, reputed warrior, and physical threat to them—to be able to hear the talk regarding the Tribunes? It makes sense to have them spatially marginalized (as they are socially, economically, and politically) by the presence of the formidable figure now dominating the stage.

Like Brecht's, Shakespeare's play directs our attention toward the mistreatment of the "common people" under the elitism and selfishness of the ruling body. Even if the stage direction ("Citizens steal away") is only meant to acknowledge that the situation has changed since the beginning of the scene—when the stage direction reads: "Enter a company of mutinous Citizens, with staves, clubs, and other weapons"—the entire scene suggests that it is dangerous for a country to have leaders who do not consider the welfare of its commoners. As Brecht eloquently puts it, "The wind has changed, it's no longer a favorable wind for mutinies; a powerful threat [the approaching war with the Volscians that was just made known] affects all alike, and as far as the people goes this threat is simply noted in a purely negative way" (1964, 261). But, unlike the commoners, Coriolanus does not have a negative perception of war: "I am glad on't," he declares, "then, we shall ha' means to vent / Our musty superfluity" (1.1.224–225; cf. *Coriolan* 66). He looks forward to the war as an opportunity to dispose of the unhappy "common people" whom he sees as the country's dispensable surplus.

Coriolanus is often described in *Coriolanus* and *Coriolan* as a great warrior, even godlike, especially after he defeats the attacking Volsces almost single-handedly; thus many characters see him as a tremendous asset to his country. Cominius holds that, "The man I speak of [Coriolanus] cannot in the world / Be singly counter-pois'd" (2.2.86–87, see also 2.2.168; cf. *Coriolan* 92). Yet, to Coriolanus' dismay, being "prov'd best man i'th'field" (2.2.97; cf. *Coriolan* 92) and being able to "Turn terror into sport" with "his sword, death's stamp" (2.2.105– 107; cf. *Coriolan* 92) are not enough; they are not the qualities required to be an adequate ruler of Rome and to gain the majority's approval. As the Third Citizen says, "if he would incline to the people, there was never a worthier man" (2.3.38–40); but for him to do this, because it would mean going against his own beliefs, his own code, he would have to "perform a part" (3.2.109) in a "wolvish toge" (2.3.114)—a false "napless vesture of humility" (2.1.232)—as the fabled wolf wears the sheep's clothing (Brockbank 1964, 185). Rather, Coriolanus prides himself as someone "never / [to] be such a gosling to obey instinct, but stand / As if a man were author of himself / And knew no other kin (5.3.34–37; cf. *Coriolan* 140). He insists uncompromisingly on his own self-fashioning and self-reliance, and his irreplaceability.

Thus, unlike in Plutarch, Shakespeare's and Brecht's Coriolanus refuses to display his wounds for the people. It would be traumatizing for him to "stand naked" and entreat people whom he sees as inferior to him, whom he calls "curs," "rats," "dissentious rogues," "quarter'd slaves" (2.2.137; 93). Doing so would require admitting to himself as well as revealing to the masses that he too has to work according to society's conventions to achieve his goals; that he too is a human being susceptible to injury; that "he too has a mouth, that he is a dependent creature" (Adelman 1980, 137);. And, therefore, in his view, that he too is replaceable like the "common people." Symbolically, by submitting to and thereby aligning himself with the "common people," which would require him to act just as they desire, he would also be revealing to the audience that he too is an actor, that like a professional actor he pretends to be someone else for profit. As Donald Hedrick puts it, "'performance for pay' would for Coriolanus constitute the most abject realm of loathing, like mercenary soldiership" (Hedrick 2000). Moreover, having been identified as an actor by an audience living in Jacobean England, a social world that discriminated against people for being actors even while it simultaneously supported them at the theater, Coriolanus would be revealing that he too (like the actor playing him) is capable of being wounded by society, that he is subject to its laws and prejudices. Hence, for the early modern audience, the performance frame would be disrupted, the fourth wall broken, and the actor playing Coriolanus would emerge prominently as an actor, a real person. However, I believe this situation occurs nevertheless, and more strikingly, through Coriolanus' emphatic refusal to act. His controversial, adamant refusal to act as the "common people" want makes the concepts of acting and identity performance the focus of the scene. His refusal breaches the performance frame and compels the audience's awareness and contemplation of performance as an operative sociopolitical mechanism in the real world. In effect, the audience is also encouraged to consider, inversely, its role in the world of the theater.

Chief Enemy to the People

Adelman's observation about today's American audience's participation in this drama is especially apt, the second clause of which is applicable to the early modern audience as well: "Nor is it only our democratic sympathies that put us uncomfortably in the position of the common people through-out much of the play: Coriolanus seems to find our love as irrelevant, as positively demeaning, as theirs; in refusing to show the people his wounds, he is at the same time refusing to show them to us" (1980, 144). In his refusal to perform, Coriolanus aligns the audience with the "common people," thereby disparaging the audience as well. As a result, he sets himself apart physically, morally, and spiritually from all people (the characters, the actors, the audience), as so many monarchs and dictators have done throughout history, including those who ruled over Shakespeare and Brecht (James I and Stalin, respectively).

Shakespeare's Coriolanus seems to correspond to Elizabeth I, who distinguished herself by her claim to virginity and her excellence in leadership. He might even be compared to Sir Walter Raleigh, who was said to have been an exceptional soldier but may have had treasonous transactions with Spain, as Coriolanus has with the Volscians. Yet the figure that most likely occurred to the early modern audience is James I, who was in power when the play was written and stands out because of his renowned erudition, his steadfast belief in the doctrine of Divine Right, and his resistance to public appearances. Because James was educated in Roman rather than English constitutional law, and because he wrote several theoretical works intended to legitimize and foster the absolute power of Christian kings, such as *The Trew Law of Free Monarchies* (1598) and *The Basilicon Doron* (priv. pr., 1599; public ed., 1603), as Albert H. Tricomi explains, "James awakened suspicions early on that he had little regard, foreigner that he was, for English rights and liberties": instead, he "inspired fears that he might become tyrannical, or had tyrannical designs" (1989, 54; 56).

In *The Trew Law of Free Monarchies*, one of many places in which James' views are documented, James maintains that:

> [The] allegeance of the people to their lawful King, their obedience, I say, ought to be to him, as to Gods lieutenant in earth, obeying his commands in all thinges, except directly against God, as the commands of Gods Minister, acknowledging him as a Iudge set by God ouer them, hauing power to judge them, but to be judged onely by God. (1982, 69)

Later he adds that the "King make daily/statutes & ordinances, inoyning such paines thereto as he thinks meet, without any advise of parliament or estates" (1982, 71). James' perception of the "Nature of a King" and "Christian Monarche" is similar to Coriolanus' own self-concept. And the fear of James shared by members of the Parliament and English populace is comparable to the fear of Coriolanus experienced by many of the play's characters. Although James' style of monarchy fell far short of the autocratic ideal articulated in his writings, his writings caused much anxiety in the realm. On March 21, 1610, for example, James was compelled to respond to the people's fear of his alleged tyrannical aspirations with a speech to Parliament delineating his ideas on Divine Right. Instead of placating the unrest among its members, however, the address provoked Parliament to confront James with the Petition of Right (May 1610): a declaration of their rights as English citizens, which James ignored. From a letter written by Lord Chamberlain dated May 24, 1610, we learn some of the effects of James' speech:

> I heare yt bred generally much discomfort; to see our monarchicall powre and regall prerogative strained so high and made so transcendant every way, that yf the practise shold follow the positions, we are not like to leave to our successors that freedome we receved from our forefathers. (1939, 301)

Inasmuch as the conflict between James and his subjects was serious when *Coriolanus* was written, and it was very serious, it is easy to compare James to Coriolanus and see *Coriolanus* as an anticourt drama.[17]

In regards to *Coriolan*'s topicality, it is similarly easy to imagine Joseph Stalin and Adolf Hitler as models for Brecht's Coriolanus, the former serving for Brecht's audience a dissident perspective on Coriolanus whereas the latter serves a conservative one. Like Coriolanus, Stalin and Hitler were both despotic pathological egotists who tried to give the impression that their greatness surpassed all. According to historian Isaac Deutscher, "Each established himself as an unchallengeable master ruling his country in accordance with a rigid *Führerprinzip*" (1949, 566). Considering the historical context in which Brecht wrote *Coriolan,* as Darko Suvin points out, "now, in that era of High Stalinism, the great leader [Coriolanus] running berserk and believing himself to be indispensable could not fail to be associated with Generalissimo Joseph Stalin (and possibly the lesser Stalins that Stalinism bred)" (1984, 200). Unfortunately, because *Coriolan* did not reach the stage for the Berliner Ensemble until 1964, eight years after Brecht's death, and in a very different Germany, we can only speculate on the kinds of response it would have gotten a decade earlier. In the communist Germany of 1964 the play was a wonderful success.

Like Coriolanus, Stalin was a great military leader, famous for his accomplishments in both the Russian Civil War and World War II, and he was eponymous to the city of Stalingrad, as Coriolanus is to Corioli. Most significant, however, is that Stalin not only believed himself irreplaceable, but also like Coriolanus—who wishes for the opportunity to kill "thousands" of rebellious plebeians (1.1.97–99; cf. *Coriolan* 64)—he sought the destruction of all people who represented the potentiality of an alternative government; and, like Hitler, he murdered millions of his country's own citizens.

Hitler's perception of war and his role in the army are also much like those of Coriolanus (recall, 1.1.224); John Keegan notes from Hitler's diary, "Hitler found the war [WWI—the only war in which he fought] 'the greatest of all experiences'" and he thought himself "'the first soldier of the Reich'" (1989, 236; 235). In relation to Hitler, as Margot Heinemann writes:

> [Brecht's potential] spectators many of whom were still under the influence of Nazi myth and glamour, brought up in SA or Hitler Youth, could all too easily see the story [of *Coriolan*] in terms of the true patriot and military hero [Coriolanus or Hitler], stabbed in the back by the cowardly masses under Red labor leaders. The production must show that no leader, however talented, is indispensable. (1985, 221)

Brecht's textual changes ensure that his play cannot be misread as profascist or right wing, that it cannot be readily appropriated as Shakespeare's *Coriolanus* has been, such as by T. S. Eliot in his overtly fascist poem *Coriolan*. This safeguarding is most pronounced in the short but nonetheless powerful final scene that Brecht adds to act 5. The scene makes it clear that "the world goes on without the hero" (125), who "aimed to make himself dictator" (126), by having the "Consul, senators, [and] tribunes" deliberating together over "current business" (126). He even has them forbid the public mourning of Coriolanus (146). This change in endings stresses the perspective, as Brecht explains, that "society can defend itself" from the individual who has risen up against it—"who has wrongly thought of himself as irreplaceable" (Brecht qtd. in Suvin 1984, 192).[18]

Similar to Stalin and Hitler, as well as James I, Coriolanus desperately endeavors to keep his fantasy alive: he works to maintain his dream of being self-reliant, greater than all other men, and an irreplaceable necessity to his country. Trying to maintain a self-image on such grandiose terms, nevertheless, places Coriolanus in an awkward contradiction to himself (as a member of a society) and to his overall social world. Coriolanus directs himself against the people, he establishes a binary opposition between himself and those people from whom he differentiates himself, and he does this to secure what he sees as his own extraordinary identity. For him to be the "heroic" politician the Romans want he would need to negotiate and make compromises; he would have to be capable of playing the necessary roles. But since such performing would cause him to lose touch with his own resolute sense of self, a self that can no longer exist if he must flatter and "be rul'd" (3.2.90) by commoners—or at least treat them congenially—he can never be their consul. Instead, as an antiperformer of sorts, a kind of antitheatricalist, he holds that he would rather "play / the man I am" than feign to be the man the people desire (3.2.15–16; 105). In fact, it is impossible for him to do otherwise, as when he fails to perform the part of, and thereby pass as, a commoner in Antium (4.5). His predicament reflects critically on the artificial nature of theater and the theatricality of politics and social life in general. It puts into question the relationship between self and social performance, asking if there is as an inherent or constant true self. It suggests implicitly that one's social identity might contradict this true self; it suggests that identity and self, however interconnected or similar, are always constrained and must be performed to be socially affirmed. Hence Coriolanus' revelation near the play's conclusion: "Like a dull actor now / I have forgot my part and I am out, / Even to a full disgrace" (5.3.40–42).

Transversal Territory

In the plays, Coriolanus is criticized as "too unbending" (106) and "too absolute" (3.2.39) in his devotion to his ideals and idealized self-image; and it is this persevering characteristic that most informs his inability to empathize with and relate to the "common people." This characteristic also explains why Coriolanus could not act successfully as a commoner in Antium; he cannot think and feel beyond the rigid boundaries of what I call his own "subjective territory." Subjective territory is my term for the scope of the conceptual and emotional experience of those subjectified by what I call "state machinery," which includes all inculcating forces in society, such as the educational, juridical, religious, and familial structures, that support the beliefs of the dominant classes and the government. In agreement with its investment in cultural, social, political, and economic fluctuations and determinations, this organizing machinery functions over time and space, sometimes consciously and sometimes unintentionally, to consolidate social and state powers in order to construct a society of subjects and thus "the state": the totalized state machinery. Subjective territory is therefore delineated by conceptual and emotional boundaries that are normally defined by the prevailing science, morality, and ideology. These boundaries bestow a spatiotemporal dimension, or common ground, to an aggregate of individuals, and work to ensure and monitor the coexistence of this social body. In short, subjective territory is the existential and experiential realm in and from which a given subject of a given hierarchical society perceives and relates to the universe and his or her place in it.[19]

Coriolanus' subjective territory is constructed less in the interest of a greater social body of "common people" than in a ruling oligarchy, and mostly in the interest of consolidating his own personal power in the world. As one of his own men, the First Officer, says of him: "That's a brave fellow; but he's vengeance / proud, and loves not the common people" (2.2.5–6; cf. *Coriolan* 90); "he seeks their hate with / greater devotion than they can render it him, and leaves nothing undone that may fully discover him their opposite" (2.2.18–21). Coriolanus' compulsion to maintain the integrity of his subjective territory, which is of course an unconscious undertaking, extends well beyond his endeavors to define himself against the plebeians to a more wholesale self-defining against the patricians, whom he includes with the plebeians as people of lesser worth than himself:

> You [patricians/senators] are plebeians
> If they [plebeians] be senators; and they are no less
> When, both your voices blended, the great'st taste
> Most palates theirs.
>   By Jove himself,
> It makes the consuls base; and my soul aches
> To know, when two authorities are up,
> Neither supreme, how soon confusion
> May enter 'twixt the gap of both. (3.1.100–110)

Launched moments before this passage, Brutus' accusation against Coriolanus, "You speak o'th'people / As if you were a god to punish, not / A man of their infirmity" (3.1.79–81), reveals that others are aware that Coriolanus thinks himself of divine stature as well as one of Rome's "Real necessities" (3.1.146). Coriolanus informs Sicinius that he himself, "Shall remain! / Hear you this Triton of the minnows? Mark you / His [meaning his own] absolute 'shall'?" (3.1.87–88). Yet to claim absolute power like James I was unacceptable in ancient Rome. This probably explains Cominius' abrupt response to Coriolanus' comment: "'Twas from the canon" (3.1.89). As Samuel Johnson says, and Brockbank agrees with his view, Coriolanus' remark "was contrary to the established rule; it was a form of speech to which he has no right" (Brockbank, 1976, 200).

Coriolanus' determination always to present himself superior to others through the arbitrary negation and denigration of others works to assert a self-constancy that he imagines presumptuously for himself. It is this steadfast determination, however, that makes it both impossible and possible for Coriolanus to engage in what I call "transversal movement." People move transversally when they cross the boundaries of their subjectification through the experience and deliberation of alternative perspectives and emotions, that is, when they breach and move beyond the parameters imposed onto them socially, conceptually, and/or physically by any organizational social structure. Such movements require engagement with and at the very least a passing through "transversal territory," which is "the non-subjectified region of one's conceptual territory [of one's imaginative range]. It is entered through the transgression of the conceptual boundaries and, usually by extension, the emotional boundaries of subjective territory" (Reynolds 1997, 149). Coriolanus' transversal movement occurs in the contradictory space of incompatibility between his investment in the Roman state (his duty) and his own self-interestedness. The more constraints are imposed onto him the more he actively slips unpredictably into this space in-between, this liminal space that is transversal to official culture, and thus challenges the subjective territories of both the plebeians and the Tribunes. Yet, he is consistent in his articulation of his self-concept, a self-concept he could only achieve by moving transversally beyond the parameters of his state-prescribed identity as devoted warrior/politician and consequently in opposition to Rome's organizational structure. Despite the tragic consequences in the play, it is precisely this consistency that some critics celebrate, such as Bradley (1912), Ide (1980), and Rossiter (1961). For these critics, the appeal of Coriolanus' resolute individualism supersedes its ultimate destructiveness to both Coriolanus and the state (I will return to this point). Nevertheless, with the character of Coriolanus, regardless of however praiseworthy his consistency might be, Shakespeare's play criticizes the idea of monarchical supremacy and the doctrine of Divine Right. Coriolanus is representative of a monarch or dictator whose egotism makes him dangerous to his nation. His obvious military usefulness is undermined by his arrogance.

The "common people" of *Coriolanus* and *Coriolan* initially give Coriolanus their vote for consul, and they do this because of his impressive military achievements. Then, after considering what they have done, Shakespeare's plebeians realize that they permitted, as Sicinius declares, an "ignorant election" (2.3.217), and Brecht's citizens never allow the election to become final (101). When Coriolanus opposes the offering of corn gratis and verbally assaults the "common people" for the last time without repercussions (3.1.120–170; cf. *Coriolan* 101–102), his egotism and sheer hatred for them are made explicit; it is confirmed that he is a "Fast foe to th'plebii" (2.3.182), their "fixed enemy" (2.3.248). "The people are incens'd against him" (3.1.30) and they determine that he deserves "present death" (3.1.209; cf. *Coriolan* 104). The contradictions in Coriolanus' character are thus reflected in the people's conflicting needs. They want protection against alien armies, and this is why they want Coriolanus. However, freedom from war means little to people who are starving and oppressed, circumstances that Coriolanus actively promotes.

By causing the audience to identify with the "common people," as discussed above, the audience is made to move transversally into the contradictory space as well. The subjective territories of its members, as the plebeians would have it, are made to "lay all flat" (3.1.196; cf. *Coriolan* 104). They are equalized and blurred into the subjective territories of the plebeians to the extent that the audience's members expand their own conceptual and emotional range. This allows them to relate to the direness of the situation. Thus, the audience also censures Coriolanus for not acting as the people want, for not being transversal enough. Acting is transversal. It requires movement outside of one's own subjective territory and entrance into the subjective territory of someone else, even if that someone is only a fictional character. Such engagement exposes the actor to thoughts and emotions that might differ hugely from those he or she experiences in everyday life. With this exposure, comes challenge, expansion, and possibly significant transformation of the actor's own subjective territory. To uphold his radically individuated subjective territory and possess state-sanctioned sociopolitical power, Coriolanus must simultaneously maintain his own sense of self and yet transverse it to meet, much less comprehend, the demands of the plebeians and the Tribunes.

It is this paradox that prevents Coriolanus from achieving the disciplinary control of the Roman populace that he so aggressively pursues. The people realize that he "affects / Tyrannical power" (3.3.1–2) and charge him appropriately:

> you have contriv'd to take
> From Rome all season'd office, and to wind
> Yourself into a power tyrannical;
> For which you are a traitor to the people. (3.3.63–66; cf. *Coriolan* 111)

The people decide that Coriolanus is a traitor and determine his punishment by democratic method: their conclusions are "Set down by th'poll"

(3.3.9) and presented through "chairmen of the electoral districts" who carry "a list of all the voters they represent" (109; cf. *Coriolanus* 3.3.7–11). Again, as in the first scene, the audience is invited to experience the uniting of the plebeians in their communal action against their oppression and in their progress toward establishing a democratic republic. All the plebeians exclaim, "Our enemy is banish'd! He is gone! Hoo! Hoo!" and the stage direction reads, "They all shout, and throw up their caps" (3.3.137; 113). This marks the third victory for the "common people." Cominius, Menenius, and the other patricians—who make many remarks suggesting that Coriolanus is out of line—now accommodate (though not reluctantly in Brecht) the people's wish to banish Coriolanus, just as they do earlier by appointing the people Tribunes: they "all forsook me" says Coriolanus to Aufidius (4.5.77; cf. *Coriolan* 123).

Only Coriolanus does not acknowledge his defeat. Instead, pathetically and desperately, he retorts: "I banish you" (3.3.123; 113). He predicts: "I shall be lov'd when I am lack'd" (4.1.15), which can be interpreted as Brecht's Coriolanus says, "They'll love me when they need me" (114). To prove this, Coriolanus joins the Volscians and marches with them against Rome, and in Shakespeare, as well as in Brecht, this further illuminates the plebeians' conflicting attitudes toward Coriolanus. They are panic-stricken and some regret Coriolanus' banishment. Yet before Volumnia convinces Coriolanus not to fight, the majority of Brecht's plebeians report for military duty and are given arms by Cominius (137). In Shakespeare, Coriolanus is quickly persuaded by his mother and we are never permitted to see the outcome of the people's confusion. Still, Coriolanus' behavior shows that his pathological individuality, exacerbated by his quest to prove his masculinity—that he does not have "a pipe / as Small as an eunuch" and "schoolboy's tears" (3.2.113–116; cf. *Coriolan* 108)—has far exceeded society's expectations. To demonstrate his indispensability and magnanimous manliness, Coriolanus betrays his family, others who care about his well-being, and the nation's "common people"; his wilful jeopardizing of their lives—given that such jeopardizing contradicts his sociopolitical ideals—testifies to the great extent to which he has moved transversally beyond the parameters according to which he is expected to live and operate.

In the end, however, we learn once and for all that Coriolanus is hardly the individual he imagines himself to be. As Brecht's Volumnia tells him, "You are no longer indispensable" (142), and Shakespeare's Aufidius keenly observes that he is not the quintessential embodiment of masculine prowess but rather a mere "boy of tears" (5.6.100). The case of Coriolanus suggests that martial expertise, sociopolitical acumen, and emotional intelligence are both related and evaluated relatively within the world of the play. In addition to *Coriolanus'* sympathizing with the "common people" and its critique of sociopolitical indispensability, as Dollimore argues, "a radical *political* relativism is advanced" (1984, 229). In his soliloquy concerning the fortunes of Coriolanus, Aufidius concludes that,

> our virtues
> Lie in th'interpretation of our time,
> And power, unto itself most commendable,
> Hath not a tomb so evident as a chair
> T' extol what it hath done. (4.7.49–53; cf. *Coriolan* 132)

Here Aufidius speaks of people's "virtues" (rather than, say, reputation) as socially constructed (Dollimore 1984, 229). This opposes the view held by the early modern Church of England that people's virtues are essential attributes bestowed by God. Again, Shakespeare seems to have anticipated Karl Marx. In his preface to *A Contribution to a Critique of Political Economy,* Marx maintains that, "It is not the consciousness of men that determines their existence, but on the contrary it is their social existence that determines their consciousness" (1904). Marx reiterates this in *The German Ideology:* "Consciousness is from the very beginning a social product, and remains so as long as men exist at all" (1978, 158). For Marx, consciousness is produced socially and exists in our relationships to our environment; it is through consciousness that we interpret these relationships, relatively, as individuals who live in society. Both Marx and Aufidius claim that our virtues are sociohistorically determined rather than inherently possessed or furnished by God.

However controversial Aufidius' view would seem to have been, because there is no decisive proof for a production of *Coriolanus* during Shakespeare's own lifetime, there is no way for us to know how Coriolanus was originally received by its Jacobean audience. Albeit the stage directions show the play ready for the theater, the play may not have been staged then. It may have been censured for its politics. The radical potential we have seen in the play, a potential that exists in *Coriolanus* prior to any alterations made by Brecht—consider Brecht's own query regarding *Coriolanus,* the last entry in his research notes, "Couldn't one do it just as it is, only with skilful direction?" (quoted in Heinemann 1984, 219)—powerfully emphasizes the value of reconsidering established readings of Shakespeare's plays.

As we have seen in the case of *Coriolanus,* it is especially important to (re)examine those plays that have been used to support political ideologies. To further stress this point, I want to conclude this essay by returning briefly (as I promised several pages ago) to the celebration of the character Coriolanus by some critics. Rather than discuss the varying opinions of critics, however, I want to conclude with the words of one influential critic, Nazi supporter H. Hüsges, from his introduction to a 1934 German edition of *Coriolanus.* Hüsges' reading epitomizes the kinds of political employment of Shakespeare about which I am most concerned; it justifies my pleas that political criticism/use of Shakespeare needs to be taken seriously. According to Hüsges:

> The meaning of this last and most mature of Shakespeare's works for the new Germany lies in the heroic features inherent in it. The poet treats the problem of *Volk* [people] and *Führer* [leader]; he portrays the true nature of a Führer in contrast to the indiscriminating masses: he portrays a misled *Volk,* a false democracy whose representatives give in to the wishes of the *Volk* for the sake of egotistical goals. The figure of the true hero and Führer Coriolanus towers high above these weaklings; he wants to lead the misdirected *Volk* to recovery, as Adolf Hitler wants to lead our beloved German Fatherland today (1934, 157).

Notes

I am grateful to Elaine Scarry, David Perkins, Tony Kubiak, Kim Savelson, Nina Venus, Don Hedrick, Ian Munro, John Rouse, Julia Lupton, and the members of Harvard's Renaissance Colloquium for their many helpful comments throughout the writing of this essay.

1. Bertolt Brecht, "Big Time, Lost" in *Die Gedichte von Bertolt Brecht in einem* (Austria: Suhrkamp, 1984), 1010. Translated by me and Nina Venus.
2. To avoid confusion, I will refer to Shakespeare's play and its protagonist as Coriolanus (like the traditional Latin spelling in Shakespeare), while Brecht's version will be called *Coriolan* (as in German) yet its protagonist will still be referred to as Coriolanus.
3. On censorship and the politics of early modern English drama, see: Martin Butler, *Theatre and Crisis 1632–1642* (Cambridge: Cambridge University Press, 1984); Janet Clare, "'Greater Themes for Insurrection's Arguing': Political Censorship of the Elizabethan and Jacobean Stage," *RES* 38 (1987): 169–83; Philip J. Finkelpearl, "'The Comedians Liberty': Censorship of the Jacobean Stage Reconsidered," *ELR* 16 (1986): 123–38 and

"The Role of the Court in The Development of Jacobean Drama," *Criticism* 24 (1982): 138–58; and Alvin Kernan, *Shakespeare, the King's Playwright: Theater in the Stuart Court 1603–1613* (New Haven: Yale University Press, 1995).

4. See V. R. Berghahn, *Modern Germany: Society, Economy and Politics in the Twentieth Century* (Cambridge: Cambridge University Press, 1989), 217–219.

5. For a thorough description of the uprising of June 16, 1953 see Henry Ashby Turner, Jr., *The Two Germanies Since 1945* (New Haven: Yale University Press, 1987), 116–124.

6. Though the exact date that Brecht stopped revising *Coriolan* is unknown, most scholars agree that it was between 1952 and 1955. See Darko Suvin, *To Brecht and Beyond: Soundings in Modern Dramaturgy* (New Jersey: Barnes and Noble, 1984), 200; and Margot Heinemann, "How Brecht read Shakespeare" in *Political Shakespeare: New Essays in Cultural Materialism,* eds. Jonathan Dollimore and Alan Sinfield (Ithaca: Cornell University Press, 1985), 221, and John Willett, *The Theatre of Bertolt Brecht* (London: Methuen, 1977), 63; 121.

7. In his 1979 biography of Brecht, *Brecht* (London: Marion Boyars), Klaus Volker provides an insightful investigation of Brecht's affinity for Marxism and his interest in establishing a Communist regime in Germany. See also Willett, *The Theatre of Bertolt Brecht*.

8. Translated by me and Nina Venus.

9. See note 6 above, and Bertolt Brecht, *Brecht on Theatre: The Development of an Aesthetic,* ed. and trans. John Willett (New York: Hill and Wang, 1964).

10. For a discussion of the date of composition and original production of Shakespeare's play, see E. C. Pettet, "Coriolanus and the Midlands Insurrection of 1607," *Shakespeare Survey* 3 (1950): 34–42; Philip Brockbank in Shakespeare, *Coriolanus,* ed. Philip Brockbank (London: Methuen, 1976), 24–29; and Annabel Patterson, *Shakespeare and the Popular Voice* (Cambridge: Basil Blackwell, 1989), 135–146.

11. As noted by E. C. Pettet in "*Coriolanus* and the Midlands Insurrection of 1607," the insurgents that participated in the Midlands revolt were "commonly described as 'Diggers' and 'Levellers,'" which are the same names that "not more than a generation later" were perpetuated by those radicals whose "ideas so shocked the Commonwealth leaders" (35). For an account of the roles that people called Diggers and Levellers played in the English revolution of the 1640s, see Christopher Hill, *The World Turned Upside Down: Radical Ideas During the English Revolution* (Harmondsworth: Penguin, 1975), 126–128.

12. For more on the damage caused by the early modern protesters, see Pettet, "*Coriolanus* and the Midlands Insurrection of 1607," 34.

13. For a detailed investigation of Shakespeare's sources, see Philip Brockbank ed., William Shakespeare, *Coriolanus,* 29–35.

14. Philip Brockbank, ed., William Shakespeare, *Coriolanus;* Samuel Taylor

Coleridge, *Biographia Literaria;* Willard Farnham, *Shakespeare's Tragic Frontier;* Günter Grass, *The Plebeians Rehearse the Uprising;* Edwin Honig, "*Sejanus* and *Coriolanus: A Study in Alienation*"; C. C. Huffman, *Coriolanus in Context;* Richard Ide, *Possessed with Greatness: The Heroic Tragedies of Chapman and Shakespeare;* Samuel Johnson, ed. *The Plays and Poems of Shakespeare;* M. W. MacCallum, *Shakespeare's Roman Plays, and Their Background;* E. C. Pettet, "*Coriolanus* and the Midlands Insurrection of 1607"; James Emerson Phillips, *The State of Shakespeare's Greek and Roman Plays;* Norman Rabkin, *Shakespeare and the Common Understanding;* A. P. Rossiter, *Angel With Horns;* Simmons, J. L., *Shakespeare's Pagan World: The Roman Tragedies;* W. Gordon Zeeveld, "*Coriolanus* and Jacobean Politics."

15. "*Coriolanus:* Body Politic and Private Parts," *Shakespeare Quarterly* 41 [1990]: 455–69, by Zvi Jagendorf, discusses the play's preoccupation with body metaphors without making any explicit claims about the play's politics. "Drama, Politics, and the Hero: *Coriolanus,* Brecht, and Grass," *Comparative Drama* 24 (Winter 1990–1991): 322–41, by Martin Scofield, discusses the aesthetic merits of Brecht's adaptation without addressing the politics of Shakespeare's play.

16. All quotations from Shakespeare's *Coriolanus* follow the new Arden edition, ed. Philip Brockbank (London: Methuen, 1976), and all quotations from Brecht's *Coriolan* are taken from *Collected Plays,* eds. Ralph Manheim and John Willett (New York: Random House, 1973). In addition, from here on, when citing Shakespeare's text I will give the act, the scene, and the line numbers, and I will refer to Brecht's play by page numbers only. Also, because Brecht modernizes Shakespeare's language for his play, to avoid needless repetition of lines I will cite Shakespeare and then give the page number(s) of the corresponding text in Brecht; for example, (2.2.137; cf. *Coriolan,* 93).

17. For discussion on similarities between Coriolanus and various people of Shakespeare's day, see P. A. Jorgensen, "Shakespeare's Coriolanus: Elizabethan Soldier," *PMLA* 64 (1949): 221– 235.

18. Suvin translated these lines from Henning Rischbieter, *Brecht II.* (Velber, 1966): 75.

19. See Bryan Reynolds, "The Devil's House, 'or worse': Transversal Power and Antitheatrical Discourse in Early Modern England," *Theatre Journal* 49.2 (May 1997): 143–167, and mine and Donald Hedrick's introduction to this collection.

Works Cited

Adelman, Janet. 1980. "'Anger's My Meat': Feeding, Dependency, and Aggression in *Coriolanus.*" In *Representing Shakespeare.* Ed. Murray M. Schwartz and Coppelia Kahn. Baltimore: Johns Hopkins. 129–149.

Berghahn, V. R. 1989. *Modern Germany: Society, Economy and Politics in the Twentieth Century.* Cambridge: Cambridge University Press.

Bourdieu, Pierre. 1993. *The Field of Cultural Production.* Ed. and Trans. Randall Jonson. New York: Columbia University Press. Cambridge: Cambridge University Press.

Bradley, A. C. 1929. "*Coriolanus:* British Academy Lecture 1912." In *A Miscellany.* London: Macmillan.

Brecht, Bertolt. 1964. *Brecht on Theatre: The Development of an Aesthetic.* Ed. and Trans. John Willett. New York: Hill and Wang.

———. 1973. *Coriolanus.* In *Collected Plays.* Ed. Ralph Manheim and John Willett. New York: Random House.

Bond, Ronald B., ed. 1987. *Certain Sermons or Homilies (1547) and A Homily against Disobedience and Wilful Rebellion (1570): A Critical Edition.* Toronto: University of Toronto Press.

Bristol, Michael D. 1987. "Lenten Butchery: Legitimation Crisis in *Coriolanus.*" In *Shakespeare Reproduced: The Text in History and Ideology.* Ed. Jean Howard and Marion O'Connor. London: Methuen. 207–22.

Brockbank, Philip, ed. 1976. William Shakespeare. *Coriolanus.* London: Methuen.

Chamberlain, John. 1939. *The Letters of John Chamberlain.* 2 Vols. Ed. N. E. MacClure. Philadelphia: American Philosophical Society.

Coleridge, Samuel Taylor. 1947. *Biographia Literaria.* New York: J. M. Dent.

Deutscher, Isaac. 1949. *Stalin: A Political Biography.* New York: Oxford University Press.

Dollimore, Jonathan. 1984. *Radical Tragedy: Religion, Ideology and Power in the Drama of Shakespeare and His Contemporaries.* Chicago: University of Chicago Press.

Farnham, Willard. 1963. *Shakespeare's Tragic Frontier.* Berkeley: University of California Press.

Gay, E. F. 1904. "The Midlands Revolt and the Inquisitions of Depopulation of 1607." In *Transactions of the Royal Historical Society.* N.S.18: 195–244.

Gildon, Charles. 1995. "The Argument of *Coriolanus.*" In *Coriolanus: Critical Essays.* Ed. David Wheeler. New York: Garland.

Grass, Gunter. 1966. *The Plebeians Rehearse the Uprising.* Trans. Ralph Manheim. New York: Harcourt, Brace and World.

Hedrick, Donald K. "Male Surplus Value." Presentation at Folger Library Shakespeare Colloquium, Washington, D.C., April, 1999.

Heinemann, Margot. 1985. "How Brecht read Shakespeare." In *Political Shakespeare: New Essays in Cultural Materialism.* Ed. Jonathan Dollimore and Alan Sinfield. Ithaca: Cornell University Press: 202–230.

Howard, Jean E. and Marion F. O'Connor, eds. 1987. *Shakespeare Reproduced: The Text in History and Ideology.* New York: Methuen.

Honig, Edwin. 1951. "*Sejanus* and *Coriolanus: A Study in Alienation.*" *Modern Language Quarterly* 12: 407–21.

Huffman, C. C. 1971. *Coriolanus in Context.* Lewisburg, 1971.

Hüsges, H., ed. 1934. William Shakespeare, *Coriolanus.* Braunschweig/Berlin/Hamburg.

Ide, Richard. 1980. *Possessed with Greatness: The Heroic Tragedies of Chapman and Shakespeare.* London: Scholar Press.

Jagendorf, Zvi. 1995. "Coriolanus: Body Politic and Private Parts." In *Coriolanus: Critical Essays.* Ed. David Wheeler. New York: Garland.

James I. 1982. *Minor Prose Works of King James VI and I.* Ed. James Craigie. Edinburgh: The Scottish Text Society.

Johnson, Samuel, ed. 1795–96. *The Plays and Poems of William Shakespeare.* Philadelphia: Bioren & Madan.

Keegan, John. 1987. *The Mask of Command.* New York: Viking.

Kishlansky, Mark. 1986. *Parliamentary Selection: Social and Political Choice in Early Modern England.* Cambridge: Cambridge University Press.

MacCallum, M. W. 1967. *Shakespeare's Roman Plays, and Their Background.* London: Macmillan.

Marx, Karl. 1904. *A Contribution to the Critique of Political Economy.* London: International Library Publishing Co.

———, and Friedrich Engels. 1982. *The Communist Manifesto.* Intro. A. J. P. Taylor. Penguin: Harmondsworth.

———, 1978. *The Marx-Engels Reader.* 2nd edition. Ed. Robert C. Tucker. New York: W. W. Norton and Company.

———, 1975. *Value, Price and Profit.* In Karl Marx and Friedrich Engels. *Collected Works.* Vol. 20. Trans. Richard Dixon. New York: International.

Pettet, E. C. 1950. "*Coriolanus* and the Midlands Insurrection of 1607." *Shakespeare Survey* 3: 34–42.

Phillips, James Emerson. 1940. *The State of Shakespeare's Greek and Roman Plays.* New York: Columbia University Press.

Rabkin, Norman. 1967. *Shakespeare and the Common Understanding.* New York: Free Press.

Reynolds, Bryan. 1997. "The Devil's House, 'or worse': Transversal Power and Antitheatrical Discourse in Early Modern England." *Theatre Journal* 49.2 (May): 143–67.

Rossiter, A. P. 1961. *Angel With Horns.* Ed. Graham Storey. London: Longmans.

Scofield, Martin. 1995. "Drama, Politics, and the Hero: Coriolanus, Brecht, and Grass." In *Coriolanus: Critical Essays.* Ed. David Wheeler. New York: Garland.

Simmons, J. L. 1973. *Shakespeare's Pagan World: The Roman Tragedies.* Charlottesville: University Press of Virginia.

Sorge, Thomas. 1987, "The Failure of Orthodoxy in *Coriolanus.*" In Howard and O'Connor, 225–239.

Stow, John. 1631. *Annales.* London.

Suvin, Darko. 1984. *To Brecht and Beyond: Soundings in Modern Dramaturgy.* New Jersey: Barnes and Noble.

Tillyard, E. M. W. 1943. *The Elizabethan World Picture.* London: Chatto and Windus.

Tricomi, Albert H. 1989. *Anticourt Drama in England 1603–1642*. University Press of Virginia.

Turner, Henry Ashby Jr. 1987. *The Two Germanies Since 1945*. New Haven: Yale University of Press.

Wilson, John Dover, ed. 1960. *Coriolanus*. London: New Shakespeare.

Zeeveld, Gordon W. 1962. "*Coriolanus* and Jacobean Politics," *Modern Language Review* 57: 321–334.

Part IV

Loving Otherwise

Chapter 6

Sweet, Savage Shakespeare

Laurie Osborne

In 1987, the *Detroit Free Press* produced a special bridal section, displaying wedding dresses with captions from Shakespeare's plays. The students in my Shakespeare class were delighted because I was running a contest: whoever discovered the most references to Shakespeare in popular culture won a prize. This particular entry seemed perfect to them. After all, not only was there a lot of Shakespeare, but it was all used so very inappropriately. My personal favorites were "She is a woman, therefore may be wooed; / She is a woman therefore may be won," taken from the gang rapists in *Titus Andronicus;* and "Doubt that the stars are fire; / Doubt that the sun doth move; / Doubt truth to be a liar; / But never doubt my love," taken from Hamlet's letter to Ophelia (Weddings 1987, 8, 12).[1] Neither quotation really suited the celebration of connubial bliss that the *Detroit Free Press* was promoting, yet there Shakespeare was, advocating and subverting the promise of marital happiness that anchors the American wedding industry—and the American romance novel as well.

This casual inclusion of Shakespearean verse appropriates the plays in the service of romantic love, regardless of the lines' initial context. Such quotations are the popular culture yoking of Shakespeare with transcendent love that Linda Charnes explores in the twentieth- century critical treatments of *Antony and Cleopatra*. Although Charnes' argument "isn't to say that Shakespeare has written a Harlequin romance or even anticipated it" (1992, 3), subgenres of the romance novel certainly invoke him as if he had.[2] Charnes suggests that the politics of Shakespeare's *Antony and Cleopatra* have been critically displaced by "the love story . . . one of the most pervasive and effective—yet least deconstructed—of all ideological apparatuses: one of the most effective smokescreens available in the politics of cultural production" (1992, 1). I propose to reverse the lens and show how and why Shakespeare becomes the "smokescreen" for negotiations of class and gender at the heart of the love story in its most prolific contemporary form—the romance novel.

Allusions to Shakespeare are particularly abundant in two subgenres: Regency romances, which take the rigid double standard of the early 1800s as the context for the heroine's struggle toward matrimony, and historical romances ranging from the Elizabethan period on, which offer longer, more sexual plots.[3] In the most consistently Shakespeare-ridden texts, the plays serve simultaneously to mark the historical "Otherness" required in the genre and to indicate authorial familiarity with canonical literature. Beyond such motives for referring to the plays, these novelists incorporate Shakespeare in elaborate combinations of class and gender differences. In the Anglophilic romances by American authors, Shakespeare and his plays serve a double purpose: they encode a fantasy of rigid class distinctions and fixed, separate gender roles, and they enable the erasure of those distinctions, most often using class mobility in apparent resolution of patriarchal strictures on women.

These functions loosely parallel the Shakespearean references in classic detective fiction, recently analyzed by Susan Baker (1995). She suggests that Shakespeare's pervasive appearance in mystery fiction calibrates guilt and innocence against class issues and problems of authenticity. Not only do Shakespearean references underscore class distinctions, according to Baker, but anti-Stratfordians are typically villains or morally suspect. Detective fiction in effect embeds its Shakespearean references within ideologically bounded, class-driven plots so that allusions to the plays or Shakespeare himself ratify both the hero-detective and the literary value of the genre (Baker 1995, 438–44).[4]

Romance novelists have even more extreme problems affirming the validity of their chosen literary form; using Shakespeare self-evidently displays the literary credentials of a romance novelist. Consequently Shakespearean references appear on several levels, from the title and identified quotations, to actual visits to the theatre or involvement with actresses. However, the result is not the ratification of Shakespeare's author-function as the touchstone for virtue, as Baker argues of detective fiction. Although romance novelists do use "'Shakespeare' as thesaurus or reservoir, as catalogue, menu, or fund of readily available transhistorical types," their allusions differ noticeably from detective fiction because these novels do not unambiguously reinscribe "Shakespeare as god-like—authoritative—creator of memorable characters" (Baker 1995, 434).

Instead, regencies and historicals often employ the Bard at the juncture of the contradictory resistance and submission to patriarchy that several feminists have noted in the romance novel. Tania Modleski (1982) frames the conflict between the female protagonist and the patriarchal society— exemplified and resolved by her relationship with the hero—in terms of Frederic Jameson's cultural unconscious:

> The so-called masochism pervading these texts is a "cover" for anxieties, desires and wishes which if openly expressed would challenge the psychological and social order of things. For that very reason, of course, they must be kept hidden; the texts after arousing them, must, in Jameson's formula, work to neutralize them. (30)

Other critics who address these genres—Janice Radway (1984), Carol Thurston (1987), and Anne Barr Snitnow (1983)—are equally intrigued with the romance novel's contradictory blend of challenges to male power and submission to the system. Drawing on Nancy Chodorow's object relations, Radway (1984) suggests an infantilization of the female reader, seeking an all-satisfying maternal relationship in the naive heroine's relationship with the dominant male (135–40). According to this argument, these novels offer narratives of maternal nurturance rather than of submission to patriarchal masculinity. Moreover, she argues that such reading itself constitutes resistance to patriarchal control. Both Snitnow and Thurston identify these novels as negotiating with "our culture['s] . . . pathological experience of sex differences" (Snitnow 1983, 247) and issues of female sexual response (Thurston 1987). Thus mass market romance both expresses and challenges hierarchies of power and sexual difference, working through conflicts that belie the love story's supposedly straightforward participation in ideology.

Despite the oft-stated determination not to devalue the genre, most of these books and essays are faintly apologetic about their subject matter, though in apparently complimentary terms. Modleski (1982), for example, suggests that "these fantasies, as complex as we find them to be, do not employ as elaborately as 'high' art the psychological and formal devices for distancing and transforming the anxieties and wishes of their readers" (31). In other words, female novelists communicate with a largely female readership without the sophisticated strategies of high art. Both the female readership and authorship are crucial to feminist interests, often despite subject matter that feminists frequently deplore.

The engagement with female authors and readers with "high art"

Shakespeare appears in Marianne Novy's recent work on Shakespearean reception. Both her essay collection, *Women's Revisions of Shakespeare* (1990), and her book, *Engaging Shakespeare* (1994), argue the importance of specifically female authors' responsive revisions of Shakespeare.[5] However, these "responses" are either those of now-canonical female authors or those of would-be canonical "serious" novelists of the twentieth century, not the Shakespeare appropriated in the largest publishing venue available to female writers. I take up a different challenge: exploring how Shakespearean appropriations work in the mass market world of paperback romance dominated by women authors and women readers. I read their complex uses of Shakespeare not as the less elaborately distanced fantasies Modleski envisions, but as the negotiations between writers explicitly excluded from the canon and the current premier male high culture phenomenon, Shakespeare. Although Novy's general observations about Shakespearean allusions could apply equally to romance novelists, romance fiction arrives and disappears from print under strikingly different conditions from other fiction. Its very transience and breadth of audience have laid romance fiction open to feminist critique and even dismissal.

Romance writers have responded vigorously to both. Jayne Ann Krentz recently edited *Dangerous Men and Adventurous Women* (1992), a collection of essays by numerous widely published romance writers. Almost every essay in the collection laments the critical disdain for the romance and objects to feminist worries about the obligatory narrative resolution in marriage. Why should romance readers be more perniciously enmeshed in their popular fiction than those who read detective stories, ask romance writers throughout this book. Again and again these writers point to the empowerment of their female characters, the heroine who "brings the most dangerous creature on earth, the human male, to his knees," from which Krentz in her introduction argues that "the subversive nature of the books is fundamental and inescapable" (Krentz 1992, 6–7), a position her contributors support.

Both academics and Krentz's essayists deal most often with either Harlequin romances (Snitnow 1983, Modleski 1982) or the so-called sexy spectaculars (the Krentz collection 1992, Radway 1984, Thurston 1987). The historical / regency novels, where Shakespeare figures so prominently, differ significantly from other subgenres, in large measure because of the historical setting:

> The first function of the setting of a romance novel is to be Other, to transport the reader somewhere else. The setting often provides the reader with

the first and clearest signal that fantasy follow. . . . The settings of romance are important for more than just their Other-ness. Particular settings are associated with particular fantasies . . . Regencies tell of a polite, ordered society in which gunfights are elegantly staged duels governed by an elaborate code. (Seidel 1992, 207–08)

The deeply coded Regency society functions as a radically repressive patriarchy with which the heroine must struggle. In that context, Regency-historical novels often incorporate Shakespearean texts with apparent casualness, as cultural shorthand—*Othello* for jealousy, *Hamlet* for indecision, *Romeo and Juliet* for love at first sight, etc. Such brief references may affirm Shakespeare's author function, as Baker (1995) suggests of detective fiction, but they serve to characterize the hero's (or heroine's) emotional state. Ultimately, Shakespeare's authorial access to transhistorically authentic human emotions is less important than the emotions themselves, which the author describes in several ways, only one of which is Shakespearean.

Still more often these novels incorporate Shakespeare within transformations of individuals, relationships, and the plays themselves. In Vanessa Gray's *A Lady of Property* (1988), Marcus North takes on the brotherly role of Sebastian to the crossdressed heroine he names Viola, but he seeks to exchange that name for Orsino by the end of the novel. Shakespeare's *Twelfth Night* provides the pseudonyms that the pair adopt as Marcus/Sebastian and Charlotte/Viola, but their interaction in disguise also transforms the arranged match between the two, which Charlotte has fled, into a love match that ultimately she accepts. On the one hand, the novel employs Shakespeare as a device enabling the heroine to marry the same man she was told to marry at the beginning—triumph to patriarchy. On the other hand, *A Lady of Property* both rewrites Sebastian's abrupt marriage for wealth and explains Viola's and Orsino's mutual affection, this time with "Orsino" knowing the gender of his cross-dressed companion. The play becomes the pivot for the evolving relationship of hero and heroine and its resolution—Marcus signals his reconciliation with Charlotte by exclaiming, "No more Sebastian!" (Gray 1988, 221).

By positioning (and often revising) Shakespeare's plays within the central romance plot, American regency novelists *use,* rather than merely praise, Shakespeare in their negotiations with social hierarchies and gender restrictions. Unlike Baker's analysis of detective fiction, which suggests that Shakespeare helps to create social hierarchies between classes and value-laden distinctions between guilt and innocence, my analyses of American romance fiction suggest that Shakespearean allusions mediate class boundaries in order to efface or mask rigid gender double standards (Baker 1995, passim). Instead of marking the hierarchies and distinctions typical of detective fiction, Shakespeare serves the integration and union that romance novelists claim as characteristic of their genre (Kinsale 1992, 49). Moreover, the plays function this way through transformation—in the forms of revision and interpretation—as much as through accurate quotations.

A novel that handily points out the differences by closely paralleling Baker's model is Alicia Rasley's *Poetic Justice* (1994). The "villain" who threatens Jessica Seton's patrimony is a secret anti-Stratfordian. The novel's plot centers around the missing text of *Sir Thomas More,* partially in Shakespeare's hand, which lays the groundwork for unusually numerous Shakespearean references. The chapters headings are quotations from the plays, and the hero, a noble by-blow and book pirate, establishes mutual interests with the heroine and bridges their class differences through sharing quotations. Baker's analysis certainly fits their efforts to rescue the manuscript in Shakespeare' s hand from the Baconian curator who wants to steal her inheritance, the Parnham collection. Distaste for monetary value and reverence for Shakespeare's autograph abound (Baker 1995, 430–33).

However, the romance plot also uses and reworks *The Merchant of Venice*'s "the will of a living daughter curb'd by the will of a dead father" (1.2.23–25). Jessica can only receive her inheritance, the library collected by her parents, if she marries soon and with her uncle's consent. He has already turned down six suitors; there is no way he will approve of John Dryden [*sic*], who is not only a bastard nobleman but involved in trade. When her uncle unexpectedly accepts Dryden's suit, Jessica imitates her Shakespearean namesake and flees. Since Dryden is simultaneously kidnapped by the villainous Baconian, society assumes that they have eloped together. With these two plot movements—the heiress obeying the will of the dead father and the apparent flight of the daughter with an inappropriate suitor, Jessica combines Portia's and Jessica's experiences.

The variations here are instructive. Caught in the patriarchal will, Jessica seeks to use marriage to achieve her real goal—control over her father's neglected book collection. Her motives are both monetary, since the collection is valuable, and altruistic, because she values the books for themselves. Her ruthlessness in pursuing her own inheritance matches the hero's commitment to pirating valuable texts. Like Jessica, John is appalled that the curator has neglected her father's collection in order to pursue his obsessive belief that Bacon wrote the plays attributed to Shakespeare.

As in *Merchant,* the arbitrary guardian blocking Jessica's marriage unexpectedly chooses the right suitor. His approval, however, explicitly denies the class differences that both Jessica and John expect to be permanent boundaries between them. In fact, the pair have devised their courtship and his interview with the guardian with the understanding that John is totally ineligible—lower class, illegitimate, and engaged in trade; the threat that she will marry him should, they assume, force the uncle into approving another suitor. Their class differences are bridged by their mutual love of books and especially of Shakespeare, explicitly positioning the bard as part of what enables the relationship to flourish. Moreover, Jessica's disappearance upon John's rather testy assertion that they must now marry to save the collection reveals her need to make sure, possibly by risking her inheritance, that he is marrying her for personal as well as professional reasons. The danger he faces as the accepted bridegroom casts the anti- Shakespearean curator as the real block to their union, not the class differences that apparently evaporate.

As Rasley's novel suggests, the characters may quote accurately, but romance novels actively revise Shakespeare when they engage his texts thoroughly. Thus Shakespearean appropriations in female-dominated popular culture are quite different than Shakespeare in detective fiction or Shakespeare in the action films and pornography.[6] Subtly or blatantly, historical and Regency romances invoke Shakespeare in mapping out class and gender hierarchies that are envisioned as historically specific obstacles to the love story. At the same time, his works help to resolve and dissolve those boundaries, not because Shakespearean narratives and characters are universal, but because they are appropriable and revisable.

For example, one typical narrative that incorporates Shakespeare is the "actress novel," where an amateur or professional actress is the heroine. Marlene Suson's *The Fair Imposter* (1992) not only employs the actress playing Shakespeare, but also revises *Romeo and Juliet* as an integral part of the plot. Actress Sally Marlowe looks startlingly like Lady Serena Keith, who has eloped with another man rather than marry her betrothed, Garth Traymor. Actually, Garth doesn't want to marry her either. Equally offended by his family's social climbing and by Lady Serena's barely concealed contempt for his comparatively low status, Garth escaped to the diplomatic corps and has now returned home, determined to convince Lady Serena to "cry off," breaking the engagement. Since she has run away, her family—in debt to Garth—wants to present Sally as Serena. When Garth and Sally meet, Shakespeare becomes an equalizing feature in a novel whose central problems are profoundly tied to class.

Both Sally and Serena (her twin as it turns out) are interlopers, the latter transposed into the upper class in gratitude to a noble lady whose baby died at birth, and the former playing the substitute and falling in love with Garth. Sally's "role" is to convince Garth to cry off so that the family will not have to repay their debt. The more he falls in love with her and she with him, the more insuperable she finds the class barriers that divide her from a baronet. However, she first charmed him when she appeared (heavily disguised) as Cleopatra in *Antony and Cleopatra* with her traveling troupe, and she utterly enchants him with departures from conventional ladylike behavior. For example, she completes his quotation from *Henry VI, Part 1*:

> "For what is wedlock forced, but a hell,
> An age of discord and continual strife?"

Recognizing the lines, Sally completes:

> "Whereas the contrary bringeth bliss,
> And is a pattern of celestial peace."

> (Suson 1992, 62–63)

Garth is amazed and pleased with her knowledge, while the quotation itself affirms sentiments that have led him to try ending his betrothal. This interchange apparently affirms the universalizing authority that Baker attributes to Shakespeare in detective fiction; however, Suson's incorporation of Shakespeare is more elaborate.

Unexpectedly, Shakespeare also becomes the mark of the disruption of the romantic relationship. When Sally finally reveals the deception, Garth's rage and Sally's subsequent return to the stage revive the Shakespearean quotations that have all but disappeared in the body of the novel. Sally has her big chance; she is to play Juliet at Drury Lane. Unfortunately Garth shows up with another woman and completely destroys Sally's performance—she can only think about him and so muffs her lines "'O Romeo, Romeo! Wherefore art thou . . .' she could not stop herself from looking toward Garth, her heart crying out her own love to him" (Suson 1992, 203). He, of course, kisses the hand of his companion and completely demoralizes Sally, who promptly flees London. Her apparent class transgressions not only destroy their relationship, but also ruin the fictive performance—both the play and Sally fail because of her overidentification with the role.

The recuperation of the relationship coincides with both the restoration and loss of Shakespeare. When she returns to her old travelling troupe, her former boss seeks to restore her confidence by casting her as Juliet again and rehearsing with her. Persuaded by Serena's sister-in-law that Sally was not just tricking him into matrimony, Garth steps into the performance during the balcony scene—which Sally still cannot do because she can only think of him. Now he declares his love in Shakespearean language:

> " . . . and Juliet is the sun.
>   Arise, fair sun, and kill the envious moon."
> Sally froze, convinced her heartbreak was robbing her of her reason.
> Preston Walcott suddenly sounded like Garth.
> The rich, caressing voice continued:
>   "It is my lady, O, it is my love!
>   "O, that she knew she were!"
> Sally's eyes flew open. Garth stood before her.
>
> (Suson 1992, 214)

Reviving her Juliet not only restores the Shakespearean performance, but also occasions the loss of Sally's career to marriage.

Even more important, class as an issue becomes explicit, identified through the Shakespearean text and ostensibly banished by its enactment. He claims her for his wife, of course, but now she insists that the obstacles to their union are insuperable. Transforming the Montague/Capulet feud into a class conflict, she thinks that "just as Romeo and Juliet had been torn apart by feuding families, she and Garth could never close the chasm between social classes that separated them" (Suson 1992, 216). He finally convinces her by exposing the "flaw" of class differences in his preference of her over her identical twin, raised as a lady of quality and destined to bore him. Providentially, class becomes completely malleable: not only is the lower- class woman (Sally) naturally more interesting, lively, and intelligent without upper class nurture, but also that nurture readily gives the lower class woman (Serena) the characteristics of the upper class, however undesirable those characteristics might be. The twin mechanism thus offers multiple reassurances that those outside the highest level of the Regency class system (the ton) will prevail—they can either mimic the behaviors and pass as upper class or they can retain their "natural" lower-class liveliness and marry their way into higher status. That the readers are also inevitably outside these social codes offers another layer of fantasy and reassurance.

Significantly, this triumph over class boundaries rewrites *Romeo and Juliet* for Garth and Sally. Garth demands Sally's with Romeo's lines:

"You have not told me whether you will marry me, fair Juliet. 'Exchange thy love's faithful vow for mine.' "

" 'I give thee mine before thou didst request it.' " Sally tipped her head and smiled at him. "And like Juliet's for Romeo, my love for you is infinite."   (Suson 1992, 217)

This denouement uses *Romeo and Juliet*'s balcony scene: the hidden lover listening to his beloved and speaking when she does not expect it, her anxiety about his intentions (Sally first thinks that Garth offers her carte blanche as his mistress), the declarations and worries about obstacles, and "Romeo's" final, but redundant request that she offer her faithful vow (Sally has already told Garth several times that she loves him). Shakespeare's play becomes the discourse through which problems of class are articulated and apparently dismissed here.

In Suson's actress-novel, despite the acknowledged destruction of her promising career on the London stage, the only real quandary Sally seems to face is the loss of Garth. In *The Toast of the Town,* Margaret Evans Porter (1993) takes the career and self-sufficiency of the actress—and her future employment after marriage—much more fully into account. Her Flora completely resists losing her career and her financial independence. A nobleman falls for her when he sees her as Olivia in *Twelfth Night* and pursues her with Orsino's obsessiveness and Cesario's skill, but she refuses him until she has tired of the London theater scene and decides to write for the theatre instead. Isabella Gellée of Mary Balogh's *Christmas Belle* (1994) is a professional actress whose emotional life parallels and revises *Othello;* she finally manages to marry her noble lover because she could not identify with Desdemona nor behave as she did.[7] Suson's Sally is not as deeply involved in her career as these other actresses, but both class issues and their resolution through Shakespeare persist. Whereas these other novels explicitly revise the Shakespeare that they invoke, Suson's novel merely ends on the semi-ambiguous note that Garth and Sally love each other as Romeo and Juliet did. And we know what happened to them.

The actress-heroine's use of Shakespeare transgresses class structure because she shares knowledge with her noble, well-educated hero. Her familiarity with Shakespeare's plays echoes his and thus undercuts their class differences by establishing the actress as implicitly of a higher class than she first appears. The problems of financial differences, birth, and so forth become insignificant in the context of intellectual kinship that allies the actress with the hero through an emergent high culture registered in Shakespeare.

When Shakespeare explicitly mediates socially enforced *gender* differences in the Regency or historical romance, the heroine is frequently a version of a "bluestocking," an inappropriately well-educated woman often perceived as masculine and unmarriageable. In Joan Overfield's *A Spirited Bluestocking* (1992), the heroine is a self-identified intellectual, in part because she loves Shakespeare: "'And a bluestocking,' Mr. Sailing supplied eagerly. 'She was throwing Shakespeare and Milton at my head when she wasn't spouting Latin at her brother'" (30). The woman who quotes Shakespeare can be either extremely eccentric, like Kate Glyn of Michelle Martin's *The Hampshire Hoyden* (1993) or more discreetly odd like Deirdre Wheaton of Brenda Hiatt's *The Ugly Duckling* (1992). Such a heroine violates the social expectations of Regency upper crust; her intelligence, very often revealed by a knowledge of Shakespeare, sets her apart from the other women in her class. Consequently, these heroines may be acceptable by birth, but they appear as outsiders within their own social class and are often considered just as ineligible as the actress-heroines.

The bluestocking novels typically identify a gender double standard rather than class differences as the obstacle to romantic union; however, the heroine's struggle with gender discrimination that reserves intellect, scholarship, and published serious writing for men becomes a class issue as well as a gender problem. The heroine who quotes Shakespeare either emerges from a nonaristocratic lower class, like the actress, or she stands in exile within her class, as an intellectual when women were supposedly not concerned with study. In both cases, her knowledge of Shakespeare makes her a match for the hero, who typically heads the gender and class hierarchy. By restructuring gender obstacles as class differences, these novelists reveal a paradox at the heart of their use of Shakespeare: invoking his texts can raise *or* lower a heroine's status.

In a few of cases, he does both in the same novel, revealing his ideological function in mapping supposedly malleable class differences onto historically intractable gender distinctions. In Joan Wolf's *His Lordship's Mistress* (1982), Jessica O'Neill explicitly lowers her class position by becoming an actress to raise money without having to marry and suffer under the authority of a man she detests. Articulating her own rejection of Sir Henry Bolton in Juliet's violent rejection of Paris, Jessica establishes herself as an actress available to a protector, from whom she intends to get funds. Shakespeare becomes both the expression and the means for her self-imposed lower social position. As an actress, she engages the interest of the Earl of Linton who finds in her both a sexually available mistress and an intellectual equal. Her involvement with Shakespeare (first *Romeo and Juliet* and later *Macbeth*) provides the backdrop for his desire to marry her, thus also enabling her supposed class shift upwards.

However, the obvious "class shifting" soon turns out to be deeply intertwined with gender inequality. Though the Earl thinks her rejection of his proposal arises from class differences, Jessica is very much of his class. Her flight from him has more to do with gender disparity. More precisely different gender expectations become encoded as a class obstacle: the unmarried peer may take a mistress before marriage without harming his social status, but the unmarried lady may not take a lover without losing all her status and marriageability, even if her only lover has been the man who wishes to marry her. As *His Lordship's Mistress* reveals most pointedly, Shakespeare's conflicting functions as a mechanism for raising and lowering class positions ultimately disguises the actual problem: unequal social burdens and expectations for men and women.

Carla Kelly's *Miss Grimsley's Oxford Career* (1992) treats educational differences facing Regency men and women quite explicitly in terms of Shakespeare. As the internal cover blurb, with the bold title of "BEYOND THE BARD," puts it:

> Miss Ellen Grimsley looked upon Shakespeare as her supreme source of information and inspiration. She had learned how amusing love in disguise could be from *A Midsummer Night's Dream*. She had learned how beautiful young love could be from *Romeo and Juliet*. She had learned how ruthlessly ravening a man's lust could be from *Measure for Measure*.
>
> (Kelly 1992, Frontispiece)

All this learning is far more accurately portrayed in the novel. Miss Grimsley knows *Dream* well enough to realize that there are no disguises in it (except perhaps Bottom's unwilling one); the hero is as far from "ravening" as the Duke in *Measure*. The publicity, despite its inaccurate representation of both the plays and the novel, pitches Shakespeare's plays as precisely the stuff of the romance novel—but only with emendations.

In Kelly's novel, Ellen Grimsley, who yearns to be a student at Oxford, ends up learning embroidery and French at Miss Dignam's School rather than the geography and Shakespeare that she desires. In order to rescue her nonscholarly brother at Oxford, she agrees to don his robes, sneak into his tutorial on *A Midsummer Night's Dream,* and write his paper for him. Aided by James Gatewood, whom she takes to be a charity student, and provoked by a mysterious Shakespearean scholar, Lord Chesney (a.k.a. Gatewood), Ellen writes two research papers that her brother presents to considerable acclaim; one treats *Dream* and the other, more radically, *Measure for Measure,* a play that she must borrow from Gatewood because the material is inappropriate and unavailable for young ladies. These essays earn her brother thoroughly undeserved praise for "his" work and land Ellen in trouble because of the difficulties she undergoes, often cross-dressed, to gain access to the books and materials she needs.

Kelly's portrait of the constraints on Ellen enacts fictionally the lament Virginia Woolf (1929) offers in *A Room of One's Own.* Not only is Oxford's library unavailable to her, but she also suffers severe humiliation because she does not have a room of her own. As her brother goes off to deliver her third paper, her tale-bearing roommate at the school discovers her male clothes and promises to expose her behavior. So Ellen defiantly goes to hear her work read in Oxford commons. The results are not pleasant. She not only discovers that her charming friend Gatewood is actually the illustrious Lord Chesney, but she must also disclaim her own work publicly, announcing to the assembled men (who don't believe a woman could write such papers anyway) that she has only copied out the paper for her brother. She is also summarily thrown out of the lecture and banned from Oxford campus. The only bright spot, besides Gatewood's marriage proposal, has been her writing about Shakespeare's plays, finally, if surreptitiously, pursuing the scholarship she has been denied.

The readings that Ellen offers are only partially available in Kelly's novel, and *Measure for Measure* has the most bearing on the plot, since Ellen is constantly called upon to rescue her various brothers. In fact, by the end of the novel, even though she has been steadfastly resisting the proposals offered by Gatewood, her youngest brother sneaks to see her and beg Gatewood's intervention with their social-climbing father. From his comments to Gatewood, Ellen realizes suddenly that all the negotiations are really between the men—she is the convenient occasion for her male relatives to interact with a lord, and her sexual choice is irrelevant because influence belongs to men.

As Kelly (1992) explores the limited educational possibilities available to young female scholars, her novel offers as much Shakespeare as the actress-novels but concentrates on the heroine's thwarted academic ambitions rather than class differences or sexual dangers of the theater. Furthermore, Ellen's insights into the relative powerlessness of women who function as tokens of exchange between men male parallel the end of *Measure for Measure;* like Isabella, she does not instantly or obviously take up her allotted place as bride in the narrative. In fact she rejects the Lord who has manipulated her through disguising his rank and hiding as the poor scholar while he arranges for her work to be read and pursued. Her resistance offers a reworking of Isabella's dilemma when faced with the Duke's proposal. Though Ellen has only saved her plagiarist brother's reputation, her choice to humiliate herself for her brothers leads to a consideration of whether to marry Lord Chesney, despite his deception. She ultimately agrees when she realizes that he is as trapped as she in his public role as Duke without any-one among his family or friends who understands his scholarship.

Miss Grimsley's Oxford Career overtly frames Shakespeare as both the mark of patriarchal power (unavailable to women who wish to study) and the measure of Ellen's resistance and nascent feminism (she masters the texts that her privileged brother cannot). In this novel, like many others, Shakespeare becomes the method for overcoming class and gender obsta-cles between hero and heroine, as well as the historical distance between Regency characters and twentieth-century authors and readers. However, the strategy does not reify Shakespeare as the ultimate cultural authority, largely because it proves as necessary to rewrite the plays as to use them. In fact these novels either extend the emotional logic of the plays they invoke, as Kelly's novel (1992) does with Isabella's decision in *Measure,* or Gray's *Lady of Property* (1988) does with *Twelfth Night.* In some cases the novels completely revise the plots so that Romeo and Juliet survive (Suson's *Fair Imposter* 1992) or the heroine becomes the Hamlet figure (Deanna James' *Acts of Passion* [1992a] and Christina Dodd's *The Greatest Lover in England* [1994]).

As these examples demonstrate, while American romance novelists, often well-educated and demonstrably popular writers, use Shakespeare to display their literary credentials, they also freely adapt and change the plots and characters they employ in working through the class and gender obsta-cles in their particular subgenres. They explain characters' reactions more fully; they revise tragic endings that do not accord with the unions dictated by their genre; they transform plots and endings to augment the deficien-cies of the woman's part in Shakespeare. When Deanna James (1992a) claims Shakespeare as "the master writer of all time" and points out that she has modeled her plots for *Acts of Passion* (1992a) and *Acts of Love* (1992b) on Shakespearean five- act structure, she appears to be claiming a secondhand literary glory. However, the avowed adulation and mimicry of Shakespeare go hand in hand with her recasting of the role of Hamlet as a woman and her working through of the aftermath of revenge by revis-ing *The Tempest* in the second novel. These writers and readers *must* change Shakespeare to recover and foreground female perspectives silenced or lacking entirely.

On a superficial level, the familiar Otherness of Shakespeare and the authorial pleasures of proving one's high culture credentials make Shakespeare appealing to American romance novelists. His supply of available character types gives him further cachet. More subtly and significantly, however, his plays mediate class and gender obstacles for historical romance. Shakespeare within romance novels chronically both raises and lowers the heroine's social status. Knowing Shakespeare on the stage either establishes her as lower class or lowers her class, but, at the same time, her knowledge of Shakespeare enables her to marry into the aristocracy because she shares knowledge with the hero. In the bluestocking novels, the academic leanings of our heroine toward Shakespearean study lower her status and even render her ineligible, a spinster. At the same time, however, her knowledge matches the hero's, and her marriage to him invariably raises her social position and assures her independence—with his help. The question this paradoxical function raises is why Shakespeare so insistently mediates class, enabling changes of status. The answer is only partly that Shakespeare functions as both popular and high culture.

The more important reason is that Shakespeare enables romance novelists to rewrite patriarchal gender inequalities as class or status obstacles. The advantage to this strategy is that class differences can ostensibly be resolved through marriage; gender inequity cannot. In fact, marriage arguably reemphasizes gender hierarchy and inequality because only the man's authority over the heroine gives her access to the higher class/status position. As a result, only by revising the hero can the heroine use her marriage in pursuit of her intellectual and personal independence. Fortunately, the hero typically possesses all the features of high class (money, social position, and power) as well as features that he can be brought to understand as gender inequity (sexual adventuring that would definitively compromise the heroine and educational/professional opportunities that she lacks). The American romance novelist thus finds Shakespeare's class mediation especially enabling because class is assumed to be flexible and fantasies of transcending class are particularly potent.

If this narrative sounds like the romance novelist's relationship to Shakespeare, it is. As the romance heroine marries into the aristocracy, simultaneously resolving her status problems and apparently disabling gender discrimination, the romance novelist weds her work to Shakespeare's. His dual influence as popular culture and high elaborated art offers a mechanism for raising the status of popular romance fiction. This use of Shakespeare effectively disguises the gender bias that consistently underwrites dismissal of this particular genre from the canonical status now provisionally granted detective fiction and even science fiction. To use this smoke-screen, however, these novelists must also rework patriarchal biases in the plays that potentially expose gender inequalities of the most brutal sort. Sweet, savage Shakespeare, indeed.

Notes

1. *Titus Andronicus* 2.1.82–83 and 2.2.19. All references to Shakespeare's play come from The Norton Edition (1997).
2. Even in the Harlequin romance, Shakespeare surfaces. The best example in relation to Charnes' argument is Kay Thorpe's *Curtain Call* (1971). Thorpe's characters wrestle with interpretations of *Antony and Cleopatra* during a production of the play, and the hero handily anticipates Charnes' assertions about the romanticizing of the role of Cleopatra.
3. References to Shakespeare do appear in other subgenres, but not with the same startling consistency. Helpful members of RRL-A (Romance Readers Anonymous list) and other groups provided titles of regencies and historicals. Nonetheless, the 500+ romance novels I have read is a fraction of those published, so this argument addresses only genres where I have found the most examples.
4. See also Susan Baker's "Comic Material: 'Shakespeare' in the Classic Detective Story" (1994) in *Acting Funny: Comic Theory and Practice in Shakespeare's Plays,* ed. Fran Teague (Cranbury, NJ: Associated University Presses, Inc.).
5. Novy (1994) argues three principal appropriations: "first, using his cultural association with sympathy, second, rewriting his characters and plots with significant differences, and, third, developing characters' cultural and political location in part through their attitude toward Shakespeare" (138).
6. See R. Burt's *Unspeakable Shaxxxpeares* (New York: St. Martin's Press, 1998).
7. For a fuller analysis, see my "Romancing the Bard."

Works Cited

Balogh, M. 1994. *Christmas Belle.* New York: Signet.

Barlow, L. and J. A. Krentz. 1992. "Beneath the Surface: The Hidden Codes of Romance." In *Dangerous Men and Adventurous Women: Romance Writers on the Appeal of the Romance.* Ed. J. A. Krentz. Philadelphia: University of Pennsylvania Press.

Baker, S. 1994. "Comic Material: 'Shakespeare' in the Classic Detective Story." In *Acting Funny: Comic Theory and Practice in Shakespeare's Plays.* Ed. Fran Teague. Cranbury, NJ: Associated University Presses, Inc.

———1995. "Shakespearean Authority in the Classic Detective Story." *Shakespeare Quarterly* 46: 424–48.

Burt, R. 1998. *Unspeakable ShaXXXspeares.* New York: St. Martin's Press.

Charnes, L. 1992. "What's love got to do with it?" *Textual Practice* 6: 1–16.

Dodd, C. 1994. *The Greatest Lover in England.* New York: HarperCollins.

Evans, M. P. 1993. *The Toast of the Town.* New York, Signet.

Gray, V. 1988. *A Lady of Property.* New York: Signet.

Hiatt, B. 1992. *The Ugly Duckling.* New York: Harlequin Books.

James, Deanna. 1992a. *Acts of Passion.* New York: Zebra Books.

———. 1992b. *Acts of Love.* New York: Zebra Books.

Kelly, C. 1992. *Miss Grimsley's Oxford Career.* New York: Signet.

Kinsale, L. 1992. "The Androgynous Reader." In *Dangerous Men and Adventurous Women: Romance Writers on the Appeal of the Romance.* Ed. J. A. Krentz. Philadelphia: University of Pennsylvania Press.

Krentz, J. A. 1992. "Introduction." In *Dangerous Men and Adventurous Women: Romance Writers on the Appeal of the Romance.* Ed. J. A. Krentz. Philadelphia: University of Pennsylvania Press.

Martin, M. 1993. *The Hampshire Hoyden.* New York: Fawcett Crest Books.

Modleski, T. 1982. *Loving with a Vengeance: Mass Produced Fantasies for Women.* Hampton, Connecticut: Archon Books.

Novy, M. 1994. *Engaging Shakespeare: Responses of George Eliot and Other Women Novelists.* Athens: University of Georgia Press.

———, ed. 1990. *Women's Revisions of Shakespeare.* Urbana: University of Illinois Press. Radway, J. 1984, rpt. 1991. *Reading the Romance.* Chapel Hill: University of North Carolina Press.

Osborne, L. 1999. "Romancing the Bard." In *Shakespeare and Appropriation.* Eds. Christy Desmet and Robert Sawyer. New York: Routledge.

Overfield, Joan. 1992. *A Spirited Bluestocking.* New York: Zebra Books.

Porter, M. E. 1993. *Toast of the Town.* New York: Signet.

Rasley, A. 1994. Poetic Justice. New York: Zebra Books.

Seidel, K. G. 1992. "Judge Me by the Joy I Bring." In *Dangerous Men and Adventurous Women.* Ed. J. A. Krentz. Philadelphia: University of Pennsylvania Press.

Shakespeare, William. 1997. *The Norton Shakespeare.* Ed. S. Greenblatt, K. E. Maus, J. E. Howard, and W. Cohen. New York: W. W. Norton & Co.

Snitnow, A. B. 1983. "Mass Market Romance: Pornography for Women is Different." In *Powers of Desire.* Ed. A. Snitnow, C. Stansell, and S. Thompson. New York: Monthly Review Press.

Summerville, M. 1992. *The Improper Playwright.* New York: Signet.

Suson, M. 1992. The Fair Imposter. New York: Avon.

Thorpe, K. 1971. *Curtain Call.* New York: Harlequin Enterprises.

Thurston, C. 1987. *The Romance Revolution.* Urbana: University of Illinois Press.

Veryan, P. 1995. Never Doubt I Love. New York: St. Martin's Press.

"Weddings: Dressing for Your Starring Part." *Detroit Free Press,* March 1, 1987, Special section.

Wolf, J. 1982. *His Lordship's Mistress.* New York: Signet.

Woolf, V. 1929. *A Room of One's Own.* New York: Harcourt, Brace.

Chapter 7

No Holes Bard: Homonormativity and the Gay and Lesbian Romance with *Romeo and Juliet*

Richard Burt

"Romeo, O, Romeo, wherefore art thou Rome(hom)o?"

The gay and lesbian performance history of *Romeo and Juliet* ranges across various forms of mass media, including film, comics, and novels. Perhaps most obviously, the play has attracted the attention of several gay film directors, George Cukor (1934), Franco Zeffirelli (1968), and, most recently, Baz Luhrmann (1996). Somewhat less well-known is the fact that the gay film director Todd Haynes' first film, made when he was nine, was *Romeo and Juliet,* inspired by the Zeffirelli version (see Holden 1998, 13). (Haynes played all the parts). The gay actor Laurence Harvey played Romeo in a film version of the play directed by Renato Castelanni (1954). There are also a number of gay and lesbian inflected spin-offs, some familiar, some obscure, including *Romanoff and Juliet* (dir. Peter Ustinov 1954) and Leonard Bernstein's *West Side Story* (dir. Robert Wise and Jerome Robbins 1953), the cult film *Tromeo and Juliet* (dir. Lloyd Kaufman 1996), in which Mercutio is gay and the Nurse lesbian, and two gay male pornographic film spin-offs *Romeo and Julian: A Love Story* (dir. Sam Abdul 1993) and *Voyage á Venise* (dir. Jean Daniel Cadinot 1986).[1] Ralf Koenig's German "graphic" novel (of the soft-core porn variety) entitled *Iago Comic* (1998) tells the story two gay actors in Shakespeare's troupe who have love affairs with a black man, conflating *Othello* with *Romeo and Juliet.* *Romeo and Juliet* has also been cited in recent gay-themed mainstream mall films such as *In and Out* (dir. Frank Oz 1997) and *The Object of My Affection* (dir. Nicholas Hytner 1998). And in 1998, an all male cast of four actors performed off-Broadway a widely admired theatrical retelling set, a la Peter Weir's *Dead Poets Society* (1986), at a boy's Roman Catholic prep school entitled *Shakespeare's R & J,* and the adaptation then went into film production.[2] Gay director Franco Zeffirelli's semi-autobiographical film *Tea With Mussolini* (1999) has Zeffirelli's surrogate, young Luca (Charlie Lucas, II) act out part of the balcony scene with his caretaker and mother figure (Joan Plowright). There are lesbian recodings as well, including a porn spin-off entitled *Where the Boys Aren't 10* (dir. F. J. Lincoln 1998), adapted from *West Story Story* (rival gangs the Jets and the Sharks are here the Blondes and the Brunettes), Naomi Mitchison's science fiction novel *Solution Three* (1975) and Kasi Lemmon's film *Eve's Bayou* (1997).[3] Vincenzo Bellini's bel canto opera adaptation *I Capuleti e i Montechhi* (1830) casts a woman mezzo soprano as Romeo and is hence open to being read as a lesbian romance.[4] And the gender-bending comedy *It's Pat* (Dir. Adam Bernstein 1994), based on the Pat character (Julia Sweeney) of *Saturday Night Live* fame, makes two references to *Romeo and Juliet.*[5]

How are we to account for this rather extensive gay and lesbian performance history of *Romeo and Juliet?* And while we might expect *Romeo and Juliet* to have been of interest to gays and lesbians when same-sex desire was still closeted or when it was still, as in Oscar Wilde's case, a practice that could not yet speak the name "homosexual," we might wonder why the gay and lesbian romance has persisted well after the need for a masked way of expressing gay and lesbian desire has significantly dissipated, at least when it comes to an increasingly queer-positive, mass-marketed cinema, theater, and fiction.6 One way to address these questions would be to follow out the logic of queer theory and identify and uncloset a gay subtext, usually centered in Mercutio's desire for Romeo (Porter 1988; Donaldson 1990; Smith 1991), or to "queer" the play by showing how heterosexual desire in the play is "sodomitical" (Goldberg 1994).[7] One would write a history of gay and lesbian performances of *Romeo and Juliet* in terms of the celluloid closet, pre- and post-Stonewall versions marking gay and lesbian desire more or less openly, more or less explicitly.

Such a history might have its detractors, however. The gay and lesbian reception of *Romeo and Juliet* might give some queer theorists pause, given that the reception would seem to limit the representation of gay and lesbian desire to closeted modes: that is to say, it would seem to do exactly the reverse of what queer theory does, reading homosexual desire in terms of heterosexual desire, upholding heterosexual romance as the norm, homosexual romance the failed imitation. (It is worth noting that the queer filmmaker Monika Treut has been highly critical of lesbian audience demands for Hollywood-style lesbian romances.[8]) Queer theory attempts to divorce gay and lesbian sexuality from heterosexuality, denying the latter the status as original (which the former, as a copy, fails to imitates properly) so that gender norms can be resignified, as Judith Butler (1991) has it, in parodic and therefore supposedly subversive ways (such as drag). Moreover, queer theory seeks to rehabilitate promiscuous, anonymous, and explicit public sex as a "counterintimacy" (Berlant and Warner 1998) or, in Leo Bersani's more radical terms, an anticommunitarian "relationality" (1994, 76), to be opposed to the privatized intimacy of the heterosexual domestic married couple.[9] In these ways, queer theory contributes to a Foucauldian and Habermasian-inflected critique of what Michael Warner (1993) calls "heteronormativity."[10] Berlant and Warner (1998) offer this economic definition of the term:

> By heteronormativity we mean the institutions, structures of understanding, and practical orientation that make heterosexuality seem not only coherent—that is, organized, as a sexuality—but privileged. . . . Heteronormativity is . . . a concept distinct from heterosexuality. One of the most conspicuous differences is that it has no parallel, unlike heterosexuality, which organizes homosexuality as its opposite. (548, n1)

Queer-identified critics of the Renaissance who follow out this critique typically criticize feminist critics of the Renaissance for imposing gender on sexuality, regarding the homoeroticism of the boy actor in terms of the boy's ability to mime femininity, thus reconstituting (in homophobic and heterosexist fashion) homoeroticism as heteroeroticism (Traub 1992, 93–94; Goldberg 1992, 105–43; Wilson 1998).

Gay and lesbian versions of *Romeo and Juliet,* in contrast to the aims of queer theory, take a heterosexual married couple to be the norm and measure of successful, happy same-sex erotic relations. One might argue that, like films such as Cukor's *Camille* (1936), Shakespeare's *Romeo and Juliet* and its spin-offs are less of interest to gays and lesbians because of any same-sex material that may be "outed" than because its story of forbidden love between a heterosexual couple serves as a means by which (forbidden) same-sex erotic relations might be safely expressed (with the death of the principal characters serving pathetically as the inevitable punishment for the expression of gay desire). The persistence of gay and lesbian interest in Shakespeare's play after Stonewall might be regarded, then, as the unfortunate reinstallation of an internalized homophobic, closeted mode of representing gay and lesbian desire in which that desire must always, like Romeo at the Capulet ball, be masked, and in which the fulfillment of that desire, like Romeo and Juliet's, is lethal. To buttress this account, one could point out that even the gay and lesbian spin-offs, which conclude happily, mimic heterosexual spin-offs, which tend to conclude the same way. The gay and lesbian spin-offs do not simply mime what I take to be the master plot of heterosexual romance but, more precisely, mime the heterosexual reception of Shakespeare's tragedy, turning it into a comedy, a generic transformation that extends as far back in heterosexual culture as Fanny Burney's *Cecilia* (1782) and Charles Dickens' *Nicholas Nickleby* (1839), and which has continued on into contemporary harlequin romance novels like Natalie Bishop's *A Love Like Romeo and Juliet* (1993) and mainstream films such as *Mississippi Masala* (dir. Mira Nair 1992), *Valley Girl* (dir. Martha Coolidge 1986), *Love Is All There Is* (dir. Joseph Bologna 1996), and James Cameron's *Titanic* (1997).[11]

However persuasive such an account of the gay and lesbian reception of *Romeo and Juliet* might be, it fails to acknowledge the ways in which that reception offers resistance to the typical moves to queer Shakespeare, and it is this resistance that I find compelling.[12] Rather than either dismiss the extensive gay and lesbian performance history of *Romeo and Juliet* as regressively fixated on heterosexual norms, a homophobic disavowal of homosexuality or, alternatively, celebrate those adaptations that might be said to have brought out the play's "gay subtext" or queer, antiheteronormative, sodomitical meanings, I wish to consider the history of gay and lesbian adaptations of *Romeo and Juliet* as a same-sex utopian impulse, a dream of what I call *homonormativity*. Far from mimicking heteronormative norms in order to resignify and possibly subvert them, these replays of *Romeo and Juliet* give expression to a gay utopian fantasy whereby a no longer forbidden practice of gay male or lesbian sex is represented as "normal," heterosexualized, that is, according to the (queer) conventions of the genre of romance fiction.

At stake in this homormative performance history is a dream of designifying gender and hence sexuality as well, not of resignifying gender in some subversive way. The dream is of a world in which gender doesn't mean and hence doesn't matter; hence, sexuality doesn't mean or matter either. Homonormativity is not, in other words, about the assimilation of gays to "normal" or "average" heterosexuals (as in gay marriage) that many conservative or liberal gay commentators (Sullivan 1997) have called for; nor is the dream a matter of "degaying" gayness, as Leo Bersani (1994) puts it, erasing it and making it again invisible. Whereas what I have called "Shakesqueer cinema" (Burt 1998, 29–76) disrupts the categories by which gay and straight sexuality are legible, homonormative Shakespeare adaptations and spin-offs evade the same categories either by seeking to be unlegible as gay or by designifying gender difference.[13]

Rather than displaying merely a conservative, regressive gay interest in heterosexual romance, homonormative gay and lesbian performances of *Romeo and Juliet* throw into relief the limits of current strategies to gay or queer a given text. In assuming that same-sex desire has to be (re)signified, made legible or risk lethal erasure, queer theorists inadvertently confine the queering of gay desire to a parodic, campy troping, whether subversive or not, of heteronormative culture. Whereas queer theorists might want to deconstruct heteronormative culture and queer critique by making homonormativity just a another version of kitsch—a nineteenth-century construction of domesticity (so that everything is queer)—one could argue that the opposite is actually the case: homonormativity shows that a queer (public sex) scene is itself just as liable to being regarded as cliched and predictable as any scene of domestic romance (so that everything is normal). I want to argue, however, not that homonormativity is merely a deconstruction of heteronormativity and queer critique but that same-sex desire is inevitably homonormative because it is embedded in gender difference. Gay and lesbian desire, insofar as it is legible, is thus bound to heteronormative culture. The homonormative move to designify rather than resignify desire and gender can best be understood as a way of addressing the fact that gay and lesbian desire will always be read, insofar as it is signified and read at all, through the lens of heteronormativity.

Setting Shakespeare Straight

Before examining how homonormative *Romeo and Juliet* adaptations and spin-offs designify gender and how that designification paradoxically enables the entry of gay desire into representation rather than its erasure, we need first to understand how both they and heteronormative replays deconstruct the opposition between heteronormative culture and queer critique. The dream of transcending gender is, to be sure, utopian. To represent gayness and lesbianism as a norm seems, on the face of it, impossible to do without introducing a corrosive comic irony that would always introduce quotations marks around the word "normal" when it comes to homosexuality. Consider, for example, Naomi Mitchison's science-fiction novel *Solution Three,* a story about a future society in which everyone is either gay or lesbian, people reproduce through cloning, and only "deviants" are heterosexual. One class of deviants, the "Professorials," are "normalized" through literature:

The essential was to get at the females and so much more could be done through a slanting of their favourite reading. But the Professorials tended to like literature of the kind which was fixed and could not be slanted, although much critical work was being done on Shakespeare, Dante, the Kama Sutra and in fact all the classics. There had also been a steady build up of the already appropriate authors, from Plato, Proust, Gide, Cavafy, Forster and many others. The excitement of finding the hidden Leonardo note-book! (1975, 23)

Shakespeare (and nearly all canonical authors) are presumptively heterosexual; the humor of this passage arises from the fact that he has to be made gay. Gay readings of canonical figures are marked as such by their "slanting."

Similar humor arises when a "normal" lesbian character named Lilac (who is dismayed by her heterosexual fantasies) speculates on her own biological origins before musing on *Romeo and Juliet:*

What would it be like to have a really [*sic*] child with one's own genes? But that would mean—before one could do it—this thing with a man—no, one couldn't! Even to think of it made her a little queasy about the stomach. And yet her Mum must have—with her Dad. Ever so long ago before people knew. But they can't have liked it. Well, one couldn't. Or could one have long ago? There were some of the old books she had read. Shakespeare. But of course she knew that Romeo was just as much a girl as Juliet. It was only that in those cruel times there had to be this pretense. (91–92)

Lilac here reveals the labor done to the classics to produce what seems to be a kind of "compulsory homosexuality," to reverse Adrienne Rich's terms. The comic ironies attendant upon imagining a world in which heterosexuality is actively discouraged and homosexuality is the norm would seem to subvert any claim for the utopian status of such a world.

If Shakespeare's gayness cannot be imagined as normal without producing comic effects, we ought not to forget that labor also has to be performed on *Romeo and Juliet* to make it receivable for heterosexual culture, often producing its own kinds of humor and irony.[14] This labor involves not only turning the tragedy into a comedy but keeping Shakespeare, when a literary character, straight. Consider the genre of the romance. While the romance, typically produced for a putatively female audience, tends to leave any hint of homosexuality unraised, as it were, Shakespeare as a character in romance fiction and films almost inevitably introduces it, thereby calling into question the extent to which *Romeo and Juliet* can be held up as a model of heterosexual romance.

We may pursue this point by turning now to two romances that seek to reconcile Shakespeare as character (whose sexuality is a problem) with the romance of *Romeo and Juliet,* an early twentieth-century novel, *Shakespeare's Sweetheart* (1903) by Sara Hawks Sterling, and the well-received film, *Shakespeare* (dir. John Madden, Jr. 1998). Sterling, in true Edwardian fashion, makes Anne Hathaway the heroic narrator of a romantic and sometimes quite painful (for Anne) story of her marriage to Shakespeare. *Romeo and Juliet* is the model for their relationship. Shakespeare woos Anne by citing Romeo's line and by climbing up a balcony to her window:

> It was a young man's voice that I heard, mellow and joyous:
> "Her beauty hangs upon the cheek of night
> Like a rich jewel in an Ethiope's ear;
> Beauty too rich for use, for earth too dear."
> At the same instant the speaker came in sight. He looked up and saw me in the window, framed about with blossoming vines. I knew him at once. It was young Will Shakespeare. . . . As for him, he bared his head and bent it low, just breathing words which I afterwards found were those of his Italian Romeus when he looked on the love of his life: "It is my lady! Oh, it is my love!" (31; 32)

Later, after Anne follows Shakespeare to London (without his knowledge) disguised as a boy and joins his acting company in order to determine whether or not he has actually left her for another woman, she plays Juliet to his Romeo. Yet the distance between these two versions of *Romeo and Juliet* immediately shows how far away Romeo and Juliet's love is from Will and Anne's. As she says of the performance:

> The rehearsal began . . . as this was Will's own play, he himself was to act Romeus. How bittersweet this last arrangement made the part of Juliet to me! Sometimes it seemed as if I were reliving my own love story. Had it not also begun in rapture and ended in despair? Again, the contrast between Will's falsehood and the faith of Romeus would cut me to the heart so deep that I found my double part passing difficult to play. (127)

The distance between person and theatrical part is so great that Anne fears she may go mad, and as if to confirm that, Burbadge [*sic*], after complimenting her on her first performance as Juliet, invites her to consider playing the role of Ophelia (186).

To be sure, the novel closes with a court performance of *Romeo and Juliet.* As it turns out, Shakespeare has been faithful to his wife, only wooing the Dark Lady, a courtesan referred to as "the Countess," for his friend, Count William. Anne and Will reunite happily. So by the time of the court-ordered performance (at which Shakespeare knows that Caesario is Anne), the passion of the actors Anne and Will mirrors the passion of the characters Juliet and Romeo:

> And of all my glad remembrances I have locked within my memory, there is none more delightsome than that afternoon at the palace when, my sex unknown, I played a double part before the Queen and the court. And those love scenes with Will, formerly such torture, what delight they were now! . . . "Let love devouring death do what he dare, / It is enough I may but call her mine." So Will, as Romeus, cried with passion, thinking of me, I knew, and in my heart the words devoutly were echoed. (255)

Yet in closing the gap between historical and literary characters, Sterling introduces a significant degree of homoeroticism through the female characters, miming the plot of *Twelfth Night,* with Anne as Caesario and the Countess as Olivia. When Shakespeare sends Anne/Caesario off to obtain a necklace from the Countess for Shakespeare, the Countess, like Olivia in *Twelfth Night,* falls in love with the messenger rather than the one who sent him: "With a sudden, sweeping movement, she was beside me, and ere I was aware of her intention she kissed me lightly on the mouth. 'I have kissed thee on the lips,' she whispered. 'Has woman ever done the like before?'" (171). The Countess' love for Caesario continues even after his/her secret has been discovered:

> She came toward us, and gave Will her hand to kiss. He bent over it obediently. Then suddenly she leaned forward, and once again, for the last time, her lips touched mine. "Farewell, my shadow love," she said, smiling sombrely, "and farewell, Mistress Shakespeare. Love and loyalty are not altogether dreams, though I have thought them so. Your secret is safe—Caesario?" (233–34)

Similarly, the royal female gaze of Queen Elizabeth disturbs Anne's account of her happy reunion with Shakespeare in the court performance of *Romeo and Juliet,* as Elizabeth's gaze focuses on Anne/Juliet in a way that mirrors the Countess' homoerotic attention to Anne/Caesario:

> The Queen had been watching me with special interest from the beginning. . . . When . . . Juliet drank the Friar's potion . . . the Queen's gaze again met mine. . . . The play drew near its close . . . but I felt the Queen's

bright, steady eyes still upon me. A few moments later, while I searched for Romeus' dagger, I noted that her gaze yet intently followed all my actions. (256–57)

Unlike the Countess, however, Queen Elizabeth sees through Anne's disguise. Yet instead of straightening things out, the disclosure of Anne's gender takes a queer form as Elizabeth repeats the Countess' earlier gesture of kissing Caesario on the lips: "She bent forward in stately fashion, and kissed me on the mouth. 'There Mistress Shakespeare,' she went on, 'thou canst say until thy dying day that thou bearest a Queen's kiss upon thy lips'" (258). Drag permits Anne and other female characters to feel and experience desire for other women. Sterling also departs from its *Twelfth Night*-based subplot by making the ending of her novel significantly less heteronormative than Shakespeare's comedy. Unlike Olivia, the Countess' homoerotic attraction to Viola/Caesario is not redirected to a heterosexual object choice. The Countess does not marry but remains single, with Count William as a friend rather than lover.

Shakespeare in Gay Love

The recent film *Shakespeare in Love* in many respects is a rewriting of Sterling's novel: it similarly combines material from *Romeo and Juliet* and *Twelfth Night* and also includes Elizabeth I (Judi Dench) as a character. When the film begins, Shakespeare is supposed to be writing a play called *Romeo and Ethel, the Pirate's Daughter*. But he has both writer's block and is sexually impotent (he lives apart from his estranged wife and is unhappy with his mistress Rosalind, who he discovers *in flagrante* with Richard Burbage). Things begin to move creatively for Shakespeare, however, when he falls in love with an aristocratic woman named Viola de Lessups (Gwyneth Paltrow). Their love becomes the inspiration for *Romeo and Juliet*. Like Romeo and Juliet, the two lovers are star-crossed: Shakespeare is married, and Viola is betrothed to an aristocrat, Lord Wessex (Colin Firth), who plans to take her to Virginia. The film redoes the balcony scene from the play with Shakespeare wooing Viola, calling to her from below as she says from the balcony "Romeo, Romeo, a young man from Verona." In one sequence, Shakespeare and Viola have sex in bed while delivering lines from the aubade scene, and in a subsequent and celebrated sequence, scenes of the lovers kissing behind the stage curtain are intercut with scenes of a rehearsal of the play. Functioning, happy heterosexuality is thus made tantamount to literary creativeness: performing as a heterosexual enables

Shakespeare to perform as a writer, bring to fruition the plays we recognize as Shakespeare's.

Yet the film complicates any easy pairing of Shakespeare and Viola to Romeo and Juliet by introducing a great deal of "queer" material. I find it difficult to tell whether the film wants to closet questions about Shakespeare's sexuality or "out" its censorship of such questions, a censorship one presumes the makers found necessary to give the film such mainstream appeal. One the hand, the fact that Viola, like her *Twelfth Night* namesake, is given to cross-dressing, disturbs the equation of literary creativity and well-oiled heterosexual desire.[15] When Viola auditions for the part of Romeo, for example, she fools even Shakespeare into believing she is a boy. In the first sequence discussed above, Viola reads Romeo's lines and Shakespeare reads Juliet's, and in the second sequence wonderfully implies an equation of same-sex desire and heterosexual desire, as shots of a very short-haired Juliet as Romeo, complete with moustache, beard, and bean bag penile prosthesis, kissing Shakespeare are intercut with a very Viola as Juliet rehearsing with a boy playing Juliet. On the other hand, this gender confusion is "straightened" out in the film's conclusion when the play is performed on stage with Shakespeare as Romeo and Viola as Juliet. Moreover, Marlowe is hardly recognizable as gay. There are no boys or tobacco about.

Though some might argue that the film contains potentially disruptive gay material, the argument that the play draws attention to its own censorship seems to me just as compelling. Even after the final performance of *Romeo and Juliet,* gender confusion persists: the Master of the Revels, who has been alerted that the actor playing Romeo is really a girl, mistakes the man playing the Nurse for a woman. Moreover, Shakespeare is indebted to Marlowe for crucial elements of the play, including Mercutio, and if the film wanted to closet Marlowe, why cast the "out" gay actor Rupert Everett to play him? And one could argue that Shakespeare is more gay than Marlowe, remarking of his gay rival in a stereotypically bitchy manner: "Lovely waistcoat. Shame about the poetry."

Far from serving as an exemplary model of heteronormativity, then, Shakespeare's presence as a character in romance films and novels like the ones I have discussed suggest that Shakespeare and his plays are hardly a normative ideal when it comes to heterosexual culture. The point holds for *Romeo and Juliet* as a marker of romantic failure and/or sexual transgression in all genres of mass media. In *Lucas* (dir. David Seltzer 1986), for example, a male *wunderkind* named Lucas (Corey Haim) falls in love with a kind, friendly girl in high school named Maggie (Kerri Green) who does not reciprocate his desire for her, and he explains the failure to another girl, Rina (Wynonna Ryder), who is in love with him, by saying that his story is not like *Romeo and Juliet*.[16] And if "Romeo" frequently serves as a signifier of young, pure love, the name also often signifies a predatory, Casanova-like seducer of women, and references to this understanding of Romeo crop up frequently in discussions of sexual harassment, as in Anne Bernay's *Professor Romeo* (1989), a novel about a Harvard Psychology professor accused (legitimately) of sexually harassing some of his students, a reference in a women's support group to Romeo as a stalker when under Juliet's balcony in the film *Jerry Maguire* (dir. Cameron Crowe 1996); and Elise Title's *Romeo* (1996), a thriller about a serial killer "who'll seduce you to death." Julie Beard in *The Romance of the Rose* (1998) has a young foppish character recite, usually incorrectly, lines from Romeo and from Juliet as he tries unsuccessfully to woo the heroine. It's hardly an accident that Monica Lewinsky thought of *Romeo and Juliet* when composing her personal ad meant for President Bill Clinton's eyes.[17] Her citation of the play is of course meant to license adultery.[18] Similarly, in Frank Oz's film *In and Out* (1997), the forbidden love of Romeo and Juliet is a model for a love between a teacher and her (former) student. And according to Nancy Spungen's mother, Deborah, the "press portrayed Sid [Vicious] and Nancy as Romeo and Juliet in black leather" (1983, 273).

Passing as Romeo and Juliet

Having seen how both homonormative and heteronormative versions of *Romeo and Juliet* call into question the opposition between queer critique and heteronormative cultural practices, we are now in a position to examine how homonormative replays represent gay desire through the designification of gender difference. In saying that heterosexual replays fail to make *Romeo and Juliet* a heteronormative romance, I do not mean to imply that this labor is symmetrical or equivalent to the labor of gaying Shakespeare's play. I do mean, however, that the inevitable failure to make a gay or lesbian version of *Romeo and Juliet* seem "normal" is tied to the problem of signifying gay desire. The very legibility of lesbian desire in *Solution Three*, for example, is what enables the novel's satire of a futuristic world in which only same-sex couples are regarded as normal. Making gay and lesbian desire meaningful limits its representation to parody, camp, kitsch, all of which would be reduced to being either "subversive" or homophobic. This limitation arises precisely because the legibility of gay and lesbian desire is bound to the legibility of gender difference (same-sex desire equals, quite obviously, same gender). The range of effects produced by homonormative spin-offs of *Romeo and Juliet* is, however, quite extensive, precisely because it seeks to free gay desire from legible meanings made available by gender. That range of effects implicitly challenges, I suggest, two crucial assumptions queer theorists make about the relation between the normative and the queer: first, that gay and straight sex are securely legible in so far as they are produced as normative (their legibility can be disrupted by being queered), and, second, that sex is *the* sign of gay desire since the literal, explicit embodiment of that desire (in porn and elsewhere) is precisely what homophobes cannot accept and seek to forbid and erase wherever possible.[19] The degree to which a given performance is queer would be measured by its sexual explicitness, pornography being perhaps the most queer form of representation. Yet homonormativity complicates this account of the normative and the queer insofar as its response to the always indirect representation of gay and lesbian desire through heterosexuality is to move either toward the unlegible or to the designified (desire is universalized, moved outside of a specific gender).

To understand this complication, we may turn first to a version of *Romeo and Juliet* by the closeted director, George Cukor. The usual approach to a film like Cukor's would be to read it either as closeted or as (perhaps obliquely) marked as gay. To be sure, the film lends itself to either critical approach. On the one hand, the film seems to disavow gayness altogether. Indeed, as a casualty of the closet and Hays Code censorship (*Romeo and Juliet* was made in 1936, two years after the Code came into effect), George Cukor might seem to confirm some readers in the view that homonormative romance is really internalized homophobia. Cukor frequently portrayed homosexuals in homophobic terms (McGilligan 1994, 115); he could imagine gay sexuality only through female characters; and he went into the closet as a director (Levy 1994, 49; McGilligan 1991, 114; Ehrenstein 1998, 72–80). As Patrick McGilligan writes in his biography of Cukor, *A Double Life:*

> There were certain pockets of the movie business where homosexuality thrived; among the creative crafts—sketch and design, decoration and sets, costume and makeup—it was almost ghettoized. However, at the top of everything in Hollywood, in creative authority, stood the director, among whose first rank there was only one homosexual—this "woman's director." Other homosexual directors, distinctly second rank, were more flamboyant about their sexual orientation: the horror specialist James Whale was "obvious," widely dubbed "The Queen of Hollywood." (1991, 115)

The comparison with James Whale, remembered chiefly for *Frankenstein* and *Bride of Frankenstein,* makes clear that Cukor chose to go into the closet, and a recent film about Whale entitled *Gods and Monsters* (dir. Bill Condon 1998), with Ian McKellen as a Shakespeare-citing Whale, makes much of the contrast between the way the two directors expressed their sexuality.[20] Cukor might be regarded as so closeted, then, that his *Romeo and Juliet* might seem not to be marked by gayness at all. Mercutio (John Barrymore), for example, is pointedly made heterosexual: he regularly flirts with the local single women. As a so-called "woman's director," Cukor's identification might be thought to be cross-gendered, with Juliet, not Romeo.

Alternatively, one could point to a number of features in Cukor's *Romeo and Juliet* as signs of its gayness. Gay desire is marked in this film not, as in his *Camille,* through the presence of gay stars (in contrast to Greta Garbo and Robert Taylor, Leslie Howard and Norma Shearer were both straight), nor by a subtext introduced by parts the principal actors had played in previous films, nor, as in Zeffirelli's film version, by a gaze that is directed more at Romeo's naked body than Juliet's.[21] It is marked rather by the set design (the sets were the most expensive ever for a production of the play [see McGilligan 1994, 378]), particularly the balcony and aubade scenes, along with lighting and music that make for a notably idealized view of Romeo and Juliet. The English and gay design consultant Oliver Messel was brought over to Hollywood at considerable expense to give the production a gauzy revue look.[22] The night Romeo and Juliet consummate their marriage, their union is represented first by a kiss on the balcony and then by a turn away from Juliet's bedroom (into which the lovers withdraw) up to the sky. The consummation scene is accompanied by the music of a gay composer, the famous opening theme from Tchaikovsky's "Pathetique" (Symphony No. 6 in B Minor, Op. 74). This music continues past the kiss in a stunning montage of dissolving shots (taken outside the bedroom) of the garden, the sky, and a fountain, followed by shots of birds as the night turns to day. In this montage, images of nature function as metonyms of the lovers' desires. This very substitution of outside, "innocent" nature for an unrepresentable consummation happening off-screen behind closed doors has the effect, however, of also suggesting that heterosexuality is anything but natural; rather, heterosexual desire is rather highly conventional and artificial, its representation repressively codified.[23] The film's gayness is also marked, one could argue, by the casting of actors much too old for their parts, most obviously a middle-aged Leslie Howard (44 at the time), and by Howard's death register, a wish registered by the fact that he rarely looks at Shearer and stops doing so altogether after the aubade scene. One could also point to the film's reception history. Cukor's version, not Zeffirelli's, was the model for the gay-inflected *Tromeo and Juliet,* and close-ups of Howard and Shearer from the film also showed up on television screens in the rap duet Sylk E Fyne's music video "Romeo and Juliet" that aired on Black Entertainment Television (BET) in 1997.

Yet what is more interesting about Cukor's film than whether it tries to mark itself as gay or disavow the marks of its (perhaps unconscious) gayness is the way the film passes as straight so that any knowledge of gay desire that it secretes comes as a surprise to its audiences. By making knowledge of gay desire a surprise, Cukor's film might be thought to resist the typically homophobic strategies (that have persisted well after Stonewall) for policing gay desire. As D. A. Miller (1998) writes in his book on the Broadway musical:

> Not only does a dread of being caught, not to say taken, by surprise where male homosexuality is concerned—which as matters stand can hardly be anything other than a dread of what will already have occurred—seem to incite the entire multiform social will to knowledge of an entity called "the gay man" . . . , it also tends to put such knowledge, be it popular or academic, homophobic or progressive, in the service of a mere knowingness whose only aim is, by reducing him to a set of signs, to display, amulet-like, its own mastery of reading them. . . . So those of us in whom this experience is still being lived remain not far from where we were before: feeling if anything more forsaken now that everyone knows what it signified than when no one did (for we shared in the ignorance as we cannot share in a knowledge that ignores what Barthes calls the "obtuse" dimension of the signifier). (1998, 19–20)

Cukor's desexualization of the heterosexual, who are limited to kisses in which Juliet is on the bed and Romeo kneels next to her, one foot on the floor (in accordance with the repressive Hays Code), paradoxically collaborates with cinema censorship in order to install a gay fantasy about romance that resists such homophobic censorship precisely by passing as heterosexual.

Masked Balls

If making gay desire unlegible presents one problem with homonormativity, namely, its virtual reclosing of same-sex desire (masking it as heterosexual to the point of erasing it), two gay male pornographic *Romeo and*

Juliet spin-offs, *Romeo and Julian* and *Carnival in Venice,* might seem to present the same problem even more forcefully in inverse, seeming to confirm the notion that homonormative romance is at best a heterosexist mode of representing gay male desire, since gay desire is made legible only through a heterosexual couple. In my view, however, these porn spin-offs complicate queer theory's critique of heteronormativity by deconstructing an opposition between romance as normative and pornography as queer. Homonormativity in these replays of *Romeo and Julian* is not about making gay desire unlegible as it is about normalizing that desire by dissolving gender difference altogether.

Neither spin-off has much directly to do with Shakespeare's play. None of the text is cited by either film, and the plots bear no resemblance to Shakespeare's (both films end happily, for example). *Romeo and Julian* centers on Julian (Grant Larson), who we see is single and without a date at the film's opening. In the film's first song, Julian expresses his desire to find "one man" with whom he can share his life. Julian soon gets his wish as he meets Romeo (Johnny Rey) at a local gay bar and the two hook up and move in together. Their first sex scene is followed by a sequence of the two men as happy lovers wearing skimpy cut-off jeans or speedo bathing suits, kissing, hugging, and playing on the beach or by a pool, going out for brunch, taking in a Sam Abdul porn flick called *Cut or Uncut,* Julian picking a flower and giving it to Romeo. During this sequence, the film's theme song is sung by a woman about the exemplary love of the two men. The first verse and chorus go as follows:

Have you ever felt a magic when you take somebody's hand,
Walking down the streets or walking in the sand?
Have you ever seen the darkness lifting when you look into their eyes?
You feel the world stop spinning, it comes as no surprise.
Have you heard the words "I love you?" Did your heart skip a beat?
Did you feel the passion building in the moment and the heat?
Chorus:
Who can say how long it takes to find
A love that can withstand the test of time?
A love that never ends,
A love like Romeo and Julian's. (Abdul 1993)

This sequence is followed, however, by romantic disappointment. Romeo starts cheating on Julian and successfully cruises the local gay bars. Finally, Romeo and Julian go to an orgy, but Julian is uninterested and leaves alone. After a few moments, however, Romeo decides that he loves Julian after all and leaves the orgy to find him. The two men end up at home and have sex. *Carnival in Venice* similarly focuses on Julien (Yannick Baud). He is visiting Venice on holiday with his parents and is initially chased by Romeo (Benjamin Fontenay), who because of his costume, mistakenly thinks he is a girl. Romeo is straight, has a reputation as a ladies' man, and is engaged to be married. Julien fantasizes having sex with him, but his parents lock him in his hotel room. After agreeing to let the bellman essentially rape him, however, Julien escapes to attend an orgy orchestrated by a local member of the Venetian elite. Julien is then raped at the orgy, but the film ends happily when Romeo shows up and decides that he is gay after all. He and Julien have sex and Julien remains in Venice after his parents return to France.

Both films might appear to code gay desire in heterosexist terms, then, achieving happiness for a gay couple only by making the man/man couple equivalent to a male/female couple. Indeed, Romeo is a top and Julian/Julien is a bottom in both films. The coding of the bottom as female is explicit in *Carnival in Venice*. As I mentioned above, Julien is initially mistaken by Romeo for a girl. Once Julien's true gender is discovered, Romeo loses interest, but Romeo accepts a blow job from Julien on condition that Julien keep it a secret.

Yet neither film is as heterosexist as some readers might think. *Carnival in Venice* normalizes Julien's desire for Romeo (and vice versa) not by reinstating gender difference as the model for a same-sex couple but the opposite: the dissolution of gender differences is the pathway to the realization and fulfillment of "normal" gay desire. Julien persuades Romeo to accept a blow job by saying that he will not be able to tell the difference between Julien and a girl. Moreover, Romeo is not "really" gay, in the film's logic. He arbitrarily happens to fall in love with a boy. Any anxiety about losing his reputation as a ladies' man dissipates as the film moves toward its happy ending.

Homonormativity in *Romeo and Julian* takes a more complex form. The film is not so much about a domestic romance or about explicit gay sex that is clearly legible, in your face, so to speak, as it is about a romance with porn, about mourning a sex scene that is no longer there in a post-AIDS era. Mourning the loss of gay male sexual possibilities gets displaced onto mourning the loss of what D. A. Miller (1998) argues is a specifically gay genre, the musical. *Romeo and Julian* departs from the kind of music played in heterosexual spin-offs of *Romeo and Juliet*. In Paul Thomas' *Romeo and Juliet II* (1988), Bach's first Brandenburg Concerto and Mozart's Symphony 29, respectively, open and close the soundtrack; similarly, Renaissance style music (usually with a harpsichord) plays during the sex scenes in A. P. Snootsberry's *The Secret Sex Lives of Romeo and Juliet* (1968), Joe D'Amato's *Juliet and Romeo* (1996), and Michael Zen's *Censored* (1996).²⁴ And in the recent postapocalyptic porn spin-off *Exile* (dir. Brad Armstrong 1998, starring Jill Kelly and Armstrong in the leads), a *Romeo and Juliet* meets *The Time Machine* meets *Metropolis*), pseudoclassical music is played whenever scenes take place with Juliette [*sic*] or above ground (Romeo is a worker who is exiled below ground). In these straight versions, European classical music is affiliated with Shakespeare as another form of high culture.

By contrast, *Romeo and Julian* adapts the American "low" popular form of the musical without falling into camp or kitsch (though the film is unbelievably sappy). *Romeo and Julian* is about the belatedness of contemporary gay desire, in other words, a belatedness it registers by making itself into an art form that, as D. A. Miller (1998) suggests, is no longer there for gay men in the way it was before Stonewall (though, oddly, *Romeo and Julian* does not cite *West Side Story*). The displacement of mourning a sex scene onto mourning the loss of an art form effectively enables the redemption, through fantasy at least, of gay desire as harmless to gay men. Rewriting Shakespeare's tragedy as a musical with a happy ending, *Romeo and Julian* retells the play to show that desire does not equal death. This porno musical (the first, it points out) doesn't really endorse the domestic couple as the alternative to cruising but, as porn, attempts to keep alive a romance of cruising, of orgies, no longer available to most viewers except on film and video. The movie is meant to arouse its viewers, after all, and Romeo and Julian pointedly take in a porn flick. Moreover, the sex scenes, as Linda Williams (1989) has suggested of porn in general, operate as alternative musical numbers. If *Romeo and Julian* mourns a past cultural moment for many gay men, then, it also displaces that moment into contemporary porn in order to save it, paradoxically, as lost.

Iag(h)o

Like the gay porn spin-offs, Ralf Koenig's soft-core "graphic" novel *Iago Comic* makes gayness perfectly legible. Unlike them, however, Koenig's novel is an antiromance, a critique on the one hand of supposedly happy domestic couples, rather than a homonormative romance. Its de-idealizing look at both the romance of the domestic couple and the romance of cruising is nevertheless useful in that it throws into relief the definition of the homonormative. Narrated by the actor Thomas (Tom) Poope (after the actor Thomas Pope), *Iago Comic* tells the story of a gay black man from

Africa named Gronzo who sleeps with two gay members of Shakespeare's acting troupe, Tom and the cross-dressing Augustine (Gus) Phillips (who plays Ophelia but longs to play Hamlet). Gronzo and Tom fall in love at first sight at the end of a performance of *Hamlet,* and the two are later compared by a character to Romeo and Juliet: "[Sam Sandwich] hat die wei auf Toms Balkon beobachtet. [Gronzo] war wohl herzzerreissend wie bei Romeo und Julia [Sam Sandwich observed the two on Tom's balcony. Gronzo was heartrending like Romeo and Juliet]" (114). Yet Gronzo has a self-confessed weakness for blonde boys (a consequence of his first sexual experience with a Portuguese blonde seaman), and one night he sleeps with Gus (who is a blonde). Gus falls in love with Gronzo after they have sex, and plots to steal Gronzo as his lover. Gus, citing lines of Lady Macbeth's "unsex me here" speech, gets Sam Sandwich to murder Tom's father in the hope of blaming it on Gronzo, but Tom is instead sent to the Tower. When it comes time to perform Iago's part in the final scene of the premiere, however, he, like Macbeth when confronted by Banquo's ghost, sees the ghosts of the people he has murdered, and confesses his crimes on the stage. His severed head winds up sitting on a long pole, ironically confirming the witches' prophecies about his fame. Invoking the end of *Romeo and Juliet, Iago Comic* seems to conclude tragically after the two lovers appear to die: Gronzo enters a tomb, has oral sex with the seemingly dead Tom before drinking a potion, and then Tom wakes up and stabs himself, thinking Gronzo is dead. In the next and final chapter, however, we see that Tom and Gronzo have left England for Gronzo's native tropical island, where they live happily ever after—er, sort of. While at first they have lots of hot sex, and Tom even reads to an inattentive Gronzo from *Romeo and Juliet* (Romeo's lines over what he thinks is Juliet's corpse), Gronzo soon takes off with blonde seamen whenever they appear on the island. In the final page of the comic book, Tom says, "Ich lebe mit dem geilsten aller Maenner in einem warmen, bunten Paradies. Ich muesste gluecklich sein. Aber . . . wenn Romeo und Julia ueberlebt haetten . . . waeren sie gluecklich geworden? [I live with the coolest of men in a warm, colorful paradise. I must be happy. But . . . if Romeo and Juliet had survived, would they have been happy?]" (182).[25] Tom then acknowledges his disappointment in Gronzo by reciting Sonnet 129 and ending the graphic novel with the sentence "I want to go home" (182). Furthermore, *Iago Comic* uses *Romeo and Juliet* to deconstruct the contrast between Gus and Tom, making the faithful Tom unhappy with the promiscuous Gronzo. Whereas Tom plays male parts and is familiar with the local scene, Gus plays female parts such as Ophelia, cites lines by Lady Macbeth when undertaking a murder, and is called a "Tunte" (German slang for "fag," but with a connotation of girl-ishness and transvestism, something akin to "queen").

Yet *Iago Comic*'s antiromance satire does not confine itself to the domestic couple. It also turns a sardonic eye on the gay bar and theater scenes. In a gay leather bar called "Faggots Aglow," for example, gay men sit around and sing together rude songs like "You don't have to love me. Just sit on my face," and all vie to sleep with Gronzo. Gronzo, playing to stereotype, has a rather huge penis. The theater scene, in which various gay actors lust for fame, is likewise lampooned. Shakespeare is a bisexual celebrity hounded by autograph seekers who buy merchandise such as *Romeo and Juliet* cups. He is represented as a man who has been disappointed by love, who views it reluctantly with a jaundiced eye. One of his poems, for example is about love turning to shit: "Was Liebesglueck uns auch verheisse—was bleibt, ist doch nur, grosse Scheisse. Es waerauf Erden schon der Himmel, gaebs keine Moes' und keine Pimmel [Whatever love promises, all that remains is shit. Heaven would be on earth if there were no cunts and cocks]" (25; 26). A line by Friar Laurence in *Romeo and Juiet*—"Young men's love then lies / Not truly in their hearts, but in their eyes" (2.2 67–68)—is paraphrased as follows: "Mir scheint, der jungen Maenner liebe liegt in den Hosen nur—nicht in des Herzens triebe [It seems to me that young men's love lies in their pants, not in their heart's urge]" (8).

Koenig's graphic novel resists any coherent allegorization of gay desire in Shakespeare's plays through a postmodern strategy of fragmenting them into quotations and then reassembling them into various gay motifs. For example, Koenig conflates *Romeo and Juliet* with *Hamlet*. Gronzo and Tom fall in love at first sight at the end of a performance of *Hamlet,* and Tom cites Hamlet's line "the rest is silence" when he kills himself in "Juliet's" tomb. And the comparison of the two lovers to Romeo and Juliet is actu-ally a misreading by Sam Sandwich. In fact, Tom and Gronzo had had a spat over Gronzo's sleeping with Gus, and Gronzo is made analogous to Oth-ello when he offers Tom a handkerchief and advises him never to lose it. The analogy with *Othello* is highlighted by a quotation from Iago serving as epigraph to the chapter in which this scene occurs. Similarly, Gus echoes a number of Shakespearean characters, including Lady Macbeth, Richard III, Macbeth, and Iago. Shakespeare as icon/character/text offers no stable point of reference for a gay reading, then.

Even Shakespeare is satirized for disavowing his homosexual desires. The actors are all gay and believe Shakespeare is bisexual and that his son-nets are addressed to the Earl of Southampton. (Shakespeare protests that he is not a sodomite, that he is in love with Emilio Bassanio, the lover of the Earl of Southampton.) Yet Koenig also satirizes gay readings of Shake-speare and gay attempts at self-legitimation through the colonization of high culture authors like Shakespeare. Gus wants to play Hamlet, for exam-ple, because of the sexual implications of Hamlet's line to Laertes during the fencing scene: "Come for the third, Laertes, you but dally. I pray you pass with your best violence" (5.2. 241–42). (The German translation of "pass" as "stoost zu mir" activates the meaning of "pass" as "thrust.") A gay reading of Hamlet's line about kissing Yorick's lips he knows "not how oft" (5.11. 175) is similarly satirized. Activism on the part of the actors is sim-ilarly lampooned. Although the actors wish that Shakespeare would come out as a sodomite so that the heterosexual audience would view sodomites more positively, they also counsel him to revise his plays so that they are acceptable to his heterosexual audience. When Shakespeare says he will end *Othello* by having Othello and Iago become boyfriends and then vacation in Ibiza, the actors protest: "Willi! Da draussen sind alle heterosexuell! Keiner will sehen, wie ein Mohr und ein Spanier zusammen Urlaub machen! . . . Erinnere dich an die erste version von *Romeo und Julia!* Julia tot in der Gruft und Romeo wird gluecklich mit seinem Freund Balthasar! Das wollen die Leute nicht sehen, Willi, das ist . . . . [Willi! Everyone out there is heterosexual. None of them wants to see a Moor vacation with a Spaniard! Remember the first version of *Romeo and Juliet!* Juliet dies in the tomb, and Romeo gets lucky with his friend Balthazar! The people don't want to see that, Willi, it's . . .]" (151; 152). After reasserting that he is het-erosexual, Shakespeare caves in to their caution, and rewrites the ending in the form we have it: "Sterben am Schluss eben Alle! [Everyone dies in the end!]" (152). *Iago Comic* thus radically calls into question the force of any queer critique of heteronormative reading of Shakespeare: the gay scene in the theater and in clubs has its own normative aspects, and the only norm in the sad, harsh world of this graphic novel is infidelity and romantic dis-appointment.

Bard On

The homonormative replays of *Romeo and Juliet* discussed thus far might appear to represent opposite ends of a spectrum, making same-sex desire normal by virtue of its being unlegible (Cukor), on the one hand, or mak-ing it normal by virtue of gender difference being dissolved (the porn spin-offs). Perhaps so, but they do not exhaust the strategies by which homonormative romance can engage a heteronormative culture of roman-tic sentimentality. In my view, the most daring and forceful examples of the ways in which homonormative citations and adaptations of *Romeo and Juliet* designify gay desire and gender difference are the film *The Object of My Affection* and the theatrical production, *Shakespeare's R & J.* In both replays, gay sexuality is not signified in stereotypical terms; instead, it is played straight, so to speak, un-marked, designified, and thereby normalized.[26] Consider first *The Object of My Affection,* a film that gives new meaning to the genre of "screwball comedy" as it uses Shakespeare to chart a gay utopia. Though no one in the film is at all homophobic and though all gay people in it appear to be "out" with comfort, the first act of the film indulges a heterosexual woman's romantic fantasy about turning a gay man straight. After deciding that they are in love, the protagonists, George Hanson (Paul Rudd) and Nina Borowski (Jennifer Aniston), decide to continue living together and raise her baby without the biological father's involvement (George wants to have a child himself; apparently, the thought of raising a child with another man has never occurred to him). In a sex scene with the couple, the film seems to go all the way in erasing gayness. But just as George and Nina are about to have sex, the phone rings with George's ex-lover Dr. Robert Joley (Timothy Daly) on the line. George then declines Nina's offer to continue where they left off and decides to go with Joley to a "critic's convention" at George's old college in order to reunite romantically.[27]

Shakespeare enters the film as it takes a turn to affirm gayness in what I call "homonormative" terms.[28] Gayness and Shakespeare are equated. At the critic's convention, Joley, a professor who has just published a book on George Bernard Shaw, sides with Shaw, Shakespeare *(Romeo and Juliet),* and Berlin is avant-garde cabaret against American musicals, while his English antagonist, Rodney Fraser, loves both musicals and Shakespeare and has no patience with contemporary theater, at one point dismissing a *King Lear* he and his young friend Paul James (Amo Gulinello) will see as one full of hunky men undressing. At this conference, George meets Paul. The two have sex and quickly fall in love. As the men form a couple, a modern dress production of *Romeo and Juliet*—starring Paul as Romeo and complete with sitar music, dark lighting, and an interracial, tattoo ornamented and seminaked cast—becomes the means by which they disentangle themselves from Nina and Rodney. When Nina finally throws a fit because she can no longer deal with George and Paul sleeping together in her apartment, she signals her loss by calling Paul "Romeo."

Gay characters have a monopoly on Shakespeare in the film, and the appropriation of *Romeo and Juliet* by the younger gay characters yields a comedy in which the truly happy couple is gay and has sex. There are several postcoital scenes with George and Paul, and, with the exception of George's Lothario-like brother Frank (Steve Zahn), no one else in the film, especially the heterosexuals, is having sex. In one particularly funny moment, Nina, after having discussed not having sex with George, asks George as she lies on top of him in bed whether married couples are as happy as they are. And even at the heteronormative occasion of George's brother's wedding, George and Nina, not the married couple, are the stars, dancing by themselves while everyone else stops to admire their skill, and constituting the ideal couple for everyone there.

In calling the film's citation of *Romeo and Juliet* homonormative, I mean in part to call attention to the way *The Object of My Affection* constructs homosexual romance in heterosexual terms. Like the heterosexual characters, all of the gay characters are looking for a romantic lover. Except for the gay Dr. Goldstein, an "ear, nose, and throat" specialist, himself a beefy caricature whose advances George spurns repeatedly, no one cruises in this film. *Object* allows gay male sex to be represented only under the rule of the couple. Yet *Romeo and Juliet* in particular and Shakespeare in general contribute to the designification of gay desire in the film instead of operating as the master signifier of gay male desire. Same-sex desire is not entirely governed by the *Romeo and Juliet* model such that man is to woman as man is to man. It's Nina who applies the Romeo interpretation, and she does not complete the analogy by identifying George with Juliet. George is not explicitly paired up with Paul, then, as female to male (as is the case in of the gay porn spin-offs *Romeo and Julian* and *Carnival in Venice*). Rather than using Shakespeare to produce a single romantic meaning, *The Object of My Affection* does the reverse through extradiegetic references to Shakespearean roles played by two of the actors. Paul Rudd makes an in-joke about his role as Paris in Baz Luhrmann's *William Shakespeare's Romeo + Juliet* (1996) when he tells Nina in jest that he and a possible date are leaving for Paris that night. Paris has been recoded as the site of romance rather than of exclusion from it. Similarly, Nigel Hawthorne's mention of a production of *King Lear* may recall to some viewers his performance as King George III playing King Lear in Hytner's earlier film *The Madness of King George* (1994). (Hawthorne's role as Malvolio in Trevor Nunn's *Twelfth Night* [1996] is also mildly hinted at insofar as he is the jilted lover.) Rather than provide an alternative romantic model for same-sex male desire, then, *Romeo and Juliet* (and Shakespeare generally) fails to impose itself as master plot.

It is precisely the process of unmarking gay desire in *The Object of My Affection* that ends up giving that desire a lot of power to disrupt heteronormativity, extensively queering Nina's "heterosexual" family. Rather than letting go of the female fantasy of marrying a gay man after Nina and Paul's "living together without sex" experiment fails, the film does not return us to traditional heterosexual couplings. When Nina's baby is born, for example, Vince, the baby's biological father, shows up at the hospital as if to claim his "rightful" place, but as the camera pans right we see that George is already there, holding the baby (named Molly) in his arms. And the film closes with a flash forward scene of a new first grade student theatrical production staged by George (starring Molly). As the camera tracks right down a row of seats, our expectation that the characters are all arranged in couples is repeatedly unsettled: we first see Vince and Nina, but then we see Nina holding hands with her new boyfriend Lewis, an African American cop she met earlier in the film; we then see Nina's step-sister and husband with their now punk rock daughter; and finally Paul with Rodney. After the show, Rodney arranges to babysit Molly at a future time, and Nina, Uncle George, and Molly go off to have coffee. Through the citation of Shakespeare, *The Object of My Affection* opens up a utopian fantasy designed more for heterosexuals than for gays, in which the family is no longer constructed in terms of who is in and who is out of it: instead of the married couple at the head of the family, we have an extended family run by a number of "uncles" (of whom the biological father is considered to be one) and a single mother.

Joe Caralco's adaptation *Shakespeare's R & J* goes even further than Hytner's *The Object of My Affection* in unmarking gay desire, and by turning to this example I can begin to clarify what I mean by a "post-queer" adaptation of Shakespeare's play. Rather than recontextualizing Shakespeare within a contemporary setting, this stage adaptation largely limits itself to Shakespeare's verse. *Shakespeare's R & J* activates a homoerotic reading of *Romeo and Juliet* by situating its performance in a boys' Roman Catholic prep school (so that all the female characters are played by young men) and by framing the adaptation through *A Midsummer Night's Dream*. The play begins as the boys march on stage and conjugate together the Latin verb "to love," and then recite what appear to be the school's three commandments: "Thou shalt not steal, kill, lust." Finally, they recite very sexist passages about the different roles members of both genders are supposed to play from a nineteenth-century etiquette book entitled *The American Code of Manners*. A school bell rings then repeatedly, and the boys begin reciting, again taking turns, Puck's lines at the opening of the final scene of *A Midsummer Night's Dream*:

Now the hungry lion roars
And the wolf behowls the moon,
Whilst the heavy ploughman snores;
All with weary task foredone.
Now the wasted brands do glow
Whilst the screech-owl, screeching loud,
Puts that wretch that lies is owed
In remembrance of a shroud.
Now it is the time of night. (5.2.1–8)

This comic frame returns at the end when the boys recite Puck's epilogue:

If we shadows have offended,
Think but this, and all is mended:
That you have but slumbered here,
While these visions did appear;
And this weak and idle theme,
Nor more yielding but a dream. (1–7)

Shakespeare's R & J reworks the generic indefinition of both *A Midsummer Night's Dream* and *Romeo and Juliet* to open up a school night's dream of homoerotic liberation through a performance of *Romeo and Juliet* by "faeries." When Puck's lines are read at the beginning of the performance, one of the boys (who will play Romeo) opens a chest and pulls out a play-book of *Romeo and Juliet*. This same boy then cites Romeo's line "I dreamt a dream tonight" (1. 4. 49) and the four boys then begin to read out of it, taking turns. At the end of the play, after Puck's epilogue is recited, the boy who played Romeo again recites the line "I dreamt a dream tonight" as the other boys leave the stage (the bell has rung and morning has arrived) and he stays alone on stage repeating "I dreamt" several times, each time more plaintively. The stage then goes dark and the performance ends.

Caralco's adaptation thus introduces a gay subtext whereby the union between Romeo and Juliet becomes a metaphor for the (forbidden) union of the two boy students playing them. At the ball when Romeo and Juliet kiss, the other boys begin shouting "Thou shalt not kill, steal, lust" and then separate the two lovers. Similarly, the Friar separates them when he first encounters them, and Mercutio breaks up the wedding scene at Juliet's line "my true love is grown to such excess. . . . My love is boundless as the sea" (2.5.33). And the gay subtext is made available by the "faeries'" frame. When the Friar first appears, two of the boys recite the chorus again and the Friar appears to get his idea about bringing the houses together from these two faeries.

A marriage scene between Romeo and Juliet is interpolated and constructed along gay lines. Becoming upset when Romeo and Juliet begin to pledge their love, Mercutio takes away the playbook from Romeo, who gets up, retrieves it, and then gives it to Juliet; but then the actor playing Tybalt takes it away from Juliet. Romeo improvises and begins to recite Sonnet 18 to Juliet, but this move is parodied by the other boys, who mockingly hum the theme song from Zeffirelli's film version of *Romeo and Juliet*. These boys then pull Romeo and Juliet apart after the two lovers recite the sonnet together. Then Mercutio begins to recite Sonnet 116 and Juliet gets up and takes his hand and the hand of the other boy. Romeo then gets up and joins hands and they all four form a circle and finish reciting the sonnet together: "If this be error and upon me proved, / I never writ, nor no man ever loved." Gay marriage, then is not founded on the couple but instead includes all four boys present, putting them on equal footing.

What is really striking about *Shakespeare's R & J*, however, is how little it marks itself as openly gay. For one thing, the adaptation distances itself from gay camp when it comes to performing the women's roles. The roles of the Nurse and Lady Capulet are initially performed as parodies (as if the boys were budding drag queens). But the boys quickly drop that act and play the women straight. Juliet is done straight throughout. As the director writes: "*Romeo and Juliet* is a sexy play, so by using just men, it is by definition going to be a homoerotic piece. But I didn't want it to be a celebration of homoerotic imagery. These characters learn what pure love is, which is genderless" (Lipton 1998).

I would not say that Caralco's adaptation (or play, for that matter) actually transcends gender, however. It is after an all-male production. And what might appear to be a genderless representation of love is of course a performance of heterosexual romance. There is no strict contrast between character and actor in *R & J* because there is virtually no extra-Shakespeare dialogue (and what little there is never assigned to individual actors but is instead recited collectively by the four boys). The male actors thus fold themselves into female characters as easily as they do into the male characters. The more interesting moments are the ones in which the gay subtext is not really apparent, such as their first kiss or their kisses in the aubade scene. Instead of heightening the extent to which gender is a performance, the naturalism of the theatrical style suggests that emotionalism isn't tied to a particular gender, that a man can express his feelings just as well as a woman and without embarrassment. The adaptation is "post-queer" in having the boys purposely transgress the commandments against stealing, lying, and lusting and the code of manners about gender roles, suggesting that one can steal parts from another gender without penalty. The boys' rebellion against conventional gender roles allows for homoerotic feelings to be expressed, but it also allows the expression of those feelings not to seem off, weird, or, in the current transvalued idiom, queer.

In their different relations to Shakespeare, one citing *Romeo and Juliet* and the other adapting it, *The Object of My Affection* and *Shakespeare's R & J* return us to an initial observation about the persistence of Shakespeare in a post-closeted era. Next to no attention has been paid to homonormativity in queer theory, presumably because the concept is thought to be antiqueer; that is, queer theory celebrates public, anonymous sex and explicit representations of gay and lesbian sexuality, while liberal and conservative gay commentators celebrate gay marriage and prefer modest representations of gay and lesbian sex. The normal and the queer fall on opposite sides of a very large divide. Yet the performance history of gay and lesbian adaptations of *Romeo and Juliet* makes clear, I hope, that homonormativity is not about what queers despise and liberal or conservative gays embrace. The homonormative does not involve, in conservative fashion, the mimicry of heterosexist practices of normalization since it dismantles the notion of a coherent norm. Homonormativity does not, that is, reinforce normalcy across the board. To be sure, homonormativity does not fully transcend homophobia (any more than queer practices do). And some readers might scoff both at gay and lesbian interest in a play like *Romeo and Juliet,* which inevitably replays a homophobic disavowal of gay desire as lethal, and at the notion of an unlegible same-sex desire as offering resistance to mass culture censorship of that desire, given that mass culture tends not to acknowledge gay desire anyway. What use is a homonormative knowledge of homosexuality that is not "mere knowingness," some critics might ask, if that knowledge remains largely inaccessible to academic and mass audiences alike? I do not want to minimize the force of these questions. Yet if replays as diverse as Cukor's *Romeo and Juliet,* romances like *Shakespeare's Sweetheart* and *Shakespeare in Love,* the gay porn spin-offs, and *The Object of My Affection* and *R & J* suggest that things can never be as queer as some queer theorists hope, they also suggest the contrary, namely, that things can never be as normal as they fear either.

Notes

1. I discuss *In and Out, The Object of My Affection,* and *Tromeo and Juliet* in my book *Unspeakable ShaXXXspeares.* (See Burt 1998, 67–71; 90–91; 104–05;229–31; 255, n. 10.)

2. Rave reviews of *Shakespeare's R &J* have appeared in the *New York Times, The New York Post,* the *Washington Post,* and the *Wall Street Journal.* On the film production, see Shtier 1998.

3. On *West Side Story* and *Where the Boys Aren't 10,* see Wood 1998). On *Eve's Bayou,* see Burt 1998, 256, n. 16; 265, n. 16.

4. This potential is exploited in a recent RCA recording with Vesselina Kasarova and Eva Mei as Romeo and Julia. On the cover is a black and white glamour shot of the two women, with a very butch-looking Kasarova. On the lesbian reception of opera divas, particularly those who do cross-dressed parts, see Castle 1993.

5. Both references are made by a heterosexual (?) male character whose wife leaves him after he develops an unrequited crush on Pat, whose gender and hence the nature of his desire for her/him he is never able to determine during the film.

6. What some critics would call either homosexual or sodomitical desire in Shakespeare's life and works was, in a closeted era, read through the genre of heterosexual romance, particularly, though not exclusively, through *Romeo and Juliet.* In Oscar Wilde's *Portrait of Mr. W. H.,* for example, Shakespeare's homosexuality is proved by his love for a young actor in his troupe, Willy Hughes, "the boy-actor for whom he created Viola and Imogen, Juliet and Rosalind, Portia and Desdemona, and Cleopatra herself" (1979, 147).

    And even earlier, in eighteenth-century masquerades, Shakespeare served as a model for homosexual liasons. As Terry Castle (1989) writes: "Several contemporary accounts of masquerading and homosexuality describe scenes of homosexual flirtation, though usually between men only, and always in extremely coy terms. Typically a sartorial error is invoked to explain such incidents, but only after piquant images have been presented to the reader. As on the Shakespearean stage, men fall in love with 'boys' at the masquerade who turn out to be women; 'women' who are really men in disguise are approached by other men" (1986, 47). And Castle goes on to mention another account in which a man dressed as a "Female Quaker" is compared to "Sir John Falstaff" (48) and points out that in his account of Elizabeth Inchbald's life, James Broaden describes an incident where Inchbald cross-dressed at a masquerade, putting her in mind of "the beautiful equivoque in the character of Viola"—a reference, as Castle notes "to the female-female attractions in Shakespeare" (48).

7. Though Donaldson focuses on Zeffirelli's film version, his reading of gay desire as antipatriarchal folds his reading into Coppelia Kahn's (1981) read-

ing of the play, implicitly feminizing gay male desire. The other, less common approach has been to cede the play to heterosexual culture, an approach taken to an extreme by a lesbian head teacher, Jane Brown, at the Hackney School in East London. Brown caused a row that received international journalistic coverage when she refused to take her students (under 11) to a ballet of *Romeo and Juliet* at Covent Garden on the grounds that the story was heterosexist (see Anon 1994 and Anon 1994a). Brown apparently conflated the play with the ballet, ignoring the possibility that the male dancers might have been gay. She also ignored, it appears, the possibility that Mercutio may have had a homosexual desire for Romeo.

8. In an interview with Monika Treut, the German lesbian filmmaker, we can see both responses. Interviewer Colin Richardson asks her to describe reactions to her work from lesbian audiences, about what they expect from her as a director, what they expect from a lesbian film. She responds:

> They are very explicit in what they want to see, though it's changed a bit since the mid- 1980s. My nasty take on it is this: they want to see love scenes on screen, they want to see attractive girls on screen, they want to see girl meets girl, girl has romance with another girl, girl has wonderful sex with another girl and maybe the highlight would be at the end. Mom and Dad approve and they all live happily ever after. . . . A huge part of the lesbian audience wants to see some kind of a heroine, somebody who is bigger than they are, bigger than life which, for me, is a kind of caricature thing. . . . I myself am unable to cater to these expectations. It's all about fulfilling the Hollywood studio formula. I don't see cinema . . . as a representative or stand-in for real life experiences. (1995, 178; 179)

Judith Butler (1993, 126) also dismisses mainstream heterosexual cinema such as *Victor / Victoria* and *Some Like It Hot*. It would appear that lesbians (or gays) who like romance want to be "normal," while those who do not want to be "queer." For a positive account of the lesbian romance and an attempt to make sense of the discrepancy between lesbian audiences (who like romances) and academic lesbians (who do not), see Stacey 1995.

9. See (1989), Butler (1993), Warner (1993), Bersani (1994), and Berlant and Warner (1998).

10. In contemporary queer theory, there is next to no room for the concept, much less the practice, of homonormativity. As Lauren Berlant and Michael Warner (1998) write:

> Because homosexuality can never have the invisible, tacit, society-founding rightness that heterosexuality has, it would not be possible to speak of "homonormativity" in the same sense. (548, note 1)

I would agree. Homonormativity is not the inverted opposite of hetero-normativity. But the question then remains: how are we to speak of homo-normativity? And we might ask the following related questions: why have queer theorists not theorized homonormativity? Would theorizing it significantly alter existing critiques of heternormativity?

11. On *Titanic,* see Brown and Ansen 1997, 66: "It's *Romeo and Juliet* on a sinking ship" (that's how Cameron first pitched it to Fox). Some readers might want to claim this film as partly gay given the casting of Leonardo di Caprio, a gay icon who has played gay characters in previous films.

12. Shakespeare and his works have frequently been read by modern critics, writers, and filmmakers as signifiers of gayness. Gregory Woods includes a chapter entitled "William Shakespeare" in his recent survey *A History of Gay Literature: The Male Tradition,* and a number of queer-identified New Historicist and cultural materialist critics have focused on same-sex desire or the practice of sodomy in the first 126 sonnets and four plays, *Othello* (Iago's desire for Othello), *The Merchant of Venice* (Antonio's desire for Bassanio), *Troilus and Cressida* (Achilles and Patroclus' desire for each other), and *Twelfth Night* (Antonio's desire for Sebastian), as well as plays that activate the homoeroticism of the boy actor (chiefly, the comedies *Twelfth Night* and *As You Like It*). Attention to Shakespeare's gayness or homosexual desire has been read, then, in terms of same-sex desire, usually male.

13. On the queer as the disruption of the legibility of categories, see Burt 1998, and on the figurality of any gay sex, see Burt 1994.

14. Terry Castle (1989) sees Shakespeare's citation and adaptation in Burney's novel *Cecilia* as being on the side of a comic narrative at odds with both the feminist utopian and melancholic, gothic impulses of the novel. (See 265–68; 286) But Castle thereby minimizes the work that heterosexuals have to do on the play when adapting it for their purposes.

15. On Stoppard's inclusion of gay material in the theatrical and film versions of his earlier *Rosencrantz and Guildenstern,* see Burt (1998, 30). For a fuller discussion of this fim, see Burt forthcoming.

16. The role of Juliet licenses statutory rape in a novel about a young actress named Miranda (who also goes on to perform Ophelia) entitled *Acts of Passion* by Deanna James (1992). An older man plays Romeo. Also, there are lesbian hints in *A Love like Romeo and Juliet.* In Amarantha Knight's *The Darker Passions: The Picture of Dorian Gray,* an S&M porno rewrite of Oscar Wilde's novel, the narrator, a cross-dressing woman named Doria Gray is initially bisexual and lusts after the actress performing Juliet in a production of *Romeo and Juliet.* Police encountered "an operatic version of "Romeo and Juliet" play[ing] eerily and endlessly over stereo speakers" when they arrived at the home of mass murderer Kip Kinkel (Anon 1998, 46).

17. See Isikoff and Thomas 1998, 47 and Morton 1999, 67.

18. It is interesting that Lewinsky cites Romeo's line rather than Juliet's.

19. See, for example, Bersani 1994.

20. In the film, Whale makes two Shakespeare references. At a party hosted by Cukor, which Whale attends with a young man as his date, Whale cites Hamlet's "O that this too to solid flesh would melt." And later in the film, when Whale nearly faints he cites Lear, asking the young man "pray you, undo this button." The film implies a parallel between McKellen and Whale, both British actors (Whale also worked in Shakespeare) whose recognition in Hollywood movies eclipsed their theatrical careers. And depending on how much credit one gives McKellen as auteur, there may also be a parallel with Branagh, another Shakespearean actor who went to Hollywood and who redid one of Whale's films as *Mary Shelley's Franken-stein.* There are also references to Shakespeare in the novel *Father of Franken-stein,* on which *Gods and Monsters* is based. See Bram 1995.

21. One might try to recuperate Howard as gay, based on the stereotypical equation of effeminate and gay. He typically appears less than fully mascu-line in whatever role he plays.

22. Set design was of interest in the gay reception of Reinhardt's *A Midsummer Night's Dream,* as well. As Tony Howard tells me, Reinhardt's notion of bal-letic male/female, dark/light *Dream* ensembles was much picked up in the U.K. by stage directors who were gay, and in the 1940s and 50s the Puck/Oberon relationship was overtly so. Key figures in this respect were Robert Helpman and his director/lover Michael Benthall. They planned a film in 1949–50, but it was never made.

23. One other feature that resonates in this post-AIDS age: an interpolated scene about the "pestilence" that keeps Balthazar from delivering Friar Lau-rence's letter further links the lovers with a deadly disease. The transmission of desire is figured as a diseased contagion.

24. Other straight porns do not have classical music. On these films, see Burt 1998, 77–126.

25. All translations from the German are mine.

26. Here they depart from the film *In and Out,* which is all about finding signs (and hence evidence) of gay desire.

27. The film veers away from typical representations of the gay man as the woman's confidant in presumptively heterosexual romantic melodramas such as *Melrose Place.* Desire always trumps intimacy in *Object.* When George agrees to go to the convention with Joley, for example, he does so not because he loves him or wants to get back together but because he still desires him.

28. These references are the film's addition (they are not in the novel). There is a reference in the novel to a performance in the middle ring of a Ringling Brothers Circus show, however. (See McCauley 1987, 266.)

Works Cited

Anon. 1994. "'Romeo' Too Heterosexual for Children." *Washington Post,* January 20: G5.

Anon. 1994a. "Principal Apologizes for 'Romeo' snub." *Washington Post,* January 21: G3.

Anon. 1998. "A Suspected Shooter Up Close." *Newsweek,* October 12: 46.

Beard, Julie. 1998. *The Romance of the Rose.* New York: Berkeley Publishing Group.

Berlant, Lauren and Michael Warner. 1998. "Sex in Public." *Critical Inquiry* 24 (Winter): 547–66.

Bernay, Anne. 1989. *Professor Romeo.* Hanover and London: University Press of New England.

Bersani, Leo. 1995. *Homos.* Cambridge: Harvard University Press.

Bishop, Natalie. 1993. *A Love Like Romeo and Juliet.* New York: Silhouette Books.

Bram, Christopher. 1995. *Father of Frankenstein.* London: Penguin Books.

Brown, Connie and David Ansen. 1997. "Rough Waters." *Newsweek* 130.24 (December 15): 64–68.

Burney, Fanny. 1986. *Cecilia, or Memoirs of an Heiress.* Introduction by Judy Simons. New York: Penguin Books Virago Press.

Burt, Richard. 1993. "Baroque Down: the Trauma of Censorship in Psychoanalysis and Queer Film Revisions of Shakespeare and Marlowe." In *Shakespeare and the New Europe.* Ed. Michael Hattaway et al. Sheffield: Sheffield Academic Press, 328–50.

———. 1998. *Unspeakable ShaXXXspeares: Queer Theory and American Kiddie Culture.* New York: St. Martin's Press. 2nd ed., new preface, 2000.

———. Forthcoming. "*Shakespeare in Love* and the End of the Shakespearean: Academic and Mass Culture Constructions of Literary Authorship." In *Shakespeare, Film, Fin de Siecle.* Ed. Mark Burnett and Ramona Wray. London: Macmillan.

Butler, Judith. 1993. *Bodies That Matter: On the Discursive Limits of Sex.* New York and London: Routledge.

Castle, Terry. 1986. *Masquerade and Civilization: The Carnivalesque in Eighteenth-Century English Culture and Fiction.* Stanford, CA: Stanford University Press.

———. 1993. *The Apparitional Lesbian.* Stanford, CA: Stanford University Press.

Crimp, Douglas, ed. 1989. *AIDS: Cultural Analysis, Cultural Activism.* Cambridge, MA: MIT Press.

Dickens, Charles. 1839. *Nicholas Nickleby.* London: Penguin Books, rpt. 1978.

Donaldson, Peter. 1990. *Shakespearean Films, Shakespearean Directors.* Boston: Unwin Hyman.

Ehrenstein, David. 1998. *Open Secret (Gay Hollywood 1928–1998).* New York: William Morrow and Company, Inc.

Goldberg, Jonathan. 1992. *Sodometries: Renaissance Texts, Modern Sexualities.* Stanford, CA: Stanford University Press.

————. 1994. "*Romeo and Juliet*'s Open Rs." In *Queering the Renaissance*. Ed. Jonathan Goldberg. Baltimore: The Johns Hopkins University Press, 218–35.

Holden, Stephen. 1998. "Focusing on Glam Rock's Blurring of Identity." *New York Times,* Sunday, November 8: 13, 22.

Isikoff, Michael and Evan Thomas. 1998. "The Secret War." *Newsweek* 131.6 (February 9): 37–47.

James, Deanna. 1992. *Acts of Passion*. New York: Zebra Books.

Kahn, Coppelia. 1981. *Man's Estate: Masculine Identity in Shakespeare*. Berkeley and Los Angeles: University of California Press.

Knight, Amarantha. 1996. *The Picture of Dorian Gray*. New York: Masquerade Books, 1996.

Koenig, Ralf. 1998. *Iago Comic*. Berlin: Rowolt Verlag.

Jong, Erica. 1995. *Shylock's Daughter: A Novel of Love in Venice*. New York: Harper Paperbacks. First published as *Serenissima,* 1986.

Levy, Emmanuel. 1994. *George Cukor, Master of Elegance*. New York: William Morrow and Company, Inc.

Lipton, Brian Scott. 1998. "Passionate Kisses." *Encore: The Off-Broadway Theatre Magazine* March. (*R & J* theater program). New York, NY.

McCauley, Stephen. 1987. *The Object of My Affection*. New York: Washington Square Press.

McGilligan, Patrick. 1991. *George Cukor: A Double Life*. New York: St. Martin's Press.

Miller, D. A. 1998. *Place For Us [Essay on the Broadway Musical]*. Cambridge, MA: Harvard University Press.

Mitchison, Naomi. 1975. *Solution Three*. London: Dobson.

Morton, Andrew. 1999. *Monica's Story*. New York: St. Martin's Press.

Porter, Joseph A. 1988. *Shakespeare's Mercutio: His History and Drama*. Chapel Hill: University of North Carolina Press.

Richardson, Colin. 1995. "Monika Treut: An Outlaw at Home." In *A Queer Romance*. Ed. Paul Burston and Colin Richardson. London and New York: Routledge.

Smith, Bruce. 1991. *Homosexual Desire in Shakespeare's England: A Cultural Poetics*. Chicago: Chicago University Press.

Spungen, Deborah. 1983. *And I Don't Want to Live this Life*. New York: Ballantine Books.

Shteir, Rachel. 1998. "Making Juliet One of the Guys in a Macho Verona." *New York Times* Sunday, June 14: 6; 23.

Stacey, Jackie. 1995. "'If you don't play, you can't win': *Desert Hearts* and the Lesbian Romance Film." In *Immortal Invisible: Lesbians and the Moving Image*. Ed. Tamsin Wilton. New York: Routledge, 92–114.

Sterling, Sara Hawks. 1905. *Shakespeare's Sweetheart*. Pictured by Clara Elsene. Philadelphia, G. W. Jacobs & Co.

Sullivan, Andrew. 1996. *Virtually Normal: An Argument about Homosexuality*. New York: Vintage.

Title, Elise. 1996. *Romeo.* New York: Bantam.

Traub, Valerie. 1992. *Desire and Anxiety: Circulations of Sexuality in Shakespearean Drama.* New York and London: Routledge.

Warner, Michael. 1993. "Introduction" to *Fear of a QueerPlanet: Queer Politics and Social Theory.* Minneapolis: University of Minnesota Press, vii–xxxi.

Wilde, Oscar. 1882. *The Portrait of Mr. W. H.* In *The Complete Shorter Fiction of Oscar Wilde.* Oxford: Oxford University Press, 139–69.

Williams, Linda. 1989. *Hardcore: The Frenzy of the Visible.* Berkeley: University of California Press.

Wilson, Richard, ed. 1999. *Marlowe: A Casebook.* London: Macmillan.

Wood, Ken. 1998. "Spotlight Pick." *Adult Video News* 14.13 (December): 138.

Woods, Gregory. 1998. *A History of Gay Literature: The Male Tradition.* New Haven and London: Yale University Press.

Films, Videos, and Operas Discussed

Abdul, Sam, dir. 1993. *Romeo and Julian.* USA. Forum Studios. Sound, col., 120 mins.

Armstrong, Brad, dir. 1998. *Exile.* USA. Wicked Pictures. Sound, col., 60 mins.

Bellini, Vinenzo. 1830. *I Capuleti e i Montechhi.* Libretto by Felice Romani. RCA recording 1998.

Bernstein, Adam. 1994. *It's Pat.* USA. Sound, col., 112 mins.

Bologna. Joseph. 196. *Love Is All There Is.* USA. Miramax. Sound, col., 105 mins.

Cadinot, Jean Daniel, dir. 1986. *Le voyage a Venise.* Fr. Videomo. Sound., col., 89 mins.

Cameron, James. 1997. *Titanic.* USA. Twentieth Century Fox. Sound, col., 194 mins.

Caralco, Joe, dir. 1998. *Shakespeare's R & J,* The John Houseman Studio Theater, New York.

Condon, Bill. 1998. *Gods and Monsters.* USA. Lion's Gate Films. Sound, b&w and col., 105 mins.

Coolidge, Martha, dir. 1983. *Valley Girl.* USA. Valley 9000. Sound, col., 96 mins.

Crowe, Cameron, dir. 1996. *Jerry MacGuire.* USA. Sound, col., 138 mins.

Cukor, George, dir. 1936. *Romeo and Juliet.* USA. MGM / UA. Sound, col., 126 mins.

D'Amato, Joe, dir. 1996. *Juliet and Romeo.* It. Excel. With Stephania Satori and Mark Davis. Sound, col., 90 mins.

Haynes, Todd, dir. 196?. *Romeo and Juliet.* USA. Silent, b&w. ? mins.

Hytner, Nicholas, dir. *The Object of My Affection.* USA. 20th Century Fox. Sound, col., 112 mins.

Kaufman, Lloyd, dir. 1996. *Tromeo and Juliet.* USA. Troma Entertainment. Sound, col., 102 mins.

Lemmons, Kasi, dir. 1997. *Eve's Bayou.* USA. Trimark. Sound, col., 108 mins.

Lincoln, F.J. dir. 1998. *Where the Boys Aren't 10.* USA. Vivid Video. Sound, col., 81 mins.

Luhrmann, Baz, dir. 1996. *William Shakespeare's Romeo and Juliet*. USA. 20th Ct. Fox. Sound, col., 120 mins.

Madden, Jr., John, dir. 1998. *Shakespeare in Love*. USA. Miramax. Sound, col., 122 mins.

Nair, Mira, dir. 1992. *Mississippi Masala*. USA. Sound, col., 118 mins.

Oz, Frank, dir. 1997. *In and Out*. USA. Paramount. Sound, col., 92 mins.

Seltzer, David, dir. *Lucas*. 1986. USA. Twentieth Century Fox. Sound, col., 104 mins.

Stoppard, Tom, dir. *Rosencrantz and Guildenstern Are Dead*. USA. Cinecom. Sound, col., 117 mins.

Stootsberry, A. P., dir. 1968. *The Secret Sex Lives of Romeo and Juliet*. USA. Global Pictures. With Foreman Shane and Dierdre Nelson. Sound, col., 90 mins.

Thomas, Paul, dir. 1987. *Romeo and Juliet*. USA. Western Visuals. With Kim Alexis, Jerry Butler, and Nina Hartley. Sound, col., 85 mins.

———. 1988. *Romeo and Juliet II*. USA. Western Visuals. With Nikki Randal and Jaquline Roberts. Sound, col., 88 mins.

Ustinov, Peter, dir. 1954. *Romanoff and Juliet*. USA. Sound, col., 103 mins.

Wier, Peter, dir. 1987. *Dead Poet's Society*. USA. Touchstone. Sound, col., 128 mins.

Wise, Robert and Jerome Robbins, dir. 1953. *West Side Story*. USA. MGM. Sound, col., 151 mins.

Zeffirelli, Franco, dir. 1968. *Romeo and Juliet*. It. Paramount. Sound, col., 152 mins.

———.1999. *Tea With Mussolini*. UK/ It. MGM. Sound, co., 116 mins.

Part V

Disfilming Power

Chapter 8

"Where's the Master?":
The Technologies of the Stage,
Book, and Screen in *The Tempest*
and *Prospero's Books*

James Andreas

> *"This is* writing that conquers."
>
> —Michel de Certeau

Art: Tomorrow's Technology Today

Even if *The Tempest* is *not* the play Bardolatry suggests it is—Shakespeare's farewell to the stage in the role of Prospero, Western *magus*—it ought to be.[1] More than any other play, *The Tempest* sums up Shakespeare's ideas about theater as medium, method, and magic while it explores the major technologies of the period in collision: the stage, the book, the visual arts, and the pseudoscientific arts collectively called "magic." Its mood at times may be nostalgic and sentimental, but its examination of the generation and uses of chirographic and theatrical power for entertainment, educational, and political ends is rigorous, even ruthless. The catchphrase for *The Tempest* is the repeated cry of Alonso and Antonio in the opening lines of the play, "where's the master?"—an interesting interjection for a king and a usurping duke. We may expand the query to ask, *who* is the master and how does he or she—remembering Prospero's island was for a time the possession of the African witch, Sycorax—maintain what becomes his political and imaginative power over unwilling and often unruly subordinates, not to mention new colonial subjects or one's own children? What is the medium—the technology of mastery—of the lord's magic or power that creates and maintains class structures on the island? The bookish Gonzalo and Shakespeare himself used the essays of Montaigne to help the shipwrecked travelers ponder these questions, just as the new world was "discovered" by Europe and smartly mastered by the technologies of scripting, mapping, and the theatrical manipulation of truth that are the real subjects of the play. What gave Westerners a sense of superiority and a "manifest destiny" of dominion over the "East"? According to Samuel Purchas in the early seventeenth century, it was the "literall advantage" enjoyed by Europeans, the advantage of writing. To the "divine endowment" of speech, which distinguishes human beings from animals, "God hath added herein a further grace, that as Men by the former exceed Beasts, so hereby one man may excell another; and amongst Men, some are accounted Civill, and more both Sociale and Religious, by the Use of letters and Writing, which others wanting are esteemed Brutish, Savage, Barbarous" (quoted in Greenblatt 1991, 10).[2] The reconstitution of the class system in post-American Europe was determined and empowered by literacy. Reading and writing distinguished between the classes and conferred class with decisive authority. Orality came to be associated with the primitive and savage "other," and, back home, dramatic and oral performance were activities rapidly being displaced by the book. Consequently, as Michael Harbsmeier has shown, the itinerant professionals who practiced these oral and theatrical arts were considered déclassé.

Peter Greenaway in his perplexing screenplay and film, *Prospero's Books,* released during the quincentennial celebration of Columbus' voyage to the New World, adapts Shakespeare's play by investigating the imaginative and political power of his own art, film, and the theatrical and scripted sources that gave rise to it as the master technology—and the technology of mastery—in the twentieth century. Early on in his career Shakespeare turned quite deliberately away from the newly available power of the text and page as a lyric poet to the open, vulgar technology of the stage—a medium "without class" if there ever was one, in spite of recent, anachronistic attempts by Alvin Kernan and others to reappropriate it for royal and elitist ends.[3] Greenaway, well aware that all screen *play* begins in script and dramatic illusion and that the aesthetic of cinematography, following Eisenstein and Panofsky, is literary in origin, uses film to illustrate the power of the medium to *become* the very message itself. If Shakespeare promotes the thesis in this play that all media *are* magical in their influence and impact—books, stage, science, and the discipline itself called "magic," which is based on scripted formulas and the power of theatrical illusion to bring them to life—Greenaway simply extends the investigation the play conducts to a new technology. This new technology in not simply visual art, which Shakespeare's era knew more about than we do, but to the emerging technology of moving pictures and the often questionable ends to which our century has deployed them for the system of mystification, promotion, and propaganda that perpetuates and extends the class distinctions first suggested in the text itself.

The Tempest is Shakespeare's anatomy of ancient, rediscovered, and current media and the powers for stasis or change that are implicit in and generated by them. The play itself is a multimedia spectacle and extravaganza that serves as an illustration of its own speculations about technological power and its uses and abuses. The medium is the message in *The Tempest*. Its argument is circular: theater is magical; magic is theatrical; books, out of which plays may be taken and which may come to contain and subsequently shape them in the long run, are mystical, but create tangible influences on populations of the new and the old worlds; politics is a theatrical art, and theater has political impact and effect. The stage represents the ritual arena where antagonists, masters and slaves, old and new worlds, old and new gods, the colonizer and the colonized, those empowered and those dominated by power, father and daughter or son, brother and other, males and females, the polite and the *vulgus,* native and alien, compete dialogically and symbolically for a share in the powers granted temporarily by the stage and permanently by the larger institutions generated by the medium of political theater. The business of art, whether literary, theatrical, or cinematic, is first to *affect,* and then *effect.* As Bertolt Brecht asks of epic theater, which looks a lot like Greenaway's film with its kaleidoscopic mix of drama, music, dance, graphic art, captions, film within film, etc.:"Why shouldn't art try, by its *own* means of course, to further the great social task of mastering life?"[4] Prospero's art, derived like Shakespeare's and Greenaway's from books and a theatrical projection of bookish powers, is a technology not only for describing but for prescribing things. For good or ill, art reconceived and implemented as technology may be used tomorrow to reconstitute the res in the res publica.

Voice: The Stage and the Mother Tongue

If there is a basic datum of theatrical experience, a primary medium that is the exchange of dramatic illusion, we might all agree it is speech—plain talk in the "mother tongue." The crucial element in a dramatic text is "dialogue," human conversation delivered in "play" between characters or between characters and audience, not written descriptions of sets or stage direction of action and gesture or elaborate prefaces provided by a proper "authority" on the "work" like Ben Jonson or Bernard Shaw. The *sine qua non* of stage presence, whether dramatic or operatic, is the human voice. There is mime, of course, as we have in the dumb show before *Hamlet*. But no one, I think, would dispute that the "thing" the play can be boiled down to is the human voice animating a dialogical or conversational text. To this day we call those folks who sit down to "watch" or "see" a production of Shakespeare an *audience,* a listening community. A Shakespeare play, unlike a football or basketball game, never developed fully into a "spectator sport," even during the eighteenth century when scenic spectacle dominated productions, or in the twentieth, when film versions of the plays are all the rage. One of the real curiosities of the career of William Shakespeare is his early abandonment of what Chaucer called the "House of Fame"—where classical authors endure because the books through which they "speak" endure as physical objects—for the "House of Rumor," his anticipation of the Globe Theatre, perhaps, with its swirling cacophony of vulgar human voices and the echoing innuendoes of popular gossip. (I have discussed the evolving relationship of orality and literacy in my article, "'Lewedly To a Lewed Man Speke:' Chaucer's Defense of the Vulgar Tongue," in a Festschrift for Walter Ong that is, in fact, devoted to this very topic.) As concerned as Shakespeare might have been about the publication of the sonnets or the narrative poems, he left his dramatic texts fluid, like Prospero's drowned books, unpublished, and, as it were, "unauthorized," which they remain to this day. His "play" never really became a "work."

Perhaps Shakespeare found his inspiration for privileging live dialogue over dead books in the attack of Socrates—a purely dialogical voice if there ever was one—on the "disgrace" of writing in the *Phaedrus:*

(W)hether Lysias or any other writer that ever was or will be, whether private man or statesman, proposes laws and so becomes the author of a political treatise, fancying that there is any greater certainty and clearness in his performance, the fact of his so writing is only a disgrace to him, whatever men may say. For not to know the nature of justice and injustice, and good and evil, and not to be able to distinguish the dream from the reality, cannot in truth be otherwise than disgraceful to him, even though he have the applause of the whole world. (Plato 1928, 326–27)

Socrates explains that while writing, which is engraving externally on the page, may produce Chaucer's "fame" and the political power that attends celebrity, oral exchange engraves the lessons of justice and goodness on the individual human soul—and on the popular collective that it reproduces—like the "track" of an acoustic recording on vinyl or tape:

> (E)ven the best of writings are but a reminiscence of what we know. . . . (O)nly in principles of justice and goodness and nobility taught and communicated orally for the sake of instruction and graven in the soul, which is the true way of writing, is there clearness and perfection and seriousness, and that such principles are a man's own and his legitimate offspring:—being in the first place, the word which he finds in his own bosom; secondly, the brethren and descendants and relations of his idea which have been duly implanted by him in the souls of others. (Plato 1928, 27)

Socrates is saying here, I think, that the page on which script appears externalizes justice and power. By projecting and reconstituting legal and moral "authority" out there through the authoring of texts, script robs the individual of the power to communicate with self and "the brethren and descendants and relations of his idea which have been duly implanted by him in the souls of others" through dialogue, through human speech. According to Michel de Certeau in *The Writing of History,* "(w)ith writing, the Westerner has a sword in his hand which will extend its gesture" and power. "The power that writing's expansionism leaves intact is colonial in principle. It is extended without being changed. It is tautological, immunized against both any alterity that might transform it and whatever dares to resist it" (de Certeau 1988, 216). Writing is derived from the colonial imperative that demands obedience to an invisible "authority" by displacing the local, oral "word" with dictates and imperatives that it is so perfectly fashioned to deliver *in absentia,* through the scriptural commandment, moral fiat, and political bull. In Shakespeare's case, however, theater circumvents what Elspeth Stuckey calls the "violence of literacy" by restoring human speech to its rightful medium in the congregation of voices that constitute a dramatic and social community in the play of presence.

In *Prospero's Books,* Peter Greenaway *underscores,* as it were, Shakespeare's subtle indictment of the "disgrace of writing" in his revealing and undermining of Prospero's "dominion" through the magical power of the book and the political climate of tyranny it spawns on the island and in the magus' own home.

Book: Script and Patriarchal Authority

Herb Coursen, in an early extended scholarly review of the film, pans *Prospero's Books* because he feels its titular subject—books—has nothing to do with the play or the film adapted from it. "The books (depicted in the film) themselves are, for the most part, curiosities and have little if anything to do with *The Tempest,* whether it be Shakespeare's play or, as here, Prospero's" (Coursen 1993, 168). But books are both the subject of the film and the medium of technological mastery historically investigated by the film. Peter Greenaway made this implicitly clear in the introduction to the screenplay he produced after filming *The Tempest:*

> The project deliberately emphasizes and celebrates the text as text, as the master material on which all the magic, illusion and deception of the play is based. Words making text, and text making pages, and pages making books from which knowledge is fabricated in pictorial form—these are the persistently forefronted characteristics. (Greenaway 1991, 146)[5]

However, our society is so implicated "in the knotty entrails" of the book like the animals and insects and plants folded into the books of nature in Greenaway's film that we can't even talk about the problems books can represent in a society that print technology structures, commands, evaluates, punishes, and rewards.

The colonial reading of *The Tempest* as a vying by Europeans for economic and political power over the native populations of the New World—whether during Shakespeare's time or our own or Huxley's envisioning of the future in *Brave New World*—is well grounded in history and in twentieth century political movements.[6] Lately, however, probably due to the crush of studies approaching the play as a vehicle for colonial assumptions and a target for postcolonial critique, scholars have begun to question such monolithic readings, as well they should. William Hamlin sets passages side by side of celebrated Renaissance ethnographers Alvar Núñez Cabenza de Vaca (1542), Jean de Léry (1578), José de Acosta (1589), William Strachey (1612), and John Smith (1624) to demonstrate that the ethnicities of the different travel writers, and the widely divergent cultures they were reporting on, produced a broad view of the "primitive" mentality and ethos. "To the extent that these descriptions register plurality and allow a varied yet specific cultural inheritance to the native groups introduced they represent anti-*tabula rasa* views and thus stand in opposition to such bald and overarching characterizations as Samuel Purchas' that American natives are 'bad people, having little of Humanities but shape, ignorant of Civilitie, of Arts, of Religion'" (Hamlin 1994, 27). Although Stephen Greenblatt is charged by Hamlin, along with Todorov, of perpetuating a "polarizing rhetoric" in his characterization of the collision of native and European cultures, he tempers his views of the travel literature as well in *Marvelous Possessions: The Wonder of the New World,* particularly in terms of our topic, the violence of literacy. "(T)here seems to me no convincing evidence that writing functioned in the early encounter of European and New World peoples as a superior tool for the accurate perception or effective manipulation of the other" (Greenblatt 1991, 11–12). I would respond, however, that the subject of this paper is not ethnic context, not the actual historical conflict between Europeans and aboriginal peoples, but the characterization of the confrontation of Old and New World cultures by two dramatic artists, Shakespeare and Greenaway, both of whom attribute enormous power to script and represent the book, for better or for worse, as a technological weapon to be reckoned with.

Drawing on Montaigne through the translation of John Florio, Shakespeare had abundant evidence that native populations of the New World were not only intelligent and civilized, but that their social and educational organizations offered viable alternatives to old political structures that were found wanting in the political commentary of his day and in his own chronicle plays. The "commonwealth" that "holy Gonzalo" would "execute," where all things would be held in common and where there would be no government, no traffic, no "riches, poverty, / And use of service, none; contract, succession, / Bourn, bound of land, tilth, vineyard, none" (2.1.151–53)[7] is drawn not only from idealized accounts of the mythical "golden world" of the ancient world, but from suppositions and predictions about behavior in the new, as Montaigne makes perfectly clear. After claiming that the West judges all customs and practices divergent from its narrowly circumscribed norms as barbaric and savage, Montaigne states that the "caniballes" actually *live* the natural life of harmony and fraternity (Montaigne 1910, 219). This experiment with wealth held in common was practiced and had succeeded in a place that had been observed, a place where all were treated as *kin,* in other words, kindly, and dominion held no sway: "Those that are much about one age, doe generally enter and call one another brethren. . . . These leave this full possession of goods in common, and without division to their heires, without other claime or title, but that which nature doth plainely impart unto all creatures, even as shee brings them into the world" (Montaigne 1910, 224). What also may be said to be held in common by the native population was oral language and the "common law" it articulated, a common law abrogated by the textual legalism that swept into the New World with the arrival of Columbus. If such a paradise indeed existed among the native population on what has by play's entry become Prospero's island, it was contaminated by the political presumptions and fraternal hatreds this Western leader has carried with him in the twin viruses of literalism and legalism inherited from the Old World. And in our own times *The Tempest* has been rewritten many times as a parable of the primeval golden age perverted: in *Brave New World,* in the science fiction film adaptation *Forbidden Planet,* and most notably in Aimé Césaire's bald colonial parable of the exploitation of native slaves by Western master, *Une Tempête.* What had not yet been explored in the play until Greenaway's film was the examination of the medium through which Prospero and by extension, the West, demanded, claimed, and solidified their power over native subjects: script and the whole weighty "burden" of patriarchal authority script carries with it. And, as a corollary to patriarchal authority, we have matriarchal orality. Paul Zumthor asserts that "(S)peech is female, a 'co-naturalness' connects woman to it; a ring set in the lip assures its innocuousness" (Zumthor 1990, 47). Mother tongue/father script. We needn't rehearse the arguments of Jacques Derrida and Geoffrey Hartman here regarding pen and page, pen and sword, ink and semen, all of which are allegorically projected in the painting of naked, female America in the face of European explorer by Jan Van der Straet discussed below (Hartman 1981, 105–07).

Critics such as C. L. Barber, Linda Bamber, and Jeanne Roberts have noted that the dominion of Prospero politically on the island, like Lear in his kingdom, has its domestic implications as well. In *The Tempest* Shakespeare, so fond of revisiting and manipulating text- bound plots, even his own, reviews and revises the ultimate fantasy of old Lear: Cordelia is resurrected in Miranda, and father and daughter have an island paradise all to themselves. Yet *"The Tempest,"* Barber says, "is centered in a dominant male figure, a manipulative, all-but-all- powerful magician, sometimes troubling for a certain arrogance or egocentricity, even at times a smugness. From beginning to end, Prospero is the consummate artist in firm control of his plot. He jealously maintains for himself all the power there is on the island, including the power to provide his daughter with the husband he has chosen for her" (Barber 1986, 334–35). What really distinguishes *The Tempest* as a romance from *The Winter's Tale* and *Pericles,* Barber concludes, is that "for Prospero, as for Lear, there is no wife to recover through his daughter." As Linda Bamber quips, "Prospero's dead wife stays dead" (Bamber 1986, 171). Jeanne Roberts argues that the whole island in *The Tempest* "seems more like a perfected male fantasy than a genuine Wild." Miranda is firmly under Prospero's control, the mother is dead, Sycorax but a ghost, and Naples' daughter Claribel is "the object of successful male exchange with the African king of Tunis." The island is "effectively de-Natured of its feminine essence" (Roberts 1991, 51). In *Prospero's Books,* Greenaway in a sense kills off Prospero's dead wife *again* in the flashback of medical anatomy where the pregnant woman, already identified as Prospero's young bride and Miranda's mother "Susannah," is shown nude and eviscerated to reveal the anatomical secrets of pregnancy.

So what went wrong on this remote island and, by thematic extension, in the New World that is still, of course, fighting the so-called "Indian wars" from the top to the bottom of the Western hemisphere? How was Prospero able to *dominate,* to rule the house in the primitive paradise Caliban eloquently describes his island was before the intrusion of the usurping master (1.2.331–44)? According to Shakespeare, Prospero rules the island and its inhabitants "by the book," by writing and controlling the "scripts" the aboriginal people he cultivates must be taught to follow and implement. Caliban grasps this fact intuitively when he reminds Stephano and Trinculo in the plot against Prospero not to forget

> First to possess his books; for without them
> He's but a sot, as I am; nor hath not
> One spirit to command: they all do hate him
> As rootedly as I. Burn but his books. (5.2.92–95)

Prospero commands the spirits and the island by the letter of the law; he runs things by the book. Through books, the real power behind the staff or scepter (which is after all only a symbol of primitive power and no longer the mechanism itself) Prospero not only describes but inscribes and prescribes what was once done, what is to be done, and what shall be done by and for the islanders and his daughter. As Michel de Certeau generalizes about the function of writing in the colonial agenda, "(a) structure already appears to be in place. From festive, poetic, ephemeral speech are delineated the tasks of conserving, of verifying, and of conquering. A will to power in invested in its form" (de Certeau 1988, 217). Prospero is the power of patriarchal authority— that is, literalism and legalism—embodied. Coursen wonders why Greenaway's Caliban swims up to grab the First Folio, which is bobbing on the surface after the master tries to drown his books. He suggests it might be for "grace," but it is more likely for desecration, remembering he shits on his master's books in an early scene, or more likely still, for empowerment, a sobering thought indeed. On a happier note, we all know the third world has embraced the Bard with a fervor that leaves the purists among us a bit bewildered.

Writing with a Camera: From Script to Screen

Script and the authority that springs from "scripture" are the subjects Peter Greenaway sets out to explore in what is entitled a "film adaptation" of Shakespeare's play, an adaptation I find much more faithful to its scripted source than any of the science fiction treatments of the play mentioned above, and even truer than Franco Zeffirelli's "readings" of *Taming of the Shrew, Romeo and Juliet,* and *Hamlet* are to Shakespeare's plot and style, or Federico Fellini's film version of the *Satyricon* is to Petronius.[8] Greenaway is true to the plot because the plot "thickens" in books, it becomes fixed in any scripted delineation of it, and Greenaway tries to reveal the literalist mechanism that atrophies the text. The film, as opposed to the play, is about the authoring of the play, about Prospero producing the "sentences" that are executed on Ariel and Caliban, Miranda and Ferdinand, and his own brother and dearest friend, as the action "unfolds," which only scripted action can. The script of the film not only follows the plot of the play accurately and sequentially, the scripting of the play is the subject of the film. This is a film about a very real source for film, script itself, the visual roots of the cinematic medium according to film aestheticians such as Eisenstein who, using the films of D. W. Griffith, celebrated Dickens and Dostoevsky as the true inventors of film montage and structure. "Griffith arrived at montage through the method of parallel action, and he was led to the idea of parallel action by— Dickens!" (Eistenstein 1979, 395). Charlie Chaplin, for one, was so captivated by bookish influence and method that he characterized his early film ventures as "writing with a camera," which they decidedly were not.

Prospero's Books deals generally with the Gutenberg revolution brought about by print technology in a sustained examination of some 20 books from antiquity that reveal the practical power of textual memory to fix and focus intellectual and political "subjects"—anatomy, mapping, mythology, medicine, botany, zoology, physics, mathematics, etc. However, the most striking sequences of *Prospero's Books* are about the scripting of the play, which is "bound" to become a book like all the other books anatomized in the film. The film and the play are both about *authority,* but the film deals exhaustively with the authoring act itself and with the power of chirographic magic—what we might call the rise to power through scripted language. To write is might. Access to power is through literacy that, as Shakespeare must surely have known, is an access easily controlled and manipulated by the powers that be and would be. The maps, which are highlighted in the Book of Maps sequence, not only charted the New World, they chartered, as Blake might say, the land and the people whose destinies were tied up in that land.[9] This detail is nicely recalled in a film produced about the same time as *Prospero's Books, The Piano,* where the colonial master naively asks the question that the West hasn't answered after 500 years of exploiting aboriginal peoples: Why should the natives have the land? How do they know they own it? They haven't burned off the trees or marked off their property—only their faces. And, of course, where are the written contracts that prove and legalize ownership and authorize property rights?

Greenaway steals the screen device Pier Pasolini used to get the sense of authoring in his film adaptations of literary classics, *The Decameron* and especially *The Canterbury Tales,* where the director himself plays Chaucer at a writing desk scripting the tales as they are related on screen (a most un-Chaucerian image, I must interject). Similarly, Sir John Gielgud as Prospero writes out the crucial lines enacted in a dumbshow with voice-over on screen, and we see and hear the scratching of the pen and hear the recitation of each part as it is written mono-tonically, if not monotonously in Gielgud's solo voice. Prospero is *dictator,* he who dictates, delivers, and interprets the script that inscribes then enforces his power. The calligraphy on the screen alone is worth the price of admission, as are the visualizations of the various Renaissance books presented. The voice-overs are not delivered dramatically or dynamically, even by a John Gielgud, but often simulate the monotonous descriptions of the books anatomized on screen. They are, in Brecht's terms, lines delivered narratively rather than dramatically, and they alienate us from the monologic dictates they convey. Gielgud as actor himself seems alienated from his own lines, not to mention the lines of the other characters, to encourage a critical reaction to those words in the listener, rather than automatic empathy. Gielgud's voice-overs seem contrived to sound like the mumblings we call "reading aloud." It is a stroke of brilliance that Greenaway chooses to "drown out" Miranda's lines, indeed all the characters' parts, with his own, for that is what happens when a single reader voices or dictates the lines of a dramatic script. That is how oral polyphony and the counterpoint of live theater are converted whole cloth into the monotonous—the single-toned stuff—students complain of as they read Shakespeare or any literary classic when it is folded artificially into one great uniform text and published in a *Great Books* series or a Norton anthology. All vocal difference, intonation, and dialect are subsumed in the single reader's "monotone," which is then reified as the universal norm we celebrate in that decidedly provincial series of regularized and sanitized classics—the Western canon—the great syllabus of "canned" classics designed to convey "class" and status on those who are privileged to read and licensed to master it.

We watch Prospero writing and imagining the illusions projected by his writing, because script is the source of his power that is being examined in the film. Yet writing is, in a sense, the source of the agony of Caliban and Ariel, and, ironically, of the lonely melancholy of Prospero himself at play's end. For Prospero—like Antonio (another normative character who would lord it over the "other") in *Merchant of Venice* and Malvolio (a text-bound literalist who would use the text to advance his rank) in *Twelfth Night*—is not paired off sexually at the end of the play or film.

The Screen in Search of a Text

Rousseau notes in wonder that "Writing is nothing but the representation of speech; it is bizarre that one gives more care to the determining of the image than to the object" (quoted in Derrida 1974, 27). Likewise, the cinema, which has so preoccupied the media attention of the twentieth century, may be considered the visual offspring of writing and theater. The horizontal tracking of film is based on the methodology of writing and reading so brilliantly recreated in the incessant procession of John Gielgud from screen left to right in *Prospero's Books*. Peter Greenaway reviews the history and the genesis of film aesthetics in *Prospero's Books*. While the subject of the film is obviously the power of books to dominate, predict, and control a given people through chirographic techniques, its subtheme is the genesis of film in literary and dramatic structures. As Coursen notes, Greenaway even references historical materials in the development of the medium, namely Eadweard Muybridge's experiments with the Morey wheel, in which a man in a birdsuit jumps around on screen, and the first film record of a heavyweight championship fight, the Fitzimmons–Corbett match (Coursen 1993, 168).

If literary texts with their montage of simultaneous narrative scenes were the paradigm for the structure of the screenplay, the obvious model for cinematographic method and composition was the theater as it was visually reinvented after the playhouses were closed down by those literal-minded Puritans in the middle of the seventeenth century. In early film experimentation, the camera was stationary in front of a stagelike set, and the characters performed to it as if it were the audience. Actors passed back and forth in front of the camera like they do in Greenaway's film. Film-makers and theorists who created the visual medium of "moving pictures" chose drama as a model for cinematographic method, because the theater itself had been progressively visualized in England and Europe after Protestant interference in the sixteenth century. What could not be controlled in live theater then and now is the unruly spontaneity inherent in oral exchange. Sets, costumes, props, not to mention books, physical objects one and all—these elements could be prescribed, licensed, and checked beforehand, whereas orally delivered scripts could be tampered with and even improvised whole cloth on stage with an audience geared up to festive pitch.[10] When the theaters were reopened in the late seventeenth century, they became largely visual affairs and their plays, as Samuel Pepys remarked, were celebrated as "spectacles;" their audience became "spectators" accordingly—viewers like deaf mutes and therefore nonparticipants in the dramatic action (quoted in Patterson 1989, 52–53). The proscenium stage, which anticipated the framing and probably the technology of motion pictures and television, was an invention designed to modulate the dominant medium of theatrical presentation from an oral, dialogical, communal event to a visually private and monologic event. Of course these spectacles, like the blockbuster high-budget, special effects films of today, were exorbitant to produce and therefore expensive to attend. Theaters, born in free folk event, became exclusive and "classy." We need look no further than Prospero's own masque in *The Tempest* and compare it to the sheepshearing pageant in *The Winter's Tale* for an example of the top-down dramatic control that the weighty technology of the highly visual masque demands and affords. We also know that these visual extravaganzas were the exclusive province of the privileged class of Shakespeare's time.

I want to wrap up this essay with a consideration of the most conspicuously visual element in *Prospero's Books,* even more graphically visual than the technology of bookmaking and reading: " 'tis (the) nudity" that Herb Coursen underscores in the title of his essay on the film, that downright nakedness paraded incessantly before us with an unsettling sense of variety and spontaneity. 'Tis the mapping of the human body. The first time I saw the film, I heard one perplexed Elderhostel student rush out of the theater complaining that he didn't like the costumes. Who noticed? From one shot to the next in *Prospero's Books* we have no idea what body part—male or female, old or young, attractive or repulsive—will be swimming or jogging or bobbing before our eyes. What this proliferation of bodies represents, of course, is the native population of Prospero's island and, in terms of our theme, the "cast of thousands" that wide-angle lens photography makes possible. If a film set is a stage, it's a stage of epic proportions made for the vigilant armies of the West holding off hoards of native heathen on the rampage. The islanders are conveniently invisible on Shakespeare's relatively shrunken dramatic stage, but they are resurrected strategically in most productions to furnish forth a tune or a meal when ordered to do so by their master. Like Prospero's islanders, the aboriginals in the film are always obedient and, more importantly, mute, with the conspicuous exception of Caliban, presented by Aimé Césaire as an unruly "field Negro" and found to have some "gross deformity" by Coursen in his discussion of the film.

The exclusively visual representation of the aboriginals—for they have no voices scripted for them by Prospero—is historically accurate, not from the viewpoint of what native populations anywhere must have looked like in themselves during the fifteenth or sixteenth centuries, but historically accurate for how they appeared and were portrayed to the sensibilities of the Europeans of the times. The aborigines were depicted in their first illustrations as miraculously just like us, apparently white, with Caucasian almost classical features representing a whole range of body types. What shocks us visually about Greenaway's film is not the nudity of thousands. We're used to looking at naked natives representing the full range of body types possible in the human race; we're just not accustomed to seeing what we choose to classify as Caucasian bodies naked: perfect, posed, poised, "classical" white bodies culled from the pack, yes, but the naked profusion of real physical difference and irregularity is more than most of us can bear, or should I say "bare."

Of course Greenaway invested a lot of energy in dressing his Western potentates to the nines. The hats, the collars, the buttons, the bows, the pumpkin pants, the boots of Spanish leather are truly spectacular, as they should be for the lords of the spectacle. Of course, the transgressive European visitors must go naked as part of their punishment before reconstitution by the scribal magus, and even Prospero himself eventually must have to stand naked in the film when he is stripped of the Emperor's old clothes. The bath scene that opens the film unnerves viewers from the outset, as some of Shakespeare's audience must have been put off by the orally induced imaginative leaps required to visualize a tempest in a theater. I think Greenaway gives us the paradigm for Prospero's chirographic power in this initial scene, as Shakespeare does orally in the opening lines of *The Tempest*. Prospero isn't in the bath; like a playwright or screen-playwright he writes himself into the bath and orders Ariel to pee himself up a storm. Film is closer to "reality" than script ever could be; at least we are in the water in that opening scene of the film, in a blue pool, not just an inkwell of blue ink that represents—which is what symbols do—the ocean. Prospero has his Ariel pee up a storm with his little phallus over a model boat, just as Prospero with his true staff and book, the pen and the pages on which he writes, is writing down (as Dogberry knows, the vector here of writing *down* is important) the storm that we are to imagine. This is all hilarious stuff to be sure, just as hilarious as the little dramatic scenarios, the plays within the plays, Shakespeare scatters throughout his plays to mock and tease his own medium and all of us who mistake it for the real thing. But the point here is modeling, what we might call using the media "mojo." The head mojo in the West is the page on which we draw the maps that parcel out the world into territories that are then acknowledged as real countries and principalities to be defended by military action, if necessary. The mojo is the book that describes a people in so compelling a way that it conditions and prescribes a view of those people *a priori,* in prejudicial fashion. The mojo of the book makes the macrocosmic world microcosmic and manageable, and when we look up from the book we project and recreate the world in the book's image. This is an awesome power, especially when we realize that the dream of equal access to the mojo of the book is a fiction because of the physical nature of the book itself (expensive and locked away in libraries) and the considerable and expensive skill it requires to master the medium (an expensive education in an ideologically controlled environment at best, and an intellectual vacuum, at worst).

Beyond the Historiography of the Other

Michel de Certeau opens his own book on the writing of history with an allegorical etching by Jan Van der Straet for Jean-Théodore de Bry's book (books begetting books), *Americae decima pars,* published in 1619, just ten years after the appearance of *The Tempest* and during the very year the first African slave was sold in Charleston, South Carolina. The painting depicts Amerigo Vespucci the voyager arriving in the New World. Certeau extrapolates from the painting an allegorical explanation that neatly characterizes the Prospero of Shakespeare and Greenaway, the magus who conquers and subdues with the power of unilateral meaning inscribed on the body of the natives living there by writing:

> Amerigo Vespucci the voyager arrives from the sea. A crusader standing erect, his body in armor, he bears the European weapons of meaning. Behind him are the vessels that will bring back to the European West the

spoils of a paradise. Before him is the Indian "America," a nude woman reclining in her hammock, an unnamed presence of difference, a body which awakens within a space of exotic fauna and flora. (1988, xxv)

Certeau allegorizes the painting: "It represents the beginning of a new function of writing in the west. . . . But what is really initiated here is a colonization of the body by the discourse of power. This is *writing that conquers.* It will use the New World as if it were a blank, 'savage' page on which Western desire will be written" (de Certeau 1988, xxv). Paul Zumthor itemizes the consequences of European colonization by writing and its offspring, literature, in terms of the decimation of oral languages:

> Since the seventeenth century, Europe has spread itself over the world like a cancer: surreptitiously at first, but for a long time now it rampages, an already insane ravaging of forms of life, animals, plants, countryside, languages. Each day that passes, several languages disappear from the world: repudiated, snuffed out, dead with the last old person, voices never tainted by writing, pure memory with no defenses, windows once thrown wide open upon the real. Without doubt, one of the symptoms of the evil was, from the very start, what we call literature, and literature has taken on consistency, prospered, become what it is—one of the most vast dimensions of human beings—by challenging voice. (Zumthor 1990, 225)

Prospero prospers by the force of the letter, declares and authorizes property by the book, strips Caliban of his own language, and silences the natives of the island who are mute in both the play and the film.

Peter Greenaway's *Prospero's Books* is an unsettling film adapted from an eerily prophetic play that treats an unsettling phenomenon—colonization and the chirographic power that drives it, a project very much still underway in the West. The medium of any presentational object is difficult to discuss, much less perceive, because its function is to create the illusion of transparency. There is nothing real about a book but the pages, ink, and glue that constitute it. But we are embedded in the technology of script, as Marshall McLuhan, Eric Havelock, and Walter Ong began teaching us decades ago, and really have lost the ready ability to distinguish between the signifier and the thing signified. For instance, the newest presentational technology, the computer, has, as most theoreticians have already noted, been tyrannized by the assumptions and conventions of literacy. On the computer we "write programs," which consist of scripts that usually are presented visually on screen in the form of textual messages, although the basic binary language of the computer is no more biased than our own brains to a single visual, aural, tactile, or metaphysical mode of communication. Nevertheless, there is a non-linear, hypertextual, multimedia revolution underway in the computer world and, I submit, the presentation of Shakespeare in this format yet to be designed, will look, sound, and maybe even feel a lot like Greenaway's zany film adaptation of Shakespeare's synaesthetic language. We can also be sure that the ultimate function of computer power, like the power of the ritual stage and the printed book before it, will be to recreate and circumscribe the social world in its own technographically biased image.

Notes

1. It was probably Edward Dowden who first identified Prospero with Shakespeare himself, and the renunciation of his magic and abandonment of the island as "the abandoning by Shakespeare of the theatre, the scene of his marvelous works" (380). For a survey of the critical reception of *The Tempest,* see Arthur Eastman and Thomas Berger (147–188).
2. Samuel Purchas, "A Discourse of the diversity of Letters used by the divers Nations in the world; the antiquity, manifold use and variety thereof, with exemplary descriptions of above threescore severall Alphabets, with other strange Writings" (quoted in Greenblatt [1991] 10).
3. Kernan discusses—quite persuasively—the development of Shakespeare as a "patronage dramatist putting on his plays before King James I and his court after James came to the English throne in 1603" (xv).
4. "The A-effect (alienation effect of epic theater) was achieved in the German epic theatre not only by the actor, but also by the music (choruses, songs) and the setting (placards, film, etc.). It was principally designed to historicize the incidents" (Brecht 1978, 96).
5. The screenplay itself is examined extensively in Claus Schatz-Jacobsen's article. Shatz-Jacobsen and I, quite independently, arrived at many of the same conclusions about the nexus of text and film explored by Greenaway in his screenplay.
6. Recent discussions of colonial and postcolonial themes in *The Tempest* include studies by Huston Baker, Paul Brown, Stephen Greenblatt (1976 and 1991), William H. Hamlin, Peter Hulme, Mary Louise Pratt, Tzvetan Todorov, Alden T. and Virginia Mason Vaughan, and G. A. Wilkes. See especially the article by Jonathan Baldo, which uses *The Tempest* to explore memory and writing as elements of European colonialism.
7. All quotations from the play are taken from *The Riverside Shakespeare.*
8. Initial reviews of the film appeared in *Commonweal, New Republic,* and *People's Weekly.* More probing discussions of Greenaway's controversial film include articles by Vernon Gras, Harlan Kennedy, Peter Schwerger, and Geoffrey Wall.

9. On the control over distant territories the technology of mapping provided Western political powers, see the studies of David Buisseret.

10. We might argue that videotape had to be invented for the same reason. Early television was "live" and unpredictable, as any of us who watched the *Show of Shows* or the *Jackie Gleason Show* well remember. Video technology developed the kinoscope and then videotape to pretape shows so orally explosive material could be cut or "bleeped," if the desired effect was "live."

Works Cited

Andreas, James, Sr. 1998. "'Lewedly To a Lewed Man Speke': Chaucer's Defense of the Vulgar Tongue." In *Time, Memory, and the Verbal Arts: Essays on the Thought of Walter Ong.* Ed. Dennis Weeks. Cranbury, NJ: Associated University Press, 134–154.

Baker, Huston. 1986. "Caliban's Triple Play." *Critical Inquiry* 13: 182–96.

Baldo, Jonathan. 1995. "Exporting Oblivion in *The Tempest.*" *Modern Language Quarterly* 56: 111–44.

Bamber, Linda. 1986. *Comic Women, Tragic Men: A Study of Gender and Genre in Shakespeare.* Stanford: Stanford University Press.

Barber, C. L. and Richard P. Wheeler. 1986. *The Whole Journey: Shakespeare's Power of Development.* Berkeley: University of California Press.

Berger, Thomas. 1988. "Miraculous Harp: A Reading of Shakespeare's *The Tempest.*" In *Second World and Green World: Studies in Renaissance Fiction.* Berkeley: University of California Press.

Brecht, Bertholt. 1978. "Alienation Effects in Chinese Acting." In *Brecht on Theatre.* Trans. John Willett. New York: Hill and Wang.

Brown, Paul. 1985. "'This thing of darkness I acknowledge mine': *The Tempest* and the Discourse of Colonialism." In *Political Shakespeare: New Essays in Cultural Materialism.* Ed. Jonathan Dollimore and Alan Sinfield. Ithaca: Cornell University Press, 48–71.

Buisseret, David. 1990. *From Sea Charts to Satellite Images: Interpreting North American History Through Maps.* Chicago: University of Chicago Press.

———, ed. 1992. *Monarchs, Ministers, and Maps: The Emergence of Cartography as a Tool of Government in Early Modern Europe.* Chicago: University of Chicago Press.

Coursen, Herb. 1993. "'Tis Nudity': Peter Greenaway's *Prospero's Books.*" In *Watching Shakespeare on Television.* Rutherford: Fairleigh Dickinson University Press.

Caesaire, Aimé. 1969. *Une tempaete; d'apraes "La tempaete" de Shakespeare.* Paris: a Editions du Seuil.

De Certeau, Michel. 1988. *The Writing of History.* Trans. Tom Conley. New York: Columbia University Press.

Derrida, Jacques. 1974. *Of Grammatology.* Trans. Gayartri Spivak. Baltimore: Johns Hopkins University Press.

Dowden, Edward. 1899. *Shakespeare: A Critical Study of His Mind and Art.* New York and London: Harper.

Eastman, Arthur. 1968. *A Short History of Shakespearean Criticism.* New York: Norton.

Eisenstein, Sergei. 1979. "Dickens, Griffith, and the Film Today." In *Film Theory and Criticism.* Ed. Gerald Mast. New York: Oxford University Press, 370–80.

Gras, Vernon. 1995. "Dramatizing the Failure to Jump the Culture/Nature Gap: The Films of Peter Greenaway." *New Literary History* 26: 123–43.

Greenaway, Peter. 1991. *Prospero's Books: A Film of Shakespeare's "The Tempest."* London: Chatto & Windus.

Greenblatt, Stephen. 1976. "Learning to Curse: Aspects of Colonialism in the Sixteenth Century." In *First Images of America: The Impact of the New World on the Old.* Ed. Fredi Chiapelli. Los Angeles: University of California Press, 561–80.

———. 1991. *Marvelous Possessions: The Wonder of the New World.* Chicago: The University of Chicago Press.

Harbsmeier, Michael. "Writing and the Other: Travellers' Literacy, or Towards an Archaeology of Orality." In *Literacy and Society.* Ed. Karen Schousboe and Morgens Trolle Larsen. Copenhagen: Akademisk Forlag, 1989.

Hamlin, William H. 1994. "Men of Inde: Renaissance Ethnography and *The Tempest.*" *Shakespeare Studies* 22: 15–44.

Hartman, Geoffrey H. 1981. *Saving the Text: Literature, Derrida, Philosophy.* Baltimore: Johns Hopkins University Press.

Havelock, Eric. 1982. *The Literate Revolution in Greece and Its Cultural Consequences.* Princeton: Princeton University Press.

———. 1963. *Preface to Plato.* Cambridge: Harvard University Press.

Hulme, Peter. 1986. *Colonial Encounters: Europe and the Native Caribbean, 1492–1797.* London: Methuen.

Huxley, Aldous. 1946. *Brave New World.* New York: Harper.

Kennedy, Harlan. 1992. "Prospero's Flicks." *Film Comment* 28: 45–49.

Kernan, Alvin. 1995. *Shakespeare, the King's Playwright: Theater in the Stuart Court 1603–1613.* New Haven: Yale University Press, 1995.

McLuhan, Marshall. 1962. *The Gutenberg Galaxy: The Making of Typographic Man.* Toronto: University of Toronto Press, 1962.

Montaigne, Miguel de. 1910. "Of the Caniballes." In *The Essays of Michael Lord of Montaigne.* Trans. John Florio, vol. 1, 215–229. London: Dent, 1910.

Ong, Walter. 1982. *Orality and Literacy: The Technologizing of the Word.* London and New York: Methuen, 1982.

———. 1971. *Rhetoric, Romance, and Technology.* Ithaca and London: Cornell University Press.

Palombo, Stanley R. 1995. "*Prospero's Books:* The Unconscious Realized." *Journal of the American Academy of Psychoanalysis* 23: 693–707.

Patterson, Annabel. 1989. *Shakespeare and the Popular Voice.* Cambridge: Basil Blackwell.

Plato. 1928. "Phaedrus." In *The Works of Plato.* Ed. Irwin Edman. New York: Modern Library.

Pratt, Mary Louise. 1985. "Scratches on the Face of the Country; or, What Mr. Barrow Saw in the Land of the Bushmen." *Critical Inquiry* 12: 119–43.

Purchas, Samuel. 1905. *Hakluytus Posthumus, or Purchas His Pilgrimes,* 20 volumes. Glasgow: James MacLehose & Sons.

"Review of *Prospero's Books.*" 1992. *Commonweal* 119 (January 31): 25–26.

———. 1992. *New Republic* 206 (January 20): 29.

———. 1992. *People's Weekly* 36 (December 9): 21.

Roberts, Jeanne. 1991. *The Shakespearean Wild: Geography, Genus, and Gender.* Lincoln and London: The University of Nebraska Press.

Schatz-Jacobsen, Claus. 1994. "Knowing I Lov'd My Books': Shakespeare, Greenaway, and the Prosperous Dialectics of Word and Image." In *Screen Shakespeare.* Ed. Michael Skovmand. Aarhus: Aarhus University Press, 132–47.

Schwerger, Peter. 1994. "*Prospero's Books* and the Visionary Page." *Textual Practice* 8: 268–78.

Shakespeare, William. 1974. *The Riverside Shakespeare.* Ed. G. Blakemore Evans. Boston: Houghton Mifflin.

Stuckey, Elspeth. 1991. *The Violence of Literacy.* New York: Heinemann/Boynton Cook.

Todorov, Tzvetan. 1984. *The Conquest of America: The Question of the Other.* Trans. Richard Howard. New York: Harper & Row.

Vaughan, Alden T. and Virginia Mason. 1991. *Shakespeare's Caliban: A Cultural History.* Cambridge: Cambridge University Press.

Wall, Geoffrey. 1994. "Greenaway Filming *The Tempest.*" *Shakespeare Yearbook* 4: 335–39.

Wilkes, G. A. 1995–96. "The Text and the Discourse of Colonialism." *Sydney Studies in English* 21: 42–55.

Zumthor, Paul. 1990. *Oral Poetry: An Introduction.* Ed. Kathryn Murphy-Judy. Minneapolis: University of Minneapolis Press.

Chapter 9

Additional Dialogue: William Shakespeare, Queer Allegory, and *My Own Private Idaho*

Matt Bergbusch

Introduction[1]

> *If a monument should be penetrated by the mob, it will be rapidly transformed into a place of passage, where everyone enters and exits, brings to and takes away.*
> —Paul Virilio, *Speed and Politics.*

G us Van Sant's road movie *My Own Private Idaho* has quickly become a cult film for youth, and in particular for queer youth. It has at the same time been attacked by the arbiters of good taste for its liberal adaptation of character and aspects of theme from Shakespeare (most notably, *Richard II, 1&2 Henry IV, Henry V*). Thus Terrence Rafferty writes in the *New Yorker* that "there's something glib and imprecise about Van Sant's appropriation of Shakespearean motifs in *My Own Private Idaho*" (Rafferty 1991, 101), and J. Simon, in the *National Review,* argues that "neither Shakespeare's ideas nor his language can be made to apply to Van Sant's present-day hustlers, and the parallels pressed on the plot are much too vague to come across as anything but the vagaries of a cultural parvenu" (Simon 1991, 61). Similarly, in *Film Comment,* Donald Lyons maintains that Van Sant's "acoustic and emotional touch" in incorporating Shakespearean material into his film "is blunt . . . He rewrites Shakespearean dialogue in an oafish way. . . ." (Lyons 1991, 7). These high culture critics imply that the seeming clumsiness with which *My Own Pri-*

vate Idaho deals with its Shakespearean materials is a consequence of its director's unsophisticated, low-cultural grasp of Shakespeare. Perhaps inevitably, given their apparent commitments, Lyons, Rafferty, and Simons fail to grasp the critical understanding of disciplinary authority that frames Van Sant's use of Shakespeare. For ironically, if the treatment of Shakespearean materials in *My Own Private Idaho* appears "clumsy," this effect of clumsiness partakes of a specifically allegorical and politically "sophisticated" clumsiness with which the film as a whole is infused. This self-reflexive clumsiness both opens a space for the production of counterhegemonic meanings, and promotes an insistent awareness of ethical responsibility in the production of meanings. *My Own Private Idaho* indirectly theorizes its own relationship to dominant culture precisely in the way in which it plays with Shakespeare, who it takes as a functional equivalent for dominant tradition in general. In so doing it demonstrates the limits, possibilities, and necessity of an undeluded yet recalcitrantly subversive and "sophisticated" praxis.

"Resemblance and Menace": Allegory, Film, Queer Praxis (Part 1)

Terrence Rafferty's fascinated but mostly negative critique of *My Own Private Idaho* unintentionally reveals Van Sant's allegorical narrative method. Rafferty objects to the accretion of "puzzling bits," and is troubled by an impression that what he calls "Van Sant's meanings" have somehow escaped their author's control. In the end, he argues, *My Own Private Idaho* leaves one feeling "empty" and "cheated" (Rafferty 1991, 101). His critique amounts to an accusation that the film promises a far more coherent, rationally translatable epiphany than it achieves.

As Walter Benjamin knew, allegory reveals that the structures with which human beings attempt to stabilize meaning inexorably fail, and in failing must appear always to have been too rigid and limiting. By "clumsily" foregrounding the "failure" of their own artifice, allegories suggest an irreversible rupture between *physis* and meaning (Benjamin [1963] 1977, 179–187; Eagleton, 1981). Maureen Quilligan's summary of the relation between critical commentary and allegory helps to place Rafferty's objections in context: all critical commentary, she argues, is in effect "allegoresis, whereby the critic treats the text in front of him as a veiled offering of a hidden message," and it is for this reason that "it is specifically the allegorical critic who does not like allegory" (Quilligan 1979, 224). One scene in particular typifies the indeterminacy that Rafferty so much objects to in *My Own Private Idaho*.

In the film's final plot sequence, the central protagonist, homeless gay street hustler Mike Rivers, is alone once again on the Idaho highway he claims as his own. He has been abandoned by Scott who, like Shakespeare's Hal, has run headlong into his inheritance. Mike, who is about to pass out in the last of many narcoleptic seizures, mumbles: "I'm a connoisseur of roads. I've been tasting roads my whole life. This road will never end. It probably goes all . . . around . . . the world." He collapses onto the edge of the highway. Two men in a truck pull up, steal Mike's shoes and duffel bag, then leave. A car then stops, and an unidentifiable man drags Mike inside. As the car drives off, the Pogues' song "The Old Main Drag" begins to play. The caption "have a nice day" scrolls in white across the middle of a black screen as Shane MacGowan sings his bleak tale of poverty, sexual exploitation, and death.

In an interview with Van Sant, Graham Fuller stresses the uncertainty conveyed by *My Own Private Idaho*'s closing sequence: "Mike's lying on the road and someone drives up and takes him away. . . . [Y]ou don't know whether this person is going to save him or hurt him" (Fuller 1993, xiv). Van Sant responds,

> You're not supposed to know, really. . . . In a way it's either you who's the person picking him up or you're him, just being asleep. Or it's just a non-ending, and you assume he will go on in his quest. He's a character that has a hard time changing, so he's just going to go on like that forever—wandering and searching. (Fuller 1993, xiv)

Van Sant's description of the interpretive quandary with which *My Own Private Idaho* leaves its viewer meshes neatly with Maureen Quilligan's assertion that allegory ends, "on an elliptical note, moments before the apocalyptic explosion of meaning" (Quilligan 1979, 220). In typically allegorical fashion, *My Own Private Idaho*'s self-reflexive terminal ambiguity impels readers to choose an ending, and in so doing to locate themselves as "ethical decision-maker[s] outside the realm of the [text] in [their] relation to the world . . ."(Quilligan 1979, 275). To choose a "happy" ending for Van Sant's film, as in the screenplay, where it is Scott who picks Mike up, may seem to be a choice for an emotionally and also politically pacifying escapism in the face of the kinds of "realworld" social problems with which *My Own Private Idaho* engages, and of which the Pogues' "The Old Main Drag" is a closing reminder. To assume that it's "you who's the person that's picking [Mike] up" is to acknowledge the responsibility and risk that attend interpretive freedom. To assume that "you're him, just being asleep"—in many ways akin to suggesting that "it's just a non-ending"—is to shy away from the challenge posed.

As Quilligan notes, one of the characteristic opening gestures of allegory is the offer of a "threshold text" marked off from the body of the ensuing narrative. Threshold texts appear to supply a key to interpretation. However, the function of the threshold text is not so much to provide a helpful template for interpretation as to "undermine the reader's confidence in his ability to translate landscape, character, or action into statement" (Quilligan 1979, 227). Dream visions, as in the opening of Dante's *Inferno,* are a common form of threshold text. In *My Own Private Idaho,* the opening-shot definition of narcolepsy as "a condition characterized by brief attacks of deep sleep" forms a composite threshold text with Mike's initial seizure, which occurs scant minutes into the action. When Mike first collapses viewers may be inclined to assume that the definition has served its purely explanatory purpose. But as the film moves into the terrain of historical nostalgia and abrupt spatiotemporal displacements—reflecting Mike's experience as he shifts between dream and waking states—and of the quasi-Freudian psychosexual dynamics involved in Mike's narcoleptic fantasies about his mother, the significance of the word "narcolepsy" and of the idea of dreaming acquire increasing symbolic weight. Indeed, taken together with the film's self-reflexive (inter)textuality, the composite threshold text evokes doubt as to where, finally, the dreaming stops. Are the film's viewers, as Van Sant suggests, "just asleep," like Mike? In this film so "full of the look and feel of words" (Als 1991, 16), is the opening conjunction of filmic dream vision and written text the first move in a developing, self-reflexive commentary on the dreamlike textuality of the narrative's construction, or even on the dreamlike space of cinematic experience in general? Hilton Als argues that

> [Mike's] attacks . . . are an obvious metaphor for Van Sant's movie-making process: the director is emotionally "uncontrolled" in his response to the cinema's ability to convey the dream state and subliminal desire. . . . . The film's brilliant conceit . . . sets Mike in an internal world of non-control, where images in memory and images in "real" time overlap. A house with interesting angles, or a woman in the street who resembles Mike's mother as he remembers her, can provoke an attack of sleep and dreams, which is where movies live: in the mind that dreams. (Als 1991, 16)

But if, in *My Own Private Idaho,* "narcolepsy, as dreaming, becomes a metaphor for film" (Roy 1992, 70; my translation), a sense of self-conscious guilt attaches to the vicarious dreaming of viewer-consumers before this medium, which has been described by Benjaminian critic Anne Friedberg (Friedberg 1993) as a model of privileged consumerist *flânerie*. After all, as Gary Indiana correctly emphasizes, *My Own Private Idaho* is concerned with homelessness, and with the social structuration of economic and cultural dispossession (Indiana 1991, 64). It is worth remembering, in this context, that the wandering of most of the film's characters is not the privileged *flânerie* of the Baudelairean petit-bourgeois consumer, with which Friedberg aligns film's "mobilized 'virtual' gaze"—the vicarious commodified experience of an elsewhere and an elsewhen—but the enforced nomadism of the disenfranchised. If Friedberg's tensely pessimistic yoking of *flânerie* and homelessness limns the ethical risks of televisual tourism (Friedberg 1993, 108–112), Van Sant's film, which Rafferty has accused of irresponsibly romanticizing the experience of destitution (Rafferty 1991, 101), self-reflexively elicits criticism on this point. Furthermore, in light of Rafferty's accusation of negligent romanticism and more particularly in regard to both his and Simon's insistence that *My Own Private Idaho* falls short of its ostensible Shakespearean model, it is worth remembering that it is in large part the self-naturalizing romance of the *ur*-Shakespeare that Van Sant's film challenges. For if Van Sant's use of Shakespeare runs the risk, to use Homi Bhabha's terminology, of mere "resemblance" and "colonial subjection," of submission to the historical values encoded in the dominant tradition's icons, it also harbours the "menace" of an inappropriate imitation, of "mimicry" that is "at once resemblance *and* menace" (Bhabha 1994, 199; emphasis added).

Queering Bill

The title *My Own Private Idaho* implies a question: how do you make Idaho, that is, an entire state within the American Union, your own? Or, more generally, how do you privatize, make personally significant, a public space? Within the context of the issues engaged by *My Own Private Idaho,* the conundrum the title poses veils a further question: how do you etch a vector of effective resistance across a disciplinary map that enjoins, even as it devalues, certain forms of proprioception (for instance, "I am gay")? Within the broad terms of *My Own Private Idaho*'s questioning of dominant culture, Mike's search for his Mother, whom he identifies with the related ideas of a home and a "normal" family, is a quest fraught with danger and probable disappointment.

Same-sex couples have repeatedly been denied the full legal and social benefits accorded heterosexuals partly because of a blinkered sexual essentialism, which maintains that, since same-sex couples cannot produce offspring, they do not qualify as Family. As Patrick Crowe explains, the definitional nexus Family-Home-Origin-Identity renders "queerness" as homelessness. For Crowe, the challenge gay men and lesbians face involves a redefinition of the terms Home and Family:

> [T]he idea of home typically evokes strong emotional associations since exile from the biological family is a common rite of passage for gay people and the necessary challenge of developing alternative identities posed by this fracture is a recurring focus of attempts to define gay experience. . . . The reproductive motive commonly attributed to heterosexual practice defines the association with home in terms of ancestral origins. Queer denial of the facile relationship between reproductive sex and home founded in the biological family is a necessary step towards a reappraisal of the significance of home. (Crowe 1994, 68)

This queer redefinition of terms is for many, one might add, a necessary step toward an acceptance of self.

Despite the sympathy that it elicits for Mike in his quest for his Mother, *My Own Private Idaho* reminds viewers that for gay persons, the ideal of a self-respect conferred by lineal placing and by procreation with a life partner is in practical terms not available. Thus Mike's Mother remains always just out of reach, her elusiveness emblematizing the exclusion of gays by conventional definitions of family. The film dreams an alternative solution to the psychosocial disorientation (metaphorized by Mike's narcolepsy) initially produced in many gay people by their exclusion from such biologistic reifications as "Family" and "Home." The film's subtextual mantra is encapsulated in a speech from the screenplay that River Phoenix does not deliver in its entirety in the film, but which echoes throughout nonetheless. At the end of the screenplay, as Mike wanders the Idaho highway, he says to himself,

> I suppose a lot of kids like me think that they have no home, that home is a place where you have a mom and a dad. But home can be any place you want. Or wherever you can find . . . . (Van Sant 1993, 186)

Home is wherever you can find, any place you want. You make your own home. But the idea of "home" has then shed its common understanding as stable, lineally determined ab-original place where identity is first formed and the self's historical integrity guaranteed. In symbolic terms, Mike's

tragedy, and the tragedy of many others as well, is that he is unable to aban-
don his quest for biologistic legitimacy, unable to cast off the definitional
model that inscribes his body as incomplete, inadequate, homeless, wrong.
It is perhaps because Mike's speech rings somewhat hollow that Van Sant
chose not to include it in the film. If *My Own Private Idaho* was initially
seen by some gay men and lesbians as a pessimistic and depressing film
(Taubin 1992, 37), this may be because Mike fails in the end to throw off
the discursive bonds of heterosexism, remains lost.

I would like to suggest, however, that if *My Own Private Idaho* does not
depict the overcoming of metaphysical heterosexism, in its engagement
with Shakespeare—the accepted type of a collective cultural home or
foundation—it reveals the ethical potential of the kind of queer-critical
deconstruction of terms exemplified by Mike's wishful assertion that
"home can be anywhere you want." *My Own Private Idaho*'s measured optimism, that is to say, is framed by the recognition that "making your own
home" is a gradual and difficult process, and by the profoundly ethical realization that the conversion of language from prison to home is a pressing
responsibility precisely because it can never be complete in a world in
which, as Richard Rorty (Rorty 1989) has so forcefully argued, specifically
human, interpersonal cruelty and suffering are ubiquitous.

Throughout *My Own Private Idaho,* the desire for a place you can call
home, a place where you belong and that defines you as quintessentially
yourself, is attached to and simultaneously disseevered from the idea of a singular and immutable point of origin. Interspersed with Mike's narcoleptic
visions of his lost home and absent Mother is a recurring image of salmon
swimming upstream to their ancestral spawning pools, their individual and
collective point of origin. Narcoleptically to dream your own home is
thus, metaphorically, to make your own and your culture's origin (it is more
than coincidental that Mike wears a salmon-pink jacket). But the act of
conceiving one's origin depends upon a kind of self-hypnosis, a dream-
state (il)logic, for it remains useful only if the origin continues to be perceived, in its assumed perfection, as necessarily external and temporally
prior to the opposed "imperfection" and "instability" of the here and now.
As dreamed by Mike, the constructed home, the idea of inventing a home,
trades on ideas of biological heredity and reproduction, of the nuclear, biological Family, even as it contravenes them.

My Own Private Idaho's final credits include this odd tribute: "Additional
Dialogue, William Shakespeare." This quiet yet deliberately impertinent
gesture suggests that Shakespeare is to be taken as supplementary to Van
Sant's creative act, rather than as in any sense its legitimating or authoriz-

ing point of origin. At the same time, there are subtly self-reflexive moments in the film that appear to acknowledge the strategic usefulness of Shakespeare's cultural authority for Van Sant's creative practice. This is particularly noticeable where that traditional cultural authority is being overtly abused and the dominant structure of value it (nominally) entrenches (apparently) contravened.

In an early scene, the street kids with whom the viewer is soon to be more fully acquainted speak from the covers of erotic magazines with such titles as "Honcho" and "Joyboy." The magazine cover Mike adorns bears the subtitle, "Go down on History," while other magazines sport such phrases as "King Leer," "Julio and Ron Dewett," "Pleasure for Pleasure." The magazine subtitles rely for their impact upon a simultaneous reinstalling and subversion of Shakespeare's cultural authority. *My Own Private Idaho* is here self-reflexively ironic about the use it makes of Shakespeare's authority: the film goes down on Shakespeare, drags him out of "His" historical remoteness into the messy, exciting present, self-mockingly "outs" the rumoured "gay" Shakespeare. Playing on the idea of Shakespeare as legitimating origin, as resting place of meaning and of value, as the noble Patriarch at the root of the Family tree, *My Own Private Idaho* proclaims that it is "making" Shakespeare, taking Shakespeare home, if only for the night.

But perhaps my use of the word "home" here still seems unclear: how, after all, do you bring your cultural home, home?

When Mike and his friend Scott arrive at the roadside motel near Boise, Idaho where Mike's mother has been living, she has already left for Italy, ostensibly to locate her family origins. The motel is named The Family Tree.

The Family Tree Motel is a roadside stop, a temporary habitation where one rests before resuming one's journey. None of the rooms in the motel is a permanent home. Through the Family Tree Motel, *My Own Private Idaho* links the familiar idea of the family tree, with its connotations of specifically "natural," biologistic, or genetic legitimacy, continuity, and belonging, with the idea of the motel, entailing ideas of impermanence, transitoriness, constructedness. The film suggests that while one may make an historical home, an origin, for oneself, by locating others (or a mother) in various rooms of the Family Tree Motel, the motel is never, finally, a satisfactory, stable, entirely dependable, or convincing "home," as that term has come to be ideally defined in Western, and more specifically American, culture. This may be especially true if, like Mike or Van Sant, one's sexual preference means that one is culturally constituted as not-family. The link established between the family tree and the motel acquires additional crit-

ical force by implying that the notion of "home" as a biologically determined location is itself only a cultural construct, a conceptual motel, and
not an absolute Truth.

Mike then to a certain extent stands in for Van Sant because he occu-
pies the subject position of a gay man. *My Own Private Idaho* reinforces this
connection symbolically. In one of the film's early scenes, Mike, dressed up
as a "little dutch boy," furiously cleans his john's apartment with a can of
"Old Dutch" cleanser. As Mike scrubs, the john becomes increasingly
excited, inciting Mike to ever greater efforts with the exhortation, "Scrub,
little Dutch boy, scrub!" Mike, who metaphorically puts the older gay man's
house in order as he scrubs, may here be thought to represent the gay, Dutch-
American filmmaker Van Sant's efforts to put his own cultural house in
order, to discover/construct a temporary home for his gay American subjectivity in and through *My Own Private Idaho*. That this project is extremely
difficult within the current cultural context, depending, for its success,
upon a special kind of cultural magic/sleight of hand, is further suggested
by what is clearly a ritually scripted initiatory exchange between the john,
"Daddy Carol," and Mike:

Mike: This place is a mess!
Daddy Carol: Yes. Let's make it immaculate.

Here, the special magic of "immaculate conception," with all its politically
retrograde baggage, is parodically invoked in the service of an "unholy"
marriage. A special irony is operative here, for an immaculate conception,
that is, the profoundly metaphysical longing for the birth of a discursive
framework beyond the prison house of inherited concepts, a brand new
idea unsullied by lineal indebtedness (the vitiation enacted by inherited tradition), yet bound to "the" great foundational Truth, has always been the
objective of both radical politics and of the "strong" artist or poet (Bloom
1973; Rorty 1989, 23–43).

As a recent interview with Graham Fuller makes clear, Van Sant is very
sensitive to the question of cultural indebtedness, commenting, in connection with Mike's narcoleptic vision of the salmon run and the process of
his own artistic creativity, "maybe I am also swimming back to . . . where I
came from" (Fuller 1993, xliii). Accordingly, it seems fitting that in both the
screenplay and the film, Mike is subtly identified not only with Van Sant,
but also with Shakespeare.

In the screenplay's opening scene Mike wears a gas station attendant's
shirt bearing the name Bill (in the film, the name has been changed to Bob,

the name given by Van Sant to his version of Falstaff). Later in the screen-play, in the midst of servicing clients in a public washroom, Mike pulls out of his pockets, among other things, a penknife bearing the initial W—or an "upside-down" M (in the film, the knife has become a scribbled-upon band-aid). In addition to standing in metaphorically for a homeless, orphaned, homosexual Van Sant, as Bill or Will Mike figures a homeless, orphaned, homosexual Shakespeare. Through the figure of Mike, Van Sant and Shakespeare enter into a complex relationship with each other; they are family. Shakespeare is Van Sant's cultural parent figure by virtue of her/his inscription as necessarily "homeless" gay person. The family "resemblance" seemingly claimed by Van Sant lies precisely, and paradoxi-cally, in the sense of homelessness or orphanhood felt by gay persons exiled by conventional definitions of family. But there is another level of irony here, for Mike's body, which, as I have already suggested, is also Bill's or Will's body, is a commodity that is bought and sold, made use of and exploited for the pleasure and in fulfillment of the needs of others. If char-acters in the film make use of Mike's body, Van Sant's suturing of Mike and Bill acknowledges the use made in the film of at least a slice of Shake-speare's corpus/corpse. So that the film subverts its own figuration of Shakespeare as family, or as Home, thereby acknowledging that *My Own Private Idaho* partakes of a long tradition of self-naturalizing productions of Shakespeare.

As Leah Marcus (1992) has shown, Shakespeare has come to embody the idea of a transhistorical cultural Home nonetheless functionally detached from any final, single, or precise sociopolitical location or cultural practice. *My Own Private Idaho* reminds viewers that it is Shakespeare's enduring status as cultural Home that, paradoxically, renders "Him" such an attractive candidate for adaptation, or perhaps, I might say, adoption. Indeed, in so far as it treats "Shakespeare" as allegorically emblematic of tradition in general, *My Own Private Idaho* suggests that the only way of "going against" tradition is by a "going beyond" that is also a playing with(in) and upon tradition. There is no outside, no such thing as an immaculate conception, no complete or final overcoming of inherited cul-tural values and the icons in which they are encoded.

"Have a Nice Day:" Allegory, Film, Queer Praxis (Part 2)

My Own Private Idaho simultaneously makes fun of and sympathizes with what Marjorie Garber describes as an almost ineluctably American image of Shakespeare as "phallic mother . . . the navel of the dream of originary cultural wholeness" (Garber 1990, 250). But *My Own Private Idaho*'s self-reflexive caution concerning the oneiric space of film, and in general the temptations of romantic escape into securitizing configurations of the past (of which, again, the Shakespeare myth is a prime example), encodes a broad warning against excessive cultural nostalgia.

An adjunct of the twentieth century experience of vicarious spatiotemporal mobility, and a legacy of the idealization of the past in nineteenth-century historicism, is an excessive nostalgia for the past as a safe or stable place (Friedberg 1993, 186–190). As Anne Friedberg explains,

> Nostalgia (from Greek, nostos = a return; algos = painful) means a painful return, a longing for something far away or long ago, separated by distance and time. An etymological history of the word nostalgia demonstrates that its first usage in the late seventeenth century was to describe the longing for a space, a technical term for "homesickness." By the late nineteenth century, as the discourses of history produced a concomitant idealization of the past, nostalgia also came to mean a time past. (Friedberg 1993, 188)

Friedberg suggests that in its extreme romanticizing incarnation, *nostomania,* nostalgia "falsifies, turning the past into a safe, familiar place" (Friedberg 1993, 188). In other words, as Gianni Vattimo puts it, societal nostalgia for "the world of our infancy," the oneiric space of fulfilled desire, "is in continual danger of turning into neurosis" (Vattimo [1985] 1988, 8). Mike's homesickness is for an inculturated ideal of familial-lineal belonging and the sense of psychic integration purported to flow therefrom; *My Own Private Idaho*'s scanty dream-mediated depictions of Mike as a child—the product of an incestuous mother-son relationship who must be "institutionalised" in order to protect him from his "unsafe" mother—reveal the hollowness of Mike's fragile screen memory of this sort of conventional "home." The longing for an *ur*-Shakespeare parodied by *My Own Private Idaho,* and which underlies Rafferty's and Simon's criticisms of the film's Shakespearean gestures, is a similarly nostomanic dream, and, to loosely paraphrase Walter Benjamin (Benjamin [1963] 1977), similarly mistakes "Shakespeare," the monogram that unveils an absence, for a masked presence.[2]

Allegory does not discover in the historical past a safe place. For the allegorical intuition history is a "petrified landscape" of hypostatized class values (Benjamin [1963] 1977, 166). Allegory redeems the dead matter of history into (new, revolutionary) meaning (Benjamin [1963] 1977, 217) by dislodging "sign systems" from "the historical maps commissioned by the dominant classes" (Seyhan 1991, 246); moments of "revolutionary promise" are thereby saved by allegory from "stagnation and death in history" (Seyhan 1991, 243), and "released into a new freedom with which fresh 'iconic' correspondences may be constructed" (Eagleton 1981, 41). As Mike says, "You make your own home."

The cover of the erotic magazine Mike adorns, as already noted, bears the title, "Go down on history." Mike is the character in *My Own Private Idaho* most centrally aligned with the progressivist quest for a lost historical origin—the recovery of which, it is imagined, will impel a better future; he is also the character most closely associated with the idea that official history is a marginalizing and exclusionary discourse: official heterosexist history, it is implied, has etched an unbridgeable rift between Mike and the fulfillment of the dream of an origin. But "going down" on history is in general the self-conscious signature gesture of allegory itself, and of *My Own Private Idaho* in particular.

Walter Benjamin (Benjamin [1963] 1977, 207) observed that allegory is characterized by subversive punning. Maureen Quilligan and Craig Owens have in turn argued that the pun is not simply a cog in the machinery of allegory, but allegory itself in miniature (Quilligan 1979, 22–26, 42, 223; Owens 1980, 54–55). Allegories, on these views, are "[w]hat puns might be if taken seriously: illustrations of the inherent instability of language and the power of uncodified linguistic relations to produce meaning" (Culler 1988, 3). Oppositional allegories pun on dominant discourse, thereby opening history to what it excludes and represses in fashioning its narrative authority. Punning on history, recontextualizing its hypostatized monuments, subversive agencies reveal that "history is not a set of immoveable past achievements but a discourse, open, as are all discursive practices, to reinterpretation" (Slemon 1989, 164). *My Own Private Idaho* includes two exemplary instances of this self-conscious allegorical "disfiguration and rehabilitation" (Seyhan 1991, 241) of historical materials.

In the opening shot of the first scene set in Portland, the camera performs a slow tilt down from statue of an "Indian" seated astride an elk. At the statue's base—which reads: "The Coming of the White Man"—Mike sleeps soundly in Scott's arms. An interview with Van Sant by David Handelman provides the screen image with a rich gloss: "Moving on, [Van Sant] describes a statue in a section of nearby Washington Park that used to be a gay pickup scene: 'It's of two Indians, one pointing off into the distance,

and it's called Coming of the White Man. I always thought it was ironic'"
(Handelman 1991, 61). Handelman explains that

> Van Sant wanted to get the pun into . . . *My Own Private Idaho,* but the statue
> was surrounded by too much greenery for his taste, so he found an elk statue
> downtown, enlisted a crew member to be covered with patina-tone makeup
> and Indian garb and hung a placard reading, The Coming of the White
> Man—all for a shot that's on-screen for only a few seconds. (Handelman
> 1991, 61)

The crucial phrase, "The Coming of the White Man," which echoes the
promise invested in the birth of the myth of rugged individualism, is visually recontextualized in *My Own Private Idaho* so that it refers instead to the
sexual identity of a group marginalized by the official discourse of American history; or else, more tendentiously, refers to the colonization of the
New World as "rape"—through the association of white men "coming"
with the image of a native person—and by implication suggests an analogy
between the colonization of Native peoples and the cultural oppression of
"sexual deviants" in mainstream American culture. In this emblematically
subversive moment, a monument directed specifically to the historical
interests of the "dominant classes" is thus allegorically (punningly) redirected to suit the present needs of a subversive agency.

Direct address is a typically inclusive allegorical device whereby the alle-
gorist "signals his intention to have the reader participate in the fiction by
making choices" (Quilligan 1979, 242). *My Own Private Idaho* features only
one clear instance of direct address, but it casts a long shadow over both
the narrative that precedes it, and the space of interpretation opened for
the reader by the film's ambiguous resolution. This single instance of direct
address is the final quarter of the second particularly notable "moment" of
self-reflexive historical disfiguration in *My Own Private Idaho.*

The film's gently ironic closing address, "have a nice day," is a caption
that typically accompanies the "smiley faces" still ubiquitous in American
consumer culture. But this closing address is already the fourth invocation
of the smiley face in *My Own Private Idaho.* I will review in reverse order
the earlier three invocations of the smiley face, which taken together with
the fourth contribute tellingly to the film's ambiguous resolution.

The smiley face makes its third appearance at the precise moment that
the film most forcefully undermines the myths of family and home. The
mobile home in which Mike's brother-father Dick lives, and where Dick

paints the family portraits that his patrons often in the end choose not to buy, features an overhead lamp festooned with yellow and red smiley faces. Symbols of optimism allied to the idea of an universal and comforting "family-values" normality, these smiley faces reflect ironically upon the short-circuited trajectory of Mike's lineage. How nice are the days, the faces seem to ask, of Mike's Alpo-nourished brother? How nice are Mike's days? Who, within the America depicted in *My Own Private Idaho,* might in good conscience admonish either of these marginal figures to "have a nice day"?

The smiley face features for a second time in the film as its own negative reflection, as Mike and Scott are travelling to Idaho to see Mike's brother. As Scott tries to restart their stalled motorcycle, Mike connects the "fucked-up face" he sees on the horizon and the motto "have a nice day." Staring down the highway he says, "I've been on this road before. Looks like a fucked-up face. Like it's saying 'have a nice day' or something."

The first smiley face in *My Own Private Idaho* is virtually identical to the already-mentioned negative reflection of a smiley face that Mike sees on the journey to his brother's place, the "fucked-up face" etched upon the horizon where the highway disappears from view. In the film's opening sequence, Mike says, looking down the highway, "There's not another road, anywhere, that looks like this road, I mean exactly like this road. It's one kind of place. Like someone's face. Like a fucked-up face." The camera picks out the fucked-up face as Mike uses his hands to frame the image he describes. The camera's (audience's) point of view and Mike's are one. Turning away from the fucked-up face Mike sees a rabbit scampering away. The words he yells after the no longer visible rabbit are a veiled address to the viewer also: "Where do you think you're running man, we're stuck here together you shit!"

Conclusion

Thierry Jousse suggests that the image of the road in *My Own Private Idaho* "is above all the image of an unpredictable, freely moving film which branches off at leisure, with little attention to linearity, and the unfolding of which is not preestablished: the pleasure of a film whose trajectory we discover as it seems to invent itself on screen" (Jousse 1992, 20; my translation). Within the broader context of *My Own Private Idaho*'s allegorical engagement with issues of history and identity, the Idaho highway on which Mike finds himself at both the beginning and the end of the film, and down which, finally, he disappears, is also the image of the defining, transient, yet never wholly original trajectory each life traces. The fucked-up face at the end of the road is indeed partly the smiley face of the "American Dream" seen through the disfiguring lens of allegory, a subversive scarring (although not, significantly, erasure) of the operative ideological maps of meaning. But more broadly, that fucked-up face is the face of a purely secular history out of and into which the car carrying Mike, who is also, figuratively, Van Sant/Shakespeare/the viewer/this critic, journeys. Mike and the viewer are thus located within a process and an experience of historical becoming whose only possible "end" is death. But death, paradoxically, is a nonending for the subject insofar as it is the moment that sets a limit to the subject's capacity to know and to judge, and thus cannot itself be subjectively experienced and evaluated as an ending. *My Own Private Idaho*'s resistance to closure, its refusal to "end" satisfactorily by making an appeal to a greater foundational Truth beyond the gateway of death, is thus a refusal to foreclose on the ethical domain, the domain of a living, revolutionary human history that is always in the making. On the view only half-facetiously elaborated by *My Own Private Idaho,* "Shakespeare" is but one of Truth's or official history's many aliases. *My Own Private Idaho* "makes" Shakespeare to make history.

Notes

1. I would like to thank the McGill Shakespeare in Performance Research Group for financial support in the spring of 1995, during which time the larger project from which this paper is distilled was written.
2. Benjamin writes: "In the field of allegorical intuition the . . . false appearance of totality is extinguished. . . . [E]very image is only a form of writing. . . . The image is only a signature, only the monogram of essence, not the essence itself in a mask."

Works Cited

Als, Hilton. 1991. "The Cave: Hilton Als on Gus Van Sant's *My Own Private Idaho.*" *Artforum* 30.15: 15–16.

Benjamin, Walter. [1963] 1977. *The Origin of German Tragic Drama.* Trans. John Osborne. Reprint, London: New Left Books.

Bhabha, Homi K. 1994. "Of Mimicry and Man." In *The Location of Culture.* London: Routledge, 85–92.

Bloom, Harold. 1973. *The Anxiety of Influence.* New York: Oxford University Press.

Crowe, Patrick. 1994. "No Place Like Home: Homelessness, Identity and Sexuality in American Queer Cinema." *Cinéaction* 35: 66–72.

Culler, Jonathan. 1988. "The Call of the Phoneme: Introduction." In *On Puns: The Foundation of Letters*. Ed. Jonathan Culler. New York: Basil Blackwell, 1–16.

Eagleton, Terry. 1981. *Walter Benjamin: Or Towards a Revolutionary Criticism*. London: Verso.

Friedberg, Anne. 1993. *Window Shopping: Cinema and the Postmodern*. Berkeley: University of California Press.

Fuller, Graham. 1993. "Gus Van Sant: Swimming Against the Current, An Interview by Graham Fuller." In *Gus Van Sant: Even Cowgirls Get the Blues & My Own Private Idaho*. Ed. Graham Fuller and Gus Van Sant. Winchester: Faber, vii–liii.

Garber, Marjorie. 1990. "Shakespeare as Fetish." *Shakespeare Quarterly* 41.1: 242–250.

Handelman, D. 1991. "Gus Van Sant's Northwest Passage." *Rolling Stone* 616 (October 31): 61–62.

Indiana, Gary. 1991. "Saint Gus: From Portland to Hollywood, the Director and his Camera Remain Candid." *Village Voice* 36.54: 57+.

Jousse, Thierry. 1992. "Sentiers qui bifurquent." *Cahiers du cinéma* 451: 20–21.

Lyons, Donald. 1991. "Gus Van Sant: Lawless as a Snowflake." *Film Comment* 27.5: 6–12.

Marcus, Leah. 1988. *Puzzling Shakespeare: Local Reading and its Discontents*. Berkeley: University of California Press.

My Own Private Idaho. 1991. 35mm, 105 minutes: AAA.

Ostria, Vincent and Laurence Giavarini. 1992. "Gus Van Sant, un cinéaste de Portland." *Cahiers du cinéma* 451: 22–23.

Owens, Craig. 1980. "The Allegorical Impulse: Toward a Theory of Postmodernism. Part I." *October* 12: 67–86.

Quilligan, Maureen. 1979. *The Language of Allegory: Defining the Genre*. Ithaca: Cornell University Press.

Rafferty, Terrence. 1991. "The Current Cinema: Street Theatre." *New Yorker* (October 7): 100–103.

Rorty, Richard. 1989. *Irony, Contingency, and Solidarity*. Cambridge: Cambridge University Press.

Roy, André. 1992. "L'Idaho des rêves." *24 Images* 59: 70–71.

Seyhan, Azade. 1991. "Allegories of History: The Politics of Representation in Walter Benjamin." In *Image and Ideology in Modern/Postmodern Discourse*. Ed. David Downing and Susan Bazagan. Albany: State University of New York Press, 231–248.

Simon, J. 1991. "Urban Blight, Slightly Varnished." *National Review* 43 (December 2): 58–60.

Slemon, Stephen. 1989. "Post-Colonial Allegory and the Transformation of History." *Journal of Commonwealth Literature* 23.1: 157–168.

Taubin, Amy. 1992. "Beyond the Sons of Scorsese." *Sight and Sound* 5: 37.

Van Sant, Gus. 1993. *My Own Private Idaho: A Screenplay.* In *"Even Cowgirls Get the Blues" and "My Own Private Idaho."* Ed. Graham Fuller and Gus Van Sant. London: Faber, 106–187.

Vattimo, Gianni. [1985] 1988. *The End of Modernity.* Trans. Jon R. Snyder. Reprint, Baltimore: Johns Hopkins University Press.

Part VI

Teaching Transversally

Chapter 10

Rehearsing the Weird Sisters: The Word as Fetish in *Macbeth*

Leslie Katz

Among the supernatural entities that issue from the trap in Shakespeare's plays to meddle in human affairs, the witches in *Macbeth* precipitate an especially disorienting brand of linguistic crisis. Macbeth treats their sly, riddling reference to the future as a supernatural speech act, as though the words themselves, rather than his actions, had brought about his ascendancy. Confusing semantics and magic, he elides the capacity of words to predict the future with their power to intervene directly, like charms or fetishes, in the processes of fate. Supposing the witches' speech to proffer the future in the form of a reified image, Macbeth fails to understand the specific way that words encode magic, that is, how they depend on tricks to unlock their content (such as being pronounced backward or penned in blood); how, by rendering semantic interpretation inadequate, they mimic the complex, illusive movements of providence that, in Shakespearean drama, are full of ironies and reversals, especially for those who struggle to oppose them.

In April 1994, I conducted two "witch workshops," one at Amherst College, the other at the University of Rochester. The Amherst participants were undergraduate theater majors; the students who took part at Rochester were enrolled in a graduate English seminar on Renaissance magic. Through each practicum, I proposed a general style of reading *Macbeth,* using physical games and exercises to analyze cross-sections of speech and dramatic action. More specifically, however, I was hoping to dislodge Shakespeare's language from its ordinary linguistic context (its connection to individual speakers, and to ideas about authority and intention), to turn it into something more magical and tactile, thereby causing the distinction between sign and thing, word and flesh, representation and the flow of matter, to oscillate. The result was a repertoire of do-it-yourself rituals, aimed at exploring what, adopting a phrase from Michael Taussig, I would like to call the witches' "carnal and ritualized" relationship to speech, to the word as fetish, or the flip side of Macbeth's compulsive bids to block the flow of life and kill the passage of time.[1]

At Amherst, we started from scratch, looking for ways to embody the witches so as to make sense of their function, both as stage devices and dramatic metaphors. By metaphor, I mean something whose theatrical dimensions—like patterns of physical movement, degrees of conscious and unconscious role-playing, stage position, etc.—unfold so as to echo in the structures of Shakespeare's text. As a starting point, the three actresses and I chose a brief exchange in 1.3., the scene on the heath in which, following their choral prelude in 1.1., the weird sisters pledge to reconvene at nightfall. The first witch greets the others by initiating a kind of roll call or inspection ("Where hast thou been, sister?"), to which each witch answers by offering an account of her recent activities and whereabouts.

> *Third Witch:* Sister, where thou?
> *First Witch:* A sailor's wife had chestnuts in her lap,
>   And munched and munched and munched. "Give me,"
>   quoth I.
>   "Aroynt thee, witch!" the rump-fed runyon cries. (1.3.4–6)[2]

The form of the first witch's rejoinder makes it difficult to know whether she is telling a story or intoning a rhyme, reporting facts or casting a spell. In our first attempt at embodying the speech, the actresses playing the second and third witches sat, listening greedily, while the first witch spoke, delivering her lines as though she were giving the blow-by-blow of a particularly succulent adventure. When the raconteuse paused in her thumbnail narrative, the second witch rose from the floor and set the story into motion again, saying—this time to the third witch— "Give *me!*" The third witch, miming the sailor's wife's showy, open-mouthed munching, turned on her sister, as though casting a spell, 'Aroynt thee witch!' The second witch, seized by the sound of the words, squatted, distending her buttocks. Waddling away, she muttered over her shoulder, in a retaliatory curse, "Rumpfed runyon, rumpfed runyon." The third witch sidled over to the first, holding out her hand and demanding in a gluttonous, if not lewd, voice, "Give *me!*" And thus the sequence recommenced.

In the discussion that followed the exercise, gender-related questions instantly arose. For example: How does covetous desire, generally speaking, play on stereotypes, so that women are imagined as embodying envy in a gender specific way? How does the embodiment change when the parts are distributed among a triumvirate of bearded witches, rather than played solo, in the form of fainthearted Macbeth, who envies the future that the weird sisters have promised to Banquo's heirs? I hoped to work toward answers, but slowly, through the logic of the situation and the actresses' physical discoveries. As the example above illustrates, the idea of physical realization came alive as a technique when the actresses and I discovered how the words recited by the first witch to her sisters could operate as the basis for an action-reaction exercise. The five-word dialogue, embedded in her tale, formed the kernel around which each actress took her turn playing a role in the miniature drama. The key to animating the text lay in the fact that the witches were *three* in number: the narrative, passing from one paired configuration to another, mutated freely, generating a spectrum of ripostes that ranged from playful aggression to genuine mockery. In the course of the rotation, the actresses began to experiment with more subtle gestures: gestures that burlesqued the sailor's wife, brought the witch and the sailor's wife into closer communion, or turned the appetitive greed of the original encounter into a more open, though not less complex, erotic business. In one round, for example, the actress playing the witch, imitating the sailor's wife, tried using the vernacular, "aroynt thee, bitch," to emphasize the secular connotations of the seventeenth-century terminology. This, in turn, led us to imagine a version of the duel performed by male actors, where the witch's "give me" might be spoken as mock solicitation, to which a gay sailor's "wife" would answer, simultaneously expanding his chest and affecting disdain: "Aroynt thee bitch; SNAP! SNAP! SNAP!"

First Witch. Where hast thou been, sister?
Second Witch. Killing swine. (1.3.1–2)

Now we started over, this time from the top of the scene. I asked the actresses to choose a position, requiring only that the members of the trio establish physical contact with each other. The women experimented with several different ways of sitting before finding one they liked. The first witch sat on the floor and spread her legs. The second witch, seated behind, wrapped her legs around her sister's waist. The two women rocked slightly, their position both relaxed and provocative. The fact that the first witch could not see her sister made the pose even more intimate (eye to eye contact would have been too much of a test), while the legs of the second witch, planted in the open space between her sister's thighs, made possible—within the erotic dyad—a wider, more subtle range of aggressive interactions: distrust, goading, withholding, and seduction. The question ("where hast thou been, sister?") expressed a mixture of curiosity and suspicion (possibly a hint of sibling rivalry), but the first witch's physical position, turned toward the audience, sheltered her face from her sister. Her movements worked their way into a conglomeration more intricate than one-on-one dialogue, because her body, together with the other actress's, comprised an organism of four feet, four hands—a form that both countenanced and contained the text's host of shifting voices. The second witch's answer, "Killing swine," provoked hunger, then envy, in the other's face. Meanwhile, this look migrated into the reaction of the third witch, who, suddenly appearing from her hiding place behind the second, accused the first witch, suspiciously, "Sister, where *thou?*"

At Rochester, the students' preparation included reading several transcripts of early modern witch trials, including the case of Ursula Kemp, a woman accused of witchcraft at St. Osyth's in 1582. In the evidence taken against her, Kemp's eight-year-old son, Thomas, testifies that his mother has four familiars: "Titty is like a little grey cat, Tiffin is like a white lamb, Piggin is black like a toad, and Jack is black, like a cat. And he saith, he hath seen his mother at times to give them beer to drink, and of a white loaf or cake to eat; and saith that in the night- time the said spirits will come to his mother and suck blood of her upon her arms and other places of her body" (Rosen 1991, 110).

In the world of sixteenth-century witch trials, small things are dangerous. Thomas's testimony is the slander of a live-in tattler, a little boy who not only enjoys spying on his mother, but also hangs on to small details: minutia that are as plain (bits of white loaf) as they are perverse (sucking blood upon her arms). His testimony foregrounds the malignant possibility of other small things, such as the familiars themselves, demons imagined to run Ursula's spiteful errands. Titty, Tiffin, Piggin, and Jack form a fellowship of plagues, incarnated in the shape of domestic pets that live together in homely vessels: boxes, kettles, or urns. Thomas says that Ursula once loaned the familiars to his godmother Newman in an earthen pot, "the which she carried away with her under her apron" (Rosen 1991, 110). In Thomas's eyes, it is the small things, the petty things, which constitute the most fascinating, yet least accessible part of his mother's secret arts—both magical and domestic.

The testimony of Ursula's neighbors reveals women who, although sharing more fully in her secrets, and by extension, in a network of female relations, harbor suspicions of other women, not to mention hostilities toward certain women who they perceive as seeking to pry into the sanctum of their domestic lives. Witchcraft emerges at a provincial level, out of conversations in a doorway: where one woman seeks to rebuff another's visit, turns down her offer of service, or refuses to trade with her. "The said Ursula fell out with Grace Thurlow, for that she [Grace] would not suffer [Ursula] to have the nursing of her child" (Rosen 1991, 107). On another occasion, Grace turns down Ursula's offer to dye a pair of hose in return for a handful of scouring sand. It is after incidents like these that a witness, in retrospect, will claim that she (or a family member) began to suffer from a mysterious ailment, a sign of the witch's reprisal. Grace Thurlow's snubs and Ursula Kemp's imagined retaliations testify, on both sides, to a long memory for little words, for passing slights. Had Grace not brought charges against Ursula, it seems perfectly possible that Ursula would have brought them against Grace—as surely as the opportunity for gossip missed on one side, seldom fails to speed its dissemination on the other.

In using Kemp's trial to historicize the rehearsal, it was the quality of smallness, if not quaintness and homeliness, that I wished to find and highlight in the witches' interactions. The particulars of Ursula's case (the particulars of a village kitchen or marketplace) echo already in Shakespeare's detail of the chestnuts, while the munching of the sailor's wife, both unmannerly and ostentatious, is resonant with the recurring interplay of village wives who covet and withhold things from each other. But I also wanted to preserve the lesson we had learned at Amherst, viz. to feel how the smallest—and most prized—of the weird sisters' possessions were morsels of contentious speech, such as those that the first witch had gained, and brought back to her sisters, from her momentous meeting with the sailor's wife. Those pieces of language, the stuff of daily greed and resentment, were—like the fetus of a secular spell—something out of which the three witches generated endless mimetic versions of a world from which, by dint of their special fellowship, they were exiled. That is to say, we found that the witches were, to a great extent, ciphers, capable in their reenactment of the "rumpfed runyon"'s stinginess, of turning her resentful speech into a medium for imitation, transformation, and parody.

We sat in a circle and "passed" the witches' words from one person to the next, trying to hear how, even within Shakespeare's text, they afforded a choral effect, never belonging to just one speaker, but reverberating, at first with two voices, but then with more, as each witch snatched her sister's phrase, tried it on like borrowed jewelry, and personalized the intonation:

Her husband's to Aleppo gone, Master o'th' Tiger. (1.3.7)

"Her husband" technically refers to the sailor whose wife was charged, in lines 4–6, with disparaging the first witch; the latter thus signals to her sisters that she is plotting revenge against the husband for his wife's abuses. But the line itself, as it moved around the circle, was transformed, by tonal shifts, into a wayward scrap of gossip: "Master o'th' Tiger," whispered the first woman to the person beside her, who upon hearing, sneered and turned to the woman on her other side, saying in a way that both mimicked and ridiculed the first speaker's snobbishness: "Master o'th' *Ti*—ger." The third woman responded with a titter, and passed the meddling talk on (Greenblatt 1993, 121).[3]

The original production of *Macbeth,* performed in 1606 at James I's court, would have traded on the style of a courtly antimasque.[4] The transcendent harmony of the monarch's microcosm (the court as a miniature version of the kingdom, the kingdom as a miniature version of the divinely ordered cosmos) was challenged, in the antimasque, by actors disguised as one of several subdivisions of the kingdom of darkness: wildmen, goblins, witches, and so on. James's emblematic victory over his assailants was regularly represented through a trick of stage machinery, which allowed the decor to open and reveal the grandeur of the court, its jewels, its lights, and its costumes, bursting through and flooding over the darkness of the fictive setting.[5] In Shakespeare's play, the witches are cast more ambivalently, making it difficult to tell whether they speed Macbeth's downfall indifferently or maliciously. In 4.1, having agreed to let Macbeth witness the future, the weird sisters conjure a spectral procession of eight kings, "the last king with a glass in his hand" [stage direction]. This mirror was probably carried into the audience and angled so that, in its frame, the spectators caught the reflection of the King himself.[6] By predicting James I's succession through this eerie trick, the witches become an ambiguous cog in the mechanism of sanctioned historical representation, demonstrating their ability to transform the trappings of king and state, in the same way they transform everyday speech, into objects that are half-ghostly amulets, half-ingenious stage devices.

By copying the speech patterns of village wives, their gossip and telltale accusations, Shakespeare's weird sisters evoke certain ideas about feminine malice and frivolity, ideas that not only underlie, aim, and focus specific accusations of witchcraft (as seen in the St. Osyth trial), but contribute to the play's broader demonization of women's language. In the original production, the weird sisters would have been played by bearded adult actors, as opposed to the boy actors or apprentices conventionally cast in female roles: thus Banquo's, "You should be women;/ And yet your beards forbid me to interpret/ That you are so" (1.3.44–6). The witches are not only, as Macbeth calls them, 'imperfect speakers,' but also imperfect simulations of women. By forcing their biological gender into an equivocal register, Shakespeare complicates the business of demonization: for a Jacobean audience, the witches work as comic feminine caricatures ("they are part of the fun of staging witchery" [Berger 1982, 68]), at the same time they challenge—even threaten to emasculate—the "tightly muscled rhetoric" (Berger 1982, 68– 69)[7] that Macbeth and the other Scottish warriors have buckled on to make up for their general lack of "manly readiness" (2.3. 130). At the end of the play, when the weird sisters' macabre prophecies reveal themselves as theatrical tricks (Birnam wood marching in the form of camouflaged soldiers), their magical powers become as suspect, if not as clunky, as their hybrid gender.[8]

Again, my purpose in turning toward history was only in part to discover the originary meanings encoded in Shakespeare's witches: it was worth knowing and discussing, for example, the ways in which the weird sisters parody feminine trickery, at the same time they mock and deflate manly virtues. But I also wished to pull the text in different directions, using its intrinsic indeterminacy as a basis for theatrical experimentation. The witches' campy, composite qualities frustrated our attempts to organize ourselves into a unified witch "community": that is, to reduce the weird sisters to a coven of cackling stereotypes or join them together as agents of a feminist rereading—in which they might conspire, *as* women, to denaturalize the male-to-male links in political succession or undermine the coherence of Duncan's patriarchal rule. Situated at opposite ends of an interpretive spectrum, these available readings crystallized a facet of the text, while failing to make enough of the dissonance internal to the witches' verse itself. Mobile, contentious, *and* shared, the weird sisters' speech elicited fluid and unpredictable emotional responses. Therefore, we aimed at propagating multiple and layered versions of a single scene, as a basis for testing, rather than demarcating, its gender implications.

In both workshops, we placed ourselves at the fulcrum of the weird sisters' double gender, at the vortex of their triple speech. The participants found that moving the particles of storytelling, hearsay, and prattle around in a circle was—like rotating the roles in the witch's story—a way of winding up the witches' charm. The actresses experienced the gathering momentum of Shakespeare's text, as lines and phrases, passing through each of the witches' mouths, became the shared property of the group. This made sense of a marked shift in the first witch's speech, where—out of the preceding specks of everyday speech—s/he yields language that is more self-consciously magical:

> But in a sieve I'll thither sail
> And like a rat without a tail
> I'll do, I'll do, and I'll do. (1.3. 8–10)

The units of paradoxical verse no longer copied the envious gossip of village wives, but rather invoked (through childish riddles)[9] the type of freakish phenomena associated through folk superstition with necromantic transformation: for example, the witch who, failing to take perfect possession of a rat's shape, becomes a deficient tailless rat. Again, we were faced with the idea that the witches, in their imperfections, were meant to give back a mocking reflection of masculine defects in the play—a joke on "nature's copy" (3.2. 38). But the potency, even the danger, of the singsong phrases drew less on the paradoxical formulations, than on the gyrating motion of passing the phrases around the circle. In place of snide titters, or perhaps building on them, each actress spoke with concentration, trying to commit the lines to memory, as she simultaneously participated in the group recitation. In place of the circular tug of war, the verse moved in a crescendo around the circle, as though, as a result of the previous exercises, the participants had become primed, as a group, to crank up the witches' curses.

At this point in the rehearsal, I brought out a box of small fetish objects, quaint and peculiar enough to pass as freaks of nature, as crusty, mummified familiars:

> a nest of blonde hair
> a sawfish snout
> the facsimile of a shrunken head
> a blowfish skeleton
> an embalmed cat

I wanted to displace the catalogue of charmed ingredients that the witches, in a later scene, would add to Hecate's magic gruel ("Eye of newt and toe of frog,/ Wool of bat, and tongue of dog,/ Adder's fork, and blind-worm's sting,/ Lizard's leg and howlet's wing" etc. [4.1. 14–17]) by turning them into material versions of the words, or charmed particles of speech, that the first witch gathers, like debris from a battlefield, in the course of her village scavenging. But this time, the power of the particles lay in their novelty: they were palpably proplike and, in the image of the singsong verse, they could be handled explicitly as toys. The objects thus oriented the witches around a new diversion, and reorganized their envious and appetitive energies within the structures of a self-conscious game.

We divided one more time into groups of three, and stitched together our own versions of the scene in 1.3. Our text began with the first witch saying to the others: "Look what I have!" then, divulging her object, "Here I have a pilot's thumb [a nest of hair, a shrunken head], etc." From there, I asked the actresses to improvise their own recreation, using the lines of the text to propel their given object around the circle.

> *Third Witch:* "Her husband's to Aleppo gone, Master o'th' Tiger."
> *Second Witch:* "Show *me,* show *me*" [at which point, the object was passed to the second witch, becoming an effigy of the sailor].
> *Second Witch:* "I'll drain him dry as hay; / Sleep shall neither night nor day / Hang upon his penthouse lid" [as if inventing a curse with which to push the game along].
> *First Witch:* " 'Give *me*' " [snatching at the object].
> *Second Witch:* " 'Aroynt thee witch!' "

And so on. The uneven rhythms of giving and seizing were neutralized when the three witches found their way back to one of the choral rhymes and fell jointly, or in orderly succession, into its cadences. "Weird sisters hand in hand/ Posters of the sea and land/ Thus do go about, about." But as pieces of spells revolved around the respective circles, their strength inevitably climaxed, then wound down. The violent redundancy of the curses culminated in their fragility, demonstrating their concomitant potential for failure. Without the stimulation of aggression and desire—the principles that held the circle in resilient tension—the spells themselves had nothing to feed on. At which point, a mischievous witch might break the increasingly embarrassing circularity by inciting curiosity or greed all over again, with the demand, "Look what I have!" The fetishes (or toys)[10] when teasingly disclosed or generously proffered, usually assisted in recharging the witches, restoring their own sense of character and motivation within the collective circle.

Through the evolution of the game, pedagogy became in Stephen Greenblatt's sense a form of witchcraft, a "space where the fantastic and the bodily . . . touch" (1993, 127),[11] and where the material effects of Shakespeare's poetry doubled as external motive powers. Our point was to explore the torque of small phrases. At a corporeal level, we experienced their equivocal power to turn the members of our weird sisterhood both toward and against each other. We did not want to deny the aggression—the lust, envy, and desire—which flavored relations in the triad, any more than we could resist the momentum of the rotating lines that prevented those aggressive impulses from solidifying. The pivoting words spun attraction around, so that it grew, through the exchange of three speakers, into hostility. Parodies of gossip evolved into flirtation. The text worked as a complex (magical?) medium for decentering gender identities, if only because the words never served as reference points in a stable or hierarchical organization of meanings. Forms of exchanging secrets, and competing for desires—forms that were recognizably "feminine"—assumed strange contours when the objects of desire were spiny skeletons and disfigured corpses. The dismembered items, which emanated a macabre aura one moment, turned shoddy and tawdry the next. One of three men participating in the Rochester group cradled the embalmed cat in his lap and nursed it with an eye dropper. In sum: the feminine origins of the weird sisters' speech emerged as integral to its dynamic power, but the dynamism encoded in the text allowed us, as a group, to destabilize by way of a half-farcical, half-sinister game the demonic stereotypes that have crystallized historically—in the moment of witchhunts, etc.—around those origins.[12]

Chapter 10 Notes

1. I am particularly indebted to Michael Taussig's account of the fetish in *The Nervous System* (Routledge, 1992).

2. All citations from the New Penguin Shakespeare will appear in parentheses.

3. In "Shakespeare Bewitched," Stephen Greenblatt describes the theatrical effects achieved when imaginative drive combines with what Aristotle calls *enargeia*: "the liveliness that comes when metaphors are set in action, when things are put vividly before the mind's eye, when language achieves visibility" (1993, 121). Tying his remarks to *Macbeth,* Greenblatt underscores the demonic dimension of language when it attains this level, not only of tangibility, but more important, of animation and praxis within the theatrical frame.

4. A good example of the genre is Ben Jonson's *Masque of Queens,* performed by the queen and her ladies at Whitehall on February 2, 1609. The anti-

masque featured 11 witches who entered the stage from "an ugly hell, which flaming beneath, smoked unto the top of the roof" (lines 21– 22). As for the witches, Jonson writes, they came "first one, then two, and three, and more . . . some with rats on their head, some on their shoulders . . . all with spindles, timbrels, rattles, or other venefical instruments, making a confused noise, with strange gestures" (lines 26–30). In order to praise the monarch, Jonson contrasted the hags' impotent magic with James's powers of reason, installing the monarch in a Chaucerian House of Fame, whose structure was supported by statues of classical poet celebrities.

5. For more on court masques, see Stephen Orgel's *The Illusion of Power* (Berkeley: University of California Press, 1975).

6. G. K. Hunter, in his introduction to the Penguin Edition, notes that performances at the Globe would have required a modification of this staging (30). For more on the glass and on the witches' riddling lies, see Stephen Mullaney, "Lying like Truth: Riddle, Representation, and Treason in Renaissance England," *ELH* 47 (1980): 32–47.

7. With regard to the bearded witches, Berger says that they are "not androgynes but bemonstered manlike images of the feminine power that threatens throughout the play to disarm the pathologically protective *machismo* essential to the warrior society."

8. To capture the clunkiness of the costume, think of Falstaff in *The Merry Wives of Windsor,* when Mistress Ford and Mistress Page stuff him into "the witch of Brainford"'s clothing and smuggle him ignobly out of Ford's house.

9. Of the weird sisters' riddling, Berger writes "They flash their credentials as symbols of transrational disorder by uttering paradoxes and inversions that sound pregnant, but are easy to unpack," 67.

10. *Macbeth*. "There's nothing serious in mortality; / All is but toys."

11. Greenblatt concludes that "to conjure such a theatre places Shakespeare . . . in the position of the witch," 127.

12. Thanks to Kathy Couch and Caroline Prugh at Amherst; Kenneth Gross and the members of his graduate seminar at the University of Rochester.

Works Cited

Berger, Jr., Harry. 1982. "Text against Performance in Shakespeare: The Example of *Macbeth.*" *Genre* 15: 68.

Greenblatt, Stephen. 1993. *New Historical Literary Study.* In "Shakespeare Bewitched." Ed. Jeffrey N. Cox and Larry J. Reynolds. Princeton University Press.

Rosen, Barbara, ed. 1991. *Witchcraft in England, 1558–1618.* Amherst: University of Massachusetts Press.

Shakespeare, William. 2000. *Macbeth.* Ed. Stephen Orgel. New York: Penguin.

Chapter 11

Shakespeare's Enduring Immorality: the Ethical vs. the Performative Turn, or Toward a Transversal Pedagogy

Donald Hedrick

The Example of Shakespeare

Critical revolutions hit teachers of Shakespeare with pronounced impact, for as "cultural capital" (Guillory 1993), Shakespeare's works constitute a Wall Street of literary study. Accordingly, the cultural specter of the Great Shakespeare Crash (for instance, Taylor 1999, 205) figures in expressions of conservative fear as well as liberal reassurance. Either produces a certain tension, if not resentment, when a Shakespearean yet again walks into class. Whether in professional jokes—a critic's remark that "it's a dirty job teaching Shakespeare. But somebody's got to do it" (Pechter 1995, 125)—or in rhetorical maneuverings, some undoubtedly infecting the present essay, we detect a nervousness about teaching Shakespeare in relation to the market value of our stock.

It would be an interminable project to trace passing mention of Shakespeare in discussions of literary value, where as limiting case, to use the "Shakespeare example" may expose one's ideological faultlines. In current interrogations of canonicity the example becomes especially problematic, since to imagine Shakespeare as *conceivably* marginal merely reinforces his centrality, confirming his role as structural symptom of literary culture. The Shakespeare example continually confirms its value along with ours as gatekeepers of the *distinctions* of culture (Bourdieu 1977), even when challenged, through such circulation and circularity.

Bracketing questions of literary value, I want to consider, through a particular dilemma, the ground and direction of our teaching, with some suggestions toward an exploratory, transversal pedagogy that can only be sketched but not systematized. The present historical moment points toward two relevant and emergent currents in the broader study of literature: the first, with a longer pedigree, is a moral emphasis; the second, more recent and less well-defined, is what I call a "performative turn"—developing bell hooks' claim that "teaching is a performative activity" (1994, 11). I want to reflect upon these shifts respectively, then place them on the same track, heading toward one another, in a transversal relation through which each must venture outside its conventionally prescribed conceptualization. In the process I hope to revise some of the anxiety described about canonicity, and perhaps even to make teaching safe for Bardolatry again, or rather Bardolatry safe for teaching.

The ramifications of our critical revolutions are especially italicized in teaching Shakespeare. Both the right-wing phobia of choice—that music videos or "obscure" postcolonial literature will be taught "instead" of Shakespeare (Berubé 1994, 172–4)—as well as the left-wing agenda—that Shakespeare be moved "off center" in literary study (Cohen 1985, 31)—frame the canonicity debate as a discourse of displacement. When a generation ago Jonathan Culler called for fewer readings of individual works and authors (1982, 220), however, the scholar-teacher of the required Shakespeare course could probably view such displacement either as irrelevance or as threat; now the issue can devolve into departmental infighting about how often Shakespeare gets taught (Smith 68). By 1978 "theory" had first intervened at a Shakespeare Association Forum, which I organized, representing marxist, feminist, and psychoanalytic approaches, as Shakespeareans themselves increasingly called for some displacement, resolving any professionalist contradiction by anticipating, for instance, future Shakespeare sessions in which "Shakespeare" was not even mentioned.

Such has come to pass, in effect taking "Shakespeare" transversally outside itself. The more lurid effects of theory, such as its disposition toward involuted self-consciousness, were inevitably accompanied by an exemplary rise of critical attention to our everyday practices of pedagogy. It is thus encouraging to note a new journal, *Shakespeare and the Classroom,* and an increase in teaching topics in *Shakespeare Quarterly* and in Shakespeare Association programs, although the interest is often relegated to workshops subordinated to major sessions. Despite the increase of salutary self-awareness, however, teaching often remains insulated from the ramifications of the critical revolution, perhaps because it tends to be viewed as private, individual artisan labor—Shakespeare, as it were, without class. This very privacy affords theorizations of an "erotics of pedagogy" (Penley 1986,

138), where teaching becomes analogous to sex or love and hence, as a figure of the transversal, less open to institutional disciplining. Yet team teaching, like interdisciplinarity for Stanley Fish, remains "so very hard to do."

Even if reflected in teaching, theoretical knowledge may not produce some one-to-one relation to it. Aside from theory courses themselves (Sadoff and Cain 1994), practical teaching often resists theory's intervention, whose consequences are often "trickle down" at best, particularly at the undergraduate level. As we progress through rigorous interrogations of methodological assumptions of "theme" (Levin 1979), "character" (Fineman 1986), "close-reading" (Rabinowitz 1987), we often revert back to such techniques when grander narratives of theory are out of sight. Such backsliding makes it all the more difficult to accept responsibility to question "Literature" itself (Smith 1994, Miklitsch 1994). If any consequence has been more general, it is probably the method of "approaches," that is, of having students understand and adjudicate theoretical models in turn. Perhaps the limitation of all this is that theory is regarded as something fixed, a method to "apply" to texts, rather than an "investigative-expansive" activity (Reynolds and Fitzpatrick, forthcoming) with the capability of transforming even itself.

One self-aware example of the problem here is Edward Pechter's "thick description" of the vagaries of teaching, taking as its starting point Gerald Graff's sensible idea to "teach the conflicts," at least those stipulated by literary study, to our students. How he describes what undercuts neat theorizing, namely, the "slime of teaching" (1990, 125), repays closer attention since it may resonate for most teachers and is important in instructive ways, though for present purposes the indefiniteness he identifies might be rethought as a virtue rather than a handicap.

Pechter's initial question is which reading of *A Midsummer Night's Dream* to teach, namely, C. L. Barber's more conservative view of the play as temporary, festive release (1959), or the New Historicist/cultural materialist view of the play as a cover for social, political, or gender inequities. Pechter usefully identifies a larger philosophical tradition (positions either separating or rendering the permeable boundaries between fiction and reality), then playfully considers this as like Edmund's dilemma in *Lear*, deciding between Goneril and Regan: "Which of them shall we take? Both? One? or neither?" (1995, 112) Pechter concludes that lack of an ultimate consensus is not a genuine problem, for we only distort critical history if we imagine some previous utopian consensus—an unexceptionable claim.

Not pretending to stand "above" the conflicts, Pechter does not present the choice in traditional, liberal humanist fashion, as an open marketplace of ideas. Instead, he emphasizes different constraints on interpretive instability, in the administrative-technical side of teaching. Beginning "Teaching Differences" with studied, commonsensical banality—"Where I teach, the book order forms for fall courses arrive in the second week of May" (106)—Pechter selects the moment when syllabus choices require pragmatic rather than intellectual rationale. Having privileged the status of the banal "slime of teaching," he goes on to enumerate a striking list of chance scenarios: switching plans to teach the materialist *Dream* for a group of sociology majors, from whom he takes "refuge" in Barberian gaiety; different circumstances resulting in teaching just the opposite; abandoning the play for another with urgent political relevance; a personal argument before class producing a state of confusion, despite which the class is "one of the best . . . you have ever taught"; or, physical attraction to a front-row student, attraction that, because of one's personal life, might go somewhere but does not.

This postmodern list of wild contingency confirms for Pechter why "sovereign reason" never fully governs teaching. And yet, Pechter views these challenges to a single pedagogic subjectivity not as possibilities for change or transformation, but as mere annoyances. Thus, we need not despair, however, since banal factors such as the same time slot or the same room for a class determine that "a story made up of episodes like these does not mean that teaching is a chaotic or anarchic activity" (123). What Pechter calls "scandalous" in his Shakespeare example is a radical contingency reducing or, viewed otherwise, elevating the teaching of literature into something like show business with its spectacular contingencies of value, anarchism in its nonpejorative political sense. I want to allow his radical insight but question his key assumptions, to revise this version of show business into something more transformative, as an opportunity for experiential alterity. One assumption or tendency is to perceive individual, local experience as definitive, with the minimal unit of teaching taken to be the single classroom performance—" the best class you've ever taught." The political hope for the single class is like the hope typically expected of the single text, reflecting in either case our inability to theorize collectivity. The scenario of a utopian hour allies Pechter with progressive scholars viewing the classroom as opportunity to create a miniaturized ideal of democratic social relations for demonstrating, say, "emancipatory authority" (Giroux 1998, 87). Another assumption, one I explore later, is that the experience is primarily intellectual, cognitive, and adjudicatory, with students applying reasoning powers to decide between positions probably furnished by the teacher, whereas a transversal pedagogy would subject this to a noncognitive, expressive other.

Less assumption than subtext, however, is the pervasive spirit of the moral in the list of contingencies Pechter lists in a sequence from public to hyperprivate. Borrowing teaching tropes from the dramatic plots he teaches, Pechter is nevertheless not as forthright as he might be, thwarting sustained ethical inquiry by teasing and allusive rhetorical play. His apparently commonsensical rejection of "anarchy" marks its own evasion of the ethical, for his undeclared versions of what different students *need* coincidentally corresponds to anarchy's political and ethical basis in *mutual aid* (Kropotkin 1986). In Pechter's subtext, it would seem, teaching's actual "slime" may turn out to be its pressure toward an ethical dimension, that uncomfortable place for modern pedagogy. The unacknowledged tension between ethical claims and the "performing" teacher calls for more rigorous theorization, if not for the possibility of their shifting places in a transformative pedagogical space.

The Ethical Turn

With the upsurge of scholarship with titles including the terms "ethical" and "moral," the Shakespearean teacher is confronted with even more reason for fragmented professional identity. To buy into the discourse of morality seems to risk recuperating the Bardolatrous tradition that views Shakespeare, as Coleridge wrote, the virtuous writer who is best able to make readers "better as well as wiser" (1992, 132). To focus on the ethical at all would thus seem to mark a backsliding from theory, a slippery slope toward belief in essentialist visions of character and conduct. Moreover, for progressive Shakespeareans, such a turn might be complicit with the tactical impoverishment of political discourse by those also attacking the "political correctness" of the academy. Of course, "anti-ethical" Shakespearean pedagogy predates the arrival of theory, for the most influential American teacher of the century, G. L. Kittredge, was well-known for his scorning Shakespeare's presumed moral uplift for students (Frey 1984, 548), though undoubtedly he never took the further step of an active alliance with what might be thought of as an "immoral" Bard. From another perspective, however, an ethical pedagogy in my sense would permit "tenured radicals" to sustain what in the formative sixties were in effect always ethical debates, both personal and national (Cohen 1987, 39).

In any case, an ethical resurgence may now generate its own "scandal" in literary studies. In *The Ethics of Criticism,* Tobin Sievers describes this legitimation conflict, observing that poststructuralists "rarely use the word 'ethical,' no doubt for fear of being unethical" (1993, 37). He deftly outlines the ethical underpinnings of modern criticism in New Criticism, whose political motives we forget in reducing it to mere formalism. Lionel Trilling's statement that we see "literary situations as cultural situations and cultural situations as great elaborate fights about moral issues" (Sievers 1993, 13), is problematic for current political criticism only if "moral" in Trilling's statement is reduced to the merely individual.

Direct moral questions now sound unsophisticated, resistant to the "gains" of theory, particularly its interrogations of agency and subjectivity. Marjorie Perloff remarks in relief that in any understanding of where theory has brought us, at least we have gone beyond asking a student, "What would you do if you were Desdemona?" (1992). But a sophisticated return to what is dismissed as "characterological" (Fineman 1986) can now be mounted (Porter 1988; 1991), and other discredited concepts may eventually require critical rethinking—sea-changes cautioning against stigmatizing *any* critical term. We might recontextualize Perloff's dismissed question more transversally, to ask, following Pechter's example of contingent need, "What would you do, Zane, if you were Desdemona?"—pedagogically a "real," transversal question for a male student's "subjective territory" (that is, a question whose answer is unknown) rather than a "test" question (Searle 1969, 66) with predetermined parameters. The case illustrates another, greater potential scandal: that in teaching literature there exists no necessary, one-to-one relationship between the forms of teaching and "progressive" uses, although given forms serve ideological functions at given historical moments. For example, New Criticism's close-reading, a suspect technique for many (although questioned early on—Eggers 1977, xii) could assist the radical paradigm of democracy defined as "paying attention" (Bellah 1991). Even the *lecture,* ostensibly a mode of domination, could be reconceived as more of a transversal, investigative mode of discourse, that is, a professor's personal inquiry within a wider, systematic controversy (MacIntyre 1990, 232). Any practice whatever could be recast to provide a transversal model, which is not to claim that all practices are simply politically neutral.

Pechter described but failed to theorize an ethical given outside a given subjectivity—the collective need for supportive aid in personal or political circumstances of some urgency. Indeed, local needs could either undermine, or in the above example motivate, teaching approaches. One thinks, for instance, of Paolo Freire's "pedagogy of the oppressed," a student-centered teaching intended to empower a Brazilian urban poor (1990). Such a pedagogy's value may be questioned, however, in different, especially U.S.

contexts. Where I have taught in a small, prestigious liberal arts college, a progressive teaching for students destined for upper managerial jobs might involve disempowering rather than empowering, that is, experiencing what it is not to be the self but to be others. Or, the class bifurcation of Lear's plea to "Expose thyself to feel what wretches feel" (3.4.34) might work transversally for some students, perhaps even discomforting them, but not for others—the very reason for citing it. It signals either a sympathetic imagination (knowing what it feels like to be wet) or a critical one (knowing that you don't know what it feels like).[1] Disjunctions of race, class, and gender, then, might call for a disjunctive teaching with local tactics differing from long-term strategies.

We may forget that interpreting students, like interpreting texts, is what constitutes a distinctively transversal basis to all teaching, likewise transversal through extension into the interpreting of their interpretation of us, as they look back at us, and thus that neither of these interpretations need be determinable in advance. My own history of teaching students in most of the categories of academic institutions recently analyzed by their social stratification (Aronowitz 1994, 245) attests to this sort of contingency, and the need to distinguish students' wants from needs. In these shifting settings, moreover, ethical questions themselves might be bifurcated and subject to specific deuniversalizations. On the other hand, student-centered models risk not only "romantic conservatism" but subsumption within consumerist models, followed by political appropriation by administrators or politicians with corporate-modeled agendas for making consumers feel good. Indeed, given these newer regimes of subjectivity, teachers are especially vulnerable now to social structures "that undermine[s] the moral concerns they profess" (Sharp 1975, 227), and hence require pedagogies of experimental alterity.

The current revolution in literary studies, particularly in its "linguistic turn," however, may have short-circuited ethical inquiry, creating registers of discourse that, apart from their technical value, may be distant from the common experiences of teachers and students. Although an ethical turn might serve as corrective, the answer is not simply to dismiss unfamiliarity: the "obvious" must itself be put under critical and moral pressure, if the ethical development of college students is conceived as an ever increasing *complexity* of understanding (Perry 1968), resisting a now prevalent authoritarian populism. The time may nevertheless be propitious to "reconceive moral reflection" in literary studies, acknowledging particularly how the broad tradition of cultural critique has sustained moral concerns (Gunn 1987, x). Literary study, which has always been indebted to the tangled relation between itself and philosophy, might again profit from examining that entanglement, an area from which poststructuralist theory has typically fled (Nussbaum, 1990, 179). Indeed, with the invigoration of ethical philosophy by such figures as Alisdair MacIntyre (1981), Martha Nussbaum (1986, 1990), Charles Taylor, Bernard Williams (1985), and Judith Jarvis Thomson (1986), there is no lack of directions for consideration.

The return inevitably encounters another phenomenon, namely, "morality" as a standardized political theme of the moment. A deeply impoverished concept in election campaigns, this theme is further distorted through domination of a society of spectacle in which, increasingly, "that which appears is good, that which is good appears" (Debord 1983, sec. 12). Significantly, the political right, either in its decorous or its more looney camps, has often captured the very discourse of "virtue," at the same time working behind the scenes to increase a number of private miseries, miseries for which it then calls for only individualist solutions. The evasion of what is moral and of moral agency may leave some theoretical positions inadequate for analyzing such phenomena, insofar as they may not be the expected Foucauldian "strategies without strategists" but rather conscious political actions and legislations, promoted by some who regard academics as the nation's worst enemies and seek to discredit universities. As "morality" increasingly falls under forces of anti-intellectualism, moreover, "Virtue" becomes a *Newsweek* cover, picturing Hillary Clinton with William Bennett as dual versions of a single, pious personality type (June 13, 1984). Such political contexts, then, considerably raise the civic stakes of an ethical turn, or at least of what is *perceived* to be an ethical turn.

If an informed return is conceivable in such an impoverished climate, three suggestions in the direction of the transversal may be offered. First, the sense of the "moral" must be continually expanded and explored, including the realms of what is taken to be "immoral," and in collective spheres rather than merely individual ones. As an example, it does not wrench *Measure for Measure* out of either its narrative or historical context to consider not simply the individualism of a hypocritical government official (an element that, I have found, tends to blind students to the play's political content), but also its equally authorized story of the state taking on responsibility for public morality. Often a fuller historicization actually returns us to a contemporary relevance, whereas "premature historicization" (Žižek 1992) merely limits inquiry of all kinds. Despite students' often stronger "pull" toward the private narrative (reinforced by everything from talk shows to high schools), one must reveal how this realm is maintained and naturalized, and whom it serves, just as in that play private moral qualities are carefully manipulated by the apparatus of the state and its imposition of subjective territory. One must not only in one's teaching resist individualism (Strickland 1990), but also use it.

In addition to the expansion of what is taken to be the individual subjective realm of morality, individual acts must also be regarded transversally outside themselves, as a collective realm of political and social relations, rather than exclusively within individual or even family ones. A double standard, for instance, is being applied when corporate decisions disrupting or destroying entire communities are not subject to the critical scrutiny some would apply (often maliciously) to an unmarried woman's decision to have a child. Compensating for the double standard of media lack of interest in how *businessmen* might themselves be raised "lacking values" (see Jacobs 1992), a cultural criticism should do so when appropriate, placing them experimentally in an alterior sphere of judgment. Along these lines, we might well explore questions of "business ethics," an interdisciplinarity often ignored in vague approvals of more liberal academic "interdisciplinarity." Our obligation to historicize ought not serve evasion of ethical inquiry; it may be that our best analogy to the privileged, inaccessible Renaissance absolute prince with his privileged distance *is* the corporate CEO, an uncanny analogue now even producing guides that find business tips in Shakespeare, the Bard (uncritically) read as a "guide to leading and succeeding on the business stage" (Augustine and Adelman 1999). *Sometimes,* it would seem, historicize.[2]

My third suggestion—always to append "inquiry" when using the term "moral"—distances me somewhat from the overtly strident politics of the preceding paragraph, limiting somewhat the very political criticism I have practiced. "Moral inquiry" may be no more than a synonym for moral philosophy, but the combination term furthers the distinction among what Bernard Williams views as different "styles" of moral philosophy (1985, 71ff.). For some poststructuralist philosophy, however, we must problematize this very notion through skepticism about the human ability to achieve distance and self-critique about moral matters. If so, the term "moral inquiry" is only an oxymoron. Nevertheless, I think "inquiry" is appropriate, just as some suspicion of the usual priority of the cognitive over the expressive may be productive in teaching, as I will address later.

While moral understandings may be unpacked throughout criticism even in its recent theoretical shapes, often they occur as givens rather than objects of inquiry. This is one reason that traditional ethical concepts might appear scandalous, not because ethical but because overt and open-ended, appearing *as questions* rather than the "obviousnesses" a political criticism would expose as ideology (Howard 1987, 4). The questions come in two types, to use Nussbaum's distinction between the terms generally conflated in the essay: the ethical ("What should I do? How should I live my life?"); and the moral (in the words of John Berryman's minstrel interlocuter, Mr. Bones: "Am I a bad man? Am I a good man" [1969, *Dream Song* No. 239]). While consideration of the "moral," with its individualist connotations, may encounter greater progressive resistance, among students moral questions are often raised from the start (Rozett, 1990). How systematic a *literary* discussion of the ethical needs to be is another important question (Nussbaum 1990, 169), but an *anti*systematicity is generally more in keeping with the traversing of subjective and conceptual boundaries.

Any actual inquiry has been more rare, the moral or ethical issues either decided in advance or omitted from disciplinary discourse. If decided in advance, they dispose the teacher of literature to serve less as an investigator, or if an investigator, more like Sherlock Holmes than Philip Marlowe (Žižek 1992, 48)—the former situated distantly above the (im)moral object of investigation, the latter complicit with it. The difference is one of styles of moral inquiry, between what Alisdair MacIntyre terms "encyclopaedic" vs. "genealogical" models (1990). But a complicit investigator would be one whose subjective territory is transversal in crossing over into the territory of the criminal and the immoral—the usual premise of *noir* fiction and film—like the transversal idea of Goethe's that there is no crime he finds himself incapable of imagining he could commit. The benefits and values of the criminal consciousness may thus be achieved, transversally, without having to have one.

As inquiry, the moral or ethical seems more in keeping with feminist criticism, all the more so in its sometime identification with the resistance of the "bad girl." Feminism, in one framework some distance from post-structuralism, could arguably be the most morally driven "approach" to teaching literature, with its investment in everyday contingencies of the "private." Having as a fundamental assumption that women are equal to men, however, might seem to render it liable to the admonition against deciding moral positions in advance. While this assumption certainly has consequences different from its opposite, it is nevertheless a claim that does not of itself necessarily determine answers to properly ethical question: "What should I do next?" The links between the personal and the political will continue to be debated, and the ethical or moral therefore need not be decided in advance, as the evolving positions and versions of contemporary feminisms are themselves evidence.

A small family moment may point up contingencies of complicit inquiry, by way of introducing how the moral responsibility of play *in* literature is complicated by the more transversal idea of literature *as* play or performance. When my daughter was growing up, our first weighty discussion was about how many Barbie dolls she could have, the question assuming a moral dimension for me from seventies critiques of media "images of women" (continuing unabated today). Should she have as many as Bridget next door? Could one have *too many?* My impulse, albeit checked, was to press the ethical toward moral absolutism, to ask, "Isn't one really enough?" Or even less gently, like Goneril reducing the pathetic Lear's number of knights—"What need one?"

Wishing at that time merely to mold responsible doll ownership, I only later saw myself complicit in the problem, by reading helpful cultural analysis by Susan Willis, explaining the communal and resistant functions of toy play, including play among males (1991, 32). Encouraged to extend my analysis outside its customary subjective space, I now realize that in this I may perhaps have been limiting the very creativity I usually tried to encourage,[3] and that doll play itself constitutes its own transversal sort of experimental alterity, i.e. transversality, for girls. Even now, the worrying question about dolls—cultural as well as D. W. Winnicott's interpretation of playthings as psychological transition objects—is not resolved, for discussion about the cultural significance of Barbie continues among postmodern consumerist defenders and dissident appropriaters (Rand 1995). The personal may be political, but we don't necessarily know how at the time, nor is politics (doll politics) necessarily in one-to-one, structuralist relation to ideology (gender assumptions) (Gramsci 1971, 376, 408–9).

Not assuming in advance the moral position within Shakespeare's plays would also seem best. It may have been Terry Eagleton who remarked once that we must teach Shakespeare as if we have something to teach him, what has been called "talking back" to Shakespeare (Rozett 1990). I am invigorated by the idea's cheek, although it may at first appear merely a different kind of deciding-in-advance, namely, the unreflective zeal dubbed "political correctness"—a teaching risk even if its notorious examples are often wrenched from context or exaggerated. Presumably directed at politics rather than playwriting, Eagleton's anti-Bardolatrous assertion, however, helpfully inverts a transcendental moral consciousness into a human one, and reverses the usual prescribed space of Shakespeare. It doesn't proscribe the traditional learning vector—Shakespeare to us—unless further radicalized as "anti-reading" or "creative vandalism" (Sinfield 1992, 22). It allows, moreover, a personal fantasy of misappropriating Shakespeare for deserving subalterns, just as Henry Clay Folger did in snubbing England to plant in

America the world's premiere Shakespeare library (Bristol 1990, 181–2), so that Shakespeare can now be proclaimed an "American institution" (Hawkes 1992, 152). Is there an Emerson to inspire, as he did Folger, other undergraduates to comparable acts of cultural activism, shifting the site of Shakespeare transversally to other groups needing *ready* capital, getting out of the subjective territory of Eurocentricism?

Yet, despite my fantasy, I have doubts about the literary-political banner I have helped raise. For Eagleton's provocation more usefully serves in British settings—witness the far more ruthless and competitive anti-Bardolatry among British cultural materialists (for instance, Aers and Wheale 1991)—than in settings where Shakespeare's "money" is taken less as tender. The institutional variety of my teaching experiences has included places where Bardolatry more than anti-Bardolatry might well inspire a more transversal inquiry productive of political dissent, as well as in places where students dutifully expect to brush up their Shakespeare as cultural veneer for their official subjective space. While seeming to encourage inquiry, Eagleton's view, requiring broader politicization, may in some cases close it off, and fail at transversal experience. We must look further at the more complicated way in which, through both Bardolatry and anti-Bardolatry, Shakespeare's role serves what we have insufficiently attended to—the social stratifications that constitute the ultimate products of academic institutions (Bourdieu and Passeron; Apple 100; Hedrick 1997, 45).

In light of the moral turn, Eagleton's reversal points toward what may be inevitable, namely, that our moral discourse inevitably gets turned upon Shakespeare himself, writer and man. Here again the ethical motives of feminist criticism are illustrative, as we observe a rough historical trajectory: from the apologetic agendas of earlier studies predicting that the new perspective on Shakespeare would "celebrate his works afresh" (Lenz, Greene, and Neely 1980, 3), to direction of the ethical searchlight onto masculinity (Kahn 1981), to a radical call for *withholding* our pleasures from plays whose aesthetics depend on assent to masculinist, patriarchal assumptions (McLuskie 1985). Given this trajectory, it was inevitable that the biographical record too would be seized and searched, as Shakespeare's last will and testament has been legally explicated to reveal an obsessive, patriarchal control (Wilson 1993)—Shakespeare's own immorality transversally revealed by a more thorough historicization.

To teach Shakespeare something enables us to think more readily of a "bad" Shakespeare, the very possibility absurd or unthinkable within traditional Bardolatry. What it opens, however, is the transversal experience of the effects of immorality achieved by other, even moral, means. The very idea poses a disturbing specter for Graham Bradshaw, who singles out cultural materialism for attack in a chapter sardonically titled "Is Shakespeare evil?"—as if the self-evident absurdity of the question (one ignoring, moreover, feminism's moral claims) were enough to derail all inquiry (of the sort the present essay tries more seriously to provide). Despite this revealing faultline, Bradshaw does, I think, unpack some problematic tendencies, such as the impulse to produce either a good "crypto-materialist" Shakespeare or a bad, authoritarian Bard (1993, 23). But he fails to recognize when such contradictions are felt, acknowledged, or even explored through their expressive rather than their mere logical dimensions. What he does not recognize, moreover, but what the entire history of criticism illustrates, is that the attempt, however sophisticated or implicit, to sort out the good from the bad Shakespeare is common to *any* criticism claiming interpretive urgency. In effect, there must perforce exist an enduringly *immoral* Shakespeare in order for us to acknowledge, identify, or construct a moral one. For this reason we find the moral turn evident now in feminist, historicist, marxist, and queer approaches, if not the common denominator within their differences.

Admittedly, any repeated approach tends to become unreflective or routinized; it has been aptly observed how ideological criticism tends predictably to read each successive work as "kinda subversive and kinda hegemonic" (Sedgwick 1993a). But this sorting and impasse constitute a generative, transversal "moral-immoral Shakespeare," the author-model sustaining canonicity/anticanonicity projects, producing a space, as Hedrick's and Reynolds' concept of "Shakespace" in the present volume, for the transformation of subjective territories. The project of teaching Shakespeare a lesson, however conceived, thus performs a more covert logic operating even in overtly canonical projects. This logic, moreover, is not a postmodern innovation. The same duality, as it happens, governs one of the earliest canon-making comments, that of Ben Jonson in his dedicatory poem in the Folio, where his hyperbolic praise is briefly undermined by noting that Shakespeare possessed "small Latin and less Greek." I emphasize that the remark denotes not merely aesthetic but also moral failing, since Jonson construed classical learning as resistance to the popular applause of the spectacle-demanding, crass multitude.

Implicitly condemning Jacobean show business, Jonson by no means stands alone as a critic for whom aesthetic factors readily stand for moral ones. Similarly designating the flaw, Lessing accounts for Shakespeare's vulnerability to applause by his position as actor (45). And if Shakespeare's dramatic irregularities represent moral failings for many eighteenth-century critics, they are transvalued into virtues by admiring Romantics such as Goethe, only to be replaced by other new faults, such as Shakespeare's use of comic relief for Schiller, recovering Sidney's abhorrence of clownery. Even Coleridge's praise of Shakespeare's unwavering virtue shows a immoral-Shakespeare unconscious, when he concludes by describing Shakespeare's twisting aesthetics as those of a *serpent's* (1992, 163).

In spite or because of these contingent transvaluations, Bardolatry proceeds by maintaining a space for immorality, a salutary, creative process deriving from Shakespeare's transversality. This process fully allows for historicization, as in liberal objections to an Elizabethan culture of violence (an editor introducing *Titus Andronicus* as "ridiculous"—Cross 1969, 825). We see this in Voltaire's objection to the influence of the English nation on Shakespeare, Englishness determining not his civilized but his barbaric part (1963, 28–41), and continuing into a modernist tradition linking Shakespeare to the barbarian in such productions as Orson Welles' "Voodoo Macbeth" (Halpern 1998), a view preparing the way for Walter Benjamin's idea that barbarism contaminates all pretenses of civilization, any document of civilization simultaneously a "document of barbarism" (256). With the now emerging "market" Shakespeare (Bruster 1992, Leinwand 1999), the earlier Romantic value of an isolated genius can be rejected or ignored, but also transvalued into a defect, compensated by the collaborative community of the repertory company or by Shakespeare's authenticity as shrewd businessman.

While to some it may seem dubious either to claim or deny moral status for artists at all, Shakespeare's function as cultural capital invariably enables some form of this project, explicitly or not. As it happens, we find what is probably the worst bad Bard in Tolstoy, whose attack on Shakespeare exposes the class formation of this cultural capital, at least at the historical moment of Tolstoy. Beginning with an aesthetic diatribe against Shakespeare's absurdities of plot and language, Tolstoy's saturation bombing shifts to a moral attack, identifying immorality not with lower-class violence but with the true barbarism of the upper classes (1963, 284). In these cases it seems that the evil Shakespeare writes is not so much interred in his bones as it is historicized.[4]

An extreme version of duality inhabits the unlikely location of textual scholarship earlier in the century by J. M. Robertson, infamous for his "disintegration" (1924). As scandalous as deconstruction today (or yesterday), was Robertson's speculation dividing Shakespeare into more and less authentic writing. By what the present consideration would view as no coincidence, Robertson was also a freethinker writing extensively on the history of morals (1957). Immorality is thus cast out as inauthentic writing, with the text split like Shakespeare into good and bad parts. Whether one accepted Robertson's performative division or not, its effect at the time, even as a hypothesis, would have been to undermine confidence in reading or teaching Shakespeare, but do so by opening up in both a space for uncertainy, with moral *inquiry* assuming the guise of editing.

In another limiting case, the editor Thomas Bowdler treated the text similarly in his nineteenth-century *Family Shakespeare* (1818), to distinguish acceptable from unacceptable passages for the inculcation of virtue (Perrin 1969)—a project with current resonance in demands for works teaching children virtue. Originating in his father's practice of reading aloud to the family while censoring passages indelicate for his children, especially daughters, Bowdler's project is not as antiquated or politically idiosyncratic as it first appears. The text, like Robertson's Shakespeare, again splits in self-mutilation, with Shakespeare a paradigm against which he himself can be found wanting. But the text was ever thus splitting in productive and unproductive ways (hence moralized "Good" and "Bad" Quartos—see Cloud 1982), suspect as editing.

All of these productions of an enduring immoral Shakespeare, therefore, allow a social space for experimental alterity. Shakespeare-specific teaching anxiety, standing on a history of these transversal doublings of Shakespeare, makes it apparent that one cannot evade the moral any more than entanglement with consequences of cultural capital. But this doubling may serve us as well in maintaining an ethical room of our own, like the back room Montaigne advises every shopkeeper keep for himself. Through historically shifting narratives of various "tragic" (sometimes comic) flaws of Shakespeare, this "Shakespace" (Hedrick and Reynolds, present volume) permits inquiry rather than absolutism, in open performance rather than editorial secrecy.

The history of strong Shakespearean criticism also illustrates that, perhaps not really all that ironically, Bardolatry may function to free such a creative space, whereas competitive anti-Bardolatry, a more facile, exhausted critical gesture, may serve only to insulate moral assumptions from investigation, self-critique, and even the public sphere, in effect cementing rather than expanding subjective boundaries and suppressing a transversal becoming. In a pure form, the anti-Bardolatrous reflex, especially if merely relativistic, removes Shakespeare's potential for consequence altogether, especially were we to accept that "Bardolatry now" means *any* institutionalization of interpretation (Felperin 1991, 141).

If "show business" needs a more articulated moral dimension provided

by the same concerns supporting traditional Bardolatry, and if literary studies now head in a moral direction, a teaching that relates the two to each
other transversally, each moving as it were outside itself, might serve us better. Such a relation might even allow more possibility of coalition between
liberal and radical, between traditional and progressive critical positions,
and between theory and teaching as well.

A morally transversal pedagogy, always capable of imagining itself outside morality, might also serve us in the public sphere. Our present paraly-
sis for this sphere is exemplified, I believe, in Robert Watson's smart essay,
"Teaching 'Shakespeare.'" Sitting by a construction worker on an airplane
while drafting a (different) Shakespeare essay, Watson finds himself
unnerved when the man asks uncertainly, "What did Shakespeare think
about marriage?" He answers anxiously but not ungenerously, offering a
few things Shakespeareans "if pressed" might say—about "the struggle to
transform the emotional bonds of childhood into heterosexual love, about
the power of love to preserve marriage through trust," and so on (1988,
133–34). What is remarkable is how Watson interprets this chance "student" and his motivating circumstances, opining that ". . . clearly he wanted
advice from a sanctioned voice of timeless wisdom about human dealings,
from a god who spoke in parables." Such speculation about the man's desire
for the oracular may seem unexceptional to self-loathing Shakespeareans,
but only, I contend, because anti-Bardolatry has grown routinely a little
smug and comfortable, like a well-worn axe handle. Like natives awed
before our deities, this tactically constructed construction worker, assumed
to be taking a "critic" for a "hierophant," must seem benighted.

Well.[5] For all I know from the anecdote, the man only spoke in hope of
a little help from the professor in a subjective role he would never assume—
that of talk-show expert or host. And the Shakespeare Teacher's response?
Watson's response is less like modesty, than like pretending not to have
money when you do, a failed opportunity at the transversal. Quote Rosalind,
or the Sonnets, on love? At least we are now far beyond that as critics, the
up-to-date Shakespearean might pronounce. For us to say "what Shakespeare
thought," or to remove the quotations around his name, might take some
expressivity rather than cognition, some tears in the performing, but that is
what we might collectively become more capable of doing—more, in short,
of what we would do outside our official subjectivities, "if pressed."

A teaching more pressed than Eagleton's might fetishize Shakespeare not
less but more. Dropping stigmas about cultural capital, we might acknowledge, after years of denial even through theoretical revolutions, how the literary is commodified in ways supporting the real economic role we play in

teaching (Apple 1995, 99), but how this might be a space for opportunity rather than a crash site. We might then let Shakespeare become what Baudrillard calls the "absolute commodity that liberates you radically from commodities" (1990, 120). Or we might teach, as John Guillory proposes in his study of cultural capital, an "aestheticism unbound" (1993, 340), making use of rather than devaluing this capital. We might still ward off a conservative capture of aesthetics, like the capture of "morality." Looking over the edge of these more creative possibilities, possibilities that would seem to lead us into that thing of darkness, i.e., "show business," I want to consider along with this new moral concern yet a second "turn" of contemporary teaching, one thought to be contradictory to the moral, which in combination with the ethical dimension might constitute a fully transversal pedagogy.

"I have no moral meaning": The Performative Turn, and Beyond

In *Resistance to Theory* Paul de Man provocatively claims that teaching is "not primarily an intersubjective relationship between people but a cognitive process in which self and other are only tangentially and contiguously involved" (1986, 4). Obliquely rejecting teaching as love—at least love conventionally understood—de Man's austere notion leaves little room even for a modern variant of the possibility of transformation—psychoanalytic transference (Felman 1982; Freedman 1980). Whether accepted or not (or qualified as more applicable to graduate education), the claim presupposes the ground of most theory, namely, that the self-evident goal of teaching literature is above all critical understanding, a premise I question here. Despite gestures toward ludic performativity, we find this in accounts of "postmodern pedagogy (for instance, Morton and Zavarzadeh 1991), although we should be chastened to learn that the postmodern pleasures of disruption are fully incorporated into the latest styles of corporate management (Newfield 1995). The same assumptions occur, moreover, in calls to go beyond the postmodern, to create "a critical subject who knows that knowledge is a social product" (Morton and Zavarzadeh 1991, 93). Of course, political critics might well register discomfort at their own assent to the idea, when recalling Marx's injunction not merely to understand the world but to change it. However, it is difficult to conceive of critical understanding, to which many of us owe allegiance, not as the point of teaching but as just another kind of teaching, as I hope to show in what follows. And it may well be that, if the claims of this volume's introductory essay are correct, namely, that love constitutes a key instance of the theory of transversality, that a transversal teaching must itself be somehow predicated on love (though perhaps not "personal" in the sense that de Man was rejecting).

A more local politics is apparent in de Man's exclusions. In a glancing swipe at schools of education, he continues, "The only teaching worthy of the name is scholarly, not personal; analogies between teaching and various aspects of show business or guidance counseling are more often than not excuses for having abdicated the task" (1986, 4).

I want to assert differently here: that there is a plausible account of teaching that encompasses or is halfway between his extreme terms of show business and cognition. To make conceivable a position not fully either, I juxtapose an offhand remark made by a Shakespearean actress on an academic residency at my university. In a discussion with theater majors, she spoke of how indispensible but difficult it is for actors on stage to respond attentively to what the other actors say and do. Noting that women often serve in social situations as such a "reflector," she went on to conclude, "Being a woman is good practice for being an actor." This extraordinary formulation, reminding us of the claim that performance is the "unifying mode of the postmodern" (Benamou 1977, 3), was made without support from authoritative models such as Joel Fineman's on subjectivity as "effect," or Judith Butler's on the subversive "performance" of gender roles. The experience described is remarkably intersubjective, cognitive, and expressive at once.

This "reflector" is a type of delicate performativity, not easily read as fully active or fully passive, cognitive or subjective, self-identical or other. An acting that at its moment transforms actor and relationship, her performativity suggests a middle way, as she returns theater to what has been theorized as an everyday "ethics of performance" (Read 1993). While her example introduces theater and acting into the discussion, and while many of us are increasingly indebted to the use of performance in the classroom, I am not directly concerned here with Shakespearean performance pedagogy (using films, actors, student performance, and so on—see Gilbert 1984). No panacea for pedagogy, some of its early hopes merely produced techniques serving a dead text, as some had earlier warned (Frey 1984, 557). Resisting the inertial, others have theorized performance pedagogy more critically and inventively, as in Simon Shepherd's carnivalesque teaching through identification of "thrills" (1991). Even so, I would relegate pedagogic styles, austere or ludic, to the propensities of individual teachers, and be suspicious of any theory commanding otherwise. I would want also to recognize, as against the "utopian classroom" model, that our effects on students are collective, combinatory, and cumulative, interdependent with classes we do not teach.

Although teaching Shakespeare through performance partly underlies my thinking, I want to pursue the more general concept of performativity overlapping the earlier "linguistic" turn of philosophy and literary study, which requires briefly relating the "double turn" of this essay to the origin of the term "performativity." Invented by the "ordinary language" philosopher J. L. Austin (refreshingly apologizing for its ugliness–1970, 233), it was further rationalized by John Searle, who systematized (thereby forfeiting poststructuralist respect) rules for "speech act theory" (1969)—the two philosophers, respectively emphasizing the performative or playful or stylistically "felicitous" and the legal or ethical or contractual—representing in their division of labor a transversal relation I wish to emphasize here. Reflecting both moral and performative turns, speech act theory thus itself originates in linking the moral with the aesthetic.

If "performative," in Austin's definition, describes verbs for which action is performed within or through the utterance itself (as in "I *hereby* promise," 1970), then it may be that the actor's performativity is a similar case of words changing something, a different state of affairs or social relations underway in the course of utterance—just as a "promise" is performed in and only in the word "promise" itself, and thus suggesting the becoming characteristic of transversal relations.

With the notion of "performativity" theoretically expanded, speech act theory was applied as "literary pragmatics" to Shakespeare, in what now seem fairly routine ways (Porter 1979, Pratt 1979, Hedrick 1979). But the broader sense of "performance" as direct and expressive experience of what might otherwise be "merely" cognitive has wider implications for our teaching. In one instance, I can recall the importance of the distinction about experience when I was amazed to learn from an offhandedly conducted classroom poll that, while most of my students "knew" what iambic pentameter was from handbooks and quizzes, very few confessed to knowing "what it sounds like." The difference here might be described as one of concrete vs. abstract knowledge, of course, but I see it as the difference between an experimental knowledge occurring through performance (where the expressive and personal effects of speaking rhythmically cannot be known in advance) and a knowledge more cognitive or propositional. To perform the rhythm is something—as I suggest about teaching itself—neither merely subjective nor merely cognitive; moreover, "what it sounds like" is the whole point of metrics, not merely one aspect.

Expanding the moral into the political, we can further apply the notion of performance: Henry Gates, Jr.'s theorization of expressivity (1988), Judith Butler's subversive performances (1990) or "queer performativity" with its "antihomophobic pedagogy" (Sedgwick 1990). Performances by the activist organization ACT UP demonstrating, for instance, the asymmetries of codes permitted homosexuals vs. heterosexuals in public, broaden the concept, which historically links to a Vietnam era legacy, namely, the *demonstration*. The idea of the latter was to represent openly to authority the bases of its power, through actions that, because acted, implied alternatives. Transferred to pedagogy, this performative mode furthers a pedagogy of dissidence (Sinfield 1992) rather than one of "empowerment," the latter a more cognitively privileged model where students, say, learn to "theorize about their experiences" (Giroux 1994, 135).

Understanding performance broadly as experiential rather than merely cognitive, and hence capable of serving the experiential alterity of transversality, I note a provocative teaching strategy described by Eve Sedgwick (1993b, 129): through the first part of one semester she instructed students not to reveal if they were heterosexual; class discussion would proceed as if *all* students were gay, as this class' stipulated "default position" of sexuality—literally an experiment, for most of the students, in transversal alterity. Of course, the instructor is by no means politically neutral in selecting such an assignment as demonstration—not everything is *not* decided in advance—but neither have the conclusions of students temporarily assuming this position necessarily been preformulated or anticipated. A performative Shakespearean pedagogy might explore adaptations of this sort of example. One might have male students play female roles nonparodically,[6] for instance, or have a male student read aloud one of the sonnets addressed to the young man, addressing it not in the usual way to the entire class but directly to another male student.[7] As in the Sedgwick technique, these tricks may provoke an creative ethical space for inquiry to develop.

Two brief examples illustrate classroom performativity with another transversal gender edge. One began as a little experiment in "comic pedagogy," after years of explicating Elizabethan "cuckold" humor to little effect, while hearing other Shakespeareans declare the concept to be culturally unrecoverable—a claim I took as a dare. I instructed students simply to laugh at the term whenever used, giving them only a limited dictionary definition. After a short time, the "canned" laughter grew spontaneous, sometimes unstoppable. Not only did the students acquire through a little cultural displacement a more rigorous sense prior to any "intellectual" investigation, but they were afterward able to develop more insightful analyses of the phenomenon in textual contexts. Too often regarded as the first if not the only level of teaching, cognition can as easily follow from the subjective as the other way around.

Another example involves the quintessentially stigmatized practice of traditional teaching—Shakespearean memorization. Violating the taboo against a practice often relegated to high schools now, I required students to memorize a passage, but selected one with a different valence than usual: Kate's submission speech at the end of *The Taming of the Shrew*. Whereas traditional memorization often assumes a posture of total submission to Shakespeare's moral authority (citing tags about mercy or money), this equally famous speech could scarcely be marshalled to reveal timeless wisdom, its own submissive posture wildly problematic. Instead, the details of the emotional contract it describes manifest a historical position—how subordination might feel. (I bracket the question, explored best through performance, of how the speech should be taken.) Not initially a "critique" of ideology, the exercise could grow into one, from a first level of teaching how ideology feels. "Aesthetic" education here produces an aesthetics with an edge, one capable of producing a genuinely creative social space, by no means a genteel "appreciation" serving to confirm the boundaries of one's subjective territory. Although the point is not to dissever critical understanding, even without an immediate understanding there would be some gain, for the speech would lodge in the memory to disturb any received opinions about Shakespeare's "timelessness." The performativity would serve to make students dysfunctional rather than automatically subscribing to Shakespearean "authority" (Hedrick 1997, Worthen 1998).

While some conceivable classroom activities might risk, if not anti-intellectualism, then a "reduction" of experiences to "feelings," I would hope that the best uses of moral performativity would encompass a range of experience, cognitive and subjective or affective, thus inspiring transversal movement. While these tentative examples probably seem anticlimactic, hardly the stuff of a pedagogical regime or revolution, I hope they encourage questioning of a teaching narrowly predicated upon propositional demonstration or even critical understanding, and encourage thinking about the value of experimental alterity. These examples admittedly depend, moreover, not only on varying teaching styles, but upon the particular moral or political commitments of the instructor, for whom sexual norms or gender assumptions may constitute the principle of selection. Although we should not expect the same lineup of commitments for every such teacher—indeed teachers of different political commitments might through this be more aligned with each other—performativity would generally not square with commitments requiring mere allegiance over inquiry.

Moreover, a performative pedagogy is itself called into question, when the ethical turn is directed not only at Shakespeare but at the instructor's own "performance" in a fully transversal relationship between instructor and student. Such a classroom of inquiry would seek to counter the disposition of teachers toward what psychologist Silvan Tomkins importantly calls the set of exceptions, or "depressive script," that turns students into either substitute parents or children and the classroom into a theater where the "depressive parent-child reproof-reward theme [is] repeated again and again with endless variations" (1995, 228).

A transversal pedagogy hardly begins to address all the questions it might raise. Are then the ethical and the performative really on all fours with each other? As poststructuralists or at least believers in contingency, do we doubt whether anyone can ever do "moral things with words"—or that the hybrid "moral performativity," like theatocracy or government by theater, is really a Nietzschean nightmare? Does hybridity remove all responsibility from the teaching of literature, leaving only the responsibility one has in, and to, *play?* Or is one of these concepts more dominant? Put otherwise, *is the play or performance of the moral itself moral?*

I want to address this crucial, recursive family of issues by returning to the initial impulse of this essay, the question of Shakespeare's canonical value, to identify "moral performativity" within the canonical text itself. We may even swerve slightly from the impossible but unavoidable issue of Shakespeare's morality, to arrive at a more empirical view about Shakespeare's own "doing moral things with words." A concordance provides data for the word "moral," and from the *OED* we learn that Shakespeare was the first to *perform* the adjective or noun by turning it into a verb, in *As You Like It,* when Jacques praises the fool's ability to "moral on the time" (2.7.24). Although Shakespeare also used the term "moralize," available from 1450 on, his play with "moral," rewriting it as performative, hints at a skepticism like that of Deleuze, writing in "Ethics and the Event" that "what is really immoral is the use of moral notions like just or unjust, merit or fault" (1993, 79).

While identifying what is in a sense an "essential" immorality attached to Shakespeare, and a transversal experience of the effects of the immoral, I do not jettison the concept of the moral altogether. Yet the discussion thus far leads me to concur with Deleuze that the ethics of the event resides *in* performance and performer, in the actor as what he terms "counteractualization" or "anti-god." The way a performative pedagogy raises experiential alternatives of subjectivity and cognition as well is itself exemplified in the paradigm of the actor, who represents the difference between the part of the event actualized vs. the part that "cannot realize its accomplishment" (1993, 81), a remark recalling Pechter's radical contingency.[8] If the implication of Jacques' remark is that performing the moral is not "serious" inquiry, such performance may be an inauthenticity that manages to undo an inauthentic moral position—the implications of a transversal rather than actual immorality.

The implication seems to hold true for Shakespeare, for what is striking about his own use of the term "moral" is its exclusive occurrence in less than expectedly "moral" ways. Indeed, of its 23 instances, all but one occur in the comedies. All, moreover, are ironic, ironic in context, jocular, applied to suspect aphorisms and posings, or even used in bawdy innuendo. The tangled reflexivity of moral and performative noted above is evident in a striking line by Margaret in *Much Ado,* joking, "Moral? No, by my troth, I have no moral meaning" (3.4.72)—where immoral meaning is performable only through the moral assurance of oaths—each in effect transversally outside itself.[9]

When the ethical and performative turns are considered transversally, as in Shakespeare's own use, they stage a collision or productive tension, which may have been where the present study was heading all along, toward a derailed rhetoric of increasingly tentative, evocative, exploratory questions—like those of literature itself. If so, the present discussion, intended as an anticipatory critique of an as yet unrealized paradigm, refers also to where we have already been, more transversal than we may have thought. Teaching literature is moral performativity, even as it threatens to undo that performativity, its moral imperative, like Shakespeare's morality, both essential and impossible. Encouraging both moral and performative turns, we may arrive at what teaching has often been about, in its actorly collision of something accomplished in the doing and a becoming unrealizable and never done. If pressed, this performativity might even turn prophetic, in an extreme form of philosophical inquiry termed "prophetic irrationalism" (MacIntyre 1981, 8) in which, with urgency but without piousness, the theatrical voice achieves its full power from expressive to cognitive—perhaps the "prophetic criticism" called for by Cornel West and described as democratically "inquiring," "unapologetically moral," and "improvisational" (West 1993, xi, xiv).

By staging the collision, here and in teaching, we see that a transversal pedagogy of moral performativity would be unapologetically moral, but as such would openly risk its own undoing; it would enact an at least temporary transformation, or at least alternative moral, or even immoral, positions essayed or tried on for size; it would expand the constraining habits of propositional and adjudicatory discourse, and indeed of an imposed subjective space itself, to link intersubjectivity and affect to cognition; it could prefer the open affect of anger to the more narrowly cognitive, intellectual hatred or resentment; it would furnish some of the urgency and moral pressure of political criticism, but without predetermined positions; its morality would be chastened by performance, but its performance would be chastened by the moral; self-limiting by virtue of these checks, its very duality could help conceive another register altogether, like Shakespeare's own wisdom effects.

A final instance of moral performativity returns us to the dilemma about Shakespeare's cultural capital. Warning about "fetishizing" Shakespeare, Marjorie Garber cites former NEH chairman Lynne Cheney's scolding of academics who forget that the humanities are about "more than politics" and social power; they are about the "ideals and practices of our civilization," and the truths "transcending accidents of class, race, and gender" (Garber 1990, 249). Toward this polemic, Cheney hijacks Maya Angelou's strong account of her formative reading of a Shakespeare sonnet: "Of course, he was a black woman. I understand that. Nobody else understands it, but I *know* that William Shakespeare was a black woman" (cited in Garber 1990, 249). While Cheney's description systematically distorts, I do not accept Garber's counterdescription that Angelou's is only a "humanistic claim," effective because the black woman in it is "*only* a figure." If in light of the moral-performative turn we attend to Angelou's entire statement (including its tamer proposition that "this is the role of art in life,") Angelou's cheekier "Nobody else understands it, but I *know* . . . ," converts the black woman declarative from mere proposition into performative—a moral and expressive one at that.

Can we convert propositions? Speak somehow outside ourselves? Pressed, can we talk like this: "Shakespeare, honey, I declare you *are* a black woman!"? Now, *that's* entertainment!

Coda

CAPITOL MADE A DOLL WHO LOOKED EXACTLY LIKE HERSELF. IF YOU PRESSED A BUTTON ON ONE OF THE DOLL'S CUNT LIPS THE DOLL SAID, "I AM A GOOD LITTLE GIRL AND DO EXACTLY AS I AM TOLD TO DO."
—Kathy Acker, "Dead Doll Prophecy" (1994, 27)

The paradox of teaching literature is like that of an interpretation that transforms, text and student, that which is interpreted. What Derrida accordingly calls "performative interpretation" (1994, 51) in his controversial (Does he turn Marxism into empty "spirit"?) *Specters of Marx* is what he attempts in response not to some imaginary crash of Shakespeare's cultural capital but to the real crash of Marx's political capital. Cannily measuring the historical moment, Derrida elects two figures signifying extreme poles of ethics and performativity. In a showy chiasmus, Derrida resurrects the ghost of Marx through the money of Shakespeare, interweaving the former with the latter's story of another ghost's heir, Hamlet. Like us, like a construction worker, Derrida would "like to become (alas, it's pretty late) a Shakespeare expert" (1992, 67). Just how late is it, to achieve the effects of experiencing an alternative professional or philosophical subjective territory?

What are "we" to do? Displacement is not the only way. We could serve Shakespeare, as the Nine Inch Nails intone: "Bow down before the one you serve. Bow down and get what you deserve." We could just play dead before him. We could treat him not as our god, but as our carnival king. In any case, as heirs of Shakespeare and literature, we may need to use the capital we have left. It is time to develop RESPONSIBILITY.

William Bennett calls his *Book of Virtues* a "how to" for developing moral literacy (11). It is be read aloud to the family, just as censor-editor Bowdler put his virtue-inculcating family moment to profit, producing a best-selling collection of virtue. Unlike the more morally responsible Bowdler, Bennett manages to blinker and evade literary disturbance in his sale of virtues. Thus, including a letter by F. Scott Fitzgerald to his daughter, Bennett glosses: "In it we see the molding of character: a father gently but explicitly telling his daughter what her duties are" (225). But reading Fitzgerald's letter, we find a list in a different tone than Bennett's smug moralizing, as Fitzgerald cheekily advises, performing something askew from the subjective territory of the Father: "Don't worry about popular opinion, Don't worry about dolls, Don't worry about the past, Don't worry about the future."

Don't worry about dolls? What does Daddy mean?

In the same chapter, the one on "Responsibility," yet another voice complicates Bennett's marketworthy enterprise to secure through painstaking selection a monolithic, nonperformative moral. Of a small poem by Eleanor Piatt (191–2) about caring for a doll, he intones austerely, "Play is the work of children and entirely suitable as an arena in which to develop habits of responsibility" (191). But a girl to whom both "stories" are read would not know whether to worry about dolls or not. What "how to" have we here? Should contradictions be read aloud to the family? Instead, let us take a moment to imagine, thank you, William Bennett performing the poem's first two stanzas, but the last four performed transversally—shrieking, angry, and pressed—by a women's alternative punk-rock band, L-7,[10] for which I will attempt to suggest expressiveness through orthography (hoping that it might, in fact, eventually inspire actual performance):

"Rebecca"
I have a doll, Rebecca,
She's quite a little care,
I have to press her ribbons
And comb her fluffy hair.

I keep her clothes all mended,
And wash her hands and face,
And make her frocks and aprons,
All trimmed in frills and lace.

[*the following, with threatening and screaming emphasis added:*]

I *HAVE TO COOK* HER BREAKFAST,
AND *PET* HER WHEN SHE'S ILL;
And *TELEPHONE* the DOCTOR
When REBECCA HAS A *CHILL*.

REBECCA *DOESN'T LIKE THAT*,
And *says* she's well and strong;
And says she'll TRY—oh! VERY HARD,
TO BE GOOD ALL DAY LONG.

BUT WHEN NIGHT COMES, she's nodding;
So into bed we *CREEP*,
And snuggle up together,
And soon are fast asleep.

I *HAVE NO OTHER DOLLY*,
For you can plainly see,
I'm *CARING FOR REBECCA*,
I'm as *BUSY* as can be!

The author wishes to thank Michael Bristol and Jean Howard for comments on this paper, first delivered at the Shakespeare Division session, Modern Languages Association, December 1994, San Diego.

Notes

1. The distinction is useful in the context of Gayatri Spivak's defense of the humanities as "the other-directedness of the Other," a critical consciousness rather than the one that invites profusions of sympathetic identification more often associated with a putatively ethical criticism. "I am not Martha Nussbaum," she thus distinguished, in the lecture regarding this idea, at the University of Washington, Seattle, March 2, 2000.

2. For a more extensive consideration of the question of a transhistorical political value in pedagogy on the early modern period, see Donald K. Hedrick, "Dumb and Dumber History: The Transhistorical Popular," in *Class Issues: Pedagogy, Cultural Studies, and the Public Sphere,* ed. Amitava Kumar (New York and London: New York University Press, 1997).

3. I am indebted to Gretchen Hedrick for this reminder.

4. This is New Historicism's posture, for which it is easier to see containment as historically bound, while seeing subversion, of which there is no end (Greenblatt 1985, 45) as more enduring—yet another enduring immorality.

5. This ignores Watson's honest self-critique, somewhat against the critical tide, about worshipping Shakespeare's ghost. As in Greenblatt's anecdote of a disturbing, emotional exercise with a passenger in the next seat (1980, 255), the new professionalist genre of the Formative Airplane Epiphany recounts a chance encounter with the public stratosphere somewhere between campus and conference, with charged significance for recognizing one's identity.

6. "Nonparodically," since, as the desire to play women is increasingly normalized by Hollywood stars doing drag, not to mention most male undergraduates with a sense of humor, the transformative potential of any such performance becomes notably less.

7. I am indebted to one actor's memorable exercise comparing an expressively read sonnet to one dramatically addressed to one female classmember.

8. Again, Gayatri Spivak's notion of the "other-directedness of the Other," may be pertinent here, but her concept appears to imply much more of a distinct subjective space of self and other rather than a permeable and indefinite one.

9. E.g., "Fortune is an excellent moral" (*H5* 3.6.32–7); ". . . while we do admire/ This virtue and this moral discipline,/ Let's be no stoics nor no stocks, I pray" (*Shrew* 4.4.77–78); "This moral ties me over to time and a hot summer" (*H5* 5.2.301); ". . . a pretty moral" (*Per* 2.1.35).

10. "Just say no to individuality./ When we pretend that we're dead/ They can't hear all that we say . . ." ("Pretend We're Dead"); "Don't preach to me, Mr. Integrity" ("Mr. Integrity").

Works Cited

Acker, Kathy. 1994. "Dead Doll Prophecy." *The Subversive Imagination: Artists, Society and Social Responsibility.* New York and London: Routledge.

Aers, Lesley, and Nigel Wheale. 1991. *Shakespeare in the Changing Curriculum.* London and New York: Routledge.

Apple, Michael W. 1995. "Cultural Capital and Official Knowledge." In *Higher Education Under Fire: Politics, Economics and the Crisis of the Humanities.* Ed. Michael Berubé and Cary Nelson. New York and London: Routledge.

Aronowitz, Stanley, and William DiFazio. 1994. *The Jobless Future: Sci-Tech and the Dogma of Work.* Minneapolis and London: University of Minnesota Press.

Augustin, Norman and Kenneth Adelman. 1999. *Shakespeare in Charge: The Bard's Guide to Leading and Succeeding on the Business Stage.* New York: Hyperion.

Austin, J. L. *How to Do Things with Words.* 1962; rpt. 1978. Cambridge: Harvard University Press.

———. 1970. *Philosophical Papers.* London: Oxford University.

Barber, C. L. 1959. *Shakespeare's Festive Comedy: A Study of Dramatic Form and Its Relation to Social Custom.* Princeton: Princeton University Press.

Baudrillard, Jean. 1990. *Fatal Strategies.* New York: Semiotext(e).

Bellah, Robert N. et al. 1991. *The Good Society.* New York: Knopf.

Benamou, Michel. 1977. "Presence and Play." *Performance in Postmodern Culture.* Ed. Michel Benamou and Charles Caramello. Madison: University of Wisconsin Press.

Bennett, William J., ed. 1993. *The Book of Virtues: A Treasury of Great Moral Stories.* New York: Simon and Schuster.

Benjamin, Walter. 1955; rpt. 1978. *Illuminations.* New York: Harcourt Brace.

Berryman, John. 1969. *The Dream Songs.* New York: Farrar, Straus and Giroux.

Berubé, Michael. 1994. *Public Access: Literary Theory and American Cultural Politics.* London and New York: Verso.

Bradshaw, Graham. 1993. *Misrepresentations: Shakespeare and the Materialists.* Ithaca and London: Cornell University Press.

Bristol, Michael D. 1990. *Shakespeare's America, America's Shakespeare.* London and New York: Routledge.

Bourdieu, Pierre. 1984. *Distinction: A Social Critique of the Judgment of Taste.* Cambridge: Harvard University Press.

Bourdieu, Pierre, and Jean-Claude Passeron. 1977. *Reproduction in Education, Society and Culture.* London: Sage.

Bowdler, Thomas. 1818. *The Family Shakespeare.* London.

Bruster, Douglas. 1992. *Drama and the Market in the Age of Shakespeare.* Cambridge: Cambridge University Press.

Butler, Judith. 1990. *Gender Trouble: Feminism and the Subversion of Identity.* New York and London: Routledge.

Cloud, Random. 1982. "The Marriage of Good and Bad Quartos." *Shakespeare Quarterly* 33: 421–31.

Cohen, Walter. 1985. *Drama of a Nation: Public Theater in Renaissance England and Spain.* Ithaca and London: Cornell University Press.

———. 1987. "Political Criticism of Shakespeare." In *Shakespeare Reproduced: The Text in History and Ideology.* Ed. Jean E. Howard and Marion F. O'Connor. New York and London: Methuen.

Coleridge, Samuel Taylor. 1992. *The Romantics on Shakespeare.* Ed. Jonathan Bate. New York and London: Penguin.

The Compact Edition of the Oxford English Dictionary. 1971; rpt. 1981. Oxford: Oxford University Press.

Cross, Gustav. 1969. "Introduction, *Titus Andronicus.*" In *William Shakespeare, The Complete Works.* Ed. Alfred Harbage. Baltimore: Penguin.

Culler, Jonathan. 1982. *On Deconstruction: Theory and Criticism after Structuralism.* Ithaca: Cornell University Press.

Debord, Guy. 1983. *Society of the Spectacle.* Detroit: Black and Red.

Deleuze, Gilles. 1993. "Ethics and the Event." In *The Deleuze Reader.* Ed. Constantin V. Boundas. New York: Columbia University Press.

de Man, Paul. 1986. *The Resistance to Theory.* Minneapolis: University of Minnesota Press.

Derrida, Jacques. 1992. *Acts of Literature.* New York and London: Routledge.

———. 1994. *Specters of Marx: The State of the Debt, the Work of Mourning, and the New International.* New York and London: Routledge.

Eagleton, Terry. 1983. *Literary Theory: An Introduction.* Minneapolis: University of Minnesota Press.

Eggers, Walter F., Jr. Ed. 1977. "Introduction." In *Teaching Shakespeare.* Princeton: Princeton University Press.

Felman, Shoshona. 1982. "Psychoanalysis and Education: Teaching Terminable and Interminable." *Yale French Studies* 63: 21–44.

Felperin, Howard. 1991. "Bardolatry Then and Now." In *The Appropriation of Shakespeare: Post-Renaissance Reconstructions of the Works and the Myth.* Ed. Jean I. Marsden. New York: Harvester.

Fineman, Joel. 1986. *Shakespeare's Perjured Eye: The Invention of Poetic Subjectivity in the Sonnets.* Berkeley: University California Press.

Fish, Stanley. 1989. "Being Interdisciplinary is So Very Hard to Do." In *Doing What Comes Naturally: Change, Rhetoric, and the Practice of Theory in Literary and Legal Studies.* Durham, NC: Duke University Press.

Freedman, Barbara. 1990. "Pedagogy, Psychoanalysis, Theatre: Interrogating the Scene of Learning." *Shakespeare Quarterly* 41: 174–186.

Freire, Paolo. 1990. *Pedagogy of the Oppressed*. New York: Continuum.

Frey, Charles. 1984. "Teaching Shakespeare in America," *Shakespeare Quarterly* 35: 541–559.

Garber, Marjorie. 1990. "Shakespeare as Fetish." *Shakespeare Quarterly* 41: 424–50.

Gates, Henry Louis, Jr. 1988. *The Signifying Monkey: A Theory of African-American Literary Criticism*. New York and Oxford: Oxford University Press.

Gilbert, Miriam. 1984. "Teaching Shakespeare Through Performance." *Shakespeare Quarterly* 33: 601–8.

Giroux, Henry A. 1994. *Disturbing Pleasures: Learning Popular Culture*. New York and London: Routledge.

———. 1988. *Schooling and the Struggle for Public Life: Critical Pedagogy in the Modern Age*. Minneapolis: University of Minnesota Press.

Graff, Gerald. 1990. "Teach the Conflicts." *South Atlantic Quarterly* 89: 51–58.

Gramsci, Antonio. 1971. *Selections from the Prison Notebooks*. New York: International.

Greenblatt, Stephen. 1985. "Invisible Bullet: Renaissance Authority and Its Subversion." In *Political Shakespeare: New Essays in Cultural Materialism*. Ed. Jonathan Dollimore and Alan Sinfield. Ithaca and London: Cornell University Press.

———. 1980. *Renaissance Self-Fashioning from More to Shakespeare*. Chicago and London: University of Chicago Press, 1980.

Guillory, John. 1993. *Cultural Capital: The Problem of Literary Canon Formation*. Chicago and London: University of Chicago Press.

Gunn, Giles. 1987. *The Culture of Criticism and the Criticism of Culture*. New York and London: Oxford University Press.

Halpern, Richard. 1977. *Shakespeare Among the Moderns*. Ithaca and London: Cornell University Press.

Hardt, Michael and Antonio Negri. 1994. *Labour of Dionysius: A Critique of the State*. Minneapolis: University of Minnesota Press.

Hawkes, Terence. 1992. *Meaning by Shakespeare*. New York and London: Routledge.

Hedrick, Donald K. 1979. "Merry and Weary Conversation: Textual Uncertainty in *As You Like It*, II.iv." *ELH* 46: 21–34.

———. 1997. "Dumb and Dumber History: The Transhistorical Popular." In *Class Issues: Pedagogy, Cultural Studies, and the Public Sphere*. Ed. Amitava Kumar. New York and London: NYU Press.

———. 1997. "War is Mud: Branagh's Dirty Harry V and the Types of Political Ambiguity." In *Shakespeare, The Movie: Popularizing the Plays on Film, TV, and Video*. Ed. Lynda E. Boose and Richard Burt. London and New York: Routledge.

hooks, bell. 1994. *Teaching to Transgress: Education as the Practice of Freedom*. New York and London: Routledge.

Howard, Jean E. and Maron F. O'Connor, eds. 1987. "Introduction." In *Shakespeare Reproduced: The Text in History and Ideology*. New York and London: Methuen.

Jacobs, Jane. 1992; rpt. 1994. *Systems of Survival: A Dialogue on the Moral Foundations of Commerce and Politics.* New York: Random House.

Kahn, Coppélia. 1981. *Man's Estate: Masculine Identity in Shakespeare.* Berkeley: University of California Press.

Kropotkin, Peter. 1992; 1986. *Ethics: Origin and Development.* Montreal and New York: Black Rose Books, 1992. Cambridge: Cambridge University, 1986.

L-7. 1992. *Bricks are Heavy.* Slash/Reprise, 9 26784–2.

Lenz, Carolyn Ruth Swift, Gayle Greene, and Carol Thomas Neely, eds. 1980. Preface. *The Woman's Part: Feminist Criticism of Shakespeare.* Urbana: University of Illinois Press.

Le Winter, Oswald, ed. 1963. *Shakespeare in Europe.* Cleveland and New York: World Publishing.

Levin, Richard. 1979. *New Readings vs. Old Plays: Recent Trends in the Reinterpretation of English Renaissance Drama.* Chicago: Chicago University Press.

Lessing, Gotthold Ephraim. 1963. "Hamburg Dramaturgy." In *Shakespeare in Europe.* Ed. Oswald LeWinter. Cleveland and New York: World Pub.

MacIntyre, Alasdair. 1981. *After Virtue: A Study in Moral Theory.* Notre Dame: University of Notre Dame Press.

———. 1990. *Three Rival Versions of Moral Enquiry: Encyclopaedia, Genealogy, and Tradition.* Notre Dame: University of Notre Dame Press.

Marsden, Jean. 1991. *The Appropriation of Shakespeare: Postcolonial Reconstructions of the Works.* New York: St. Martin's Press.

McLaren, Peter. 1995. *Critical Pedagogy and Predatory Culture: Oppositional Politics in a Postmodern Era.* London and New York: Routledge.

McLuskie, Kathleen. 1985. "The Patriarchal Bard: Feminist Criticism and Shakespeare: *King Lear* and *Measure for Measure.*" In *Political Shakespeare: New Essays in Cultural Materialism.* Ed. Jonathan Dollimore and Alan Sinfield. Ithaca and London: Cornell University Press.

Miklitsch, Robert. 1994. "The Politics of Teaching Literature: The "Paedagogical Effect." In *Margins in the Classroom: Teaching Literature.* Ed. Kostas Myrsiades and Linda S. Myrsiades. Minneapolis and London: University of Minnesota Press.

Morton, Donald, and Mas'ud Zavarzadeh. 1991. *Theory/Pedagogy/Politics.* Urbana and Chicago: University of Illinois Press.

———. 1994. "(Post)modern Critical Theory and the Articulations of Critical Pedagogies." In *Margins in the Classroom: Teaching Literature.* Ed. Kostas Myrsiades and Linda S. Myrsiades. Minneapolis and London: University of Minnesota Press.

Nancy, Jean-Luc. 1991. *The Inoperative Community.* Ed. and trans. Peter Conner. Minneapolis: University of Minnesota Press.

Newfield, Christopher. 1995. "Corporate Pleasures for a Corporate Planet." *Social Text* 44: 31–44.

Nine Inch Nails. 1988. "Head Like a Hole." *Pretty Hate Machine.* TVT, 2610–2.

Nussbaum, Martha C. 1986, *The Fragility of Goodness: Luck and Ethics in Greek Tragedy and Philosophy.* Cambridge: Cambridge University Press.

———. 1990."Perceptive Equilibrium: Literary Theory and Ethical Theory." In *Love's Knowledge: Essays on Philosophy and Literature*. New York and London: Oxford University Press.

Pechter, Edward. 1995. *What Was Shakespeare? Renaissance Plays and Changing Critical Practice*. Ithaca and London: Cornell University Press.

Penley, Constance. 1986. "Teaching in Your Sleep: Feminism and Psychoanalysis." In *Theory in the Classroom*. Ed. Cary Nelson. Urbana and Chicago: University of Illinois Press.

Perloff, Marjorie. 1992. Talk at Modern Language Association of America Convention.

Perrin, Noel. 1969. *Dr. Bowdler's Legacy: A History of Expurgated Books in England and America*. New York: Atheneum.

Perry, William G., Jr. 1968. *Forms of Intellectual and Ethical Development in the College Years: A Scheme*. New York: Holt.

Pratt, Mary Louise. 1979. *Toward a Speech Act Theory of Literary Discourse*. Bloomington: Indiana University Press.

"The Politics of Virtue: The Crusade Against America's Moral Decline." *Newsweek*, June 13, 1994.

Porter, Joseph A. 1979. *The Drama of Speech Acts: Shakespeare's Lancastrian Tetralogy*. Berkeley: University of California Press.

———. 1988. *Shakespeare's Mercutio: His History and Drama*. Chapel Hill: University of North Carolina Press.

———. 1991. "Character and Ideology in Shakespeare." In *Shakespeare Left and Right*. Ed. Ivo Kamps. New York and London: Routledge.

Rabinowitz, Peter J. 1987. *Before Reading: Narrative Conventions and the Politics of Interpretation*. Ithaca: Cornell University Press.

Rand, Erica. 1995. *Barbie's Queer Accessories*. London and Durham: Duke University Press.

Read, Alan. 1993. *Theatre and Everyday Life: An Ethics of Performance*. London and New York: Routledge.

Reynolds, Bryan, and Joseph Fitzpatrick. Forthcoming. "The Transversality of Michel de Certeau: Foucault's Panoptic Discourse and the Cartographic Impulse." *diacritics*.

Robertson, J. M. 1924. *An Introduction to the Study of the Shakespeare Canon; proceeding on the problem of "Titus Andronicus."* London: Routledge.

———. 1899. *A Short History of Freethought, Ancient and Modern*. London. New York: Russell, 1957.

Rozett, Martha Tuck. 1990. "First Readers as Moralists." *Shakespeare Quarterly* 41: 211–221.

Sadoff, Dianne, and William E. Cain. 1994. *Teaching Contemporary Theory to Undergraduates*. New York: Modern Language Association.

Searle, John. 1969. *Speech Acts: An Essay on the Philosophy of Language*. Cambridge: Cambridge University Press.

Sedgwick, Eve Kosofsky. 1993. Paper delivered at Ohio Shakespeare Conference on "Shakespeare and the Senses of Shame," Cincinnati, April.

———. 1990. "Pedagogy in the Context of an Antihomophobic Project." Ed. Darryl J. Gless and Barbara Herrnstein Smith. *South Atlantic Quarterly* 89: 139–56.

———. 1993."Socratic Raptures, Socratic Ruptures: Notes Toward Queer Performativity." In *English Inside and Out: The Places of Literary Criticism*. Ed. Susan Gubar and Jonathan Kamholtz. New York and London: Routledge.

Sievers, Tobin. 1993. *The Ethics of Criticism*. Ithaca and London: Cornell University Press.

Shakespeare, William. 1997. *The Norton Shakespeare,* ed. Stephen Greenblatt. New York: W. W. Norton. *The Complete Pelican Shakespeare.*

Sharp, Rachel and Anthony Green. 1975. *Education and Social Control: A Study in Progressive Primary Education*. London and Boston: Routledge & Kegan Paul.

Shepherd, Simon. 1991. "Acting Against Bardom: Some Utopian Thoughts on Workshops." In *Shakespeare in the Changing Curriculum*. Ed. Lesley Aers and Nigel Wheale. New York and London: Routledge.

Sinfield, Alan. 1992. *Faultlines: Cultural Materialism and the Politics of Dissident Reading*. Berkeley: University of California Press.

Smith, Paul. 1994. "The Political Responsibility of the Teaching of Literatures." In *Margins in the Classroom: Teaching Literature*. Ed. Kostas Myrsiades and Linda S. Myrsiades. Minneapolis and London: University of Minnesota Press.

Spevack, Marvin. 1969. *The Harvard Concordance to Shakespeare*. 1969. Harvard University Press.

Strickland, Ronald. 1990. "Confrontational Pedagogy and Traditional Literary Studies." *College English* 52: 291–300.

Taylor, Gary. 1999. "Afterword: the incredible shrinking Bard." In *Shakespeare and Appropriation*. Ed. Christy Desmet and Robert Sawyer. London and New York: Routledge.

Thomson, Judith Jarvis. 1986. *Rights, Restitution, and Risk*. Cambridge: Harvard University Press.

Tolstoy, Leo Nikolayevich. 1963. "Shakespeare and the Drama." In *Shakespeare in Europe*. Ed. Oswald LeWinter. Cleveland and New York: World Publishers.

Tomkins, Silvan. 1995. *Shame and Its Sisters: A Silvan Tomkins Reader*. Ed. Eve Koskofsky Sedgwick and Adam Frank. Durham and London: Duke University Press.

Voltaire. 1963. "Discourse on Tragedy." In *Shakespeare in Europe*. Ed. Oswald LeWinter. Cleveland and New York: World Publishers.

Watson, Robert N. 1988. "Teaching 'Shakespeare': Theory versus Practice." In *Teaching Literature: What is Needed Now*. Ed. James Engell and David Perkins. Harvard Studies in English. Cambridge, MA and London: Harvard University Press.

West, Cornel. 1993. *Keeping Faith: Philosophy and Race in America*. New York and London: Routledge.

Williams, Bernard. 1985. *Ethics and the Limits of Philosophy*. Cambridge, MA: Harvard University Press.

Willis, Susan. 1991. "Gender as Commodity." In *A Primer for Daily Life*. New York and London: Routledge.

Wilson, Richard. 1993. "A Constant Will to Publish: Shakespeare's Dead Hand." In *Will Power: Essays on Shakespearean Authority*. Detroit: Wayne State University Press.

Winnicott, D. W. 1964. *The Child, The Family, and the Outside World*. New York: Penguin, 1964.

Worthen, William B. 1984. *The Idea of the Actor: Drama and the Ethics of Performance*. Princeton: Princeton University Press.

———. 1997. *Shakespeare and the Authority of Performance*. Cambridge: Cambridge University Press.

Žižek, Slavoj. 1992. *Looking Awry: An Introduction to Jacques Lacan through Popular Culture*. Cambridge, MA: MIT Press.

Part VII

Afterword

Chapter 12

Afterword: Shakespace on Marloan

Julia Reinhard Lupton

In these pages we have overheard Stephen Greenblatt regretting Marc Norman's decision not to make a film about a love affair between William Shakespeare and Christopher Marlowe (Hedrick and Reynolds 2000, 25–26). In a similar mood, Richard Burt remarks that in *Shakespeare in Love,* "Marlowe is hardly recognizable as gay" (2000, 162).[1] Yet isn't a love affair between Marlowe and Shakespeare magnanimously covered in the indeterminate Proustian sweep of the film's title? Shakespeare in Love: yes, in love with Viola de Lesseps, Girrrl Actor and True Fan, but also in love with that intoxicating mix of poetry, theater, money, and fame represented by the life and work of Christopher Marlowe. Hasn't the film taken a different kind of risk—not the risk of the lurid or scandalous (a risk that, admit it, usually pays off these days), but rather the risk of allusiveness, the gamble not of *the literal,* but of *the literate?* The screen writers, that is, chose to put near the center of their film the imaginative relationship between two playwrights, a relationship composed of rivalry and debt, guarded respect and grudging exchange, heightened by the play of accident and rumor in the small world of a hot new medium. Everyone knows Shakespeare, as Laurie Osborne shows us in this volume, but the Marlowe cognoscenti dwindle rapidly to English majors and those canon voyeurs educated before the great vowel shift from Literature to Culture. To make so much depend on Shakespeare's (non)relation with Marlowe—a half-story of barroom chats, hackneyed recitations, and mistaken identities—was indeed a risk, though certainly amortized by the success of *Amadeus.*

Put otherwise, the real interest of *Shakespeare in Love* lies in its representation of "Shakespace on Marloan"—its conceptualization, for a new generation, of Shakespeare's debt to another playwright, taken as a constitutive moment in the creation of the Shakespearean as an ongoing cultural enterprise worthy of our attention and participation, our criticism and our love. According to Hedrick and Reynolds, "Shakespace" allows for transversal movement in part because of Shakespeare's own crossings in and out of the subjective territory of literary clichés defined by "Ethel, the Pirate's Daughter," an ambivalent romance with Romance whose sharpest breaks and most productive estrangements were enabled by his career-long engagement with the example of Marlowe. Yes, Norman and Stoppard map *Romeo and Juliet* onto the heterosexual affair between Shakespeare and Viola de Lesseps, yet they also transpose it onto the war of the theaters and the competition among writers, which opens up a distinctively transversal territory, a space for both creativity and criminality, emulate pride and fraternity-style brawls. In the film, Marlowe's flamboyant farcicalness, grandiloquent poetry, and short, violent life lay the groundwork for the mimetic achievements of Shakespeare, who took both his inspiration and his negative example from the extremes mapped by Marlovian virtuosity. The film even introduces a third term: the Artaudian excess of the young John Webster, who confesses in the film to having "played the head in *Titus Andronicus*," and who is thus given the historical task of enunciating within Shakespeare's early work a theater of cruelty at odds with the representational canons of the high Shakespearean tradition. Moreover, through its very liberties with history, the film manages to replicate some of the definitive moves of that most creative of historians, William Shakespeare, recreating the Shakespearean as that battery of revisionary and allusive techniques, of incessant double-plotting, that characterizes Shakespeare's relation to his own historical and literary sources, including the works of Marlowe.

Not simply Shakespeare on Marloan, but what Hedrick and Reynolds have termed "Shakespace": the film communicates and indeed enacts a sense that the shifting history of Shakespearean appropriation is itself shot through and set into motion by the originary encounter, whether physical or purely cognitive, between these playwrights. How might such a Shakespace-on-Marloan operate? Two directions are implied by the concerns running through this volume: *theatrical performance,* and *pedagogical practice.* Several essays have emphasized a modernist, absurdist, or Brechtian potential in Shakespearean drama activated in key performance traditions. Curtis Perry calls this line the Senecan absurd, which he in turn quite rightly ascribes to Shakespeare's more brutely Senecan (and absurdist) contemporary, Marlowe. William Over and Bryan Reynolds both link Shakespeare to Brecht. Over discovers in the African Theater of antebellum New York an anticipation of Brechtian political and class transversals. It is perhaps no accident that Over's chief examples are *Richard III* and *Othello*, which present two distinct moves in Shakespeare's competitive love affair with Marlowe. For Reynolds, the Brecht-Shakespeare interface is more direct, as he effects a transversal jump cut between Brecht's *Coriolan* and Shakespeare's *Coriolanus*, using Brecht's play to deposit the specter of Marx in Shakespeare's tragedy of Roman republicanism. The play's concerns with the tragic dialectic between an overlarge sovereign personality and the challenges of a political constitution certainly resonate with the work of both Marlowe and his own most potent political specter, the figure of Machiavelli. Even Ralph Koenig's *Iago Comic,* as analyzed by Richard Burt, seems to unfold the Marlovian underside of Shakespeare's golden world.

The other direction to explore Shakespace-on-Marloan is pedagogy: how does the Marlovian bent or turn within Shakespeare, the transversality of their own forever-skewed and indeterminate relationship, lend itself to classroom experiments and modes of critical analysis that resist the maxims of Shakespearean officialdom? In this volume (and it is one mark of its distinction), pedagogical exploration runs a track parallel to that of critical performance traditions, since the classroom can provide a microclimate for the staging of generative cruxes in Shakespeare and his reception. Hence Donald Hedrick presents a transversal pedagogy defined as moral performativity, a formulation that effectively combines the expository and the theatrical. Hedrick focuses on opportunities for "temporary transformation" that would "furnish some of the urgency and moral pressure of political criticism, but without predetermined positions" (2000, 264). Such a pedagogy "links intersubjectivity and affect to cognition," drawing, that is, on the transversal nature of theater itself without devolving into a performance approach to teaching, in which show biz replaces intellectual and ethico-political working through. Leslie Katz provides an extended case study of transversal pedagogy in practice, as ritualized bits of language and grim toys pass from the subjective territory of one student to that of another, changing ethical and semantic content with each perverse exchange.

To what extent is this pedagogical Shakespace, like the performance one, "on Marloan"? I'd like to try to answer this by way of a second question: to what extent is Shakespace a *civic territory,* with the civic understood not as the policing of the transversal, but rather as its fullest exercise, what Hedrick and Reynolds herald as "a collective, creative space not fully limited by [individual] interests, conceptions, or affects, and one in which new social arrangements are produced or at least become capable of becoming imagined" (2000, 3)? But why not start with Aristotle, who opens his *Politics* with a definition of citizenship reiterated throughout the treatise: "Citizens rule and are ruled in turn" (1252a); "A citizen is one who shares in governing and being governed" (1283b). Aristotle's definition does not do away with hierarchy; rather, by rotating offices from citizen to citizen, such that the citizen is the one who alternately rules and is ruled, the polis keeps hierarchy in motion, as a necessary principle of order that nonetheless cannot become fixed in a particular person or persons without tyrannous results. An *office* is not unlike a *role,* and to change offices is at least potentially to undergo a transversal transformation; in Aristotle's words, "Thus one party rules and the others are ruled in turn, *as if they were no longer the same persons*" (1261b, emphasis added).

Or, as Hedrick and Reynolds put it, "Be all you aren't" (2000, 5). Images of theatrical rotation occur throughout the essays in this volume: "moving the particles of storytelling, hearsay, and prattle around in a circle" (Katz 2000, 235-6); "moral positions tried on or assayed" (Hedrick 2000, 30); "shared space for repositionings" (Hedrick and Reynolds 2000, 5). Robert Weimann writes that "the study of the early texts of *Hamlet* is the study of a play in motion" (2000, 52), and hence of authority itself unfixed, shaken up. We might think as well here of Marx's ideal citizen, who changes offices in the course of the day: "to hunt in the morning, fish in the afternoon, rear cattle in the evening, criticize after dinner . . . without ever becoming hunter, fisherman, shepherd, or critic'" (cited Reynolds and Hedrick 2000, 11). The exchange of offices frees up subjective territory through contact with contiguous domains, creating a transsubjective region fraught with civic and communitarian promise.

The classroom is certainly capable of becoming civic in Aristotle's sense. Graduate education has long been structured on the alternating rhythm of teaching and being taught, though the civic capacities of this dynamic are in serious risk of being shut down by the increasing construction of graduate student teaching on an economic continuum with other kinds of part-time work in the university's growing labor crunch. The undergraduate seminar can certainly become such a civic space if authority is not sacrificed so much as mobilized, passed around the room. Undergraduate education has an even deeper civic potential in the newly emerging or revitalized area of "service-learning," in which students become teachers by participating in community and K-12 educational projects directed toward those caught on the dark side of America's deepening economic, cultural, and educational divides. If literacy was violent in the colonial context, as James Andreas suggests (2000, 195), illiteracy in the current moment is even more so. Literacy training has the potential to become an intellectual and ethical rather than purely technical enterprise, in which undergraduates (in concert with graduate students and faculty) work with younger students on basic skills through deep cognitive and imaginative engagement with key works of history, art, philosophy, and literature (Lupton 2000).

Like Shakespeare: one site of a transversal Shakespeare can open up between the schools and the university, driving the scores-driven anti-intellectualism of the one and the mental insularity of the other—two hierarchies, no rotation—into creative contact and interchange with each other. Shakespeare has special currency in this interspace because he remains part of "official culture," still on good standing in the syllabi of both the school and university canons, yet remaining the object of continued cultural innovation, critique, and popularization (as attested in this volume). The play of offices within Shakespeare's works makes them into a playground of unofficial culture, or rather, in my renovated Aristotelian terms, of official culture with its positions dissolved once more into a set of structural and imaginative transfers. Think here of Cicero's *De Officiis* not as a treatise about offices, but rather about the devolution and revolution of offices: de-officiis = offices de-officialized, offices in the plural, offices in motion. Such could be the subtitle of any number of Shakespeare's works, from his dramas of delegation *(King Lear, Measure for Measure, The Tempest)* to a play like *Macbeth:* what if we were to read Macbeth's replacement of Duncan as a kind of civic exercise, with Malcolm as simply the next citizen in line for the right to exercise rule? Throughout his *oeuvre,* Shakespeare's interest in the rotation of power is constitutional as well as intrinsically theatrical, even when framed within an orthodox monarchical vision.

To what extent is this pedagogical Shakespace "on Marloan"? Shakespeare, of course, has always been appropriated for putatively "civic" goals, his plays brought into line with national, patriotic, and moral agendas on both sides of the Atlantic, and in the Empire as well. This hegemonic brand of civics is certainly closer to what Hedrick and Reynolds call "state machinery" (2000, 10)—promoting conformity to subjective norms in order to maintain the current distribution of resources and authority— than to either Shakespeare or to Aristotle's radical definition of citizenship as rotational activity. Marlowe, however, is notoriously less assimilable to such educational instrumentalization—his plays are too much in love with tyranny, whether political, erotic, or cerebral, to lend support to the national programs of the modern state. Patrick Cheney has identified this current as "counter-nationhood," whose lineaments are by definition revealed only negatively: "Whatever counter-nationhood is, enigma is central to it. Even though the writer of counter-nationhood speaks of the individual's suppression by state power, he reveals its oppositional idea, freedom, only obliquely. As the term implies, counter-nationhood is less concerned with the health of the nation than with the illness of the individual" (Cheney 1997: 25). Faustus dies mourning the loss of "both Germany and the world" (V.i.51), yet the latter would seem to bear rather the more heavily on this passionate cosmopolitan. Tamburlaine's imperial sweep destroys nations in its path without itself congealing into a particular national banner; he is a "Scythian shepherd," a nomadic professional from a nomadic people who becomes the bearer not of his own Turco-Mongolian heritage, but of the high Persian culture of Iran (Lowry 1989: 2–5). Barabas, stemming from a differently scattered nation, prefers to play both sides against each other for fun and profit than to accept political power when it is offered to him.

Barabas, like Shylock after him, exists at the border between the *civil* and the *civic*. Though both words are defined as pertaining to citizens, and seem at times interchangeable, the *civic* refers more precisely to the political participation of citizens. The *civil* refers to those social, economic, and domestic associations, "civilian" rather than properly "civic," that exist outside the operation of the political per se. Excluded from the *civic* order—the political world of offices—Barabas has succeeded in *civil* society (the market), which remains his deregulated habitat to the very end. Both Marlowe and Shakespeare stage the ethical and political dangers that attend exclusions of whole groups of people from the rights and responsibilities of full citizenship. In both Malta and Venice, the *civil* divorced from the *civic* becomes a space of pure economy, of self-interest unmitigated by communitarian impulses, and of class exploitation rationalized in the name of a narrowly defined political sphere.

On loan to Shakespeare, who moderates and tempers its message within a more orthodox framework, Marlowe's counternational strand might help disable the hegemonic force field of official Shakespeare in favor a Shakespeare *de-officiis*. Such a Shakespeare might, through various kinds of community theater, literacy, and literature projects, as well as his continued currency in both high culture and mass media, of regency romances and gay porn, come to belong to the informal arrangements of civil society, and from their daily operations of interface, exchange, negotiation, and compromise help lubricate the rotation of offices in the civic order.[2] In the process, "improvisation" of a theatrical, civil, and ultimately civic nature might become one basis of a new (transversal) citizenship. The African Theatre reconstructed by William Over in this collection represents an early moment in such a history of Shakespace on the way from transversality to citizenship: a cultural institution of political importance emerging from the voluntary associations of civil society.

In Marlowe, the civic does not correspond to the national, pointing instead to a vision of citizenship as *cosmopolitical,* taken not as the consolidation of global capitalism's new hegemonies, but rather as a liberating affirmation of the universal significance of local actions. In the cosmopolitical, the local and the global coincide, but nonsynthetically—their synthesis would be the middle term of the nation, a synthesis that Tamburlaine and Barabas, from opposite ends, restlessly evade. Tamburlaine acts as a force of imperial globalization, of nomadism rendered ubiquitous. Barabas, on the other hand, operates as a force of extreme localization, of civil society forcibly disengaged from civic nationhood.[3] In Shakespeare, the figures of Shylock, Othello, and Caliban invite us to examine the counternational strains of Marlowe as they enter into the body of Shakespeare's mature drama. The wandering Jew, the extravagant and erring Moor, and the marooned pagan, all on loan from Marlowe, are subject to cosmopolitical interpretation, performance, and pedagogy. Cosmopolitics emerge most forcefully in Shakespeare when Marlowe's expansive cosmography intercepts Shakespeare's national ethnography, when the work of the two poets themselves enters into a kind of civic rotation and transversal exchange.

That is, Shakespace-on-Marloan can be brought into the current movement—the result of both intellectual efforts of conceptualization and global economic and political changes—toward what Etienne Balibar calls "a regulated extension of the notion of citizenship which breaks with the sacrosanct equation of citizenship and nationality" (1988, 728). Such an enterprise is all the more urgent when the moral and performative turns of our productions and our teaching express the practical and imaginative needs of populations composed largely of noncitizens—whether disenfranchised juridically (as "illegal aliens") or excluded de facto from large parts of civic life by economic and educational inequity. It is no accident that in 1821 the hostile white reviewer of the African Theatre parodied the language of citizenship in his attempt to ridicule the political claims of the black actors: "and thus were many of our ebony friends excluded from a participation in those innocent recreations to which they were entitled, by virtue of the great charter that declares 'all men are equal'" (cited Over 2000, 74). In the tragical short history of the African Theatre, civil society had the chance to become civic exercise without supporting state power, and local actions took on universal meaning without congealing in nationalist solutions. Therein lies the civic promise of Shakespace when we approach its pedagogic and performance entrances transversally.

Notes

1. In a kind of companion piece to the one in this volume, Burt explores further the way in which *Shakespeare in Love* "straighten out" gender confusion (2001, 19).

2. This point echoes one strain of current citizenship theory, so-called "civil society theorists," a development of the communitarian emphasis in recent debates about the legacy and future of liberalism. As Kymlicka and Norman explain, "It is the voluntary organizations of civil society—churches, families, unions, ethnic associations, cooperatives, environmental groups, neighborhood associations, women's support groups, charities—that we learn the virtues of mutual obligation. As [Michael] Walzer puts it, 'the civility that makes democratic politics possible can only be learned in the associational networks of civil society" (1994, 363).

3. In the words of contemporary cosmopolitical theorist Ulrich Beck, "Ecological crises, migration and xenophobia, crime, financial flows, tax evasion, job flight, poverty and justice, the future of the welfare state, and retirement pensions—all these are global problems, and not only in the sense that they have grown too big for the national political frame. No, they are also global in the sense of being down-to-earth, everyday problems in this locality, in this city, for this group. There is a new dialectic of the global and the local that is not easy to accommodate in national politics." (1999: 54) On cosmopolitics as an ideal of liberal education, see Martha Nussbaum. On cosmopolitics and national citizenship, see Bruce Ackerman.

Works Cited

Ackerman, Bruce. 1994. "Rooted Cosmopolitanism." *Dissent* 104: 516–535.

Andreas, James. 2000. "'Where's the Master?': The Technologies of the Stage, Book, and Screen in *The Tempest* and *Prospero's Books.*" In *Shakespeare Without Class.* Ed. Donald Hedrick and Bryan Reynolds. New York: St. Martin's Press.

Aristotle. 1984. *Complete Works.* 2 Vols. Ed. Jonathan Barnes. Princeton: Princeton University Press.

Balibar, Etienne. 1988. "Propositions on Citizenship." *Ethics* 98: 723–730.

Beck, Ulrich. 1999. "Democracy beyond the Nation-State: A Cosmopolitical Manifesto." *Dissent* (Winter): 53–55.

Bevington, David. 1989. "Timur and the Ambivalent Vision of Heroism." *Asian Art* II.2: 6–9.

Burt, Richard. 2000. "No Holes Bard: Homonormativity and the Gay and Lesbian Romance with *Romeo and Juliet.*" In *Shakespeare Without Class.* Ed. Donald Hedrick and Bryan Reynolds. New York: St. Martin's Press.

————. 2001. "Shakespeare in Love and the End of the Shakespearean: Academic and Mass Culture Constructions of Literary Authorship." Forthcoming in *Shakespeare, Film, Fin de Siecle.* Ed. Mark Burnett and Ramona Wray. London: Macmillan.

Cheney, Patrick. 1997. *Marlowe's Counterfeit Profession: Ovid, Spenser, Counter-Nationhood.* Toronto: University of Toronto Press.

Hedrick, Donald. 2000. "Shakespeare's Enduring Immorality and the Performative Turn." In *Shakespeare Without Class.* Ed. Donald Hedrick and Bryan Reynolds. New York: St. Martin's Press.

————, and Bryan Reynolds. 2000. "Shakespace and Transversal Power." In *Shakespeare Without Class.* Ed. Donald Hedrick and Bryan Reynolds. New York: St. Martin's Press.

————, ed. 2000. *Shakespeare Without Class.* New York: St. Martin's Press.

Katz, Leslie. "Rehearsing the Weird Sisters: The Word as Fetish in *Macbeth.*" In *Shakespeare Without Class.* Ed. Donald Hedrick and Bryan Reynolds. New York: St. Martin's Press.

Kymlicka, Will and Wayne Norman. 1994. "Return of the Citizen: Recent Work on Citizenship Theory." *Ethics* 104: 352–381.

Lowry, Glenn D. 1989. "The House of Timur." *Asian Art* II.2: 2–5.

Lupton, Julia Reinhard. 2000. "The New Outreach." *PMLA.* Special Millennium Edition.

Marlowe, Christopher. 1969. *The Complete Plays.* Ed. J. B. Steane. Harmondsworth, Middlesex: Penguin.

Nussbaum, Martha. 1997. *Cultivating Humanity: A Classical Defense of Reform in Liberal Education.* Cambridge: Harvard University Press.

Over, William. 2000. "New York's African Theatre: Shakespeare Reinterpreted." In *Shakespeare Without Class.* Ed. Donald Hedrick and Bryan Reynolds. New York: St. Martin's Press.

Weimann, Robert. 2000. "Performance and Authority in *Hamlet* (1603)." In *Shakespeare Without Class.* Ed. Donald Hedrick and Bryan Reynolds. New York: St. Martin's Press.

Contributors

JAMES ANDREAS is currently Professor of English at Middlebury College's Bread Loaf School of English, and Professor Emeritus at Clemson University, where he directed the Clemson Shakespeare Festival and the South Carolina Shakespeare Collaborative for ten years (www.clemson.edu/shakespeare). Recent publications include "Teaching Shakespeare's Bawdry: Orality, Literacy, and Censorship," in *Teaching Approaches to Romeo and Juliet,* and "Signifying on Shakespeare: Gloria Naylor's Mama Day," in *Shakespeare and Appropriation.* He is at work on a book dealing with African American appropriations of *Othello* and *The Tempest.* E-mail at asjames@mail.clemson.edu.

MATT BERGBUSCH, a recent McGill Ph.D., currently teaches American literature in the English Department at Dawson College in Montreal. Forthcoming work includes the articles "Pissing Contents and Water Sports: Peter Greenaway's Shakespeare," and "Sensuous Ontologies: Gurganus, White, Wojnarowicz, and the Ethical Real." He is also an anti-poverty street activist with the Montreal Anti-Poverty Action Committee and with Food Not Bombs Montreal. E-mail: verwindung@yahoo.com.

RICHARD BURT, Professor of English at the University of Massachusetts, Amherst, is author of *Unspeakable ShaXXXspeares: Queer Theory and American Kiddie Culture,* and *Licensed by Authority: Ben Jonson and the Discourses of Censorship;* editor of *The Administration of Aesthetics: Censorship, Political Criticism, and the Public Sphere,* and co-editor of *Enclosure Acts: Sexuality, Property, and Culture in Early Modern England,* and of *Shakespeare the Movie: Popularizing the Plays on Film, TV, and Video.* He is currently working on two books: *Afterlives: Reanimating the Renaissance* and *Dumb Love.* E-mail: burt@english.umass.edu.

DONALD HEDRICK is Professor of English at Kansas State University, where he was founding director of the graduate Program in Cultural Studies. He has published on Shakespeare, Jonson, Marston, Renaissance architecture, film, pedagogy, language theory, and contemporary culture. A 1998 Senior Fulbright Fellow in American Film and Literature at Charles University in Prague, he has also taught at the University of New Orleans, Cornell University, Amherst College, and Colgate University, where he held the O'Connor Professorship of Literature. He is completing a book on entertainment and valuation in Shakespeare and a study of movie trailers. E-mail: hedrick@ksu.edu.

LESLIE KATZ is currently Assistant Professor at the Graduate Centre for the Study of Drama at the University of Toronto, where she also teaches dramaturgy and dramatic literature at University College. In addition to her specializations in Renaissance theatre history and post-war avant-garde drama, she works in postcolonial African dramaturgy. Her book-in-progress is *Theatres of the Despised*.

JULIA REINHARD LUPTON is Associate Professor of English and Comparative Literature at the University of California, Irvine. She is co-author with Kenneth Reinhard of *After Oedipus: Shakespeare in Psychoanalysis* and author of *Afterlives of the Saints: Typology, Hagiography and Renaissance Literature*. She is founder of Humanities Out There, a nationally recognized outreach program. E-mail: jrlupton@uci.edu.

LAURIE OSBORNE is an Associate Professor of English at Colby College. She has published *The Trick of Singularity: 'Twelfth Night' and the Performance Editions* as well as essays on Renaissance audiences and on Shakespeare in film and popular culture. Her forthcoming work includes "Cutting Up Characters in Trevor Nunn's *Twelfth Night*" in *Shakespeare, Cinema, Spectacle: Critical Theory and Film Practice,* edited by Courtney Lehmann and Lisa Starts, and an essay on pedagogy, "Shakespeare and the Construction of Character." E-mail: leosborn@colby.edu.

WILLIAM OVER teaches English and communication at St. John's University. His recent books are *Human Rights in the International Public Sphere* (Outstanding Book Award 1999 from the International and Intercultural Division of the National Communication Association), and *Social Justice in World Cinema and Theatre*. His articles concern race and class issues in literary forms. He also studies the intercultural dimensions of human rights and group identity issues. E-mail: overw@stjohns.edu.

CURTIS PERRY is an Associate Professor of English at Arizona State University. In addition to articles on several aspects of English Renaissance literature and culture, he is author of *The Making of Jacobean Culture: James I and the Renegotiation of Elizabethan Literary Practice,* and editor of *Material Culture and Cultural Materialisms in the Middle Ages and the Renaissance.* E-mail: cperry@asu.edu.

BRYAN REYNOLDS is Assistant Professor of Drama at the University of California, Irvine. His book, *Becoming Criminal: Transversal Theater and Cultural Dissidence in Early Modern England* is forthcoming from Johns Hopkins University Press. He has published articles on the work of Shakespeare, Cixous, de Certeau, Dekker, Foucault, Guattari, Middleton, Polanski, Rousseau, and Robert Wilson. E-mail: breynold@uci.edu.

ROBERT WEIMANN is Professor of Drama at the University of California, Irvine. He is author of numerous books and essays on theater, Shakespeare, criticism, and culture. Available in English are *Structure and Society in Literary History: Studies in the History and Theory of Historical Criticism* (1976), *Shakespeare and the Popular Tradition in the Theatre* (1987), *Authority and Representation in Early Modern Discourse* (1996), and *Author's Pen and Actor's Voice: Playing and Writing in Shakespeare's Theatre* (2000).

Index

A-effect, 205
  see also Brecht, Bertolt
A Love Like Romeo and Juliet, 156
A Lady of Property, 139, 148
A Midsummer Night's Dream, 146,
  175–6
A Midsummer Night's Dream, 24, 146,
  243
A Midsummer Night's Dream,
  (Hoffman), 24
A Room of One's Own, 147
A Spirited Bluestocking, 145
Abraham, Roger D., 76
absurdism, 103
Acker, Kathy, 264
Ackerman, Bruce, 284 n. 3
acting, black "imitation" of white,
  68–9, 74–5
Acts of Love, 148
Acts of Passion, 148
Adelman, Janet, 104 n. 6, 112,
  117
African Theatre
  African-American traditions,
    76–7
  challenging authority, 78
  compared to epic theatre, 66
  disturbances, 72
  "imitation" style, 68, 74
  political themes, 67
  protests of slavery, 76

Richard 3, 75
white audience response, 71
Aldridge, Ira, 65, 67, 70, 72
Als, Hilton, 212
Althusser, Louis, 10, 78
Amadeus, 277
Anderson, Benedict, 12
Andreas, James, 280
Angelou, Maya, 264
Ansen, David, 183 n. 11
antihomophobic pedagogy, 260
Antony and Cleopatra, 135, 142
The Appropriation of Shakespeare, 7
Aristotle, 280
As You Like It, 262
audience and audience response
  and voice, 192
  American, 117–18
  antebellum, 65
  black audiences, 72
  Coriolanus, 112, 114, 126
  female readers, 138
  feminist, 235
  identification with commoners, 124
  gay and lesbian, 154
  Hamlet, 54
  heterosexual, 156
  outside London, 62
  rowdy, 70
authority
  and author, 198

authority *(cont)*
  critique of, 55
  in script, 196
Austin, J. L., 259

Baker, Houston, 205 n. 6
Baker, Susan, 136, 150 n. 4
Bakhtin, Mikhail, 87
Baldo, Jonathan, 205 n. 5
Balibar, Etienne, 283
Balogh, Mary, 144
Bamber, Linda, 190
Barber, C. L., 196, 243
Barbies, 251, 264–6
Basilikon Doron, 118
Baudrillard, Jean 77
Beard, Julie, 163
Beck, Ulrich 284 n. 3
Benjamin, Walter, 210, 219, 223 n. 2,
  226, 254
Bennett, William, 248, 265–6
Benthall, Michael, 182 n. 22
Berger, Harry, Jr., 239 n. 9
Berger, Thomas, 205 n. 1
Berghahn, V. R., 128 n. 4
Bergson, Henri, 91
Berlant, Lauren, 155, 180 n. 9, n. 10
Bersani, Leo, 155, 156, 182 n. 19
Bertram, Paul, 61 n. 3
Bhaba, Homi, 213
Bishop, Natalie, 156
bluestocking novels, 145–6
Book of Virtues, 265
Booth, Junius Brutus, 71
Booth, Stephen 104 n. 1
Bourdieu, Pierre, 12, 17
Braden, Gordon, 104 n. 1
Braden, James, 98–9, 179 n. 6
Bradley, A. C., 123
Brecht, Bertolt, 107–27, 108, 127 n. 1,
  128 n. 9, 199, 191, 205
  and A-effect 77,
Bridget, 251
Brockbank, Philip, 128 n. 13, 129 n. 16
Bronski, Michael, 77
Brooks, Cleanth, 104 n. 6
Brown, Connie, 183 n. 11
Brown, Henry, 65

Brown, Jane, 180 n. 7
Brown, Paul, 205 n.6
Buisseret, David, 206 n.9
Burney, Fanny, 156
Burroughs, William, 7–8
Burt, Richard, 21, 24, 150 n. 6, 179 n.
  1, n. 3, 181 n. 13, 277, 279, 284 n. 1
Butler, Judith, 28, 155, 180 n. 8, n. 9,
  258, 260
Butler, Martin, 127 n. 3

Camille, 155, 165
Campion, Jane, 33
Camus, Albert, 102
Canterbury Tales, The, 199
Caralco, Joe, 175
Carnival in Venice, 167
Castelanni, Renato, 153
Castle, Terry, 179 n. 4, n. 6, 181 n. 14
Cecilia, 156
Censored, 169
Césaire, Aimé, 196, 202
Chambers, E.K., 62 n. 6
Chaplin, Charlie, 198
"Characteristics of Negro Expression,"
  76
Charnes, Linda, 135, 150 n. 2
Chaucer, 192
Cheney, Patrick, 281
Cheney, Lynne, 264
Chomsky, Noam, 35
Christmas Belle, 144
Cicero, Marcus Tullius, 281
Clare, Janet, 127 n. 3
class and pedagogy, 247
Clayton, Thomas, 61
Clinton, Hillary, 248
Clinton, William, 163
Coleridge, Samuel Taylor, 111, 245,
  254
Collins, Kris, 65
Collinson, Patrick, 41 n. 9
colonization, as rape, 221
Communist Manifesto, The, 113
computers, technology of mastery, 204
concepts, key theoretical
  Alienation-effect, 205
  allegory, 221, 219–20

and author, 198
bifold authority, 57, 61
body, 201–2
camp, 177
civil vs. civic, 282
class, as flexible, 149
cosmopolitics, 283
counternational, 282
designifying gender, 156
disfilming, 5, 187
emulate pride, 96–104
fetish, 230
language as, 233
grotesque realism, 87
heteronormativity, 25–6, 155
historical depth-of-field, 23, 35, 38
homonormativity, 156, 180–81 n.10
hybrid authority, 61
imagined community, 12
instability of text, 55, 211
mimetic desire, paradox of, 91, 95
"mojo," 203
moral performativity, 203
official territory, 9
out-of-field, 38
pedagogy of the oppressed, 246
performative, 257–9
post-queer adaptation, 175, 178
queer and racial performativity,
    260
queer theory, 154–5, 157, 178, 214
see also bifold authority
see also Brecht, Bertolt
see also hybrid authority
see also Shakespace, subjective
    territory, and transversality
Senecanism, endless repetition, and,
    102
signifying, 78
state machinery, 11, 14–15
technology of mastery, 189, 204
transcendance, fantasy of, 103
violence of literacy, 195
voice, 199
*A Contribution to the Critique of Political
    Economy,* 126
Coriolan, 107–27, 279
Coriolanus, 107–27,

issue of support for plebeians, 111
staging, 114–15
irreplacability, 111, 279
Couch, Kathy, 239 n.12
Coursen, Herb, 194, 201–2
Crowe, Patrick, 214
Cukor, George, 153, 155, 164
Culler, Jonathan, 242
Cut or Uncut, 167

Davis, Mike, 34
De Officiis, 281
Dead Poet's Society, 153
Debord, Guy, 248
Decameron, The, 199
DeCerteau, Michel, 193, 197, 203
Deleuze, Gilles, 17, 19, 43 n. 13
    any-space-whatever, 30, 33
    action-image, 29
    counteractualization, 262
    dream-image, 30–31
    crystal-image, 31
    movement-image, 29
    "moral" language, 262
    time-image, 29
DeMan, Paul, 257
Dench, Judi, 33
Derrida, Jacques, 14, 196, 265
Desmet, Christy, 40–41 n. 1
Dickens, Charles, 198
Dodd, Christina, 148
Dollimore, Jonathan, 126, 128 n.6
Donaldson, Peter 179 n. 7
Donne, John, 34
Double Life, A, 164
Dowden, Edward, 205 n 1
Drama of King Shotaway, The, 67–8
Duthie, George Ian, 56

Eagleton, Terry, 16, 251–2, 256
Eastman, Arthur, 205 n. 1
Edwards, Philip, 51
Einstein, Sergei, 190
Elizabeth (film), 26
Elizabeth I, Queen, 110, 118,
    160–1
Engels, Friedrich, 110, 112–13
Esslin, Martin, 86

Eve's Bayou, 154
Exile, 169

*Fair Imposter, The,*141
family values, 222
Fellini, Federico, 198
Fiennes, Joseph, 39
Fineman, Joel, 258
Finkelpearl, Philip J., 127, n.3
Fitzgerald, F. Scott, 265
Folger, Henry Clay, 251
Folger Shakespeare Library with
    S.W.A.T. team, 6
Forbidden Planet, 196
Foucault, Michel, 71
Freire, Paolo, 246
Friedberg, Anne, 213, 219
Fuller, Graham, 211, 217

Garber, Marjorie, 22, 43 n. 18, 218–19,
    264
Gates, Henry Louis, Jr., 77, 260
gay desire, belatedness of, 169
Gielgud, Sir John, 199
Gildon, Charles, 111
Ginsberg, Allen, 7
Glucksmann, Andre, 13, 18
Gods and Monsters, 165, 182
Goethe, Wolfgang, 254
Gras, Vernon, 205 n.8
Grauerbach, James, 41 n. 2
Gray, Vanessa, 139, 148
*Greatest Lover in England, The,*148
Greenaway, Peter, 190–205
Greenblatt, Stephen, 10, 25, 44 n. 21,
    27–9, 39, 97, 195, 205 n. 6, 205 n.
    11, 238 n. 3, 267 n. 5,   277
Griffith, D. W., 198
Grimsley's Oxford Career, 146–8
Gross, Kenneth, 239 n.12
Guattari, Félix, 19, 42 n. 9, 43, n. 13
Guillory, John, 257
Gutenberg, 198
Gysin, Bryon, 7

Hamlet, 24, 54, 55, 139, 177
Hamlet (Branagh), 23
Hamlet (dir. Zeffirelli), 23, 198

Hamlin, William H., 195, 205 n. 6
The Hampshire Hoyden, 145
Handelman, David, 220
Harbsmeier, Michael, 190
Hardt, Michael, 43, n. 12
Hartman, Geoffrey, 196
Harvey, Laurence, 153
"Have a nice day," 222
Havelock, Eric, 204
Hay, Samuel, 67, 73
Hays Code, 164, 166
Hedrick, Donald, 9, 42–3 n. 11, n. 6,
    43 n. 10, 127, 267 n. 2, 278, 279
Hedrick, Gretchen, 267 n. 3
Heinemann, Margot, 120, 128 n . 6
Helpman, Robert, 182 n. 22
Henry IV, 23
Henry VI, 22, 142
Hewlett, James, 66, 68–9, 73
Heywood, Jasper, 104 n. 15
Hill, Christopher, 41 n.9, 128 n. 11
His Lordship's Mistress, 145–7
Hitler, Adolf, 117, 120
hooks, bell, 242
Hopkins, D. J., 44, n. 20
Howard, Leslie, 165, 182 n. 21
Hulme, Peter, 205 n.6
Hurston, Zora Neale, 76
Hüsges, H., 127

Iago Comic, 169–71
In and Out, 163
Ionesco, Eugene, 85–7, 91–6, 92–3,
    102–4
Irace, Kathleen, 58, 62 n. 5
Isikoff, Michael, 184 n. 17

Jagendorf, Zvi, 129 n. 15
James, Deanna, 148, 181 n. 16
James I, King of England, 118–19, 122,
    234, 239 n. 4
Jameson, Frederic, 137, 43 n. 15
Jarry, Alfred, 85–92, 97, 102–4
Jenkins, Harold, 51, 56
Jerry Maguire, 163
Johnson, Samuel, 122
Jonson, Ben, 192, 253, 238 n. 4
Jorgenson, P. A. 129 n. 17

Jousse, Thierry, 221
Juliet and Romeo (D'Amato), 24

Kahn, Coppelia, 179–80 n. 7
Kant, Immanuel, 11
Kasarova, Vessilina, 179 n. 4
Katz, Leslie, 270
Kaufman, Lloyd, 21
Kelly, Carla, 146–7
Kemp, Ursula, 232–3
Kempe, William 62 n. 6
Kennedy, Harlan, 205 n.8
Kernan, Alvin, 128 n. 3, 205 n. 3
Kerouac, Jack, 7
Kerrigan, John, 104 n. 10, n. 12
King Lear, 173, 243
Kittredge, G. L., 245
Kliman, Bernice W., 61 n. 3
Knight, Amarantha, 181 n. 16
Koenig, Ralf, 153, 169
Kott, Jan, 85
Krentz, Jayne Ann, 138
Kymlicka, Will, 284 n. 2

L-7, 266, 267 n.10
Laclau, Ernesto, 42 n. 12
Lamont, RosetteC., 104 n. 1, n. 7
Lane, Nancy, 94
Larner, Christina, 42 n. 9
Lefebvre, Henri, 11
Lemmon, Kasi, 154
Lessing, 253
Lewinsky, Monica, 163, 182 n. 18
Livy, 110
Looking for Richard (Pacino), 24
Los Angeles, as future, 34–5
Lott, Trent, 26, 29, 32
love
    and cynicism, 35
    as affiliation, 24
    class and gender, 141
    failed transversality, 39
    see also transversality
    Shakespeare as exemplar, 135
    teaching as, 243
Love's Labor's Lost, 24
Lucas, 162
Luhrmann, Baz, 153, 174

Lupton, Julia, 127
Lyons, Donald, 209
Lyotard, Francois, 29, 37

Macbeth, 22, 44, 97, 100, 146, 229–38
MacDonald, Joyce Green, 72
Macfarlane, Alan, 42 n. 9
MacIntyrre, Alisdair, 248, 250
MacLean, Sally-Beth, 60
Madness of King George, The, 174
Maguire, Laurie E., 62 n. 5
Marcus, Leah, 55, 62 n. 5, 218
Margaret Evans Porter, 144
Marlowe, Christopher, 25, 36, 97, 98, 162, 277–84
Marsden, Jean, 7
Marshall, Charles, 71
Marvelous Possessions, 195
Marx, Karl, 110, 112, 126, 257
Matthews, Charles, 69–70, 73
McGill Shakespeare in Performance
    Research Group, 223 n.1
McGilligan, Patrick, 164
McLuhan, Marshall, 204
Measure for Measure, 146, 147, 248
Mei, Eva 179 n. 4
Memoir of Ira Aldridge, 75
Merchant of Venice, The, 140, 200
Merry Wives of Windsor, The, 239 n. 8
Messel, Oliver, 165
Midlands insurrection, 1109, 10, 128
Miller, D. A., 167–9
mimetic desire, 94–5
Miola, Robert, 104 n. 8, n. 11
Mitchison, Naomi, 154, 157
Modleski, Tania, 137
Montaigne, 20, 190
Morton, Andrew, 181 n. 17
Mowat, Barbara, 61 n. 3
Much Ado About Nothing, 263
Much Ado About Nothing (Branagh), 24
Mullaney, Stephen, 239 n. 6
Munro, Ian, 127
Muybridge, Eadward, 200
My Own Private Idaho, 209–23

Nancy, Jean-Luc, 7
Negri, Antonio, 43 n. 13

New Criticism, 246
Nine Inch Nails, 265
Noah, Mordecai Manuel, 67
Norman, Marc, 25, 27
Norman, Wayne 284 n. 2
Novy, Marianne, 6, 138
Nussbaum, Martha, 248, 250, 267 n. 1, 284 n. 3

Object of My Affection, The, 153, 173, 174–5, 178
O'Neill, Jessica, 145
Ong, Walter, S. J., 204
Orgel, Stephen, 39, 239 n. 5
Osborne, Laurie, 277, 150 n. 7
Othello, 24, 70, 75, 139, 144, 153, 172, 279
Othello (Parker), 24
Over, William, 278
Overfield, Joan, 145
Owens, Craig, 220

Panofsky, Erwin, 190
Pasolini, Pier, 198
Pechter, Ed, 263
Pepys, Samuel, 201
Perkins, David, 127
Perry, Curtis, 278
Pettet, E. C., 110, 128 n. 11, n. 12
Phaedrus, 192
Phoenix, River, 214
*Piano, The,*33, 199
Piatt, Eleanor, 265
Plato, 193
Poetic Justice, 140
Polanski, Roman, 44
Porter, Margaret Evans, 144
Portrait of Mr. W. H., 179
postmodern pedagogy, 257
Pratt, Mary Louise, 205 n.6
proscenium stage, technology of, 201
Prospero's Books, 23
Prugh, Caroline, 239 n.12
Purchas, Samuel, 190, 194, 205 n. 2

Quilligan, Maureen, 210, 211, 220

Rabelais, 87
Radner, Gilda, 28
Radway, Janice, 137
Rafferty, Terence, 209, 210, 213
Raleigh, Sir Walter, 118
Rasley, Alicia, 146
Rasmussen, Eric, 62 n. 5
Records of Early English Drama, 55
Regency novel, 136, 138
  mass market and, 137
Reinhard, Max, 182 n. 22
Renais, Alain, 32
Reynolds, Bryan, 17, 42–3 n. 11, 44n. 19, 129 n. 19, 253, 278
Rich, Adrienne, 158
Richard 3, 66, 72, 75, 279
Richard 3 (Loncraine), 24
Rischbieter, Henning, 129 n. 18
Roberts, Jeanne, 196
Robertson, J. M., 254–5
Romance of the Rose, The, 163
romance novel, disdain for, 138
  triumph over class in, 143
Romeo, 163
Romeo and Julian: A Love Story, 153, 167–89
Romeo and Julian (Abdul)
Romeo and Juliet, 139, 141–4, 145, 153–78, 168, 278
Romeo and Juliet (dir. Zefirelli), 198
"Romeo and Juliet" (music video), 166
Romeo Must Die, 24
A Room of One's Own, 147
Rossiter, A. P., 123,
Rouse, John, 127
Rousseau, 200

Satyricon, 198
Savelson, Kim, 127
Sawyer, Robert, 40–41 n. 1
Scarry, Elaine, 127
Schatz-Jacobsen, Claus, 205 n. 5
Schwerger, Peter, 205 n.8
Scofield, Martin 129 n. 15
Scott, Michael, 106 n. 1
Searle, John, 259
The Secret Lives of Romeo and Juliet, 169

Sedgwick, Eve, 260
Seneca, 97–104
Sessa, Jacqueline 106 n.
"Shakespace", (versions of the
    concept), 277, 278
  acting as alterity, 258
  as civic territory, 279, 284
  as Mike, in *My Own Private Idaho,*
    217
  bardolatry as, 255
  black acting, 70
  creativity, 278
  criminality, 278
  compared to Marxspace, 14–15
  counterhegemony, 210
  defined, 8–10
  essays as, 40
  godlike authority of, 136
  lower body and, 87–88
  mimetic rivalry, 86
  purposeless playing, 58
  representational and presentational
    space blurred, 59
  unsanctioned performance, 57
  unstable identity, 58
  vs. official culture, 9, 12
  vs. Shakespeare nostalgia, 219
  witch role as transformative, 234
  see also transversality
"sexy spectaculars," 138
Shakespeare in Love, 161–2, 277
Shakespeare Our Contemporary, 85
Shakespeare's R & J, 175
Shakespeare, William
  and Anne Hathaway, 159
  author's authority, 53
  bardolatry and anti-bardolatry, 252
  as bisexual celebrity, 171
  as black woman, 264
  as contemporary, 97
  as gay, 181
  as guide to business, 249
  as home, 218
  as immoral, 252
  as love authority, 39
  as market entrepreneur, 254
  as mechanism for class-shifting, 146
  as phallic mother, 219

  as supplement, 216
  body of, 218
  displacement of, 241–2
  Hollywood as heir to, 35
  identification with, 217
  inhabited by spirit of, 22
  outing, 26
  views on morality, 262
Shakespeare Without Tears, 5–6
Shaw, George Bernard, 173–192
Shepherd, Simon, 258
Shtier, Rachel, 179 n. 2
Sievers, Tobin, 245
Simon, J., 209
Sinfield, Alan, 42 n. 9, 78, 104 n. 1,
    128 n. 6
Sir Thomas More, 140
Sisyphus myth, 102
smiley face, 221–23
Snipe, Simon, 67, 76
Snitnow, Anne Barr, 137
Solution Three, 154, 157, 163
Somerset, Alan 60
Sonnets, The, 38
Sorge, Thomas, 113
Spivak, Gayatri, 267 n. 1, n. 8
Stalin, Joseph, 118, 119
Sterling, Sara Hawks, 159
Stock, Mildred, 71
Stoppard, Tom, 26, 181 n. 15
Stow, John, 109
Stuckey, Elspeth, 193
subjective territory
  and monotonic voice, 200
  and resistance, 15
  and state machinery, 121–2
  as language transformation, 229,
    233–4
  colonial subjection, 213
  Coriolanus in, 121–2
  defined, 12
  "fucked up" smiley face,
    221–3
  homelessness, 214
  mimicry, 213
  nostalgia, 219
  through the book, 197
  vs. civic space, 280

subjective territory (*cont*)
  vs. performativity, 258
  women's language, 235
  see also transversality
Suson, Marlene, 141
Suvin, Darko, 119, 128 n.6

Taming of the Shrew, The, 261
Taming of the Shrew, The, (dir. Zeffirelli),
  198
Taussig, Michael, 230, 238 n. 1
Taylor, Charles, 248
Tchaikovsky, 165
Teague, Fran, 150 n. 4
technology, twentieth-century, 190–91
Tempest, The, 23, 148, 189–205
Texas Chainsaw Massacre, The, 21
Thomas, Evan, 181 n. 17
Thomas, Paul, 168
Thorpe, Kay, 150 n. 2
Thurston, Carol, 137
Thyestes, 97–104
Title, Elise, 163
Titus Andronicus, 21, 135, 254
Titus Andronicus (Taymor), 24
Toast of the Town, The, 144
Todorov, Tzvetan, 195, 205n. 6
Tolstoy, 254
Tom and Jerry, 68
Tomkins, Silvan, 262
touring companies, 60, 62 n.8
transversality
  acting as, 124
  and audience response and desire, 91
  and class, 247
  and contingency, 245
  and microsubversions, 16
  and new historicism, 250.
  and pedagogy, defined, 39
  and performance, 108, 112, 117–27
  and political commitment, 262
  and property, 7
  and replaceability, 112
  and the commercial sublime, 39
  and the "ethical" vs. the "moral,"
    246, 249
  as anarchist mutual aid, 245
  as authority passed around, 56, 280
  as "becoming," 19
  as counterculture, 77
  as criminality, transgression, 6, 18
  as ethical open space, 211
  as experimental alterity, 18, 261
  as immorality by other means, 252
  as literary genre, 20
  as love, 20, 258
  as misappropriation, vs. appropria-
    tion, 7
  as private and public space, 213
  as reckless subjectivity, 86
  as revision of cultural authority, 73
  as road, 222
  as "self-creating transcendence," 99
  as stripping, 94, 202
  audience expectation of, 115, 117,
    124
  black acting as criminality, 70
  early modern theatricality as, 16
  examples of Shakespeare characters,
    18–19
  illustrated, "cut-ups," 7–8
  inquiry vs. instruction, 250
  literacy as, 190
  outside individualism, 249
  teaching and theory, 245
  vs. state machinery, 10
  witches, transformative power of, p.
    234.
transversal movement
  as liminal space, 123
  between school and university, 281
  Coriolanus, between state and self,
    123; betrayal as, 125; failed
    transversality, 101
  highbrow/ lowbrow exchange, 79
  masculinity through witchcraft, 236
  mediating class and gender, 140
  revenge as transcendence, 101
  Shakespeare outside Shakespeare,
    242
transversal slogans
  "Be all you aren't" (Hedrick and
    Reynolds), 5, 280
  "BEING OTHERS" (Burroughs),
    8
  "Home is anywhere," 215

"the self was not the same"
(Shakespeare), 3
transversal territory, 121
see also Shakespace, subjective
territory, transversality
Treut, Monika, 154, 180 n. 8
Trew Law of Free Monarchies, The, 118
Tricomi, Albert H., 118
Trilling, Lionel, 246
Tromeo and Juliet, 20, 21–2, 153
Tromly, Fred B., 104 n. 9
Turner, Harry Ashby, Jr., 108, 128 n. 5
Twelfth Night, 24, 39, 139, 160, 174

*Ugly Duckling, The,*145
Une Tempête, 196

Van Sant, Gus, 209, 221–223.
Vattimo, Vianni, 219
Vaughan, Virginia Mason, 205 n.5
Venus, Nina, 127
Vespucci, Amerigo, 203
Volker, Klaus, 128 n. 7
Voltaire, 254

Wall, Geoffrey, 205 n.8
Walsingham, Thomas, 36
Walzer, Michael, 284 n. 2
Warner, Michael, 180 n. 9
Watson, Robert, 256–7

Webster, Margaret, 6
Weimann, Robert, 280
Weir, Peter, 154
Welles, Orson, 254
Werstine, Paul, 61 n. 2, n. 3
West, Cornel, 263
Whale, James, 165, 181 n. 20, 182
Wilde, Oscar, 154, 179 n. 6, 181 n. 16
Wilkes, G.A., 205 n.6
Willett, John, 128 n. 9
William Shakespeare's Romeo + Juliet,
154, 174
Williams, Bernard, 248
Williams, Linda, 169
Williams, Raymond, 41 n. 7
Willis, Susan, 251
Wilson, John Dover 62 n. 5. 115
Winnicott, D.W., 251
witch stereotypes, 231
Wolf, Joan, 145
Woods, Gregory, 181 n. 12
Woolf, Virginia, 147
Worthen, W. B., 261
Writing of History, The, 193
Wriothesley, Henry, 44 n. 20

Zane, 246
Zeffirelli, Franco, 153, 154, 198
Žižek, Slavoj, 42 n. 12, 248
Zumthor, Paul,